Lecture Notes in Computer Science 792
Edited by G. Goos and J. Hartmanis

Neil D. Jones Masami Hagiya
Masahiko Sato (Eds.)

Logic, Language and Computation

Festschrift in Honor of Satoru Takasu

Springer-Verlag
Berlin Heidelberg New York
London Paris Tokyo
Hong Kong Barcelona
Budapest

Series Editors

Gerhard Goos
Universität Karlsruhe
Postfach 69 80
Vincenz-Priessnitz-Straße 1
D-76131 Karlsruhe, Germany

Juris Hartmanis
Cornell University
Department of Computer Science
4130 Upson Hall
Ithaca, NY 14853, USA

Volume Editors

Neil D. Jones
DIKU, University of Copenhagen
Universitetsparken 1, DK-2100 Copenhagen, Denmark

Masami Hagiya
Department of Information Science, University of Tokyo
7-3-1 Hongo, Bunkyo-ku, Tokyo 113, Japan

Masahiko Sato
Research Institute of Electrical Communication, Tohoku University
Sendai 980, Japan

CR Subject Classification (1991): F.4, F.3.3, F.1.3, D.3.3-4, I.2.2

ISBN 3-540-57935-4 Springer-Verlag Berlin Heidelberg New York
ISBN 0-387-57935-4 Springer-Verlag New York Berlin Heidelberg

CIP data applied for

Printed in Germany

Typesetting: Camera-ready by author
SPIN: 10132126 45/3140-543210 - Printed on acid-free paper

Preface

Professor Satoru Takasu is scheduled to give his final lecture at the Research Institute of Mathematical Sciences (RIMS) in Kyoto at the end of March, 1994. The purpose of this volume is to celebrate Professor Takasu's career to date, and the many positive effects he has had upon theoretical computer science, both in Japan and worldwide.

Professor Takasu has been involved in pathbreaking research work, especially in constructive type theory and its relation to automatic program synthesis. He was one of the first, and perhaps *the* first, seriously to consider using the computer to derive a program automatically from a constructive proof that a problem specification is satisfiable.

Further, he has greatly stimulated Japanese theoretical computer science by his research, by his philosophy, and by advising a great many students since the time he dreamed he was building a computer (told to us many years ago). The range of areas in which he has supervised excellent work is surprisingly broad:

> automata theory, category theory, complexity theory, lambda calculus, machine learning, program synthesis, and verification; and many aspects of logic including: constructing programs from proofs, cut elimination, non-classical logics, proof theory, and logic programming.

The editors of this volume are three of Takasu's former students, and Neil Jones was his very first student (in Canada, in the time 1962-66). We were motivated to organize this volume because we feel that this outstanding level of breadth, depth, energy, and research stimulation deserves recognition. The quality of the contributions here confirms this impression and Takasu's unusual ability to inspire good research among his students and colleagues.

Biographical information

Satoru Takasu was born in 1931, and his father was a well-known professor of mathematics at Tohoku University in Sendai. He earned his B.S., M.S., and Ph.D. degrees, all in mathematics, from the University of Tokyo, respectively in 1953, 1955, and 1959, with emphasis on homological algebra and mathematical logic. After this time he worked at Nippon Telegraph and Telephone until 1964.

In the period 1962 to 1966 he was first Assistant and then Associate Professor at the newly established Computer Science Department at the University of Western Ontario in London, Canada. While there, he set the pattern for that department's further theoretical research, teaching the first courses in switching circuits, logic, and formal languages. These areas were not well recognized at the time, but later became an important part of North American computer science curricula. Further, he helped to organize a conference on General Systems Theory when in Canada, and co-edited its proceedings. The contributions Dr. Takasu made in the initial stage of that department's development and the legacy that he left behind are still greatly appreciated.

In 1966 he became Associate Professor at RIMS (Research Institute for Mathematical Sciences) at Kyoto University. He continued as Full Professor at RIMS from 1967 through 1994, and was director of the institute for two years in 1991-1993. That time was especially fruitful because RIMS was willing to devote means to organize symposia with mostly domestic but sometimes foreign researchers as well. Takasu organized or helped organize many RIMS symposia. He also hosted an IFIP Working Group 2.2 meeting, and organized several international symposia on theoretical computer science, supported by IBM Japan.

From the very beginning, when the Japanese theoretical Computer Science community was very small, he played a central role in its development throughout the country. Almost all of today's good Japanese theoretical computer scientists have some connection with him, many as direct or indirect students.

At RIMS Professor Takasu was in the right place at the right time, and most importantly, he had the right sense of direction. In particular, Takasu foresaw the fundamental role of constructive logic in theoretical computer science already in the 1960s after studying the work of Gentzen on cut elimination and the work of Gödel on dialectical interpretation. Although Kreisel and Constable published similar ideas at an early stage, it seems fair to say that Takasu was the first seriously to pursue this direction.

This book

These papers cover a wide spectrum, characteristic of Takasu's wide-ranging interests and activities. All are by former students or close colleagues. Many have to do with logic, and especially its applications and implementation on the computer. Following is a brief summary of the subjects of the various articles.

Constructive Type Theory. *Lifschitz' Logic of Calculable Numbers and Optimizations in Program Extraction*, by Susumu Hayashi and Yukihide Takayama, introduces a new approach to extract a program from a proof that an input-output specification is satisfiable. The approach starts from a logic devised by Lifschitz with quite different aims, but turns out to be closely related to earlier work by both authors. *On Implicit Arguments*, by Masami Hagiya and Yozo Toda, deals with a real problem in automation of logic: types are necessary for both theoretical and implementational reasons, but their overabundance can be distracting for human readers and writers. The authors provide a well-founded scheme for omitting many type annotations without informational or computational loss. *A functional system with transfinitely defined types*, by Mariko Yasugi and Susumu Hayashi, introduces a new formal system for constructive analysis, proves strong normalization, and describes its computational mechanisms. *The Non-deterministic Catch and Throw Mechanism and Its Subject Reduction Property*, by Hiroshi Nakano, concerns the interface between logic and functional programming. Even though the catch/throw mechanism gives nondeterministic evaluation results, it is shown to be type-preserving under reductions in a constructive type discipline.

Lambda Calculus. *Conservativeness of Λ over $\lambda\sigma$-calculus*, by Masahiko Sato and Yukiyoshi Kameyama, concerns a new functional programming language Λ that has encapsulated assignment but doesn't sacrifice referential transparency. It is shown that Λ is a conservative extension of a well-known lambda calculus with explicit substitutions. *ML with First-Class Environments and its Type Inference Algorithm,* by Shin-ya Nishizaki, and also related to explicit substitutions, describes an ML-polymorphic language with first-class environments and gives a type inference algorithm for the language. *A Simple Proof of the Genericity Lemma*, by Masako Takahashi, gives a short and elegant new proof of a classical theorem, whose usual proof is quite complex.

Logic, Algebra, and Applications. *The Logic of* FOL *Systems Formulated in Set Theory*, by Richard W. Weyhrauch and Carolyn Talcott, systematically reinterprets ideas from traditional logic with the ultimate goal of building an artificial reasoner, rather than providing a theory about what a reasoner might have done. *Well-Ordering of Algebras and Kruskal's Theorem*, by Ryu Hasegawa, shows the existence of a strong connection between a certain class of algebras and a hierarchy of ordinal notations known from mathematical logic. *On Locomorphism in Analytical Equivalence Theory*, by Shigeru Igarashi, Tetsuya Mizutani, Takashi Tsuji and Chiharu Hosono, concerns a logic for reasoning about and verifying concurrent and real-time systems. Locomorphism is a generalization of program equivalence, and can be considered as a homomorphism between acts. *Analysis of a Software/Hardware System by Tense Arithmetic*, by Kohji Tomita, Takashi Tsuji and Shigeru Igarashi, applies the framework of the preceding paper to analyze a typical (and realistic) example of a hardware/software system.

Program Transformation. *The Essence of Program Transformation by Partial Evaluation and Driving*, by Neil D. Jones, shows that some well-studied program transformation schemes may be formulated in logical terms, giving links to both the classical predicate transformer semantics and to program analysis by abstract interpretation. *Program Transformation via Contextual Assertions*, by Ian A. Mason and Carolyn Talcott, applies their 'Variable Typed Logic of Effects' to justify on a logical basis a number of program transformations that can be used to optimize functional programs with side effects, including both assignment and pointers.

Complexity and Coding. *On Coding Theorems with Modified Length Functions*, by Kojiro Kobayashi, strengthens a result by Csiszar and Körner in coding theory. *Thirty Four Comparisons are Required to Sort 13 Items*, by Takumi Kasai, Shusaku Sawato and Shigeki Iwata, establishes by a novel and sophisticated computer analysis that 13 items cannot be sorted in fewer than 34 comparisons, answering a question left open by Wells nearly 30 years ago. The result would not have been computationally feasible just a few years ago.

Acknowledgements

Many have aided production of this volume. In addition to the authors, we want to thank Peter Holst Andersen, Robert Glück, John Hart, Chetan Murthy, Hans Henrik Løvengreen, Takako Nakahara, Peter Sestoft, Morten Heine Sørensen, Carolyn Talcott, and Lisa Wiese. The DART project, funded by the Danish Natural Sciences Research Council, partly supported P.H. Andersen, N.D. Jones, and M.H. Sørensen.

Contents

Constructive Type Theory

Lambda Calculus

Logic, Algebra, and Applications

Program Transformation

Complexity and Coding

Lifschitz's Logic of Calculable Numbers and Optimizations in Program Extraction

Susumu Hayashi[1] and Yukihide Takayama[2]

[1] Department of Applied Mathematical and Informatics,
Ryukoku University,
Seta, Ohtsu, Shiga, 520-21, Japan
[2] Department of Computer Science and Systems Engineering,
Ritsumeikan University,
56-1, Kita-machi Tohjiin, Kita-ku, Kyoto, 603, Japan

Abstract. In the early 80's, V. Lifschitz presented a classical logic which can code up constructive logic [8], [9]. We will show how it is used for optimization in program extraction. We will show that the second author's extended projection method [13], [14] can be considered as a translation of constructive proofs into Lifschitz's logic. We will also give an interpretation of Lifschitz's logic into the first author's type system ATTT, which evolved from the extended projection method.

1 Lifschitz's logic and information relevance

It is well-known that classical logic can be faithfully embedded in constructive logic via so-called double-negation interpretations. These interpretations are finding applications to extraction of programs from classical proofs by means of continuation. The other way around, V. Lifschitz introduced a classical logic in which constructive logic can be coded up [8], [9].

The key idea of Lifschitz's logic is the "calculability predicate" $K(x)$, which stands for "x is a computable number." Lifschitz introduced the following realizability for his logic:

$$\begin{aligned}
r \mathrel{\mathsf{s}} K(t) &\text{ iff } r = t \\
r \mathrel{\mathsf{s}} \forall x.F &\text{ iff } \forall x.r \mathrel{\mathsf{s}} F \\
r \mathrel{\mathsf{s}} \exists x.F &\text{ iff } \exists x.r \mathrel{\mathsf{s}} F \\
r \mathrel{\mathsf{s}} t_1 = t_2 &\text{ iff } t_1 = t_2 \\
r \mathrel{\mathsf{s}} F \supset G &\text{ iff } r \downarrow \wedge \forall x.(x \mathrel{\mathsf{s}} F \supset r(x) \mathrel{\mathsf{s}} G) \\
r \mathrel{\mathsf{s}} F \wedge G &\text{ iff } r_0 \mathrel{\mathsf{s}} F \wedge r_1 \mathrel{\mathsf{s}} G
\end{aligned}$$

We assumed a surjective pairing of natural numbers and r_0 and r_1 are the first and second components of the pair represented by the number r. Lifschitz read this realizability interpretation $r \mathrel{\mathsf{s}} F$ as "r solves the problem F."

The interpretation of the first order quantifiers resembles the realizability interpretation of second order quantifiers by Kreisel and Troelstra [7], which is an origin of the so-called "simple semantics" of polymorphism and data abstraction in [11].

Lifschitz interpreted the quantifiers above as *classical* quantifiers and defined constructive (Brouwerian) quantifiers $\forall^B$, $\exists^B$ as follows:

$$\forall^B x.F \text{ iff } \forall x.K(x) \supset F$$
$$\exists^B x.F \text{ iff } \exists x.K(x) \wedge F.$$

Note that the realizability interpretations of the constructive quantifiers coincide with Kleene's realizability interpretation:

$$r \mathrel{\mathsf{s}} \forall^B x.F \text{ iff } \forall x.r(x) \mathrel{\mathsf{s}} F$$
$$r \mathrel{\mathsf{s}} \exists^B x.F \text{ iff } \exists x.r_1 \mathrel{\mathsf{s}} F(r_0).$$

Lifschitz's aim was a theory of computable (discrete) numbers. But, we may give another understanding of his theory and realizability interpretation. We may read "r s F" as "the program r satisfies the specification F" after the philosophy of "proofs as programs" or "program extraction," e.g., [1], [5], [12]. From the view point of "proofs as programs" notion, $K(x)$ can be read as "x is relevant to our computation." (This interpretation was pointed out to us by J.-Y. Girard and G. Mints.) In the next section, we will explain the significance of this interpretation and how it relates to Lifschitz's logic and the second author's extended projection method.

2 Information redundancy in program extraction

One of the main problems in program extraction is avoidance of redundant codes. The standard interpretation of the formula $\exists x.A$ in intuitionistic logic is a pair of a value v of the variable x and a witness (proof) of $A[v/x]$. Suppose a programmer/verifier developed a proof of the formula above in Nuprl system or PX system to solve the problem "develop a formally verified program p which satisfies the condition $A[p/x]$." The standard Curry-Howard interpretation says "take the first component of the proof developed." Let P be the proof. Then, P_0 is p. If the program p is evaluated by call-by-value strategy, P must be evaluated to compute the value of P_0. But, P is often of the form of pair $\langle a_1, a_2 \rangle$ and so evaluation of the second component a_2 is not necessary. By simple program transformation or call-by-need evaluation, such unnecessary evaluation might be avoidable. However, as far as we stick to the standard interpretation of constructive logic, there is no way to *specify* the irrelevance of the second component.

Let us illustrate it by an example. Suppose a client (specifier) wishes to have a program $p(n)$ computing the n-th prime number. He wishes to specify the program and hand it to a programmer. If the specification is written by means of "proofs as programs" notion, it would have to be

$$\exists x \in N.x \text{ is the } n\text{-th prime.}$$

But, this is not the specification of a function which computes primes but pairs of primes and proofs of their primeness. The second component is not relevant to the client but there is no way *not* to specify the proof part.

Several authors introduced formulas (or types) to avoid such unnecessary part in specifications. Examples of such formulas and types are subset types [1], [12], rank 0 formulas [5], and non-informative propositions [2]. These formulas and types are intended not to carry any information.

For example, in PX system, if the $\Diamond$-sign is put in front of a formula F, then $\Diamond F$ is intended not to carry any computational information. The $\Diamond$-sign kills the computational information of F. Thus, a specifier can specify information of which subformula is irrelevant to him by using this new logical sign.

Lifschitz's logic allows a dual and even finer approach. Remember that Lifschitz's K could specify which information is relevant. The specification

$$\exists x.(K(x) \wedge \text{``}x \text{ is the } n\text{-th prime''})$$

says that the prime x is relevant. If we do not use any K in the body of the existential quantifier above, this specification tells that only the prime x is relevant.

To see Lifschitz's logic is more precise (expressive) to specify necessary and unnecessary information, let us consider the following formula

$$\exists q \in N.\exists r \in N.a = b * q + r \wedge r \leq b,$$

where the quantifiers are interpreted constructively. This specifies that q and r are the quotient and remainder of division of a by b. Let us assume that we need only the quotient. Then we can put $\Diamond$-sign of PX as follows

$$\exists q \in N.\Diamond\exists r \in N.a = b * q + r \wedge r \leq b.$$

But, there is no way to specify that r is relevant and q is not, since if $\Diamond$ is put in front of $\exists q$, all information is suppressed unless the order of the quantifiers is changed. In Lifschitz's logic, this can be naturally specified by

$$\exists q \in N.\exists^B r \in N.a = b * q + r \wedge r \leq b.$$

Note that the first quantifier is non-constructive and the second one is constructive. This change of quantifiers resembles "marking" in the extended projection method [13]. Actually, this is a link between Lifschitz's logic and extended projection method.

3 Extended projection method and Lifschitz's logic

The second author has introduced a technique called the extended projection method to eliminate unnecessary information in the extraction time. The method has some advantages to the other methods.

In the extended projection method, a notion of marking on realizing variables which are place holders for realizers is introduced. The realizability used was the modified realizability interpretation and thus a formula is realized by a finite sequence of realizers. The marking is the same as marking on the strictly positive occurrences of existential quantifier and disjunction, since realizing variables correspond to the strictly positive occurrences of existential quantifiers as far as disjunction is defined by existential quantifier. (Note that this is not true if Kleene's original realizability is used.) The marked realizing variables were meant to be extracted. Correspondingly, marked existential quantifiers are meant to carry information to be extracted.

In the extended projection method, a programmer/verifier writes a proof of a specification, then marks some strictly positive occurrences of existential quantifier of the specification. For example, let us assume that $\exists x.\exists y.A(x,y)$ is proved and the first occurrence of the quantifier is marked. Let us denote the marking by $\exists' x.\exists y.A(x,y)$. This marking means that the user wishes to extract x but not y.

Then an algorithm *Mark* [13], [14] propagates marking of the specification to the formulas throughout the proof. The algorithm terminates in success or failure. When it succeeds, a program (realizer) which meets the specification with marking can be extracted and it does not include the y-part. Note that the marked specification $\exists' x.\exists y.A(x,y)$ is essentially the same as the specification $\exists^B x.\exists y.A(x,y)$ in Lifschitz's logic.

The second author proved soundness of the method by a direct analysis of the marking procedure and his extraction method. Marks were counted as annotation to formulas in proofs. Namely, marks lived outside of the logic. Now, we wish to make marks (or marked quantifiers) live in logic. To this end, we should find a logic with marked and unmarked existential quantifiers so that the proof whose formulas marked by *Mark* is counted to live in the logic. The logic we seek for is Lifschitz's logic. Then, the marking procedure *Mark* would turn to be a translation from constructive logic to Lifschitz's logic. We will show this fact below.

Lifschitz's logic HA^{k} (Heyting Arithmetic HA with K) is the intuitionistic first order logic plus the following postulates (c.f. [8]):

1. $\neg\neg x = y \supset x = y$
2. $\neg\neg\exists x.A \supset \exists x.A$
3. $\neg\neg K(x)$
4. $\neg s(x) = 0$
5. $s(x) = s(y) \supset x = y$
6. The definitions of primitive recursive functions
7. $K(0)$
8. $K(x) \supset K(s(x))$
9. $A(0) \supset \forall x.(K(x) \supset (A(x) \supset A(s(x))) \supset \forall x.(K(x) \supset A(x))$

Lifschitz's logic does not have disjunction as a primitive. Non-informative disjunction is defined as in classical logic. Constructive disjunction of A and B may be defined by $\exists x.(K(x) \wedge (x = 0 \supset A \wedge \neg x = 0 \supset B))$. $\forall$ and $\exists$ are the *non-informative* quantifiers and the unbounded variables are intended to be quantified by $\forall$. Note that the mathematical induction is *restricted* only to the informative universal quantifier.

Then, we can prove the following (formalized) soundness theorem of the extended projection method.

Theorem 1. *Let Pr be the set of the proofs of HA whose conclusions are equipped with marks on which the marking algorithm succeeds. Interpreting marked occurrences of existential quantifier as* $\exists^B$ *and universal quantifiers as* $\forall^B$ *respectively, the conclusions of Pr can be regarded as formulas of* HA^k*. Then there is a translation* Φ *from Pr to the proofs of the* HA^k *with the same conclusions. Furthermore, the realizer associated to* $\Phi(P)$ *is essentially the same as the realizer extracted by the extraction algorithm of the extended projection algorithm.*

Note that the extended projection method interprets universal quantifiers as informative ones. Thus, all the universal quantifiers must be "marked" in the conclusions of the translated proofs.

The theorem above is proved by straightforward induction on the length of the proof in HA. Note that the marking algorithm in [13], [14] is not defined for HA but for a theory with typing statement on terms. The marking algorithm uses the typing statement as an auxiliary device. Thus, we consider a non-essential "typed" version of HA by introducing a new formula $e \in Nat$ and introducing the new axioms and rules below (α is a variable or a constant).

$$\frac{}{\alpha \in Nat} \qquad \frac{t \in Nat}{s(t) \in Nat} \qquad \frac{t \in Nat \quad A(t)}{\exists x.A(x)} \qquad \frac{\exists x.A(x) \qquad \begin{array}{c}[x \in Nat \quad A(x)] \\ \vdots \\ C\end{array}}{C}$$

$$\frac{\begin{array}{c}[x \in Nat] \\ \vdots \\ A(x)\end{array}}{\forall x.A(x)} \qquad \frac{t \in Nat \quad \forall x.A(x)}{A(t)}$$

The marking algorithm propagates marking on the conclusion on a rule to markings on the premises. It marks not only the existential quantifiers but also formulas of the form $t \in Nat$. For example, the premise of the existential elimination is marked if and only if the conclusion is marked as $\exists' x.A(x)$. (The marks on the part of $A(x)$ are inherited.) This propagation is simulated by the following inferences of Lifschitz's logic:

$$\frac{K(t) \quad A(t)}{\exists^B x.A(x)} \qquad \frac{A(t)}{\exists x.A(x)}.$$

Namely, if a formula of the form $t \in Nat$ is marked, then it is simulated by $K(t)$. The marking-propagation for the other inference rules are simulated in the same way. Thus, the marked proofs are easily converted to proofs of HA^k.

Next, we have to show that the terms extracted by the extended projection method is the same as the terms extracted from the converted proofs of HA^k.

This is proved by induction on the length of proofs. Lifschitz's realizability is a variant of Kleene's realizability and realizers are first order recursive functions. On the other hand, the realizability interpretation of the extended projection is a sort of the modified realizability and so realizers are higher order recursive functions. This difference is not quite essential as Lifschitz's realizability can be modified so that the realizers are higher order functions. Another possible way is interpreting the higher order functions in HEO model and compare them with the first order recursive functions.

4 ATTT and Lifschitz's logic

The first author tried to make the extended projection method "logical" using a logic with marked quantifiers without knowing of Lifschitz's work. The authors introduced a logic resembling Lifschitz's logic and presented it and the soundness theorem above for the logic (not for Lifschitz's) [6]. Our logic did not have K, but had "marked" quantifiers as primitives.[3] Then, Girard and Mints pointed out that Lifschitz's logic will do the job better. (It seemed that Girard was not aware of Lifschitz's work and invented it by himself, when he listened to the first author's talk. Mints also pointed out relevance to his own logic with similar quantifiers [10].)

Our logic differed from Lifschitz's in the way to represent "information redundancy" in proofs. Our elimination rule for the marked existential quantifier was formulated as usual

$$\frac{\exists' x.A \quad \begin{array}{c} A \\ \vdots \\ C \end{array}}{C}$$

but with the side condition which guarantees that the information x is not included in the realizer of the minor premise C of the rule. Although its intention was very simple as "the realizer of the minor premise does not contain any free occurrences of x," this condition on *proof figures* was unnatural so that some rules are inhibited in the derivation of the minor premise C. Later T. Ito and an anonymous referee for the earlier version of this paper pointed that our logic has an anomaly and did not work well.

In Lifschitz's logic, the dual of the "side condition" can be expressed *in the logic* using K. A realizer of "$K(x) \supset C$" is (roughly) a realizer of C with possibly a free occurrence of x. The realizers of a *open* formula A in Lifschitz's logic are *closed* terms as noted in 3.3 of [8]. (This is *the* trick which makes Lifschitz's realizability work.) Thus, if one says nothing, he is saying that "there are no free variables in realizers." Thus, he has to say "$K(x)$" to say "x can be a free variable in realizers." In a sense, Lifschitz's K and axioms on it are a technique expressing the side condition "x may appear freely" internally by formulas, resembling the way one expresses side conditions by judgments in LF-technology.

[3] In the talk, the marked and unmarked quantifiers are used the other way around.

Lifschitz's technique is wise, but it is not the unique solution. In type theories of the proofs as programs notion, realizers (typed terms) are first class citizens. The side condition on realizers (terms) can be expressed naturally. Furthermore, sets of realizers of $K(x)$, and Lifschitz's universal and existential quantifiers turns to singleton types and, intersection and union types. This observation led the first author to introduce type theories ATT and ATTT which are based on Singleton, Union and Intersection Types (SUIT) [3], [4].

Our SUIT approach subsumes Lifschitz's, as HA^{k} is naturally interpreted in our type systems. Here, we will show how HA^{k} is interpreted in ATTT.

Firstly, we briefly sketch the type theory ATTT (see [3], [4] for details). ATTT is a conservative extension of the second order polymorphic lambda calculus. ATTT has the notion of *refinement types* besides the types of the second order polymorphic lambda calculus. *A refinement types of type* A is intended to be a subset of the ordinary type A.

If A is a type of the second order polymorphic lambda calculus, we introduce the refinement kind of A, which we will write *refine*(A). A refinement kind is a sort of "kind" in the sense of Barendregt's GTS (or PTS). The elements of the refinement kind *refine*(A) are intended to be the refinements of the type A. The readers who are not familiar with GTS may consider *refine*(A) as the power set of A. Namely, an element of *refine*(A) is a set of the elements of A.

ATTT has term-constructors and inference rules for them which guarantee that *refine*(A) is closed under formations of singletons, intersections, unions and a kind of function space. For example, if a is an element of A, then its singleton $\{a\}_A$ is a refinement type of A (i.e., belongs to *refine*(A)). Furthermore, if $\{R_i\}_{i \in I}$ is a family of refinement types of A, then its intersection $\bigwedge i \in I.R_i$ and union $\bigvee i \in I.R_i$ are refinement types of A. Besides the indexed intersection and union, finite intersections and unions, $R_1 \wedge R_2$ and $R_1 \vee R_2$, are also available. If R and Q are refinements of A and B, respectively, then $R \to Q$ is a refinement of $A \to B$, which is the set $\{f : A \to B | \forall x \in R.f(x) \in Q\}$.

These constructors are powerful enough to define Martin-Löf's equality type $Eq(A, x, y)$, and dependent sum and product.

$$
\begin{aligned}
Eq(A, x, y) &\text{ iff } \{x\}_A \wedge \{y\}_A \\
\Sigma x \in R.Q &\text{ iff } \bigvee x \in R.(\{x\}_R \times Q) \\
\Pi x \in R.Q &\text{ iff } \bigwedge x \in R.(\{x\}_R \to Q).
\end{aligned}
$$

Now, we give an interpretation of HA^{k} in ATTT with the type of natural numbers N presented in [4], which we will denote by $\mathrm{ATTT}_{\mathrm{N}}$. Let A be a formula of HA^{k}. Then we define a refinement A^* as follows:

Definition 2. 1. $(K(t))^*$ is $\{t\}_N$.
2. $(t_1 = t_2)^*$ is $\{a\} \wedge \{b\}_N$.
3. $(\forall x.A)^*$ is $\bigwedge x \in N.A^*$.
4. $(\exists x.A)^*$ is $\bigvee x \in N.A^*$.

5. $(A \wedge B)^*$ is $A^* \times B^*$, where $\times$ is the polymorphic cartesian product.
6. $(A \supset B)^*$ is $A^* \to B^*$.

Then the following theorem holds.

Theorem 3. *Let A be a formula of HA^k and $x_1, \ldots, x_n$ be the free variables of A. If A is provable in HA^k, then the judgment*

$$x_1 \in N, \ldots, x_n \in N \vdash t \in A^*$$

is derivable in $ATTT_N$ for a closed term t.

Proof. For simplicity, we assume that HA^{k} is formulated in Hilbert's style as in [8], [9] rather than a natural deduction system. (Note that we assumed that it is a natural deduction system in theorem 1.) The theorem above is easily proved by induction on derivations. Let us consider a critical case:

$$\frac{C \supset A(x)}{C \supset \forall x.A(x).}$$

By the induction hypothesis, there is a term t_0 for which the following is derivable in $\mathrm{ATTT_N}$:

$$x \in N, x_1 \in N, \ldots, x_n \in N \vdash t_0 \in C^* \to A(x)^*,$$

where $x_1, \ldots, x_n$ are the other free variables of $C \supset A(x)$.

Note that t_0 is a closed term. Hence the following is derivable:

$$x_1 \in N, \ldots, x_n \in N \vdash \lambda y \in C.t_0(y) \in C^* \to \bigwedge x \in N.A(x)^*,$$

and $\lambda y \in C.t_0(y)$ is a closed term. The other cases are proved similarly.

Note that the term t is essentially the same as the realizer extracted from the proof of A by Lifschitz's realizability interpretation.

5 Future work

M. Hagiya has pointed out that the extended projection method might be replaced by a partial computation technique resembling strict analysis. Furthermore, a modified realizability interpretation together with a clever lazy evaluator might do the same job. Such approaches lack devices to express and reason about the relevance and irrelevance of information explicitly. In Lifschitz's logic, the relevance and irrelevance can be expressed and reasoned about by K-predicate and non-informative quantifiers, respectively. As these features are built in logic, we can reason about irrelevance (and relevance) by means of logic deductions. On the other hand, partial evaluators, lazy evaluators and the mark-propagation algorithm of extended projection method do not do any logical deduction. (Futatmura's generalized partial evaluator is an exception.) For example, one may be able to prove that f is a constant function so that x in $f(x)$ is irrelevant although x appears as a free occurrence. But, it is not been known whether such features of Lifschitz's logic are useful in the real practice. This should be investigated by applying Lifschitz's logic and ATTT to realistic examples, and comparing them with the other approaches.

Acknowledgment We thank J.-Y. Girard, G. Mints, T. Ito and M. Hagiya for very helpful comments and/or discussions.

References

1. Constable, R.L. and others: Implementing Mathematics with the Nuprl Proof Development System, Prentice-Hall, 1986
2. Dowek, C. and others: The Coq Proof Assistant User's Guide, Version 5.6, Technical report, No. 134, INRIA, December, 1991
3. Hayashi, S.: Singleton, Union and Intersection Types for Program Extraction, Lecture Notes in Computer Science **526** (1991) 701-730
4. Hayashi, S: Logic of refinement types, in Informal Proceedings of the 1993 Workshop on Types for Proofs and Programs, Nijmegen, (1993) 157-172, the formal version of the proceedings is to appear in Springer LNCS.
5. Hayashi, S. and Nakano, H.: PX: A Computational Logic, The MIT Press, 1988
6. Hayashi, S. and Takayama, Y.: Extended projection method and realizability interpretation, a talk presented at Workshop on Programming Logic, Bastad, Sweden, 1990
7. Kreisel, G. and Troelstra, A. S.: Formal Systems for Some Branches of Intuitionistic Analysis, Annals of Math. Logic **1** (1970) 229–387
8. Lifschitz, V.: Calculable Natural Numbers. Intensional Mathematics, S. Shapiro ed. (1985) 173–190, North-Holland
9. Lifschitz, V.: Constructive Assertions in an Extension of Classical Mathematics. J.S.L. **47** (1982) 359-387
10. Mints, G. E. : Normalization of Natural Deduction and the effectivity of classical existence, in "Logicheskii Vyvod", Moscow, Nauka (1979) 73–77 (in Russian), English translation is in G. E. Mints, Selected Papers in Proof Theory, Bibliopolis, Napoli, Italia and North-Holland, Amsterdam, Distributed by North-Holland (1992) 123–146.
11. Mitchell, J. C.: Type systems for programming languages, in Handbook of Theoretical Computer Science, Volume B, J. van Leeuwen ed., (1990) 365–458, North-Holland
12. Nordström, B. and Petersson, K. and Smith, J.M.: Programming in Martin-Löf's type theory, an introduction, Clarendon Press, 1990
13. Takayama, Y.: Extended Projection: a new technique to extract efficient programs from constructive proofs, Proceedings of 1989 Conference on Functional Programming Languages and Computer Architecture, ACM Press, 1989
14. Takayama, Y.: Extraction of Redundancy-free Programs from Constructive Natural Deduction Proofs, Journal of Symbolic Computation **12** (1991) 29–69.

On Implicit Arguments

Masami HAGIYA and Yozo TODA

Department of Information Science, University of Tokyo
7-3-1 Hongo, Bunkyo-ku, Tokyo 113, JAPAN
{hagiya,yozo}@is.s.u-tokyo.ac.jp

Abstract. A typechecker for a typed λ-calculus having implicit arguments is presented. The typechecker works in such a way that the uniqueness of implicit arguments is always preserved during reduction. Consequently, when it compares two terms by reduction, it can reduce them without inferring implicit arguments. Before describing the typechecker, we analyze various situations where the uniqueness of implicit arguments is not preserved by naïvely defined reduction.

1 Introduction

When we write terms in a typed λ-calculus, we often want to omit some arguments of a function that can be easily inferred from the other arguments of the function. For example, in Calculus of Constructions, if we define `andI` (and introduction) by

$$\texttt{andI} \;=\; \lambda X{:}{*}.\lambda Y{:}{*}.\lambda x{:}X.\lambda y{:}Y.\lambda Z{:}{*}.\lambda z{:}(X\rightarrow Y\rightarrow Z).zxy,$$

the first two arguments of `andI` corresponding to the parameters X and Y can be inferred from the next two arguments corresponding to the parameters x and y, because X and Y are the types of x and y.

Some implementations of typed λ-calculi have introduced the notion of implicit arguments. In LEGO [4], for example, one can declare a function whose type is of the form

$$\Pi x \,|\, A.\Pi y{:}B(x).C(x,y).$$

A function of this type take two arguments. While the second argument corresponding to the parameter y is an ordinary explicit argument, the first one corresponding to the parameter x is an implicit argument and inferred from the type of the second one. If the type of the second argument is $B(a)$, then the first argument is inferred to be a.

A Π-abstraction of the form $\Pi x \,|\, A.B$ is called an implicit Π-abstraction in this paper. Corresponding to an implicit Π-abstraction is an implicit λ-abstraction of the form $\lambda x \,|\, A.M(x)$. By using an implicit λ-abstraction, `andI` could be defined as follows.

$$\texttt{andI} \;=\; \lambda X \,|\, {*}.\lambda Y \,|\, {*}.\lambda x{:}X.\lambda y{:}Y.\lambda Z{:}{*}.\lambda z{:}(X\rightarrow Y\rightarrow Z).zxy.$$

In this definition, arguments corresponding to X and Y are implicit, and hence we write (`andI` a b) instead of (`andI` A B a b).

In this paper, we deal with two different calculi, *explicit calculus* and *implicit calculus*. In the implicit calculus, some arguments of a function are implicit and are not written. In the explicit calculus, on the other hand, all the arguments are written explicitly, though implicit arguments are distinguished from the other arguments. Since the explicit calculus is essentially an ordinary typed λ-calculus, it has good syntactical and semantical properties. However, it seems difficult to directly give a foundation to the implicit calculus. In this paper, as in the approach taken in [10], the meaning of the implicit calculus is given by defining the translation from the implicit calculus to the explicit calculus. The implicit calculus can be considered as an informal language for humans who are lazy and do not want to write long terms in the explicit calculus. In other words, it is a user-interface for the explicit calculus.

However, using the implicit calculus as a user-interface of the explicit calculus, we humans tend to think in terms of the implicit calculus rather than in terms of the explicit calculus. Therefore it seems natural that the typechecker also works at the level of the implicit calculus and is able to directly check terms in the implicit calculus. This is the approach taken in this paper. We propose a typechecker that directly checks terms in the implicit calculus.

There are some practical benefits in our approach.

- If the typechecker directly checks terms in the implicit calculus, then it can report type errors more appropriately than a typechecker that indirectly checks terms in the explicit calculus.
- In some situations, it is more efficient to do typechecking at the level of the implicit calculus than to work in the explicit calculus after completely inferring implicit arguments.
- If the typechecker directly checks terms in the implicit calculus, it can immediately reuse terms in the implicit calculus that have already been checked and stored because implicit arguments need not be inferred before they are reused.

The problem of directly checking terms in the implicit calculus is that the uniqueness of implicit arguments may not be preserved by reduction. Assume that types A and B in the implicit calculus are translated to types A_e and B_e in the explicit calculus, and A_e and B_e must be equal for a certain term to be well-typed. Since we want to do typechecking at the level of the implicit calculus, we compare A and B by reducing them to see if A_e and B_e are equal. However, even if A and B are reduced to a common reduct C, A_e and B_e may not be equal because C may not have a unique translation. If C has a unique translation, then it must be a common reduct of A_e and B_e.

$$\begin{array}{ccccccc} A & \Longrightarrow & A_e & \simeq & B_e & \Longleftarrow & B \\ \downarrow & & \downarrow & & \downarrow & & \downarrow \\ C & \Longrightarrow & C_e & \stackrel{?}{\equiv} & C'_e & \Longleftarrow & C \end{array}$$

Related Works

LEGO [4,10] is a well-known typechecker having implicit arguments. In order to make its typechecking algorithm simple, LEGO requires that an implicit argument should precede an ordinary argument. For example, one cannot declare the constant `nil` in LEGO because it has only an implicit argument. Moreover, an implicit argument should be determined only from its succeeding ordinary arguments.

ELF [8,9] is another typechecker with implicit arguments. A characteristic feature of ELF is that it uses deterministic higher-order unification for instantiating unknowns introduced by implicit arguments. ELF has almost no restriction on the use of implicit arguments. It only requires unknowns to be instantiated by its unification procedure.

However, according to the authors' knowledge, this paper is the first that analyses the situations where the uniqueness of a translation is not preserved by reduction. Consequently, the typechecking algorithm reported in this paper is also a new one, which directly typechecks a term in the implicit calculus.

Semantics of the functional language ML is also given by translating ML into an explicit polymorphic calculus, which is called XML in [3]. Investigations have been done not on the uniqueness of a translation, but on the uniqueness of the interpretation of (possibly more than one) translations. This problem is called coherence in general.

It seems, however, difficult to solve our problem at the semantic level, because we allow not only types but arbitrary terms as implicit arguments. Uniqueness is required at the syntactic level in our approach.

Overview of the Paper

In the rest of the paper, we first describe the two calculi of this paper. We then define the translation from the implicit calculus to the explicit calculus, and the notion of validity based on the translation. Roughly speaking, a term in the implicit calculus is said to be valid if it has a unique translation.

After the definition of validity, we analyze various situations where validity is not preserved by reduction. These analyses led to restrictions and extensions of the calculi. The typechecking algorithm is also based on the analyses.

The typechecking algorithm is designed such that if a term is successfully typechecked, then it is guaranteed to be valid. Moreover, typability by the algorithm is preserved by reduction. Therefore, if the algorithm typechecks term M and M is reduced to M', then the unique translation of M is reduced to the unique translation of M'. The algorithm is explained with discussions on its correctness.

The treatment of implicit λ-abstractions is postponed until the last section of the paper.

2 Two Calculi and Translation

In this section, we define the two calculi and the translation between them.

Explicit Calculus

The explicit calculus gives a foundation to our approach, because it is a variant of a PTS (pure type system), and its consistency is an almost obvious consequence of that of an ordinary PTS [1,13].

The explicit calculus is a calculus having two kinds of application and abstraction. In addition to ordinary application and abstraction, it has implicit application and implicit abstraction. The two kinds of application and abstraction in the explicit calculus have no essential difference. Only the distinction is important.

Syntax of the explicit calculus is defined by adding the following rules to that of a PTS.

$$M \ ::= \ M \,|\, N \ \mid \ \lambda x \,|\, A.M \ \mid \ \Pi x \,|\, A.B$$

$M \,|\, N$ is called *an implicit application.* In implicit application $M \,|\, N$, N is called *an implicit argument,* though it is explicitly written in the explicit calculus. $\lambda x \,|\, A.M$ and $\Pi x \,|\, A.B$ are called *implicit abstractions.* Implicit applications have the same precedence as that of ordinary applications, and implicit λ- and Π- abstractions have the same precedence as that of ordinary λ- and Π- abstractions, respectively. The β-reduction is also defined for implicit arguments.

$$(\lambda x \,|\, A.M) \,|\, N \ \rightarrow_\beta \ M[x{:=}N]$$

The usual typing rules for a PTS are augmented by the following ones.

$$\frac{\Gamma \vdash A \in s_1 \quad \Gamma, x{:}A \vdash B \in s_2}{\Gamma \vdash \Pi x \,|\, A.B \in s_3} \quad ((s_1, s_2, s_3) \in \texttt{Rule})$$

$$\frac{\Gamma, x{:}A \vdash M \in B \quad \Gamma \vdash \Pi x \,|\, A.B \in s}{\Gamma \vdash \lambda x \,|\, A.M \in \Pi x \,|\, A.B} \quad ((s_1, s_2, s_3) \in \texttt{Rule})$$

$$\frac{\Gamma \vdash M \in \Pi x \,|\, A.B \quad \Gamma \vdash N \in A}{\Gamma \vdash M \,|\, N \in B[x{:=}N]}$$

The definition of the explicit calculus is summarized in Table 1.

For the correctness of the typechecker, we require that the explicit calculus be functional and normalizing. This means that a term has at most one type (modulo reduction) and any well-typed term is strongly normalizable.

Implicit Calculus

Terms in the implicit calculus are the terms we actually read and write. In other words, the implicit calculus is used as a user-interface between a human and a proof checker. Although the implicit calculus is natural to humans, it seems rather difficult to give it a foundation directly. In our approach, we define translation from the implicit calculus to the explicit calculus. The meaning of the implicit calculus is then given by the translation.

Syntax of the implicit calculus is defined by adding implicit Π- and λ-abstractions to that of a PTS. The definition of the implicit calculus is summarized in Table 2.

abstract syntax

$$M ::= s \mid x \mid (\Pi x{:}M.M) \mid (\Pi x \,|\, M.M) \mid (\lambda x{:}M.M) \mid (\lambda x \,|\, M.M) \mid (MM) \mid (M \,|\, M)$$

reduction rules

$$(\lambda x{:}A.M)N \longrightarrow M[x := N]$$

$$(\lambda x \,|\, A.M) \,|\, N \longrightarrow M[x := N]$$

typing rules

$$\emptyset \ \mathtt{valid} \qquad \frac{\Gamma \ \mathtt{valid} \quad \Gamma \vdash A \in s}{\Gamma, x{:}A \ \mathtt{valid}}$$

$$\frac{\Gamma \ \mathtt{valid}}{\Gamma \vdash s_1 \in s_2} \ (\ (s_1, s_2) \in \mathtt{Axiom}\ ) \qquad \frac{\Gamma \ \mathtt{valid}}{\Gamma \vdash x \in A} \ (\ (x{:}A) \in \Gamma\ )$$

$$\frac{\Gamma \vdash A \in s_1 \quad \Gamma, x{:}A \vdash B \in s_2}{\Gamma \vdash (\Pi x{:}A.B) \in s_3} \ (\ (s_1, s_2, s_3) \in \mathtt{Rule}\ )$$

$$\frac{\Gamma \vdash A \in s_1 \quad \Gamma, x{:}A \vdash B \in s_2}{\Gamma \vdash (\Pi x \,|\, A.B) \in s_3} \ (\ (s_1, s_2, s_3) \in \mathtt{Rule}\ )$$

$$\frac{\Gamma, x{:}A \vdash M \in B \quad \Gamma \vdash (\Pi x{:}A.B) \in s}{\Gamma \vdash (\lambda x{:}A.M) \in (\Pi x{:}A.B)} \qquad \frac{\Gamma \vdash M \in (\Pi x{:}A.B) \quad \Gamma \vdash N \in A}{\Gamma \vdash (MN) \in (B[x := N])}$$

$$\frac{\Gamma, x{:}A \vdash M \in B \quad \Gamma \vdash (\Pi x \,|\, A.B) \in s}{\Gamma \vdash (\lambda x \,|\, A.M) \in (\Pi x \,|\, A.B)} \qquad \frac{\Gamma \vdash M \in (\Pi x \,|\, A.B) \quad \Gamma \vdash N \in A}{\Gamma \vdash (M \,|\, N) \in (B[x := N])}$$

$$\frac{\Gamma \vdash M \in A \quad \Gamma \vdash B \in s \quad A \simeq B}{\Gamma \vdash M \in B}$$

Table 1. Explicit Calculus

Translation

The translation from the implicit calculus to the explicit calculus is defined in a natural-semantics style.

$M \Longrightarrow_{\Gamma_e} M_e$ is read: implicit term M is translated to explicit term M_e under context Γ_e. Γ_e denotes a context in the explicit calculus. We also define the translation from contexts to contexts. $\Gamma \Longrightarrow \Gamma_e$ is read: context Γ in the implicit calculus is translated to context Γ_e in the explicit calculus. See Table 3 for the translation rules.

Validity

A context or a term in the explicit calculus is called a translation of a context or a term in the implicit calculus, if the latter is translated to the former. Following are the formal definitions.

abstract syntax

$$M ::= s \mid x \mid (\Pi x{:}M.M) \mid (\Pi x \,|\, M.M) \mid (\lambda x{:}M.M) \mid (\lambda x \,|\, M.M) \mid (MM)$$

reduction rules

$$(\lambda x{:}A.M)N \longrightarrow M[x := N]$$

Table 2. Implicit Calculus: first attempt.

$$\frac{\Gamma_e\ \mathtt{valid}}{s \Longrightarrow_{\Gamma_e} s} \qquad \frac{\Gamma_e \vdash x \in A_e}{x \Longrightarrow_{\Gamma_e} x}$$

$$\frac{A \Longrightarrow_{\Gamma_e} A_e \quad B \Longrightarrow_{\Gamma_e, x:A_e} B_e}{(\Pi x{:}A.B) \Longrightarrow_{\Gamma_e} (\Pi x{:}A_e.B_e)} \qquad \frac{A \Longrightarrow_{\Gamma_e} A_e \quad B \Longrightarrow_{\Gamma_e, x:A_e} B_e}{(\Pi x \,|\, A.B) \Longrightarrow_{\Gamma_e} (\Pi x \,|\, A_e.B_e)}$$

$$\frac{A \Longrightarrow_{\Gamma_e} A_e \quad M \Longrightarrow_{\Gamma_e, x:A_e} M_e}{(\lambda x{:}A.M) \Longrightarrow_{\Gamma_e} (\lambda x{:}A_e.M_e)} \qquad \frac{A \Longrightarrow_{\Gamma_e} A_e \quad M \Longrightarrow_{\Gamma_e, x:A_e} M_e}{(\lambda x \,|\, A.M) \Longrightarrow_{\Gamma_e} (\lambda x \,|\, A_e.M_e)}$$

$$\frac{M \Longrightarrow_{\Gamma_e} M_e \quad N \Longrightarrow_{\Gamma_e} N_e \quad \Gamma_e \vdash (M_e N_e) \in A_e}{(MN) \Longrightarrow_{\Gamma_e} (M_e N_e)}$$

$$\frac{M \Longrightarrow_{\Gamma_e} M_e \quad \Gamma_e \vdash (M_e \,|\, N_e) \in A_e}{M \Longrightarrow_{\Gamma_e} (M_e \,|\, N_e)}$$

$$\emptyset \Longrightarrow \emptyset \qquad \frac{\Gamma \Longrightarrow \Gamma_e \quad A \Longrightarrow_{\Gamma_e} A_e}{\Gamma, x{:}A \Longrightarrow \Gamma_e, x{:}A_e}$$

Table 3. Translation from the Implicit Calculus to the Explicit Calculus: first attempt.

Definition 1. We say that Γ_e is a *translation* of Γ, if $\Gamma \Longrightarrow \Gamma_e$.

We identify two translations, if they become identical after implicit arguments are reduced. Therefore, a context or a term is said to have a unique translation if its translations are all equivalent *modulo reduction inside implicit arguments*.

We now want to define the validity of contexts and terms in the implicit calculus. Roughly speaking, contexts and terms are said to be valid if they have a unique translation.

Definition 2. Context Γ is said to be *valid* if one of the following two conditions is satisfied.

- Γ is an empty context.
- Γ is of the form $\Gamma', x{:}A$, where Γ' is valid, and for any translation Γ'_e of Γ', there uniquely exists A_e such that $\Gamma'_e, x{:}A_e$ is a translation of $\Gamma', x{:}A$.

Proposition 3. *If Γ is valid, then Γ has a unique translation.*

Definition 4. Assume that Γ is valid, whose unique translation is Γ_e. We say that A_e is a translation of A under Γ, if $\Gamma_e, x{:}A_e$ is a translation of $\Gamma, x{:}A$. A is said to be *valid* under Γ if A has a unique translation under Γ.

Definition 5. If $\Gamma_e \vdash M_e \in A_e$, $\Gamma \Longrightarrow \Gamma_e$, $M \Longrightarrow_{\Gamma_e} M_e$ and $A \Longrightarrow_{\Gamma_e} A_e$, then we say that (Γ_e, M_e, A_e) is a *translation* of (Γ, M, A).

Definition 6. Assume that Γ is valid, whose unique translation is Γ_e, and that A is valid under Γ, whose unique translation is A_e. We say that M_e is a translation of M under Γ and A, if (Γ_e, M_e, A_e) is a translation of (Γ, M, A). M is said to be *valid* under Γ and A if M has a unique translation under Γ and A.

The above definition of validity seems natural from the viewpoint that the implicit calculus is a user-interface. Since we specify a term in the explicit calculus by writing a term in the implicit calculus, we want the former term to be uniquely determined by the latter one. However, a more serious motivation for requiring the uniqueness of a translation is that we want to compare two terms at the level of the implicit calculus.

3 Analyses of Validity

In this and next several sections, we study the calculus without implicit λ-abstractions. Implicit λ-abstractions are later introduced and discussed in Section 6.

We want to define reduction on the implicit calculus such that if M is reduced to N and M has a unique translation M_e, then N also has a unique translation N_e and M_e is reduced to N_e in the explicit calculus. If such reduction is defined, we can compare two valid terms in the implicit calculus by reducing them and checking if the results are identical.

However, naïvely defined reduction does not preserve the uniqueness of translations in general. In this section, we examine various situations where the above definition of validity causes problems. In particular, we enumerate the situations where even if term M in the implicit calculus has a unique translation, the result of naïvely reducing M does not have a unique translation.

Consider the following context.

$$\begin{aligned}
&\texttt{Nat} : *\\
&\texttt{List} : * \to *\\
&\texttt{id} : \Pi X\,|\,*.X \to X\\
&\texttt{nil} : \Pi X\,|\,*.\texttt{List}\ X\\
&\texttt{length} : \Pi X\,|\,*.\texttt{List}\ X \to \texttt{Nat}\\
&\texttt{sum} : \texttt{List Nat} \to \texttt{Nat}
\end{aligned}$$

Notice that this context is valid. In fact, it is its only translation. The following situations assume this context or its extensions.

Situation 1

($\texttt{length}$ $((\lambda x{:}\texttt{List Nat}.x)\ \texttt{nil})$) has a unique translation:

$$\texttt{length}\ |\texttt{Nat}\ ((\lambda x{:}\texttt{List Nat}.x)\ (\texttt{nil}|\texttt{Nat})).$$

By naïvely reducing ($\texttt{length}$ $((\lambda x{:}\texttt{List Nat}.x)\ \texttt{nil})$), we obtain ($\texttt{length nil}$). However, ($\texttt{length nil}$) does not have a unique translation. It has as a translation

$$\texttt{length}\ |X\ (\texttt{nil}|X),$$

where X may be an arbitrary type available in the context.
Reason: By naïvely reducing $((\lambda x{:}\texttt{List Nat}.x)\ \texttt{nil})$ to $\texttt{nil}$, the information in ($\texttt{List Nat}$) is lost and the type of $\texttt{nil}$ becomes undetermined.
Solution: We introduce explicit coercion in β-reduction, i.e., $((\lambda x{:}\texttt{List Nat}.x)\ \texttt{nil})$ is reduced to ($\texttt{nil}$:($\texttt{List Nat}$)).

In general, $(\lambda x{:}A.M)N$ is reduced to $M[x{:=}N{:}A]$, if the information in A is needed to determine implicit arguments in M or in N. If the type A is completely determined only from N, we can reduce $(\lambda x{:}A.M)N$ to $M[x{:=}N]$.

Situation 2

Extend the above context by the following variable declarations.

$$P : \texttt{Nat} \to *$$
$$Q : *$$
$$q : Q$$

Then, consider the following term.

$$\lambda y{:}P\ (\texttt{length nil}).$$
$$\lambda f{:}(P\ (\texttt{length}\ ((\lambda x{:}\texttt{List Nat}.x)\ \texttt{nil})) \to Q).$$
$$(\lambda z{:}Q.q)\ (f\ y)$$

It has a unique translation:

$$\lambda y{:}P\ (\texttt{length}\ |\texttt{Nat}\ (\texttt{nil}|\texttt{Nat})).$$
$$\lambda f{:}(P\ (\texttt{length}\ |\texttt{Nat}\ ((\lambda x{:}\texttt{List Nat}.x)\ (\texttt{nil}|\texttt{Nat}))) \to Q).$$
$$(\lambda z{:}Q.q)\ (f\ y).$$

On the other hand,

$$\lambda y{:}P\ (\texttt{length nil}).$$
$$\lambda f{:}(P\ (\texttt{length}\ ((\lambda x{:}\texttt{List Nat}.x)\ \texttt{nil})) \to Q).q$$

does not have a unique translation, because X can be an arbitrary type in

$$\lambda y{:}P\ (\texttt{length}\ |X\ (\texttt{nil}|X)).$$
$$\lambda f{:}(P\ (\texttt{length}\ |\texttt{Nat}\ ((\lambda x{:}\texttt{List Nat}.x)\ (\texttt{nil}|\texttt{Nat}))) \to Q).q$$

Reason: In the λ-abstraction $(\lambda y{:}P\ (\texttt{length nil}).\cdots)$, the type $(P\ (\texttt{length nil}))$ does not have a unique translation if y is not referenced in the body of the abstraction. After y vanishes by reduction, there is no way to determine implicit arguments in $(P\ (\texttt{length nil}))$.
Solution: We require that type A in $(\lambda x{:}A.M,\ \lambda x\,|\,A.M)$, $(\Pi x{:}A.B)$, $(\Pi x\,|\,A.B)$ or $(M{:}A)$ be valid under the context that these terms appear, i.e., A has a unique translation. This means that implicit arguments in A are uniquely determined by only examining A.

Situation 3

We further extend the context as follows.

$$a : \Pi F{:}(\texttt{Nat} \to *).\Pi n{:}\texttt{Nat}.F\ n \to \texttt{Nat}$$
$$b : \Pi F{:}(\texttt{Nat} \to *).\Pi n\,|\,\texttt{Nat}.F\ n$$

$((\lambda F{:}(\texttt{Nat} \to *).a\ F\ 3\ (b\ F))\ (\lambda n{:}\texttt{Nat.Nat}))$ has a unique translation:

$$(\lambda F{:}(\texttt{Nat} \to *).a\ F\ 3\ (b\ F\ |3))\ (\lambda n{:}\texttt{Nat.Nat}).$$

However, $(a\ (\lambda n{:}\texttt{Nat.Nat})\ 3\ (b\ (\lambda n{:}\texttt{Nat.Nat})))$ does not have a unique translation, because it has as a translation

$$a\ (\lambda n{:}\texttt{Nat.Nat})\ 3\ (b\ (\lambda n{:}\texttt{Nat.Nat})\ |k),$$

where k is arbitrary.
Reason: The uniqueness of the implicit argument 3 in $(b\ F\ |3)$ depends on the fact that F is a variable. When $(\lambda n{:}\texttt{Nat.Nat})$ is substituted for F, the typing constraint that determines the implicit argument disappears.
Solution: We restrict the process of determining implicit arguments such that even if a bound variable is substituted for, typing constraints on implicit arguments are preserved. This means that we can decompose an equation

$$fM_1 \cdots M_n \ = \ fN_1 \cdots N_n$$

into equations

$$M_1 = N_1,\ \cdots,\ M_n = N_n,$$

only when f is a constant, i.e., a variable that is never substituted for.

Situation 4

$(\texttt{sum}\ (\texttt{id nil}))$ has two translations:

$$\texttt{sum}\ (\texttt{id}\ |(\Pi X\,|\,*.\texttt{List}\ X)\ \texttt{nil}\ |\texttt{Nat}),$$
$$\texttt{sum}\ (\texttt{id}\ |(\texttt{List Nat})\ (\texttt{nil}|\texttt{Nat})).$$

On the other hand, ($\mathtt{sum}\ ((\lambda X{:}{*}.\lambda x{:}X.\mathtt{id}\ x)\ (\Pi X\,|\,{*}.\mathtt{List}\ X)\ \mathtt{nil})$) has a unique translation:

$$\mathtt{sum}\ ((\lambda X{:}{*}.\lambda x{:}X.\mathtt{id}\,|\,X\ x)\ (\Pi X\,|\,{*}.\mathtt{List}\ X)\ \mathtt{nil}\ |\mathtt{Nat}).$$

Notice that ($\mathtt{sum}\ ((\lambda X{:}{*}.\lambda x{:}X.\mathtt{id}\ x)\ (\Pi X\,|\,{*}.\mathtt{List}\ X)\ \mathtt{nil})$) is reduced to ($\mathtt{sum}\ (\mathtt{id}\ \mathtt{nil})$) in two steps.
Reason: ($\lambda X{:}{*}.\lambda x{:}X.\mathtt{id}\ x$) has a unique translation because X is a type variable. When an implicit Π-abstraction is substituted for X, the uniqueness is not preserved.
Solution: We should not allow implicit Π-abstractions to appear at an implicit or explicit argument position of a function application.

Situation 5

Let 3 be a term of type Nat. ($\mathtt{sum}\ ((\lambda n{:}\mathtt{Nat}.\mathtt{nil})\ 3)$) has two translations:

$$\mathtt{sum}\ ((\lambda n{:}\mathtt{Nat}.\mathtt{nil}\,|\,\mathtt{Nat})\ 3),$$
$$\mathtt{sum}\ ((\lambda n{:}\mathtt{Nat}.\mathtt{nil})\ 3\ |\mathtt{Nat})$$

Therefore, the term ($\mathtt{sum}\ ((\lambda n{:}\mathtt{Nat}.\mathtt{nil})\ 3)$) is not valid according to the above definition of validity.
Reason: In the second translation, the variable nil is used without being applied to an argument.
Solution: We may require that when a variable whose type contains implicit Π-abstractions is referenced, it should be applied to an enough number of implicit arguments so that the type of the application does not contain an implicit Π-abstraction.

4 Changes to the Calculi

According to the analyses, we make the following changes to the two calculi. See Table 4 for the implicit calculus, and Table 5 for the translation rules. The explicit calculus is indirectly restricted by the changes on the implicit calculus and the translation rules.

Restrictions

As we noted before, we first restrict the calculi so that implicit λ-abstractions are not allowed. We also restrict implicit Π-abstractions according to the above analyses, particularly Situations 4 and 5. In order to state the conditions imposed on the implicit and explicit calculi, we define the notion of implicit-freedom.

Definition 7. Let M be a term in the implicit or explicit calculus. M is called *implicit-free,* if any occurrence of an implicit Π-abstraction in M is within some occurrence of an explicit Π-abstraction.

abstract syntax

$$M ::= s \mid x \mid (\Pi x{:}M.M) \mid (\Pi x \,|\, M.M) \mid (\lambda x{:}M.M) \mid (MM) \mid (M^{\dagger}M) \mid (M{:}M)$$

reduction rules

$$(\lambda x{:}A.M)N \longrightarrow M[x := N]$$

$$(\lambda x{:}A.M)^{\dagger}N \longrightarrow M[x := N{:}A]$$

$$(\lambda x{:}A.M){:}(\Pi x{:}A'.B') \longrightarrow (\lambda x{:}A.M{:}B')$$

Table 4. Implicit Calculus.

$$\frac{\Gamma \Longrightarrow \Gamma_e \quad \Gamma_e\ \mathtt{valid}}{s \Longrightarrow_{\Gamma_e} s}$$

$$\frac{\Gamma \Longrightarrow \Gamma_e \quad \Gamma_e \vdash (x \,|\, N_e^1 \cdots |\, N_e^k) \in A_e}{x \Longrightarrow_{\Gamma_e} (x \,|\, N_e^1 \cdots |\, N_e^k)} \quad \left(\begin{array}{c} A_e,\ N_e^1, \cdots, N_e^k \text{ are implicit-free,} \\ 0 \leq k. \end{array}\right)$$

$$\frac{A \Longrightarrow_{\Gamma_e} A_e \quad B \Longrightarrow_{\Gamma_e, x:A_e} B_e}{(\Pi x{:}A.B) \Longrightarrow_{\Gamma_e} (\Pi x{:}A_e.B_e)} \quad (A_e \text{ is implicit-free.})$$

$$\frac{A \Longrightarrow_{\Gamma_e} A_e \quad B \Longrightarrow_{\Gamma_e, x:A_e} B_e}{(\Pi x \,|\, A.B) \Longrightarrow_{\Gamma_e} (\Pi x \,|\, A_e.B_e)} \quad (A_e \text{ is implicit-free.})$$

$$\frac{A \Longrightarrow_{\Gamma_e} A_e \quad M \Longrightarrow_{\Gamma_e, x:A_e} M_e}{(\lambda x{:}A.M) \Longrightarrow_{\Gamma_e} (\lambda x{:}A_e.M_e)} \quad (A_e \text{ is implicit-free.})$$

$$\frac{M \Longrightarrow_{\Gamma_e} M_e \quad N \Longrightarrow_{\Gamma_e} N_e \quad \Gamma_e \vdash (M_e\ N_e \,|\, L^1 \cdots \,|\, L^l) \in A_e}{(MN) \Longrightarrow_{\Gamma_e} (M_e\ N_e \,|\, L^1 \cdots \,|\, L^l)} \quad (N_e,\ L^1, \cdots, L^l, A_e \text{ are implicit-free, } 0 \leq l.)$$

$$\frac{M \Longrightarrow_{\Gamma_e} M_e \quad N \Longrightarrow_{\Gamma_e} N_e \quad \Gamma_e \vdash (M_e\ N_e \,|\, L^1 \cdots \,|\, L^l) \in A_e}{(M^{\dagger}N) \Longrightarrow_{\Gamma_e} (M_e\ N_e \,|\, L^1 \cdots \,|\, L^l)} \quad (N_e,\ L^1, \cdots, L^l, A_e \text{ are implicit-free, } 0 \leq l.)$$

$$\frac{M \Longrightarrow_{\Gamma_e} M_e \quad A \Longrightarrow_{\Gamma_e} A_e \quad \Gamma_e \vdash M_e \in A_e}{(M{:}A) \Longrightarrow_{\Gamma_e} M_e} \quad (A_e \text{ is implicit-free.})$$

$$\emptyset \Longrightarrow \emptyset \qquad \frac{\Gamma \Longrightarrow \Gamma_e \quad A \Longrightarrow_{\Gamma_e} A_e}{\Gamma, x{:}A \Longrightarrow \Gamma_e, x{:}A_e}$$

Table 5. Translation from the Implicit to the Explicit Calculus.

We then impose the following conditions on terms in the implicit or explicit calculus.

- In abstractions $\Pi x{:}A.B$, $\Pi x \,|\, A.B$ and $\lambda x{:}A.M$, the type A must be implicit-free.
- When a term whose type contains an implicit Π-abstraction occurs, it must be applied to an enough number of implicit arguments so that the type of the application becomes implicit-free.
- In an application, the argument must be implicit-free. The type of the argument must also be implicit-free.

The notion of translation and hence that of validity are redefined according to the above restrictions.

Extensions

To overcome the problem in Situation 1, we introduce coercions in the implicit calculus. A term of the form $(N{:}A)$ means that the type of term N is coerced to type A. The typechecking algorithm assumes that some occurrences of applications in the implicit calculus have been annotated with the symbol † and have the form $M^\dagger N$. While an ordinary β-redex $(\lambda x{:}A.M)N$ is reduced to $M[x{:=}N]$, a β-redex of the form $(\lambda x{:}A.M)^\dagger N$ is reduced to $M[x{:=}N{:}A]$. This annotation can be added while terms are typechecked by the algorithm. For simplicity, however, we assume that terms are annotated before typechecking.

More rigorously, we extend the syntax of the implicit calculus by adding the following rules.

$$M \ ::= \ (M{:}M) \ | \ M^\dagger M$$

Coercions and annotated applications have the same precedence as that of ordinary applications. Annotated applications are translated to ordinary applications in the explicit calculus.

Reduction Rules

For the extended syntax, we have the following set of reduction rules in the implicit calculus.

$$\begin{aligned}(\lambda x{:}A.M)N &\to M[x{:=}N] \\ (\lambda x{:}A.M)^\dagger N &\to M[x{:=}N{:}A] \\ (\lambda x{:}A.M){:}(\Pi x{:}A'.B') &\to \lambda x{:}A.(M{:}B')\end{aligned}$$

In the last rule, we discard A' because the type of x is determined by A and information in A' is redundant.

Notice that the second rule also appears in the calculus of Tsuiki [12], although our motivation for introducing it is different from his.

This set satisfies the Church-Rosser property, which is a fundamental requirement for the correctness of the typechecking algorithm. Note that we do not allow η-reduction in the implicit calculus.

Proposition 8. *The above set of reduction rules is Church-Rosser.*

Proof. The Church-Rosser property of the implicit calculus can be proved using the well-known parallel reduction method [11]. □

Lemma 9. *If* $M \Longrightarrow_{\Gamma_e} M'$ *and* $N \Longrightarrow_{\Gamma_e} N'$*, then* $M[x := N] \Longrightarrow_{\Gamma_e} M'[x := N']$.

Proof. The substitution property of the translation is easily proved by induction on the structure of M. □

Proposition 10. *If term* M *in the implicit calculus is translated to* M_e *and is reduced to* M'*, then there exists a unique term* M'_e *in the explicit calculus such that* M' *is translated to* M'_e *and* M_e *is reduced to* M'_e.

$$\begin{array}{ccc} M & \Longrightarrow_{\Gamma_e} & M_e \\ \downarrow & & \downarrow \\ M' & \Longrightarrow_{\Gamma_e} & M'_e \end{array}$$

Proof. We prove the proposition by induction on the structure of M. Almost all the cases are trivial. We check the cases of ordinary and annotated applications. When an ordinary application is a redex $(\lambda x{:}A.M)N$, then its translation is $((\lambda x{:}A_e.M_e)\ N_e\ |N_1\ \cdots\ |N_k)$. Hence we have the following diagram.

$$\begin{array}{ccc} (\lambda x{:}A.M)N & \Longrightarrow_{\Gamma_e} & ((\lambda x{:}A_e.M_e)\ N_e\ |N_1 \cdots\ |N_k) \\ \downarrow & & \downarrow \\ M[x := N] & \Longrightarrow_{\Gamma_e} & (M_e[x := N_e]\ |N_1\ \cdots\ |N_k) \end{array}$$

When an annotated application is a redex $(\lambda x{:}A.M)^{\dagger}N$, then its translation is $((\lambda x{:}A_e.M_e)\ N_e\ |N_1\ \cdots\ |N_k)$. We can write the following diagram.

$$\begin{array}{ccc} (\lambda x{:}A.M)^{\dagger}N & \Longrightarrow_{\Gamma_e} & ((\lambda x{:}A_e.M_e)\ N_e\ |N_1 \cdots\ |N_k) \\ \downarrow & & \downarrow \\ M[x := N{:}A] & \Longrightarrow_{\Gamma_e} & (M_e[x := N_e]\ |N_1\ \cdots\ |N_k) \end{array}$$

In the above cases, we use the subject reduction property of the explicit calculus and the substitution property of the translation. □

With the existence of coercions, the head of a term is defined as follows.

Definition 11. Variable x is called the *head* of term M, if

- M is x,
- M is $M_1 M_2$ or $M_1^{\dagger} M_2$ and x is the head of M_1, or
- M is $N{:}A$ and x is the head of N.

5 The Typechecker

The typechecking algorithm is derived from the above analyses of validity.

Unification

The typechecking algorithm is based on a deterministic fragment of higher-order unification [5,6]. When the algorithm encounters an implicit argument, it replaces the argument by a term of the form $?x_1 \cdots x_n$, where ? is an unknown variable and $x_1, \cdots, x_n$ are bound variables that are active at the position of the argument. The unification procedure instantiates unknown variables according to typing constraints. Roughly speaking, if a constraint $?x_1 \cdots x_n = M$ is obtained during typechecking, the unknown ? is instantiated by the abstraction $\lambda x_1{:}A_1. \cdots .\lambda x_n{:}A_n.M$. The unification procedure is deterministic in the sense that if all the unknowns are instantiated by the procedure, then there exists no other solution.

The algorithm distinguishes three kinds of variable.

- global variable or constant
- bound variable
- unknown variable

A constant is a variable that is never substituted for. It is a variable declared in the global context. An unknown variable is a variable created by the algorithm when an implicit argument is encountered. It may be instantiated during unification. Other variables are called bound variables.

If the unification procedure is given a constraint of the form $xM_1 \cdots M_n = xN_1 \cdots N_n$, where x is a constant, it decomposes the constraint into constraints $M_1 = N_1, \cdots, M_n = N_n$, each of which is processed recursively. If x is a bound variable, on the other hand, it decomposes the constraint but does not allow an unknown to be instantiated while each constraint $M_i = N_i$ is processed.

The Algorithm

The typechecking algorithm is formulated as a set of Prolog-like clauses, which is listed at the end of the paper. It consists of definitions of the following predicates.

- $\mathtt{Type}(\Gamma_0, \Gamma, M, A, k)$ checks that term M is of type A under context Γ_0, Γ. Variables in Γ_0 are considered as constants. Variables in Γ are bound variables. It computes the type of M by calling `type` and unifies it with A by calling `unify`. Unknown variables created by `type` are not allowed to be instantiated during unification.
- $\mathtt{Type}^\dagger(\Gamma_0, \Gamma, M, A)$ is similar to `Type`, except that unknown variables created by `type` are allowed to be instantiated during unification.
- $\mathtt{Kind}(\Gamma_0, \Gamma, A, s)$ checks that A is a valid type. It also calls `type` and computes the type s of A. It finally checks that s is a sort.
- $\mathtt{Context}(\Gamma)$ checks that Γ is a valid context.

- $\texttt{coerce}(\Gamma_0, \Gamma, A, A', k)$ creates a new unknown variable if A is of the form $\Pi x \mid B.B'$. It then substitutes the unknown for x in B' and returns the result in A'. If B' is also an implicit Π-abstraction, it calls itself recursively.
- $\texttt{type}(\Gamma_0, \Gamma, M, A, k)$ computes the type of term M under context Γ_0, Γ and returns it in A.
- $\texttt{unify}(\Gamma_0, \Gamma, M, N, k)$ unifies terms M and N under context Γ_0, Γ.

The last argument k of some of the predicates is described below.

Each clause defining the above predicates must be considered as a transformation rule that transforms a sequence of goals to another sequence of goals. Each goal in a sequence is an atom whose head is one of the predicates. We assume that goal sequences are nondeterministically transformed by clauses. A goal is suspended when there is no clause applicable to the goal. In particular, a goal often waits until unknown variables in it are instantiated. When an unknown variable is instantiated by a clause, all the occurrences of the unknown in a goal sequence is replaced with the substituted term.

Unknown variables are created by the predicate `coerce` and instantiated by the predicate `unify`. In order to control instantiation of unknown variables, we assign a key to each unknown and to each typing constraint. When an unknown is instantiated by a constraint, the key of the unknown must be equal to that of the constraint. In the clauses, the statement $k' = \textbf{new}$ creates a new key and assigns it to k'. Some predicates of the algorithm including `unify` have a key as their last argument. It is the key of the typing constraint represented by the predicates. If the key of a constraint is $\perp$, the constraint is never used to instantiate an unknown because no unknown has key $\perp$.

The algorithm distinguishes between the two kinds of application as follows. In an ordinary application MN, where M is of type $(\Pi x{:}A.B)$, implicit arguments in N must be determined only from N, while unknowns in A may be instantiated from the type of N. In an annotated application $M^{\dagger}N$, on the other hand, A can be used to determine implicit arguments in N, while unknowns in A may not be instantiated from the type of N.

Given an initial goal (that contains no unknown variables), we not only require that the goal should be transformed into an empty sequence, but also require that all the unknowns created during transformation of the goal should be instantiated. This requirement is made explicit by introducing the (built-in) predicate `instantiated`. $\texttt{instantiated}(M)$ succeeds if M does not begin with an unknown.

Correctness

The following properties guarantee the correctness of the typechecker:

- If $\texttt{Context}(\Gamma)$ succeeds, then Γ is valid.
- If $\texttt{Context}(\Gamma)$ and $\texttt{Kind}(\Gamma, \emptyset, A, s)$ succeed, then A is valid under Γ.
- If $\texttt{Context}(\Gamma)$, $\texttt{Kind}(\Gamma, \emptyset, A, s)$ and $\texttt{Type}^{\dagger}(\Gamma, \emptyset, M, A)$ succeed, then M is valid under Γ and A.

The correctness of the typechecker is shown by induction on the computation of the predicate `type`. In particular, we prove by induction the existence of a translation of a term on which the typechecker succeeds. The uniqueness of a translation is a straightforward result of the deterministic unification procedure.

In principle, we can consider that the typechecker implicitly constructs a translation (and its derivation in the explicit calculus) while it checks a term in the implicit calculus. When it detects an implicit argument, it introduces an unknown for the argument, and when the unknown is later instantiated, it checks the implicit argument at that point.

The most important difference between our typechecker and the ordinary typechecker for the explicit calculus is that ours does not compare implicit arguments when it checks that two terms are equal. Therefore, in order to show the existence of a translation, one must verify that if the typechecker succeeds on M and M is reduced to M', then it also succeeds on M' (consequently, M' has at most one translation).

It is relatively easy to define a procedure that constructs the computation of the typechecker on M' from that on M. However, its termination is not obvious because one reduction step may cause several reduction steps inside some implicit argument and the procedure must be called recursively.

If M has a translation, each call of the above procedure corresponds to a reduction step in the translation. Since the explicit calculus is normalizing, reduction in the translation is always finite. Therefore, the procedure eventually terminates.

Example

Let us give an example. Consider the following context.

$$\begin{aligned}
&Q : * \\
&\mathtt{Ex} : \Pi X \,|\, *.(X \to *) \to * \\
&\mathtt{exI} : \Pi X \,|\, *.\Pi P \,|\, (X \to *).\Pi x{:}X.Px \to \mathtt{Ex}\ P \\
&R : \mathtt{Nat} \to \mathtt{Nat} \to * \\
&f : \mathtt{Ex}\ (\lambda x{:}\mathtt{Nat}.\mathtt{Ex}\ (\lambda y{:}\mathtt{Nat}.Rxy)) \to Q \\
&r : R\,1\,2
\end{aligned}$$

The algorithm successfully typechecks the following term.

$$f^{\dagger}(\mathtt{exI}\ 1^{\dagger}(\mathtt{exI}\ 2\ r))$$

Remarks

Following remarks point out some weaknesses of the algorithm. It may be difficult to understand this section without looking at the algorithm at the end of the paper.

We can compare an ordinary application $M_1 M_2$ and an annotated application $N_1^{\dagger} N_2$, because if M_1 and N_1 have a common translation and M_2 and N_2 have a common translation, then $M_1 M_2$ and $N_1^{\dagger} N_2$ also have a common translation.

However, we cannot compare a coercion term with a non-coercion term in general. For example, `sum (nil:List Nat)` and $\texttt{sum}^{\dagger}\texttt{nil}$ cannot be compared. In order to see that the two terms are equal (i.e., have a common translation), we must replace `nil` in the latter term with `nil:List Nat`. This would, however, require the unification procedure to do typechecking.

Since the typechecking algorithm is not complete, the discussion about its termination is somewhat meaningless, because in its actual implementation, it can stop at any place where there is a danger of non-termination.

The description of the typechecker, which is formulated as a set of clauses, does not contain the information on how to control the selection of clauses. Since untyped terms may not terminate in reduction, the typechecker must check that a term is well-typed before reducing it. Unfortunately, this is in general not possible because a term (and its type) may contain unknowns and it is guaranteed to be well-typed only after the unknowns have been instantiated.

6 Implicit λ-abstraction

So far, we assumed that the calculus did not have implicit λ-abstractions. In this section, implicit λ-abstractions are introduced and discussed.

As we restrict the use of implicit Π-abstractions, implicit λ-abstractions must also be used with a restriction. Remember that we only allow Π-abstractions to appear in the type of a variable. Therefore, we allow λ-abstractions only through variables defined in the global context.

In addition to a variable declaration of the form $x{:}A$, the global context may now contain a variable definition of the form $x{=}M$. For example, the definition

$$\texttt{andI} \;=\; \lambda X \,|\, *.\lambda Y \,|\, *.\lambda x{:}X.\lambda y{:}Y.\lambda Z{:}*.\lambda z{:}(X \rightarrow Y \rightarrow Z).zxy.$$

in the introduction is allowed in the global context.

When a variable x defined as above is referenced, it must be given a sufficient number of implicit arguments, so that the type of the application becomes implicit-free.

When x is applied to arguments in the explicit calculus, it can be reduced by the ordinary reduction rules. In the implicit calculus, on the other hand, in order to reduce an application of x containing implicit arguments, we must infer the implicit arguments during reduction.

The simplest approach to cope with the problem is to allow reduction only when successive steps of β-reduction eliminate all the implicit arguments. For example, when `andI` is given only two explicit arguments M and N, then (`andI` M N) is not allowed to be reduced to

$$\lambda Z{:}*.\lambda z{:}(X \rightarrow Y \rightarrow Z).zMN,$$

because X and Y are implicit arguments. On the other hand, the term

$$\texttt{andI}\ M\ N\ A\ (\lambda x{:}A.\lambda y{:}B.x)$$

is reduced to M, because all the implicit arguments are eliminated and disappear.

Another approach is to do typechecking during reduction. When an implicit λ-abstraction $\lambda x \mid A.M$ is encountered, it is reduced as follows, where ? is a newly created unknown variable.

$$\lambda x \mid A.M \ \rightarrow\ M[x{:=}?]$$

On the other hand, while reducing an ordinary β-redex

$$(\lambda x{:}A.M)N \ \rightarrow\ M[x{:=}N],$$

if A contains an unknown variable created in preceding reduction of an implicit λ-abstraction, the type of N is computed and then unified with A. This seems to work well, but typechecking makes reduction very inefficient. Moreover, the formal treatment of the entire algorithm becomes complicated.

7 Conclusions

We have presented a typechecking algorithm that directly checks terms in the implicit calculus by restricting instantiation of unknowns introduced by implicit arguments. The algorithm was derived by the analyses of various situations in which the uniqueness of a translation is not preserved by reduction.

The typechecker has actually been implemented and runs with reasonable efficiency. However, users of our typechecker sometimes find it difficult to distinguish between well-typed terms and ill-typed terms. It is therefore important to characterize the terms that can be checked by our typechecker in a style that is more natural and intuitive. With such a different style of formalization, it becomes meaningful to show the completeness and the termination of the typechecker.

Finally, we want to work on the handling of implicit λ-abstractions in the future.

Acknowledgments

We deeply thank Randy Pollack and Atsushi Ohori for their invaluable advice, and Shin'ya Nishizaki for being the first and impatient user of our typechecker. The first author would also like to thank Professor Satoru Takasu, whose continuous encouragements were like an oasis in the desert.

References

1. H. Barendregt. Introduction to generalised type systems. *Journal of Functional Programming,* Vol.1, No.2, pp.124-154, 1991.
2. V. Breazu-Tannen, T. Coquand, C. A. Gunter and A. Scedrov. Inheritance as Implicit Coercion. *Information and Computation,* Vol.93, No.1, pp.172-221, 1991.
3. R. Harper and J. C. Mitchell. On the type structure of standard ML. *ACM Transactions on Programming Languages and Systems,* Vol.15, No.2, pp.211-252, 1993.
4. Z. Luo and R. Pollack. LEGO proof development system: User's manual. Technical Report ECS-LFCS-92-211, LFCS, Computer Science Department, University of Edinburgh, 1992.
5. D. Miller. A logic programming language with lambda-abstraction, function variables, and simple unification. *Journal of Logic and Computation,* Vol.1, No.4, pp.497-536, 1991.
6. D. Miller. Unification of simply typed lambda-terms as logic programming. In K. Furukawa, editor, In *Proceedings of the Eighth International Conference on Logic Programming,* MIT Press, 1991.
7. D. Miller. Unification under a mixed prefix. *Journal of Symbolic Computation,* Vol.14, No.4, pp.321-358, 1992.
8. F. Pfenning. Elf: A language for logic definition and verified metaprogramming. In *Proceedings of the Fourth Annual Symposium on Logic in Computer Science, Asilomar, California,* 1989.
9. F. Pfenning. Logic programming in the LF logical Framework, In *Proceedings of the First Workshop on Logical Frameworks,* 1991.
10. R. Pollack. Implicit syntax. LFCS, Computer Science Department, University of Edinburgh, 1992.
11. M. H. Takahashi. Parallel Reductions in λ-Calculus. *Journal of Symbolic Computation,* Vol.7, pp.113-123, 1989.
12. H. Tsuiki. A normalizing calculus with subtyping and overloading. *Theoretical Aspects of Computer Software 94,* Lecture Notes in Computer Science, to appear.
13. L. S. van Benthem Jutting. Typing in pure type systems. *Information and Computation,* Vol.105, pp.30-41, 1993.

The Typechecker

$\texttt{Type}(\Gamma_0, \Gamma, M, A, k) \leftarrow$
$\quad k' = \texttt{new},$
$\quad \texttt{type}(\Gamma_0, \Gamma, M, B, k'),$
$\quad \texttt{unify}(\Gamma_0, \Gamma, A, B, k).$

$\texttt{Type}^\dagger(\Gamma_0, \Gamma, M, A) \leftarrow$
$\quad k' = \texttt{new},$
$\quad \texttt{type}(\Gamma_0, \Gamma, M, B, k'),$
$\quad \texttt{unify}(\Gamma_0, \Gamma, A, B, k').$

$\texttt{Kind}(\Gamma_0, \Gamma, A, s) \leftarrow$
$\quad k' = \texttt{new},$
$\quad \texttt{type}(\Gamma_0, \Gamma, A, s, k'),$
$\quad s$ is a sort.

$\texttt{Context}(\emptyset).$

$\texttt{Context}(\Gamma, x{:}A) \leftarrow$
$\quad \texttt{Context}(\Gamma),$
$\quad \texttt{Kind}(\Gamma, \emptyset, A, s).$

$\texttt{coerce}(\Gamma_0, \Gamma, A, A, k) \leftarrow$
$\quad A$ is implicit-free.

$\texttt{coerce}(\Gamma_0, \Gamma, \Pi x \,|\, A.B, B', k) \leftarrow$
$\quad \Gamma \equiv x_1{:}A_1, \cdots, x_n{:}A_n,$
$\quad$ let ? be a new unknown,
$\quad$ let ?'s type be $\Pi x_1{:}A_1. \cdots . \Pi x_n{:}A_n.A,$
$\quad$ let ?'s key be k,
$\quad \texttt{coerce}(\Gamma_0, \Gamma, B[x{:=}?x_1 \cdots x_n], B', k),$
$\quad \texttt{instantiated}(?x_1 \cdots x_n).$

$\texttt{coerce}(\Gamma_0, \Gamma, A, B, k) \leftarrow$
$\quad A \to A'$
$\quad \texttt{coerce}(\Gamma_0, \Gamma, A', B, k).$

$\texttt{type}(\Gamma_0, \Gamma, s, s', k) \leftarrow$
$\quad (s, s') \in \texttt{Axiom}.$

$\texttt{type}(\Gamma_0, \Gamma, x, A', k) \leftarrow$
$\quad \Gamma \equiv \Gamma_1, x{:}A, \Gamma_2$ or $\Gamma_0 \equiv \Gamma_1, x{:}A, \Gamma_2,$
$\quad \texttt{coerce}(\Gamma_0, \Gamma, A, A', k).$

$\texttt{type}(\Gamma_0, \Gamma, \Pi x{:}A.B, s_3, k) \leftarrow$
$\quad \texttt{Kind}(\Gamma_0, \Gamma, A, s_1),$
$\quad \texttt{Kind}(\Gamma_0, (\Gamma, x{:}A), B, s_2),$
$\quad (s_1, s_2, s_3) \in \texttt{Rule}.$

$\texttt{type}(\Gamma_0, \Gamma, \Pi x \,|\, A.B, s_3, k) \leftarrow$
$\quad \texttt{Kind}(\Gamma_0, \Gamma, A, s_1),$
$\quad \texttt{Kind}(\Gamma_0, (\Gamma, x{:}A), B, s_2),$
$\quad (s_1, s_2, s_3) \in \texttt{Rule}.$

$\texttt{type}(\Gamma_0, \Gamma, \lambda x{:}A.M, \Pi x{:}A.B, k) \leftarrow$
$\quad \texttt{type}(\Gamma_0, (\Gamma, x{:}A), M, B, k),$
$\quad \texttt{Kind}(\Gamma_0, \Gamma, \Pi x{:}A.B, s).$

$\texttt{type}(\Gamma_0, \Gamma, MN, B', k) \leftarrow$
$\quad \texttt{type}(\Gamma_0, \Gamma, M, C, k),$
$\quad C \to (\Pi x{:}A.B),$
$\quad N$ is implicit-free,
$\quad \texttt{Type}(\Gamma_0, \Gamma, N, A, k),$
$\quad \texttt{coerce}(\Gamma_0, \Gamma, B[x{:=}N], B', k).$

$\texttt{type}(\Gamma_0, \Gamma, M^\dagger N, B', k) \leftarrow$
$\quad \texttt{type}(\Gamma_0, \Gamma, M, C, k),$
$\quad C \to (\Pi x{:}A.B),$
$\quad N$ is implicit-free,
$\quad \texttt{Type}^\dagger(\Gamma_0, \Gamma, N, A),$
$\quad \texttt{coerce}(\Gamma_0, \Gamma, B[x{:=}N{:}A], B', k).$

$\texttt{type}(\Gamma_0, \Gamma, M{:}A, A, k) \leftarrow$
$\quad \texttt{Kind}(\Gamma_0, \Gamma, A, s),$
$\quad A$ is implicit-free,
$\quad \texttt{Type}^\dagger(\Gamma_0, \Gamma, M, A).$

$\texttt{unify}(\Gamma_0, \Gamma, s, s, k).$

$\texttt{unify}(\Gamma_0, \Gamma, x, x, k).$

$\texttt{unify}(\Gamma_0, \Gamma, \Pi x{:}A.A', \Pi x{:}B.B', k) \leftarrow$
$\quad \texttt{unify}(\Gamma_0, \Gamma, A, B, k),$
$\quad \texttt{unify}(\Gamma_0, (\Gamma, x{:}A), A', B', k).$

$\texttt{unify}(\Gamma_0, \Gamma, \lambda x{:}A.M, \lambda x{:}B.N, k) \leftarrow$
$\quad \texttt{unify}(\Gamma_0, \Gamma, A, B, k),$
$\quad \texttt{unify}(\Gamma_0, (\Gamma, x{:}A), M, N, k).$

$\texttt{unify}(\Gamma_0, \Gamma, MM', NN', k) \leftarrow$
$\quad M$'s head is a variable in Γ_0,
$\quad \texttt{unify}(\Gamma_0, \Gamma, M, N, k),$
$\quad \texttt{unify}(\Gamma_0, \Gamma, M', N', k).$

$\texttt{unify}(\Gamma_0, \Gamma, MM', NN', k) \leftarrow$
$\quad M$'s head is a variable in Γ,
$\quad \texttt{unify}(\Gamma_0, \Gamma, M, N, k),$
$\quad \texttt{unify}(\Gamma_0, \Gamma, M', N', \bot).$

$\texttt{unify}(\Gamma_0, \Gamma, MM', N^\dagger N', k) \leftarrow$

M's head is a variable in Γ_0,
$\mathtt{unify}(\Gamma_0, \Gamma, M, N, k)$,
$\mathtt{unify}(\Gamma_0, \Gamma, M', N', k)$.
$\mathtt{unify}(\Gamma_0, \Gamma, MM', N^\dagger N', k) \leftarrow$
M's head is a variable in Γ,
$\mathtt{unify}(\Gamma_0, \Gamma, M, N, k)$,
$\mathtt{unify}(\Gamma_0, \Gamma, M', N', \bot)$.
$\mathtt{unify}(\Gamma_0, \Gamma, M^\dagger M', NN', k) \leftarrow$
M's head is a variable in Γ_0,
$\mathtt{unify}(\Gamma_0, \Gamma, M, N, k)$,
$\mathtt{unify}(\Gamma_0, \Gamma, M', N', k)$.
$\mathtt{unify}(\Gamma_0, \Gamma, M^\dagger M', NN', k) \leftarrow$
M's head is a variable in Γ,
$\mathtt{unify}(\Gamma_0, \Gamma, M, N, k)$,
$\mathtt{unify}(\Gamma_0, \Gamma, M', N', \bot)$.
$\mathtt{unify}(\Gamma_0, \Gamma, M^\dagger M', N^\dagger N', k) \leftarrow$
M's head is a variable in Γ_0,
$\mathtt{unify}(\Gamma_0, \Gamma, M, N, k)$,
$\mathtt{unify}(\Gamma_0, \Gamma, M', N', k)$.
$\mathtt{unify}(\Gamma_0, \Gamma, M^\dagger M', N^\dagger N', k) \leftarrow$
M's head is a variablel in Γ,
$\mathtt{unify}(\Gamma_0, \Gamma, M, N, k)$,
$\mathtt{unify}(\Gamma_0, \Gamma, M', N', \bot)$.
$\mathtt{unify}(\Gamma_0, \Gamma, M{:}A, N{:}B, k) \leftarrow$
M's head is a variable in Γ_0,
$\mathtt{unify}(\Gamma_0, \Gamma, M, N, k)$,
$\mathtt{unify}(\Gamma_0, \Gamma, A, B, k)$.
$\mathtt{unify}(\Gamma_0, \Gamma, M{:}A, N{:}B, k) \leftarrow$
M's head is a variable in Γ,
$\mathtt{unify}(\Gamma_0, \Gamma, M, N, k)$,
$\mathtt{unify}(\Gamma_0, \Gamma, A, B, \bot)$.
$\mathtt{unify}(\Gamma_0, \Gamma, ?x_1 \cdots x_n, M, k) \leftarrow$
?'s type is $\Pi x_1{:}A_1. \cdots .\Pi x_n{:}A_n.A$,
M is implicit-free,
M does not contain variables in Γ
other than $x_1, \cdots, x_n$,
M contains no unknowns,
no unknowns occur in
the types of free variables in M,
?'s key is k,
$\mathtt{Type}(\Gamma_0, \Gamma, M, A, k)$,
replace each occurrence of
$?M_1 \cdots M_n$ with
$M[x_1{:=}M_1, \cdots, x_n{:=}M_n]$
$\mathtt{unify}(\Gamma_0, \Gamma, M, N, k) \leftarrow$
$M \rightarrow M'$,
$N \rightarrow N'$,
$\mathtt{unify}(\Gamma_0, \Gamma, M', N', k)$.
$\mathtt{instantiated}(M) \leftarrow$
M does not begin with an unknown.

A Functional System with Transfinitely Defined Types

Mariko YASUGI[1] and Susumu HAYASHI[2]

[1] Faculty of Science, Kyoto Sangyo University, Kita-ku, Kyoto, Japan 603
[2] Faculty of Science and Engineering, Ryukoku University, Seta, Ohtsu, Japan 520-21

Introduction

The first author formulated a system of generalized terms (called term-forms) in [9] in order to provide with the foundations to the "consistency proofs." Technically, it is a device to realize a functional interpretation of a formalized intuitionistic analysis (called **ASOD** in [9]), which has transfinite recursive definitions of predicates along some well-ordered structures and bar induction applied to "admissible formulas".

Here we present a revised version of the system of term-forms, named **TRM** and consider **ASOD** in a more general setting, renaming it as **TRDB**. **TRM** is interesting by itself (aside from proof-theoretical necessity), and **TRDB** has its place among formal systems of constructive analysis.

Our major objectives in this article are to prove the normalization theorem in **TRM** and to distil the computational mechanism of **TRDB** via a translation of **TRDB** into **TRM**. The paper is designed to be nearly self-contained.

TRM is based on a kind of parametric types, called type-forms. Among the constructors of type-forms are the transfinite recursor (along some well-ordered structure), parametric abstraction, projection to parametric objects and the conditional definition (Section 2). Term-forms belonging to such type-forms are defined in terms of abstraction, application, conditional definition, primitive recursion and bar recursion (Section 4).

Section 1 furnishes the reader with some preparatory background.

Normalizability of type-forms is proved by transfinite induction on the "degree" of type-forms (Section 3), and the same property of term-forms is proved in terms of the reducibility set, following the Tait method (Section 5). The Church-Rosser property can be established by well-known arguments (Section 6). This completes the first of our objective.

Arithmetization of the normalization proof can be executed in **TRDB** with standard technique (Section 7). The opposite direction, realization of **TRDB** in **TRM** has been demonstrated in [9] as a consequence of the modified realizability (mr-)interpretation. We thus obtain the computational equivalence of **TRM** and **TRDB**. We also present, however, a direct translation of **TRDB** to **TRM**, associating formulas with type-forms and proofs with term-forms (Section 8). We can then complete our second objecticve.

Zucker has worked on the modified realizability interpretation of an extension of HA (Heyting arithmetic) with "twice iterated inductive definitions" applied to a subfamily of formulas. Interested readers can refer to [11].Our idea of **TRM** is an expansion of the "construction principle", which was proposed in [8], in order to interpret transfinite induction up to ε_0. A type system which requires reductions is not novel. We have quoted [2] and [6] as references, although their systems are impredicative while ours is not.

We have taken much of notations, technical terms and proof techniques from [1], [3] and [5]. In the separate paper [10], we have presented interpretations of **TRM** in sets and in **TRDB**. We also plan to define an extension of **TRDB** which is complete with respect to the mr-translation.

1 Preliminaries

We first define formal expressions of number-theoretic objects and relations (in the basic language $\mathcal{BL}$), and then give an account of the continuity of functionals.

Our entire theory depends on a pre-supplied, primitive recursive well-ordered structure $\mathcal{I} \equiv (I, <_I)$ on natural numbers. That is, we identify I with the set of natural numbers, and $<_I$ is a primitive recursive well-ordering on it. For the simplicity of arguments, we assume $\mid I \mid < \epsilon_0$, where $\mid I \mid$ represents the order type of I.

We assume $\mathcal{I}$ is accessible. That is, there is a functional μ (modulus of finiteness functional for $\mathcal{I}$) such that, given any $\{i_n\}_n$, a decreasing sequence from I, for any $m \geq \mu(\{i_n\})$, i_m is in fact empty.

There can be more than one order structure $\mathcal{I}$, but we assume just one for the sake of simplicity.

Definition 1. **(1)** The language $\mathcal{BL}$ consists of the following.

(1.1) Propositional connectives.

(1.2) There are variables, say $x_0{}^n, x_1{}^n, \cdots, x_p{}^n, \cdots$, where $n = 0, 1, \cdots$. Variables with superscript n are called n-ary variables.

(1.3) Constant symbols for natural numbers, say 0, 1, 2,$\cdot\cdots$.

(1.4) Constant symbols for all the number-theoretic functions which are primitive recursive in function parameters.

(1.5) Constants for primitive recursive relations such as $=$ and $<$ (of numbers). We assume the elementary relations concerning the structure $\mathcal{I}$ (such as $<_I$) have symbols in $\mathcal{BL}$.

(2) $\mathcal{BL}$-terms are defined by (2.1) $\sim$ (2.4).

(2.1) A constant as well as a variable is a term of its arity.

(2.2) If f is an n-ary term, and if $t_1, \cdots, t_n$ are number terms, then $f(t_1 \cdots t_n)$ is a number term. (A term of arity 0 will be called a number term.)

(2.3) Terms are closed with respect to primitive recursion of the lowest type.

(2.4) Let t be a number term, and let $u_1, \cdots, u_l$ be number variables. Then $\lambda u_1 \cdots \lambda u_l.t$ is an l-ary term.

(3) The $\mathcal{BL}$-formulas are defined from $\mathcal{BL}$-terms and relational symbols by applications of the propositional connectives.

Definition 2. Let c be a new, unary function constant symbol. We can extend $\mathcal{BL}$ to $\mathcal{BL}(c)$ adding c to it. We assume the computation of primitive recursive functoins in function parameters. So, for any $\mathcal{BL}(c)$-sentence A, the truth value of A relative to c can be determined. We write $c \models A$ or simply $\models A$ when A is true in this context.

We next explain neighborhood functionals. (See, for example, [4].)

Let $\mathrm{T}(f,\ x)$ be any recursive relation with a function argument f and a number argument x. The facts below are known to hold.

(CF) If $\forall f \exists x \mathrm{T}(f,x)$ is true, then there is a neighborhood function a (recursive) such that the properties below hold.

(CF1) $\forall f \exists n (a(f\lceil n) \neq 0)$, where $f\lceil n$ represents the restriction of f up to the argument $n-1$.

(CF2) $\forall z \forall s (a(z) \neq 0 \supset a(z * s) \neq 0)$, where $z * s$ denotes the sequence $< z_1, z_2, \cdots, z_n, s >$ presuming that z represents $< z_1, z_2, \cdots, z_n >$.

(CF3) $\forall f \forall n (a(f\lceil n) \neq 0 \supset \mathrm{T}(f,\ a(f\lceil n) - 1))$.

For such an a, define

$$\mathbf{b}_a(f) = \min\{n\ ;\ a(f\lceil n) \neq 0\ \}.$$

We shall use $\mathbf{b}_a$ to define bar recursive functionals (Section 4).

Proposition 3. *Let a satisfy (CF1)-(CF3).*

(1) $\forall f \exists n \forall g (f\lceil n = g\lceil n \supset \mathbf{b}_a(f) = \mathbf{b}_a(g))$.

(2) $m \geq \mathbf{b}_a(f)$ *if and only if* $a(f\lceil m) \neq 0$.

Definition 4. Let $\mathbf{b}$ denote a functional $\mathbf{b}_a$ for a neighborhood function a as explained above. We introduce the language $\mathcal{CBL}(c)$, which is $\mathcal{BL}(c)$ augmented by functional symbol $\mathbf{b}$. (We will use the same letter $\mathbf{b}$ for a functional and the corresponding symbol.) The $\mathcal{CBL}(c)$-terms and $\mathcal{CBL}(c)$-formulas are defined similarly to those of $\mathcal{BL}$ in Definition 1. ($\mathcal{C}$ stands for "continuous functionals.") For any $\mathcal{CBL}(c)$-sentence A the truth value of A can be determined relative to c. We write $\mathcal{C} \models A$ for a $\mathcal{CBL}(c)$-sentense A if it is true in this sense.

Note. (1) An unspecified function constant is necessary in our theory to give substance to bar recursion (Definition 32).

(2) Each $\mathbf{b}$ as above is called a continuous functional.

(3) The theory of type-forms will be based on $\mathcal{BL}(c)$, while the theory of term-forms will be based on $\mathcal{CBL}(c)$.

2 Type-forms and generalized types

A scheme with parameters which is to become a (generalized) type when the parameters are filled with actual objects will be called a type-form. It was introduced in Part II of [9] but here we present a revised version, and the presentation is self-contained.

Definition 5. (1) The language of type-forms, $\mathcal{L}_{typ}$, consists of the following.

(1.1) $\mathcal{BL}(c)$ in Definition 1.

(1.2) $\mathbf{1}, N, \rightarrow$, *cond*, π, $\mathcal{R}$, ρ, $\{\ \}$, $[\ ]$.

(2) $s \sim t$ will express the fact that (terms) s and t are of the same arity.

(3) We present the construction rules of type-forms below, where x will denote a variable, i and j number terms which are supposed to belong to I, t a $\mathcal{BL}(c)$-term and A a $\mathcal{BL}(c)$-formula.

(3.1) N and $\mathbf{1}$ are (atomic) type-forms.

(3.2) Suppose α and β are type-forms. Then so are $(\alpha) \rightarrow (\beta)$ (mapping), $\{x\}\alpha$ (abstraction) and $\pi(\alpha\ ;\ t)$ (projection). ( ) will be omitted most of the time. In particular, $\beta \rightarrow (\gamma \rightarrow \cdots \rightarrow (\delta \rightarrow \kappa) \cdots)$ will be abbreviated to $\beta \rightarrow \gamma \rightarrow \cdots \rightarrow \delta \rightarrow \kappa$. The x in $\{x\}\alpha$ is called a bound variable in it, and a symbol in α is said to be in the scope of $\{x\}$.

(3.3) If α_1 and α_2 are type-forms, then so is $cond[A\ ;\ \alpha_1,\ \alpha_2]$ for any $\mathcal{BL}(c)$-formula A (case definition).

(3.4) $\mathcal{R}[i,t]$ (transfinite recursion) is a type-form.

(3.5) $\rho[\ j <_I i\ ; \mathcal{R}[j,t]]$ (restriction to i) is a type-form.

(4) Substitution of a $\mathcal{BL}$-term t for a free variable x in a type-form α, written as $\alpha[t/x]$, can be defined as usual according to the construction of α. We assume that $x \sim t$ (See (2) above.) and that x is not in the scope of an abstraction $\{y\}$ in α if y occurs free in t. (We can say, in such a case, t is "free for x in α.") In particular,

$$\mathcal{R}[i,t][s/x] \equiv \mathcal{R}[i[s/x], t[s/x]].$$

Note that $\alpha[s_1/x_1, s_2/x_2, \cdots, s_n/x_n]$ will denote a simultaneous substitution, while $\alpha[s_1/x_1][s_2/x_2]\cdots[s_n/x_n]$ will denote successive substitutions.

(5) If α and β are constructed with the same rules except for denotations of bound variables, then α and β are regarded as identical.

(6) A type-form which does not contain free occurrences of variables will be called a type.

Remark. Let us emphasize that the x in $\{x\}\alpha$ is a variable ranging over objects corresponding to x, and the t in $\pi(\alpha\ ;\ t)$ is a $\mathcal{BL}(c)$-term. Abstraction and projection are not made on type-forms.

There are *no* variables ranging over type-forms.

Lemma 6. *(1) If α is an $\mathcal{R}v$-free, type-form-like expression containing Ξ, and if β is a type-form, then $\alpha[\beta/\Xi]$ is a type-form, where $\alpha[\beta/\Xi]$ represents the result of replacement of Ξ by β in α.*

(2) If α is a type-form, then so is $\alpha[t/x]$.

By virtue of this lemma, we can define contractions of some type-forms.

Definition 7. Let η be a type-form-like expression built only by (3.1)~ (3.3) with a designated letter Ξ, which is regarded as an atomic type-form, where Ξ occurs in the context $\pi(\pi(\Xi; j); b)$. (In general, $\pi(\cdots\pi(\pi(\alpha; t_1); t_2); \cdots; t_n)$ will be abbreviated to $\pi(\alpha; t_1, t_2, \cdots, t_n)$.) We fix one such η throughout.

(1) $\alpha \Rightarrow \beta$ will denote the fact that α is contracted to β, or β is the contractum of α.

(1.1) If $x \sim t$, then

$$\pi(\{x\}\alpha \ ; \ t) \Rightarrow \alpha[t/x].$$

(1.2) If $\models A_l$, where A_1 denotes A and A_2 denotes $\neg A$, then

$$cond[A \ ; \ \alpha_1, \ \alpha_2] \Rightarrow \alpha_l.$$

(We will observe this kind of abbreviated notations.)

(1.3) $\quad \rho[\, j <_I i \ ; \ \mathcal{R}[j, \ r]] \Rightarrow \alpha_l$

if $\models A_l$, $\alpha_1 \equiv \mathcal{R}[j, \ r]$ and $\alpha_2 \equiv \mathbf{1}$, where A_1 denotes $j <_I i$ and A_2 denotes $j \not<_I i$ (the negation of $j <_I i$).

(1.4) Let $\mathcal{R}(i)$ denote $\{j\}\{x\}\rho[\, j <_I i \ ; \ \mathcal{R}[j, \ x] \,]$. Then

$$\mathcal{R}[i, \ t] \Rightarrow \eta[i/k, t/w]\, [\mathcal{R}(i)/\Xi] \,.$$

(Notice that η is $\mathcal{R}$-free, and so the contractum is a type-form.)

(2) A redex of α is a sub-type-form of α which is contractible. $rdx(\alpha)$ will denote the set of redexes of α.

(2.1) $\ rdx(N) \equiv rdx(\mathbf{1}) \equiv \phi$ (empty).

(2.2) $\ rdx(\{x\}\alpha) \equiv rdx(\alpha)$.

(2.3) $\ rdx(\alpha \to \beta) \equiv rdx(\alpha) \cup rdx(\beta)$.

(2.4) $\ rdx\,(\pi(\alpha \ ; \ t)) \equiv rdx(\alpha) \cup \{\pi(\alpha \ ; \ t)\}^*$, where $\{\gamma\}^*$ is the singleton $\{\gamma\}$ if γ is contractible and is empty otherwise. (The same applies in (2.5) and (2.6).)

(2.5) $\ rdx\,(cond[A \ ; \ \alpha_1, \ \alpha_2]) \equiv rdx(\alpha_1) \cup rdx(\alpha_2) \cup \{cond[A \ ; \ \alpha_1, \ \alpha_2]\}^*$.

(2.6) $\ rdx(\rho[j <_I i \ ; \ \gamma]) \equiv \{\rho[j <_I i \ ; \ \gamma]\}^*$.

(2.7) $\ rdx(\mathcal{R}[i, \ r]) \equiv \{\mathcal{R}[i, \ r]\}$.

(3) Write $\alpha \equiv \alpha(\beta)$ to indicate that β is a subtype-form of α, and write $\alpha' \equiv \alpha(\beta')$ to indicate that β has been replaced by β' in α. Suppose β is a redex of α and $\beta \Rightarrow \beta'$. Then write ($\alpha \equiv$) $\ \alpha(\beta) \rightsquigarrow \alpha(\beta')$ ($\equiv \alpha'$), and say α 1-reduces to α', or α' is an immediate reduct of α. This step is called a reduction of α. If there is a sequence of type-forms,

$$\alpha \equiv \alpha_0, \ \alpha_1, \ \cdots, \ \alpha_l, \ \alpha_{l+1}, \ \cdots, \ \alpha_m \equiv \alpha' \quad (m \geq 0),$$

where α_l 1-reduces to α_{l+1}, then we write

$$\alpha \rightsquigarrow\!\!\!\rightsquigarrow \alpha',$$

and say that α is reducible to α', or α' is a reduct of α.

Notice that, α and α' are distinct if $\alpha \rightsquigarrow \alpha'$, while they may be identical when $\alpha \rightsquigarrow\!\!\rightsquigarrow \alpha'$.

(4) If α has no redex, then α is said to be normal.

(5) If α is reduced to a normal type-form with respect to any sequence of reductions, then α is said to be strongly normalizable.

(6) As is seen in (2.6) and (2.7) above, ρ and $\mathcal{R}$ have priorities in reduction. (In particular, $\mathcal{R}[i,\ r]$ is infallibly its own redex due to (1.4).) We shall call these priority conditions ρ-strategy and $\mathcal{R}$-strategy respectively.

Note. (1) Finite types (in the sense of Gödel) are types defined by means of N and $\rightarrow$.

(2) Suppose α is a type-form and $\alpha \rightsquigarrow\!\!\rightsquigarrow \alpha'$. Then α' is a type-form, a variable occurs free in α' only if it does in α, and, in case α is a type, α' is also a type.

(3) We could have countably many recursors successively depending on the predecessors, but we will deal with just one $\mathcal{R}$ for the sake of simplicity.

In order to assign scales of complexity to type-forms, we expand the well-ordered structure $\mathcal{I}$. The idea of what follows in this section has been taken from the treatment of γ-degree in Section 11 of [7].

Definition 8. (1) Extend $\mathcal{I} \equiv (I,\ <_I)$ to $(I^*, <^*)$ as follows.

$$I^{\sim} \equiv \{i^{\sim}\ ;\ i \in I\}\ ;\ I^* \equiv I \cup I^{\sim} \cup \{\infty\}\ ;\ i <^* i^{\sim} <^* j <^* \infty \text{ if } i <_I j.$$

(2) The rank of an *occurrence* of $\mathcal{R}$ in a type-form γ, $r(\mathcal{R}\ ;\ \gamma) \in I^*$, will be defined as below.

Case 1. $\mathcal{R}$ occurs in γ in the form $\rho[j <_I i; \mathcal{R}[j, r]]$.

Case 1.1. i is closed. $r(\mathcal{R}\ ;\ \gamma) = i$

Case 1.2. i is open. $r(\mathcal{R}\ ;\ \gamma) = \infty$

Case 2. The $\mathcal{R}$ in $\mathcal{R}[j, r]$ does not satisfy Case 1.

Case 2.1. j is closed. $r(\mathcal{R}\ ;\ \gamma) = j^{\sim}$.

Case 2.2. j is open. $r(\mathcal{R}\ ;\ \gamma) = \infty$.

Definition 9. Let $<_*$ be the order of $I_* \equiv \omega^{I^*}$ induced from $<^*$. (We can regard this as a well-ordered structure. Since we assume $|<_I| < \epsilon_0$, $\omega^i\ {}_*\!> i$ for $i \in I^*$. For a larger I, we can use, for example, the system of ordinal diagrams based on I^* in the place of I_*.)

Let γ be a sub-type-form of γ_0. Define the degree of γ relative to γ_0, $d(\gamma\ ;\ \gamma_0) \in I_*$, as follows, and put $d(\gamma_0) = d(\gamma_0\ ;\ \gamma_0)$.

(1) $d(\gamma\ ;\ \gamma_0) = 1$ if γ is atomic.

(2) $d(\{x\}\alpha\ ;\ \gamma_0) = d(\alpha\ ;\ \gamma_0) + 1$.

(3) $d(\alpha \rightarrow \beta\ ; \gamma_0) = \max(d(\alpha\ ;\ \gamma_0), d(\beta\ ;\ \gamma_0)) + 1$.

(4) $d(\pi(\alpha\ ;\ t)\ ;\ \gamma_0) = d(\alpha\ ;\ \gamma_0) + 1$.

(5) $d(cond[A\ ;\ \alpha,\ \beta]\ ;\ \gamma_0) = \max(d(\alpha\ ;\ \gamma_0),\ \ d(\beta\ ;\ \gamma_0)) + 1.$
(6) $d(\mathcal{R}[i,r]\ ;\ \gamma_0) = \omega^{r(\mathcal{R}\ ;\ \gamma_0)}.$
(7) $d(\rho[j <_I i\ ;\ \mathcal{R}[j,r]]\ ;\ \gamma_0) = d(\mathcal{R}[j,r]\ ;\ \gamma_0) + 1.$

Lemma 10. *(1)* $r(\mathcal{R}\ ;\ \gamma[t/x]) \leq^* r(\mathcal{R}\ ;\ \gamma)$.
(2) If α *is* $\mathcal{R}$*-free, then* $d(\alpha\ ;\ \gamma_0) <_* \omega$.
(3) $d(\gamma_0[t/x]) \leq_* d(\gamma_0)$.

The proofs are straightfoward, according to the constructions and cases.

Lemma 11. $\beta[s/y][t/x] \equiv \beta[t/x][s[t/x]/y]$*, presuming that* t *is* y*-free. (We shall assume this condition for such an expression.)*

Lemma 12. *Consider a type (closed type-form)* $\mathcal{R}[i,r]$ *and put*

$$\gamma_0 \equiv \eta[i/k][r/w][\mathcal{R}(i)/\Xi]$$

(See Definition 7). Then

$$d(\gamma_0) = \sum \omega^{r(\mathcal{R}\ :\ \gamma_0)} + m$$

for some $m < \omega$*, where* $\sum$ *represents a finite sum for the occurrences of* R *in* γ_0 *and*
$(1^0)\quad r(\mathcal{R}\ ;\ \gamma_0) <^* r(\mathcal{R}\ ;\ \mathcal{R}[i,r])$.

Proof. Here i is closed.

$$r(\mathcal{R}\ ;\ \gamma_0) = r(\mathcal{R}\ ;\ \mathcal{R}(i)) = r(\mathcal{R}\ ;\ \rho[j <_I i\ ;\ \mathcal{R}[j,x]]) = i <^* r(\mathcal{R}\ ;\ \mathcal{R}[i,\mathrm{r}]) = i^{\sim}$$

So, the equation can be established easily from

$$d(\mathcal{R}(i)) = d(\mathcal{R}[j,x]\ ;\ \gamma_0) + 3 = \omega^{r(\mathcal{R}\ ;\ \gamma_0)} + 3,$$

since η is $\mathcal{R}$-free.

Proposition 13. *Let* β *and* γ *be types. If* $\beta \Rightarrow \gamma$*, then* $d(\gamma) <_* d(\beta)$.

Proof. We refer to the cases in Definition 7. (1.1) $\beta \equiv \pi(\{x\}\alpha\ ;\ t)$ and $\gamma \equiv \alpha[t/x]$.

$d(\beta) = d(\alpha\ ;\ \beta) + 2 = d(\alpha\ ;\ \alpha) + 2 \ {}_*\!\geq d(\alpha[t/x]\ ;\ \alpha[t/x]) + 2$ (by (3) of Lemma 10) $= d(\gamma\ ;\ \gamma) + 2$,

and hence $d(\gamma) <_* d(\beta)$. ($d(\alpha\ ;\ \alpha) = d(\alpha\ ;\ \beta)$ can be proved by the fact that $r(\mathcal{R}\ ;\ \alpha) = r(\mathcal{R}\ ;\ \beta)$ for any occurrence of $\mathcal{R}$ in α.)

(1.2) is trivial.

(1.3) Suppose $\beta \equiv \rho[j <_I i\ ;\ \alpha]$ and $\gamma \equiv \alpha$ (that is, $\models j <_I i$).

$$r(\mathcal{R}\ ;\ \alpha) = j^{\sim} \leq^* r(\mathcal{R}\ ;\ \beta) = i$$

for any occurrence of $\mathcal{R}$ in α, and $j^{\sim} <^{*} i$. So it follows that

$$d(\alpha \; ; \; \alpha) <_{*} d(\alpha \; ; \; \beta).$$

(1.4) $\beta \equiv \mathcal{R}[i, r]$ and $\gamma \equiv \eta[i/k][r/w][\mathcal{R}(i)/\Xi]$.
By Lemma 12 above,

$$d(\gamma) = \sum \omega^{r(\mathcal{R} \; ; \; \gamma)} + m,$$

where (1^0) there holds. But

$$d(\beta) = \omega^{r(\mathcal{R} \; ; \; \mathcal{R}[i,r])},$$

and hence the inequality.

Proposition 14. *If $\beta \rightsquigarrow \gamma$ for types β and γ, then $d(\gamma) <_{*} d(\beta)$.*

Proof. Suppose $\beta \equiv \delta(\alpha), \alpha \Rightarrow \alpha'$ and $\gamma \equiv \delta(\alpha')$. The Proposition is proved by induction on the construction of $\delta(\Xi)$, applying Proposition 13 to the bases.

Note. We assume computations of $\mathcal{BL}(c)$-terms, which are effective relative to c. So, for example, $\{x\}cond[(x+1)+1 = 0; \alpha, \beta]$ is reduced to $\{x\}cond[x+2 = 0; \alpha, \beta]$. The latter is nomal if α and β are.

3 Strong normalizability of type-forms

The objective of this section is to prove the

Theorem 15 (Strong normalizability of type-forms). *Every type-form is strongly normalizable to a unique normal form (under the ρ- and $\mathcal{R}$- strategies).*

Lemma 16. *If $\beta \rightsquigarrow \gamma$, then $\beta[t/x] \rightsquigarrow \gamma[t/x]$.*

Proof. By induction on the construction of β relative to the redex of the supposed reduction. (See Definition 7.)
1°. $\beta \Rightarrow \gamma$. We consider just one case.
(1.1) $\beta \equiv \pi(\{y\}\alpha \; ; \; s)$ and $\gamma \equiv \alpha[s/y]$. Use the fact that

$$\gamma[t/x] \equiv \alpha[t/x]\,[s[t/x]/y]\,,$$

which holds by Lemma 11 in Section 2.
2°. Inductive steps. Straightforward.

Proposition 17. *For any type-form β, every reduction sequence of β is finite.*

Proof. Suppose there is a reduction sequence of β, say $\{\beta_n\}_n$, so that $\beta_0 \equiv \beta$ and $\beta_n \leadsto \beta_{n+1}$. By the Corollary of Definition 7, a free variable in β_n must occur free in β. Let u stand for all the free variables in β, and let u_0 stand for the constants (of $\mathcal{BL}(c)$) corresponding to u. By Lemma 16 above,

$$\beta_n[u_0/u] \leadsto \beta_{n+1}[u_0/u].$$

So, $\{\beta_n[u_0/u]\}_n$ is a reduction sequence of $\beta[u_0/u]$, which is a type. Proposition 14 implies that this must be finite, which means $\{\beta_n\}_n$ be finite.

Lemma 18. *If $\beta \leadsto \delta$ and $\beta \leadsto \epsilon$, then there is a μ such that $\delta \leadsto\leadsto \mu$ and $\epsilon \leadsto\leadsto \mu$.*

More generally, if $\beta \leadsto\leadsto \delta$ and $\beta \leadsto\leadsto \epsilon$, then there is a μ such that

$$\delta \leadsto\leadsto \mu \text{ and } \epsilon \leadsto\leadsto \mu.$$

Proposition 19 (Church-Rosser property). *Every type-form can have at most one normal form. (See note in 2.)*

Proof. By induction on $lg(\beta)$, the length of the reduction tree of β, which can be defined by virtue of Proposition 17. Apply Lemma 18.

Theorem 15 is the combination of Propositions 17 and 19.

Definition 20. By virtue of Theorem 15, we can define the relation $\beta \simeq \gamma$, which holds when β and γ share a same normal form. $\simeq$ is an equivalence relation. We shall have the equivalence class of β represented by its unique normal form, which we write $\|\beta\|$.

Corollary 21. *(1) $\{x\}\beta \simeq \{x\}\gamma$ if and only if $\beta[t/x] \simeq \gamma[t/x]$ for every t.*

(2) $\beta \to \gamma$ is normal if and only if β and γ are ; $\{x\}\gamma$ is normal if and only if γ is ; $\pi(\beta\ ;\ t)$ is normal if and only if β is not of the form $\{x\}\gamma$ (In such a case we say $\pi(\beta\ ;\ t)$ is irrelevant as mentioned before.) and β is normal ; cond$[A\ ;\ \beta_1,\ \beta_2]$ is normal if and only if A is not closed and β_1 and β_2 are normal; $\rho[j <_I i\ ;\ \mathcal{R}[j, s]]$ is normal if and only if $j <_I i$ is not closed. $\mathcal{R}[i,\ r]$ is not normal.

(3) Normal types are the following. N, $\mathbf{1}$, $\beta \to \gamma$ where β and γ are normal, $\{x\}\beta$ where β is normal, and irrelevant $\pi(\beta\ ;\ t)$ where β is normal.

Lemma 22. *(1) $\|\beta \to \gamma\| = \|\beta\| \to \|\gamma\|$; $\|\{y\}\beta\| = \{y\}\|\beta\|$; $\|\pi(\beta\ ;\ t)\| = \|\pi(\|\beta\|\ ;\ t)\|$; $\|$ cond$[A\ ;\ \beta_1,\ \beta_2]\ \| = \|$ cond$[\ A\ ;\ \|\beta_1\|,\ \|\beta_2\|\ ]\ \|$; $\|\ \rho[j <_I i\ ;\ \beta]\ \| = \mathbf{1}$ if $\models j \not<_I i$, $= \|\beta\|$ if $\models j <_I i$ and $= \rho[\ j <_I i\ ;\ \beta\ ]$ if i or j is open ; $\|\mathcal{R}[i,\ r]\| = \|$ its contractum $\|$.*

(2)$d(\beta \to \gamma)\ {}_*{>}d(\beta)$, $d(\gamma)$ and $d(\{y\}\beta)\ {}_*{>}d(\beta)$.

Definition 23. A type-form is called regular if it does not contain a sub-type-form of the form $\pi(\{y\}\gamma\ ;\ t)$.

Corollary 24. *Regularity is closed under substitutions of terms and constructions of type-forms except applications of non-irrelevant* π.

Definition 25. (1) $\alpha \times \beta$ will abbreviate $\{l\}cond[\, l = 0 \,;\, \alpha,\ cond[l = 1 \,;\, \beta,\ \mathbf{1}]\,]$, $\pi_1\gamma$ abbreviates $\|\pi(\gamma \,;\, 0)\|$ and $\pi_2\gamma$ abbreviates $\|\pi(\gamma \,;\, 1)\|$.

Corollary 26. $\pi_1(\alpha \times \beta) = \|\alpha\|$ *and* $\pi_2(\alpha \times \beta) = \|\beta\|$.

4 Term-forms

Subsequently we confine ourselves to regular type-forms.

Definition 27. (1) For each n and each regular type-form β, a variable-form ${X_n}^\beta$ is supplied.

${X_n}^\beta$ *and* ${X_m}^\delta$ are said to be similar if $m = n$ and $\beta \simeq \delta$.

(2) The language of term-forms, $\mathcal{L}_{trm}$, consists of the following.

(2.1) The language $\mathcal{L}_{typ}$ in Definition 5.

(2.2) $\{{X_n}^\beta\}_n$ as above.

(2.3) μ, $*$, λ, *app*, $\mathcal{B}$, $\mathcal{P}$, *cond*, σ, $[\,]$. (μ denotes the modulus of finiteness functional for $\mathcal{I}$ as mentioned in Section 1.)

(3) $\phi : \gamma$ will represent "ϕ is of type-form γ".

(4) Construction rules of term-forms and the associated variables of term-forms are given below. $assc(\phi)$ will denote the set of associated variables of ϕ.

(4.0)

$$\text{(type equivalence)} \quad \frac{\phi \;:\; \beta}{\phi \;:\; \gamma},$$

where $\beta \simeq \gamma$.

(4.1) (Axioms) ${X_n}^\beta \,:\, \beta$, for each n and β. $assc\left({X_n}^\beta\right)$ is the set of free variables in β.

$* : \mathbf{1}$; $assc(*)$ is empty.

$\mu : \{f\}N$, where f is a $\mathcal{BL}$-variable; $assc(\mu)$ is empty

(4.2) (Axioms) Let t be an n-ary $\mathcal{BL}(c)$-term, $n \geq 0$. Then $t : \{y_1\}\cdots\{y_n\}N$, where $y_1, \cdots, y_n$ are number variables. $assc(t)$=the set of free variables in t.

(4.3) (λ-abstraction on $\mathcal{BL}$-variable)

$$(\lambda : 1) \quad \frac{\phi : \gamma}{\lambda x.\ \phi : \{x\}\gamma},$$

where x is a $\mathcal{BL}$-variable. $assc(\lambda x.\phi) = assc(\phi)$ minus x.

(4.4) (λ-abstraction on variable-form)

Let $\Gamma_0(\phi,\ \beta)$ denote the following condition.

For each variable-form Z which is similar to ${X_n}^\beta$ and which occurs free in ϕ, the associated variables of Z are not bound in ϕ (by the operation λ).

$$(\lambda:2)\quad \frac{\phi:\gamma}{\lambda X_n{}^{\beta}.\ \phi:\beta\to\gamma},$$

where $\Gamma_0(\phi,\ \beta)$ is assumed. $assc(\lambda X_n{}^{\beta}.\phi) = assc(\phi)\cup assc(X_n{}^{\beta})$.

Notice that, for all Z as in $\Gamma_0(\phi,\beta)$, $Z:\beta$. These occurrences of Z are regarded as bound by this $\lambda X_n{}^{\beta}$.

λ stands for the lambda-abstraction in both cases.

(4.5) (Application to $\mathcal{BL}(c)$-term)

$$(\mathrm{app}\ :\ 1)\quad \frac{\phi\ :\ \{x\}\gamma}{app(\phi\ ;\ t)\ :\ \gamma[t/x]},$$

where $t\sim x$. $assc\,(app(\phi\ ;\ t)) = assc(\phi)\cup$ the set of free variables in t. $app(\phi\ ;\ t)$ may be abbreviated to ϕt.

(4.6) (Application to term-form)

$$(\mathrm{app}\ :\ 2)\quad \frac{\phi\ :\ \beta\to\gamma\qquad \psi\ :\ \beta}{app(\phi\ ;\ \psi)\ :\ \gamma}.$$

$assc\,(app(\phi\ ;\ \psi)) = assc(\phi)\cup assc(\psi)$. $app(\phi\ ;\ \psi)$ may be abbreviated to $\phi\psi$.

(4.7) (Conditional)

$$\frac{\phi_1\ :\ \beta_1\qquad \phi_2\ :\ \beta_2}{cond\,[A\ ;\ \phi_1,\ \phi_2]\ :\ cond\,[A\ ;\ \beta_1,\ \beta_2]},$$

where A is a $\mathcal{BL}$-formula. $assc\,(cond[A\ ;\ \phi_1,\ \phi_2]) = assc(\phi_1)\cup assc(\phi_2)\cup$ the set of free variables in A.

(4.8) ($<_I$-restriction)

$$(\sigma)\quad \frac{\phi\ :\ \mathcal{R}[j,t]}{\sigma[j<_I i\ ;\ \phi]\ :\ \rho[j<_I i\ ;\ \mathcal{R}[j,t]\ ]}$$

$assc(\sigma[j<_I i;\ \phi]) = assc(\phi)\cup$ the set of free variables in i, j and t.

(4.9) (Bar recursion)

Let $\mathbf{b}$ be a continuous functional, and let $z*s$ denote $<z_1,\ z_2,\ \cdots,\ z_n,\ s>$ presuming that $z\equiv<z_1,\ z_2,\ \cdots,\ z_n>$. Suppose m and f are $\mathcal{BL}$-terms of respectively arity 0 and 1. Let γ be a type-form, and let z be a variable which is not bound in γ. Define

$$\alpha\equiv\{z\}\gamma \text{ and } \epsilon\equiv\{z\}\,(\{s\}\gamma[z*s/z]\to\gamma\,).$$

$$(\mathcal{B};\mathbf{b})\quad \frac{\phi\ :\ \alpha\qquad \psi\ :\ \epsilon}{\mathcal{B}\,[\mathbf{b};\phi,\ \psi\ ;\ m,\ f]\ :\ \gamma[f\lceil m/z]}$$

We call $\mathcal{B}$ the bar recursion operator of type-form δ (with respect to $\mathbf{b}$), where

$$\delta\equiv\alpha\to\epsilon\to\{m\}\{f\}\gamma\,[f\lceil m/z].$$

$assc\,(\mathcal{B}[\mathbf{b};\phi,\ \psi\ ;\ m,\ f]) = assc(\phi)\cup assc(\psi)\cup$the set of free variables in m and f.

ϕ will be called a term-form if ϕ is derived from axioms ((4.1) and (4.2)) by the construction rules ((4.3)∼(4.9)). We then write $\phi \in$**TRM**.

(5) A term-form whose *assc* is empty is called a term. A term is called a hyper-term if it does not contain variable-forms free.

(6) $||\phi||$ will denote the set $\{\beta \mid \phi \ : \ \beta\}$.

Corollary 28. *(1) Every type-form of a term-form is indeed regular.*

(2) The typing is consistent. That is, $||\phi||$ is an equivalence class of regular type-forms. We can thus represent $||\phi||$ by the normal form of this class, and shall write the normal form also as $||\phi||$. If $||\phi|| = ||\psi||$, then we write $\phi \sim \psi$.

(3) If ϕ is a term, then $||\phi||$ is a type.

Lemma 29. *If $\phi t \in$**TRM**, then $\phi \ : \ \{x\}\gamma$ and $\phi t \ : \ \gamma[t/x]$ for some γ.*

*If $\lambda x.\ \phi \in$**TRM**, then $\phi \ : \ \gamma$ and $\lambda x.\ \phi \ : \ \{x\}\gamma$ for some γ.*

*If $\phi\psi \in$ **TRM**, then $\phi \ : \ \delta \to \gamma$, $\psi \ : \ \delta$ and $\phi\psi \ : \ \gamma$ for some δ and γ.*

*If $\lambda X_n{}^\beta.\ \phi \in$ **TRM**, then $\phi \ : \ \gamma$ and $\lambda X_n{}^\beta.\ \phi \ : \ \beta \to \gamma$ for some γ.*

*If $cond[A\ ;\ \phi_1,\ \phi_2] \in$ **TRM**, then $\phi_l \ : \ \delta_l$, $l = 1,\ 2$, and $cond[A\ ;\ \phi_1,\ \phi_2] \ : \ cond[A\ ;\ \delta_1,\ \delta_2]$ for some δ_1 and δ_2.*

*If $\sigma[j <_I i\ ;\ \phi] \in$**TRM**, then there is an α such that $\phi : \alpha$ and $\sigma[j <_I i\ ;\ \phi] \ : \ \rho[j <_I i\ ;\ \alpha]$.*

*If $\mathcal{B}[\mathbf{b};\ \phi,\ \psi\ ;\ m,\ f] \in$ **TRM**, then there is γ as in (4.9) of Definition 27 and $\mathcal{B}[\mathbf{b};\ \phi,\ \psi\ ;\ m,\ f] \ : \ \gamma[f\lceil m/z]$.*

Definition 30. (1) Substitution of a $\mathcal{BL}(c)$-term for a free variable in a term-form, say $\phi[t/x]$, is defined as follows. (We can assume that t is "free for x in ϕ", since we can change the bound variables in ϕ otherwise.)

$X^\beta[t/x] \equiv X^{\beta[t/x]}$; $f[t/x] \equiv f$; $(\lambda y.\ \phi)[t/x] \equiv \lambda\ y.\ \phi[t/x]$; $(\lambda X^\beta.\phi)[t/x] \equiv \lambda\ X^\beta[t/x].\ \phi[t/x]$; $(\phi\psi)[t/x] \equiv \phi[t/x]\psi[t/x]$; $(\phi\ s)[t/x] \equiv \phi[t/x]s[t/x]$; $cond[A;\phi_1,\phi_2][t/x] \equiv cond\,[A[t/x];\phi_1[t/x]\ ,\ \phi_2[t/x]]$;
$\sigma[j <_I i\ ;\ \phi][t/x] \equiv \sigma[j[t/x] <_I i[t/x]\ ;\ \phi[t/x]]$;
$\mathcal{B}[\mathbf{b};\phi,\psi;m,f][t/x] \equiv \mathcal{B}\,[\mathbf{b};\phi[t/x],\psi[t/x];m[t/x],f[t/x]]$.

(2) Substitution of a term-form ψ for a variable-form $X_n{}^\beta$ in ϕ, $\phi\left[\psi/X_n{}^\beta\right]$, is defined when the conditions in (C) below are satisfied.

(C) (C1) $\psi \ : \ \beta$.

In the following, Z will denote a variable-form which is similar to $X_n{}^\beta$. (See (1) of Definition 27.)

(C2) The associated variables of Z are not bound in ϕ.

(C3) Suppose x is an associated variable of ψ. Then Z is not in the scope of λx in ϕ.

(C4) Suppose Y is a variable-form occurring free in ψ. Then Z is not in the scope of λY in ϕ.(We say "ψ is free for Z in ϕ" if this condition is satisfied.)

When (C1)∼(C4) are satisfied, ψ is substituted for Z for every Z as above. We write X for $X_n{}^\beta$ for simplicity.

$X_m{}^\delta[\psi/X] \equiv \psi$ if $m = n$ and $\delta \simeq \beta$, and $X_m{}^\delta[\psi/X] \equiv X_m{}^\delta$ otherwise ; $*[\psi/X] \equiv *$; $f[\psi/X] \equiv f$; $(\phi\chi)[\psi/X] \equiv \phi[\psi/X]\chi[\psi/X]$; $(\phi t)[\psi/X] \equiv \phi[\psi/X]t$; $(\lambda x.\phi)[\psi/X] \equiv \lambda x.\phi[\psi/X]$; $(\lambda Y.\phi)[\psi/X] \equiv \lambda Y.\phi[\psi/X]$; $cond[A;\phi_1,\phi_2][\psi/X] \equiv cond\,[A;\phi_1[\psi/X],\phi_2[\psi/X]]$; $\sigma[j <_I i\ ;\ \phi][\psi/X] \equiv \sigma[j <_I i\ ;\ \phi[\psi/X]]$; $\mathcal{B}[\mathbf{b};\phi,\xi;m,f][\psi/X] \equiv \mathcal{B}\,[\mathbf{b};\phi[\psi/X],\xi[\psi/X];m,f]$.

Notice that, if $(\phi,\ X,\ \psi)$ satisfies the conditions in (C), then so does $(\phi',\ X,\ \psi)$ for each ϕ', where ϕ' is used in the hypothesis of an induction step in forming ϕ. $\phi[\psi/X]$ is therefore well-defined.

We shall say that ϕ is "X-inactive for substitution" if there is no free occurrence of variable-forms similar to X.

Lemma 31. *(1) Term-forms are closed under substitutions, and, if $\phi\ :\ \gamma$, then $\phi[t/x]\ :\ \gamma[t/x]$ and $\phi[\psi/X]\ :\ \gamma$.*

(2) $\phi[s/y][t/x] \equiv \phi[t/x]\,[s[t/x]/y]$, presuming that t is y-free.

(3) $\phi[\psi/X][t/x] \equiv \phi[t/x]\,[\psi[t/x]/X[t/x]]$.

(4) $\phi[\chi/Y][\psi/X] \equiv \phi[\psi/X]\,[\chi[\psi/X]/Y]$, presuming that X and Y are not similar and ψ is Y-inactive for substitution.

The proof is by induction on the construction of ϕ, using Lemma 11 in Section 2 and the fact that $\beta \simeq \gamma$ implies $\beta[t/x] \simeq \gamma[t/x]$.

By virtue of this lemma, we can define contractions of some term-forms.

Definition 32. (1) Contractions of some of term-forms (written as $\phi \Rightarrow \psi$) are defined below. ψ is called the contractum of ϕ, and ϕ is said to be contractible to ψ.

(1.1) If $x \sim t$, then

$$(\lambda x.\phi)t \Rightarrow \phi[t/x].$$

(1.2) If $X \sim \psi$ (See (2) of Corollary of Definition 27.), then

$$(\lambda X.\phi)\psi \Rightarrow \phi[\psi/X].$$

Notice that condition $\Gamma_0(\phi,\beta)$ of (4.4) in Definition 27 implies (C). ((C3) and (C4) can be satisfied by adjustments of bound variables and variable-forms.)

(1.3) If $\models A_l$ (where $A_1 \equiv A$ and $A_2 \equiv \neg A$), then

$$cond[A\ ;\ \phi_1,\ \phi_2] \Rightarrow \phi_l.$$

(1.4) $\sigma[j <_I i\ ;\ \phi] \Rightarrow \phi$ if $\models j <_I i$, and $\sigma[j <_I i\ ;\ \phi] \Rightarrow *$ if $\models j \not<_I i$.

(1.5) $\mathcal{B}[\ \mathbf{b}\ ;\ \phi,\ \psi\ ;\ m,\ f\ ] \Rightarrow app(\phi\ ;\ f\lceil m)$ if $\mathcal{C} \models \mathbf{b}(f) \leq m$,

$\mathcal{B}[\ \mathbf{b}\ ;\ \phi,\ \psi\ ;\ m,\ f\ ] \Rightarrow \mathcal{B}\{m+1\}$ if $\mathcal{C} \models \mathbf{b}(f) > m$,

where $\mathcal{B}\{m+1\}$ abbreviates

$$app\,(app(\psi\ ;\ f\lceil m)\ ;\ \lambda k.\mathcal{B}[\ \mathbf{b}\ ;\ \phi,\ \psi\ ;\ m+1,\ (f\lceil m)*k]).$$

(1.6) Let t be a closed, $\mathcal{BL}(c)$-term.

$$t \Rightarrow s,$$

if s is the result of computation of t.

(2) $rdx(\phi)$ will denote the set of redexes of ϕ.

(2.1) $rdx(\phi)$ is empty if ϕ is a variable-form, function constant or $*$.

(2.2) $rdx(\lambda x.\phi) \equiv rdx(\phi)$.

(2.3) $rdx(\lambda X.\phi) \equiv rdx(\phi)$.

(2.4) $rdx(\phi t) \equiv rdx(\phi) \cup \{\phi t\}^*$, where $\{\theta\}^*$ is the singleton $\{\theta\}$ if θ is contractible and is empty otherwise.

(2.5) $rdx(\phi\psi) \equiv rdx(\phi) \cup rdx(\psi) \cup \{\phi\psi\}^*$.

(2.6) $rdx\,(cond[A\ ;\ \phi_1,\ \phi_2]) \equiv rdx(\phi_1) \cup rdx(\phi_2) \cup \{cond[A\ ;\ \phi_1,\ \phi_2]\}^*$.

(2.7) $rdx\,(\sigma[j <_I i\ ;\ \phi]) \equiv \{\sigma[j <_I i\ ;\ \phi]\}^*$.

(2.8) $rdx\,(\mathcal{B}[\mathbf{b}\ ;\ \phi\ ,\ \psi\ ;\ m,\ f]) \equiv \{\mathcal{B}[\mathbf{b}\ ;\ \phi,\ \psi\ ;\ m,\ f]\}^*$.

Corollary 33. *The contractum of each contraction is a term-form.*

Definition 34. (1) Let $\phi \equiv \phi(\psi)$, where ψ is a redex of ϕ and $\psi \Rightarrow \psi'$. Then we write

$$\phi \equiv \phi(\psi) \rightsquigarrow \phi(\psi') \equiv \phi',$$

and call ϕ' an immediate reduct of ϕ. (See (3) of Definition 7 for these notations.) We also say ϕ 1-reduces to ϕ'. This step is called a reduction of ϕ.

(2) If there is a sequence of term-forms $\{\phi_l\}_{l \le m}$, where $m \ge 0$, $\phi_0 \equiv \phi$, $\phi_m \equiv \phi'$ and $\phi_l \rightsquigarrow \phi_{l+1}$, then we write

$$\phi \rightsquigarrow\!\!\!\rightsquigarrow \phi',$$

and say ϕ reduces to ϕ', or ϕ' is a reduct of ϕ.

(3) If ϕ has no redex, then ϕ is said to be normal.

As is seen in (2.7) and (2.8) above, σ and $\mathcal{B}$ have priorities in reduction, the facts of which will be called σ-strategy and $\mathcal{B}$-strategy.

Lemma 35. *(1) If $\chi \Rightarrow \chi'$, then $\chi \sim \chi'$ and $assc(\chi') \subset assc(\chi)$.*

*(2) If $\phi \in$ **TRM** and $\phi \rightsquigarrow \phi'$, then $\phi' \in$ **TRM**, $\phi \sim \phi'$ and no new variables or variable-forms arise in ϕ'. In particular, $assc(\phi') \subset assc(\phi)$.*

The proofs are straightforward, according to the constructions of term-forms and the corollary above.

From the lemma it follows immediately that

Proposition 36. *If $\phi \rightsquigarrow\!\!\!\rightsquigarrow \phi'$, then $\phi \sim \phi'$ and $assc(\phi') \subset assc(\phi)$.*

Lemma 37. *(1) If $\phi \sim \psi$, then $\phi[t/x] \sim \psi[t/x]$. (A consequence of (1) of Lemma 31.)*

(2) $\lambda X.\ \phi \rightsquigarrow \psi$ if and only if $\psi \equiv \lambda X.\ \phi'$ and $\phi \rightsquigarrow \phi'$.

$\lambda y.\ \phi \rightsquigarrow \psi$ if and only if $\psi \equiv \lambda y.\ \phi'$ and $\phi \rightsquigarrow \phi'$.

(3) If $\phi \rightsquigarrow \phi'$ or $\psi \rightsquigarrow \psi'$, then respectively $\phi\psi \rightsquigarrow \phi'\psi$ or $\phi\psi \rightsquigarrow \phi\psi'$.

If $\phi \rightsquigarrow \phi'$, then $\phi t \rightsquigarrow \phi' t$.

(4) If ϕ is not an abstraction and $\phi t \rightsquigarrow \psi$,then $\psi \equiv \phi' t$ where $\phi \rightsquigarrow \phi'$. If $\phi\chi \rightsquigarrow \psi$, , then $\psi \equiv \phi'\chi$ or $\psi \equiv \phi\chi'$, where $\phi \rightsquigarrow \phi'$ or $\chi \rightsquigarrow \chi'$.

(5) $cond[A\ ;\ \phi_1,\ \phi_2] \rightsquigarrow \psi$ if and only if $\psi \equiv cond[A\ ;\ \phi_1',\ \phi_2']$ where $\phi_l \rightsquigarrow \phi_l'$ and $\phi_k' \equiv \phi_k (k \neq l)$, or $\psi \equiv \phi_l$ and $\models A_l$. $\sigma[j <_I i\ ;\ \phi] \rightsquigarrow \psi$ if and only if one of the following holds; $\models j <_I i$ and ψ is *ϕ, or $\not\models j <_I i$ and ψ* is *$*$.*

Lemma 38. *If $\phi \rightsquigarrow \psi$, then $\phi[t/x] \rightsquigarrow \psi[t/x]$ and $\phi[\chi/X] \rightsquigarrow \psi[\chi/X]$.*

The proof is by induction on the construction of ϕ relative to its redex, using Lemmas 35 and 37.

Proposition 39. *Normal terms (that is, normal term-forms without associated variables) are of the following form.*

${X_n}^\beta$, $*$, μ, function constants, $\lambda X.\phi$ and $\lambda x.\phi$ where ϕ is normal, ϕt and $\phi\chi$ where ϕ and χ are normal and ϕ is not an abstraction.

5 Reducibility and normalization

Definition 40. A term-form, say ϕ, is said to be strongly normalizable if every reduction sequence of ϕ (under σ-strategy and $\mathcal{B}$-strategy) is finite. We write $\phi \in sn$ in such a case.

Strong normalizability of term-forms is established according to the Tait method by means of a reducibility set of terms. We have referred to [3]. We define here a reducibility set for every normal type by transfinite induction on degree of type. Due to the presence of bar recursion, we are forced to work with reductions under σ- and β-strategies.

Definition 41. (1) Let β be any normal type. We define the reducibility set *Red*(β) of terms as follows. When we write $\phi \in$ *Red*(β), we assume $\phi\ :\ \beta$. (See Corollary of Definition 27.)

(1.1) β is atomic or irrelevant. $\phi \in$ *Red*(β) if $\phi \in sn$.

(1.2) $\phi \in$ *Red*$(\{x\}\gamma)$ if, for every closed $\mathcal{BL}$-term t (where $x \sim t$), $\phi t \in$ *Red*$(\|\gamma[t/x]\|)$.

(1.3) $\phi \in$ *Red*($\beta \rightarrow \gamma$) if, for every $\psi \in$ *Red*(β), $\phi\psi \in$ *Red*(γ).

(2) For any term ϕ, $\phi \in$ *Red* if $\phi \in$ *Red*$(\|\phi\|)$, and in this case ϕ is said to be reducible.

(3) A term is said to be neutral if it is not of the form $\lambda x.\phi$, $\lambda X.\phi$, or $f\phi_1 \cdots \phi_n$.

Corollary 42. *Red(β) is well-defined.*

Proof. By transfinite induction on $d(\beta)$. Consult Definition 9, Lemma 10, Definition 30, Proposition 14, Theorem 15 and Corollary of Definition 20.

As the fundamental properties of reducibility sets, we list the following reducibility conditions.
(RC)
(*Red* 1) If $\phi \in Red(\beta)$, then $\phi \in sn$ (ϕ is strongly normalizable.).
(*Red* 2) If $\phi \in Red(\beta)$ and $\phi \rightsquigarrow\!\!\rightsquigarrow \phi'$, then $\phi' \in Red(\beta)$.
(*Red* 3) If ϕ is neutral, $\phi \;:\; \beta$ and, for every immediate reduct of ϕ, say ϕ', $\phi' \in Red(\beta)$, then $\phi \in Red(\beta)$.

Notice that, in (*Red* 2) and (*Red* 3), $\phi' \;:\; \beta$ by virtue of Proposition 36.

Corollary 43. *(RC) implies the following.*

(Red 4) If ϕ is neutral and normal, then $\phi \in Red$.
(Red 5) For every variable-form X^β, $X^\beta \in Red(\|\beta\|)$ (and hence $X^\beta \in sn$).

We can thus include (*Red* 4) and (*Red* 5) in (RC) once (*Red* 1) $\sim$ (*Red* 3) are established.

The main purpose of this section is to prove the

Lemma 44 (Reducibility Lemma). *(RC) holds for all normal type β.*

(*Red* 1) will be restated as a proposition.

Proposition 45. *If $\phi \in Red$, then $\phi \in sn$.*

We will also prove the

Theorem 46. *All terms are reducible.*

We are then led to two conclusions.

Conclusion 47. *Every term is strongly normalizable.*

This follows immediately from Proposition 45 and Theorem 46.

Conclusion 48. *Every term-form is strongly normalizable.*

Proof. Suppose not. That is,
(*) there is an infinite sequence $\{\phi_n\}$ of term-forms where $\phi_n \rightsquigarrow \phi_{n+1}$. Recall that no new associated variables occur in the reducts. So, let $x_1, \cdots, x_m$ be distinct, associated variables of ϕ_0, and let $f_1, \cdots, f_m$ be any closed $\mathcal{BL}$-terms of corresponding types. Then, by Lemma 38 in Section 4,

$$\{\phi_n[f_1/x_1, \cdots, f_m/x_m]\}_n$$

satisfies the same condition as (*). But this contradicts Conclusion 47.

We now turn to the proofs of Reducibility Lemma and Theorem 46. Recall that we are dealing with terms, not general term-forms.

Proof of Reducibility Lemma. This is proved by transfinite induction on $d(\beta)$, within which by induction on $\nu(\phi)$, length of the "reduction tree" of ϕ when ϕ is known to be strongly normalizable. (The existence of such number can be proved as usual.) Lemmas in Sections 2,3 and 4 will be used without references.

(1) $d(\beta) = 1$ (β is atomic) or β is irrelevant. By definition, $\phi \in Red(\beta)$ if and only if $\phi \in sn$, and hence (RC) follows immediately. Recall that $\phi \rightsquigarrow\rightsquigarrow \psi$ implies $\phi \sim \psi$.

Suppose henceforth $d(\beta) \,_*{>} 1$ and β is not irrelevant.

(2) β is $\{x\}\gamma$. Recall that $d(\|\gamma[t/x]\|) <_* d(\{x\}\gamma)$. By the induction hypotheses applied to ϕt, (CR 1) ~ (CR 5) hold for $\|\gamma[t/x]\|$. We write (CR l') for these.

(CR 1) Suppose $\phi \in Red(\beta)$. Then $\phi t \in Red(\|\gamma[t/x]\|)$, and hence (CR 1′) implies $\phi t \in sn$. A reduction sequence $\{\phi_n\}$ of ϕ would induce the one $\{\phi_n t\}$ of ϕt, so that $\{\phi_n\}$ must be finite. That is, $\phi \in sn$.

(CR 2) Suppose $\phi \in Red(\beta)$ and $\phi \rightsquigarrow\rightsquigarrow \psi$. Then $\phi t \rightsquigarrow\rightsquigarrow \psi t$. Since $\phi t \in Red(\|\gamma[t/x]\|)$, (CR 2′) implies $\psi t \in Red(\|\gamma[t/x]\|)$. This is true with every t, and hence by definition $\psi \in Red(\beta)$.

(CR 3) Suppose ϕ is neutral and for each immediate reduct ψ, $\psi \in Red(\beta)$. $\phi t \rightsquigarrow \chi$ means $\chi \equiv \psi t$ and $\phi \rightsquigarrow \psi$. By definition, $\psi t \in Red(\|\gamma[t/x]\|)$. $\phi t \in Red(\|\gamma[t/x]\|)$ by (CR3′). This is true with every t, and hence $\phi \in Red(\beta)$.

(3) β is $\gamma \to \alpha$. (CR 1′) ~(CR 5′) hold for every $\psi \in Red(\gamma)$ and $\phi\psi \in Red(\alpha)$.

(CR 1) Suppose $\phi \in Red(\beta)$. $X^\gamma \in Red(\gamma)$ by (CR 5′). So, $\phi X^\gamma \in Red(\alpha)$ by definition, and hence, by (CR 1′), $\phi X^\gamma \in sn$, which implies $\phi \in sn$.

(CR 2) Suppose $\phi \in Red(\beta)$ and $\phi \rightsquigarrow\rightsquigarrow \psi$. Take any $\eta \in Red(\gamma)$. Then $\phi\eta \in Red(\alpha)$ by definition. Since $\phi\eta \rightsquigarrow\rightsquigarrow \psi\eta$, (CR 2′) implies $\psi\eta \in Red(\alpha)$. Thus $\psi \in Red(\beta)$.

(CR 3) Suppose ϕ is neutral and $\psi \in Red(\beta)$ for every immediate reduct ψ of ϕ. We shall show $\phi\eta \in Red(\alpha)$ for every $\eta \in Red(\gamma)$ by induction on $\nu(\eta)$; this is possible by virtue of (CR 1′) holds for η.

1°. $\nu(\eta) = 0$. The immediate reducts of $\phi\eta$ are of the form $\psi\eta$ where $\phi \rightsquigarrow \psi$ since ϕ is neutral. $\psi \in Red(\beta)$ implies $\psi\eta \in Red(\alpha)$, and hence $\phi\eta \in Red(\alpha)$ by (CR 3′).

2°. $\nu(\eta) > 0$. $\phi\eta$ 1-reduces to (i) $\psi\eta$ where $\phi \rightsquigarrow \psi$ or (ii) $\phi\eta'$ where $\eta \rightsquigarrow \eta'$. In case of (i), $\psi \in Red(\beta)$ implies $\psi\eta \in Red(\alpha)$. In case of (ii), $\eta' \in Red(\gamma)$ by (CR 2′) and hence $\eta' \in sn$ by (CR 1′). $\phi\eta' \in Red(\alpha)$ by the induction hypothesis of $\nu(\eta')$. In either case, the premise of (CR 3′) is satisfied for $\phi\eta$, and hence $\phi\eta \in Red(\alpha)$.

We have thus obtained $\phi \in Red(\gamma \to \alpha)$.

This completes the proof of reducibility lemma.

For the proof of Theorem 46, we need some more lemmas. They are corollaries of (CR).

Lemma A *(1)* $\phi_1 \in Red$ *and* $\phi_2 \in Red$ *imply* $cond[A\ ;\ \phi_1,\ \phi_2] \in Red$. *If* $\phi \in Red$, *then* $\sigma[j <_I i\ ;\ \phi] \in Red$.

(2) $\lambda x.\ \phi \in Red(\{x\}\gamma)$ *if and only if* $\phi[t/x] \in Red(\|\gamma[t/x]\|)$ *for every closed* t.

(3) Let X *be a variable-form of a type. Then,* $\lambda X.\ \phi \in Red$ *if and only if* $\phi[\psi/X] \in Red$ *for every* $\psi \in Red$ *such that* $X \sim \psi$.

(4) If $\phi \in Red$, *then* $\sigma[j <_I i\ ;\ \phi] \in Red$.

(5) If f *is an* n*-ary function constant and* $\psi_1,\ \psi_2,\ \cdots,\ \psi_n \in Red$, *then* $f\psi_1, \cdots, \psi_n \in Red$.

Proof. (1) By induction on $\nu(\phi_1) + \nu(\phi_2)$.

(2) Suppose $\lambda x.\ \phi \in Red(\{x\}\gamma)$. By definition, $(\lambda x.\ \phi)t \Rightarrow \phi[t/x]$, and hence, by (CR 2), $\phi[t/x] \in Red(\|\gamma[t/x]\|)$.

Suppose, conversely, $\phi[t/x] \in Red$ for every closed t. To claim $\lambda x.\phi \in Red$, it suffices to show that $(\lambda x.\phi)t \in Red$ for every t. $(\lambda x.\phi)t$ 1-reduces to either (i) $\phi[t/x]$ or (ii) $(\lambda x.\phi')t$ where $\phi \rightsquigarrow \phi'$ (and hence $\lambda x.\phi \rightsquigarrow \lambda x.\phi'$). $\phi[t/x] \in Red$ by the assumption, and hence $\phi[t/x] \in sn$, which implies successively $\phi \in sn$, $\phi' \in sn$, $\lambda x.\phi \in sn$ and $\lambda x.\phi' \in sn$. The induction on $\nu(\lambda x.\phi)$ can thus be used to prove $(\lambda x.\phi)t \in Red$ (under the premise of $\phi[t/x] \in Red$ for every t). Obviously $\nu(\lambda x.\phi') < \nu(\lambda x.\phi)$. $\phi[t/x] \in Red$ implies $\phi'[t/x] \in Red$ by (CR 2). So follows $(\lambda x.\phi')t \in Red$ by the induction hypothesis on $\nu(\lambda x.\ \phi')$. By (i),(ii) and (CR 3′), $(\lambda x.\phi)t \in Red$.

(3) Similarly.

(4) By induction on $\nu(\phi)$.

(5) $f \in Red$ by (CR4), and hence by definition.

Lemma B *If* $\phi \in Red$ *and* $\psi \in Red$, *then* $\mathcal{B}[\mathbf{b}\ ;\ \phi,\ \psi\ ;\ m,\ f] \in Red$ *for every closed* m *and* f.

Proof. This is established by an informal account of the bar induction. Recall that we defined $\mathbf{b}$ as $\mathbf{b_a}$ for a fixed neighborhood function $\mathbf{a}$. (See (CF) in Section 1.) For this $\mathbf{a}$, we put

$$R(z) \equiv \mathbf{a}(z) \neq 0,$$

$$A(z) \equiv \forall f \forall m\,(f\lceil lg(z) = z\ \&\ m \geq lg(z) \supset \mathcal{B}[\mathbf{b}\ ;\ \phi,\ \psi\ ;\ m,\ f] \in Red)\,.$$

$lg(z)$ denotes the length of z (presuming that z represents a finite sequence of numbers). $R(z)$ is equivalent to $lg(z) \geq \mathbf{b}(z)$.

$$A(<>) \equiv \forall f \forall m\,(\mathcal{B}[\mathbf{b}\ ;\ \phi,\ \psi\ ;\ m,\ f] \in Red)\,,$$

which expresses the conclusion of the lemma. So, it suffices to establish the four hypotheses of the bar induction (written as Hyp 1 $\sim$ Hyp 4) with respect to R and A, under the premise of $\phi \in Red$ and $\psi \in Red$.

Hyp 1. $\forall f \forall l\,(R(f\lceil l) \supset \forall m > l R(f\lceil m))$
Hyp 2. $\forall f R(f\lceil \mathbf{b}(f))$
Hyp 3. $\forall z\,(R(z) \supset A(z))$
Hyp 4. $\forall z\,(\forall k A(z * k) \supset A(z))$

Hyp 1. $\mathbf{a}(f\lceil l) \neq 0$ implies that for every $m > l$, $\mathbf{a}(f\lceil m) \neq 0$ by (2) of (CF) (Proposition 3).

Hyp 2. $\mathbf{a}(f\lceil \mathbf{b}(f)) \neq 0$ since $\mathbf{b}(f)$ is the least m such that $\mathbf{a}(f\lceil m) \neq 0$.

Hyp 3. Suppose $\mathbf{a}(z) \neq 0$, $f\lceil lg(z) = z$ and $m \geq lg(z)$. Then $\mathbf{b}(z^*) \leq m$ by definition of $\mathbf{b}$, where z^* is the function z followed by 0's. This implies $\mathbf{b}(f) \leq m$. So,

$$\mathcal{B}[\mathbf{b}\ ;\ \phi,\ \psi\ ;\ m,\ f] \Rightarrow app(\phi\ ;\ f\lceil m).$$

Due to $\mathcal{B}$-strategy, this is the only immediate reduct. (See (1.5) of definition 32.) By the hypothesis of the lemma, $\phi \in Red(\{z\}\gamma)$. So, by definition, $app(\phi\ ;\ f\lceil m) \in Red$. Since $\mathcal{B}[\mathbf{b}\ ;\ \phi,\ \psi\ ;\ m,\ f]$ is neutral, (CR 3) implies $\mathcal{B}[\mathbf{b}\ ;\ \phi,\ \psi\ ;\ m,\ f] \in Red$.

Hyp 4. Suppose $A(z * k)$ holds for every k and assume $f\lceil lg(z) = z \& m \geq lg(z)$. $A(z * k)$ is

$$\forall g \forall n\, (g\lceil lg(z * k) = z * k\ \&\ n \geq lg(z * k) \supset \mathcal{B}[\mathbf{b}\ ;\ \phi,\ \psi\ ;\ n,\ g] \in Red)\,.$$

To show that $A(z)$ holds, argue as follows. For some k, $f\lceil(lg(z) + 1) = z * k$. If we put $n = m + 1$ and $g_l = (f\lceil n) * l$, then $g_l\lceil lg(z * k) = z * k$ and $n \geq lg(z * k)$. So, by the premise,

$$\mathcal{B}[\mathbf{b}\ ;\ \phi,\ \psi\ ;\ n,\ g_l] \in Red.$$

This is true for every l. That is,

$$\mathcal{B}[\mathbf{b}\ ;\ \phi,\ \psi\ ;\ n,\ (f\lceil n) * l] \in Red$$

for every l. By (2) of Lemma A, this implies

(*) $$\lambda l \mathcal{B}[\mathbf{b}\ ;\ \phi,\ \psi\ ;\ n,\ (f\lceil n) * l] \in Red.$$

Now, if $\mathbf{b}(f) \leq m$, then

$$\mathcal{B}[\mathbf{b}\ ;\ \phi,\ \psi\ ;\ m,\ f] \Rightarrow app(\phi\ ;\ f\lceil m),$$

and this is the sole immediate reduct of

$$\mathcal{B}[\mathbf{b}\ ;\ \phi,\ \psi\ ;\ m,\ f]$$

by virtue of $\mathcal{B}$-strategy. Since $\phi(f\lceil m) \in Red$ as claimed above, (CR 3) implies $\mathcal{B}[\mathbf{b}\ ;\ \phi,\ \psi\ ;\ m,\ f] \in Red$. Next, if $\mathbf{b}(f) > m$, then

$$\mathcal{B}[\mathbf{b}\ ;\ \phi,\ \psi\ ;\ m,\ f] \Rightarrow \mathcal{B}\{m + 1\},$$

where $\mathcal{B}\{m + 1\}$ abbreviates

$$app\,(app(\psi; f\lceil m)\ ;\ \lambda l \mathcal{B}[\mathbf{b}\ ;\ \phi,\ \psi\ ;\ m + 1,\ (f\lceil m + 1) * l])\,,$$

and this is the sole immediate reduct. $\psi \in Red$ by the premise, and hence, by definition, $app\,(\psi\ ;\ f\lceil m) \in Red$.

Again, by definition and by (*), $\mathcal{B}\{m + 1\} \in Red$. (CR 3) then implies $\mathcal{B}[\mathbf{b}\ ;\ \phi,\ \psi\ ;\ m,\ f] \in Red$.

Lemma C *Let ϕ be a term whose free occurrences of variable-forms (of type) are among $\mathcal{X} \equiv X_1, \cdots, X_n$, and let $\Psi \equiv \psi_1, \cdots, \psi_n$ be reducible terms of corresponding types. Then*

$$\phi\,[\Psi/\mathcal{X}] \equiv \phi\,[\psi_1/X_1, \cdots, \psi_n/X_n] \in \mathit{Red}.$$

Proof. By induction on the construction of ϕ, according to (4) of Definitions 27, 30 and 41.

(4.1) If ϕ is X not similar to any of $\mathcal{X}$, then $\phi[\Psi/\mathcal{X}] \equiv X$ and hence $\phi \in \mathit{Red}$ by (CR 5). If ϕ is $*$, then the claim is trivial. If ϕ is $X_i, 1 \leq i \leq n$, then $\phi\,[\Psi/\mathcal{X}] \equiv \psi_i \in \mathit{Red}$.

(4.2) If ϕ is a constant f, then $f \in \mathit{Red}$ by (CR 4).

(4.3) ϕ is $\lambda x.\ \chi$. By Lemma A,

$$(\lambda x.\ \chi)\,[\Psi/\mathcal{X}] \equiv \lambda x.\chi\,[\Psi/\mathcal{X}] \in \mathit{Red}$$

if, for every t,

$$\chi\,[\Psi/\mathcal{X}]\,[t/x] \equiv \chi[t/x]\,[\Psi/\mathcal{X}] \in \mathit{Red}.$$

(Notice that x does not occur free in Ψ and x is not an associated variable of χ.) To $\chi[t/x]$ the induction hypothesis applies.

(4.4) ϕ is $\lambda X^\beta.\chi$. By (3) of Lemma A,

$$\phi\,[\Psi/\mathcal{X}] \equiv \lambda X.\ \chi\,[\Psi/\mathcal{X}] \in \mathit{Red}$$

if, for every $\theta \in \mathit{Red}$ such that $\theta \sim X$,

$$\chi\,[\Psi/\mathcal{X}]\,[\theta/X] \equiv \chi\,[\Psi/\mathcal{X},\ \theta/X] \in \mathit{Red},$$

which holds by the induction hypothesis.n

(4.5) ϕ is χt where $\chi\ :\ \{x\}\gamma$. By the induction hypothesis, $\chi\,[\Psi/\mathcal{X}] \in \mathit{Red}(\{x\}\gamma)$. So, by definition, $\chi\,[\Psi/\mathcal{X}]\,t \equiv \chi t\,[\Psi/\mathcal{X}] \in \mathit{Red}(\|\gamma[t/x]\|)$.

(4.6) ϕ is $\chi\theta$ where $\chi \in \mathit{Red}(\beta \to \gamma)$. By the induction hypothesis, $\chi\,[\Psi/\mathcal{X}] \in \mathit{Red}(\beta \to \gamma)$ and $\theta\,[\Psi/\mathcal{X}] \in \mathit{Red}(\beta)$. $\chi\,[\Psi/\mathcal{X}] \in \mathit{Red}$ implies that, for every $\xi \in \mathit{Red}(\beta)$, $\chi\,[\Psi/\mathcal{X}]\,\xi \in \mathit{Red}$. $\phi\,[\Psi/\mathcal{X}] \equiv \chi\,[\Psi/\mathcal{X}]\,\theta[\Psi/\mathcal{X}]$, and hence put $\xi \equiv \theta\,[\Psi/\mathcal{X}]$.

(4.7)~(4.9) By the induction hypothesis and Lemma A.

(4.10) ϕ is $\mathcal{B}\,[\mathbf{b}\ ;\ \theta,\ \chi\ ;\ m,\ f]$. By the induction hypotheses and Lemma B.

Now, Theorem 46 is a special case of Lemma C; let Ψ be $\mathcal{X}$ and apply (CR 5).

Definition 49. If ϕ and ψ share a normal form, we write $\phi \simeq \psi$, and the normal form of ϕ will be denoted by $|\phi|$.

6 Strong normalizability of term-forms

The uniqueness of the normal form of any term-form can be proved similarly to Proposition 19.

Here we prove the

Proposition 50. *If* $\phi \rightsquigarrow\rightsquigarrow \psi_1$ *and* $\phi \rightsquigarrow\rightsquigarrow \psi_2$*, then* $\psi_1 \rightsquigarrow\rightsquigarrow \psi$ *and* $\psi_2 \rightsquigarrow\rightsquigarrow \psi$ *for some* ψ.

As an immediate corollary we obtain the

Conclusion 51. *The normal form of a term-form is unique.*

Putting Conclusions 48 (of Section 5) and 51 together, we can conclude the

Theorem 52. *Every term-form is strongly normalizable to a unique normal form (in the sense of Definition 34).*

For the proof of the proposition, we first claim a lemma, which is parallel to Lemma 18 in Section 3.

Lemma 53. *Suppose* $\phi \rightsquigarrow \psi_1$ *and* $\phi \rightsquigarrow \psi_2$*. Then* $\psi_1 \rightsquigarrow\rightsquigarrow \psi$ *and* $\psi_2 \rightsquigarrow\rightsquigarrow \psi$ *for some* ψ.

We can follow standard arguments. For the cases where the redex of ψ_1 is itself and ψ_1 contains the redex of ψ_2, use Lemmas 37 and 38 in Section 4. Notice that $\sigma[j <_I i \ ; \ x]$ and $\mathcal{B}[\mathbf{b} \ ; \ \phi, \ \psi \ ; \ m, \ f]$ can have at most one immediate reduct due to σ-strategy and $\mathcal{B}$-strategy.

Proposition 50 can be proved by induction on the sum of the steps respectively between ϕ and ψ_1 and between ϕ and ψ_2. For the bases use the lemma above.

This completes the proof of strong normalizability of term-forms.

Note. We can define pairing and its converses as follows.

$$(\phi, \ \psi) \equiv \lambda l.cond[l = 0 \ ; \ \phi, \ cond[l = 1 \ ; \ \psi, \ *]],$$

$$\pi_1\chi \equiv app(\chi \ ; \ 0), \qquad \pi_2\chi \equiv app(\chi \ ; \ 1).$$

7 Computational strength of TRM

We first comment on an immediate consequence of the normalization theorem.

Lemma 54. *The normal form of any hyper-term (no free variables or variable-forms) of type N is a closed $\mathcal{BL}(c)$ constant.*

This can be easily established by induction on the construction of a hyper-term of type N, by referring to the definitons and Lemma 37 in Section 4.

The system of term-forms was invented originally in [9] to interpret the system **ASOD**, an intuitionistic system of arithmetic with $\forall f$ (on function variables), (iterated) transfinite inductive (recursive) definitions and the bar induction applied to "admissible" formulas. Although **ASOD** is a specific system, it is a system of general interest and the argument in [9] goes through in a more general setting. We give a brief account of it, calling the system $\mathbf{TRDB_1}$.

Definition 55. (1) The language $\mathcal{L}$ of $\mathbf{TRDB_1}$ consists of $\mathcal{BL}(c)$, the language of Heyting arithmetic, $\forall f$ and H, a predicate constant for the transfinite recursive definition along I.

(2) A formula of this language is said to be admissible if H does not occur within the scope of $\exists$ and $\vee$. In $\mathbf{TRDB_1}$, only admissible formulas are admitted as legitimate formulas. (In **ASOD**, admissible formulas formed a narrower class of formulas.)

(3) $\mathbf{TRDB_1}$ is based on Heyting arithmetic (applied to admissible formulas) with the additional axioms and inferences below.

(3.1) WF(I), the well-foundedness of I.

(3.2) Introduction and elimination of $\forall f$.

(3.3) Monotone bar induction applied to pairs of formulas $(R,\ A)$, where R is H- and quantifier-free and A is admissible. For R, Hyp 1 and Hyp 2 (in Section 5) are assumed to be true.

(3.4) Let $G(i,\ x,\ \Xi)$ be an admissible formula without H and with a designated predicate symbol Ξ, where Ξ does not occur in the scope of $\exists$ and $\vee$. (Specify such a G.) Then the axiom of transfinite recursive definition $\mathbf{TRD}(G)$ stands :

$$\forall i \in I \forall x\,(H(i,\ x) \equiv G(i,\ x,\ H[i])),$$

where $H[i]$ abbreviates the abstract $\{j,\ y\}((j <_I i \supset H(j,\ y)) \wedge (j \not<_I i \supset 0 = 1))$. (An abstract is a meta-object, and $G(i,\ x,\ H[i])$ is a formula in which substitutions for the variables j and y have been carried out.)

$j <_I i$ & $H(j,\ y)$ will be used as short for

$$(j <_I i \supset H(j,\ y)) \wedge (j \not<_I i \supset 0 = 1).$$

We will observe these abbreviated notations. $\mathbf{TRD}(G)$ is admissible.

Corollary 56. *In* $\mathbf{TRDB_1}$, $A \vee B$ *can be represented by*

$$\exists z\,[(z = 0 \supset A) \wedge (\neg z = 0 \supset B)].$$

Note. (1) We can deal with a more general system $\mathbf{TRDB}_\omega$, which is based on accessible sets $\{I_n\}_n$ and predicates $\{H_n\}_n$ of iterated transfinite recursive definitions along $\{I_n\}_n$ and the admissible formulas $\{G_n(i, x, \Xi_1, \cdots, \Xi_{n-1})\}_n$ as the defining formulas of $\{H_n\}_n$, in exactly the same way as that follows. Here, $i \in I_n$ and H_n depends at most on $H_0, \cdots, H_{n-1}$.

In the following we write **TRDB** to denote any of $\mathbf{TRDB}_m$ $(m \leq \omega)$.

(2) In [9], there occurs a formula of the form

$$\mathbf{B}: \qquad (R_1 \wedge \mathbf{A}_1) \vee (R_2 \wedge \mathbf{A}_2) \vee (R_3 \wedge \mathbf{A}_3),$$

where R_k are mutually exclusive and exhaustive decidable formulas and $\mathbf{A}_k$ contain an inductive predicate. **B** is constructively equivalent to

$$(R_1 \supset \mathbf{A}_1) \wedge (R_2 \supset \mathbf{A}_2) \wedge (R_3 \supset \mathbf{A}_3),$$

and hence the admissibility is observed. In particular, the $\vee$ in p.250 of the opening part of [9] can be dispensed with. In fact the entire proof in Part I of [9] is essentially $\vee$-free.

(3) Mathematical induction and transfinite induction along I are derived theorems in $\mathbf{TRDB}_1$. (See §1 in Part III of [9].)

(4) Notice that **TRDB** is not a specified system, but it is relative to an accessible structure $(I, <_I)$ and a defining formula G of transfinite recursion.

The soundness of **TRM**, which consists of the normalization theorems of type-forms and term-forms, can be formalized as follows.

1°. The strong normalizability of type-forms is carried out by transfinite induction along I_* applied to a formula of the form

$$\forall f\,(A(j, f) \supset \exists x B(j, f, x))\,,$$

where j is supposed to range over I_* and A and B are $\exists$-free arithmetical (hence H-free) formulas. Transfinite induction along I_* can be proved from that of I and mathematical induction.

2°. In the following, ϕ, β, *etc* in fact denote their codes $\ulcorner\phi\urcorner$, $\ulcorner\beta\urcorner$, *etc.* The reducibility predicate of term-forms can then be expressed with an admissible formula below.

$\phi \in Red(\beta,\ j) \equiv \quad d(\beta) = j$
$\wedge$ "β is normal" $\wedge$ "$\phi\ :\ \beta$"
$\wedge\ [j = 0 \supset \forall f \exists x C(x, f, \phi)]$
$\wedge\ [j > 0 \wedge$ "β is of the form $\{x\}\gamma$"
$\supset$ "for every t closed, $\phi t \in Red\,(\|gamma[t/x]\|,\ k_1)$"]
$\wedge\ [j > 0 \wedge$ "β is of the form $\gamma \rightarrow \delta$"
$\supset$ "for every ψ, $\psi \in Red(\gamma,\ k_2)$
implies $\phi\psi \in Red(\delta,\ k_3)$"],

where $\phi \in Red(\beta,\ j)$ is read "$\phi \in Red(\beta)$ and $d(\beta) = j$", $\forall f \exists x C(x, f, \phi)$ expresses "$\phi \in sn$", k_1, k_2, k_3 are determined from β, j, t, ψ and k_1, k_2, $k_3 <_I j$.

We can regard $Red(\beta,\ d(\beta))$ as $Red(\beta)$. *Red* is a predicate symbol for a transfinite recursion, and its defining formula is admissible.

3°. The arguments on reducibility and normalizability of term-forms can be taken care of by the bar induction (which enables us to employ also the mathematical induction and the transfinite induction applied to admissible formulas).

Lemma 57. *For any fixed element d of I_*, transfinite recursive definitions (on admissible formulas) up to d can be proved in* **TRDB** *with appropriate accessible sets and defining formulas. (Recall that we are assuming $|I| < \epsilon_0$.)*

Proof. $d = \omega^{2I} n + e$ for some $e < \omega^{2I}$. It is hence sufficient to show that a recursive definition up to $2I$ can be extended to the one up to ω^{2I}.

This can be done by recursive definitions along ω first and then along $2I$ by putting

$$G'(x, a, z, \Xi) \equiv G(z\#\omega^x, a, \Xi)$$

and considering the axiom

$$K(x, a, z) \equiv G'(x, a, z, K[x]),$$

where x is supposed to range over $2I$. This is a classical technique which has the origin in Gentzen's derivation of transfinite inducton up to ω_n fer each n, using mathematical induction.

This lemma together with 1° ~ 3° above implies the

Proposition 58. *Strong normalizability of each fixed term-form is verified in* **TRDB** *with some appropriate transfinite recursive definitions.*

To characterize number-theoretic functions representable in **TRM**, we argue as usual; see [3], for example. Here by a number-theoretic function we mean a function of type $\{x\}N$, x being a number variable.

Proposition 59. *The functions representable in* **TRM** *are recursive and provably total in* **TRDB** *(with some suitable transfinite recursive definitions).*

Proof. Let f be a closed hyper-term of type $\{x\}N$, and let n be a number constant. Consider *fn*, which reduces to the normal form (which is a numeral m by Lemma 54). If we put $e_f(n) = m$, e_f is a recursive function, and the termination of its computation is guaranteed in **TRDB** by virtue of Proposition 58.

For the converse, suppose $\forall x \exists y A(x, y)$ is a $\prod_2^0$-sentence and is a theorem of **TRDB**. Then, with the same argument as in [9], we can show that there is a hyper-term of type $\{x\}N$, say ϕ, such that $\forall x A(x,\ \phi x)$ is HP-valid. (See §6 of Part II in [9].) Since A is a formula of arithmetic, this means $\forall x A(x, \phi x)$ is true;

that is, a provably total function is realized by a hyper-term. (See Section 8 for an alternative proof, which is to be presented thoroughly.)

We can extend the results above to $\mathbf{TRDB}_m$ $(m \leq \omega)$ by adding successive, transfinitely defined type-forms to **TRM**, calling the resulting system of term-forms $\mathbf{TRM}_m$ $(m \leq \omega)$. So, we sum up the results into the theorem below. (We write **TRM** for any of $\mathbf{TRM}_m$.)

Theorem 60. *A function is provably total in* **TRDB** *if and only if it is representable in* **TRM**. *The defining formulas of transfinite recursive definitions and the defining forms of transfinitely defined type-forms are mutually definable.*

Note. The interpretation of **ASOD** in terms of **TRM** via modified realizability as developed in [9] involved a new predicate constant Δ (for $H(i,\ a)$) and quantifications over variable-forms. Furthermore, the semantics of the inductive definitions is quite complicated. In the next section we present an alternative treatment, which is simpler and easier to get the insight of. In fact we obtain the same (up to reductions) term-forms in both cases.

8 Translation of $\mathbf{TRDB}_1$ into TRM

Here we define a direct translation of the system $\mathbf{TRDB}_1$ into **TRM** and prove **TRM**-representability of $\mathbf{TRDB}_1$-provably total functions.

Definition 61. To each (admissible) formula A of $\mathbf{TRDB}_1$, we associate a regular type-form $[\![A]\!]$ as follows. (As was remarked before, we may assume there is no $\vee$ in A.)

(1) If A is free of $\exists$ and H, then $[\![A]\!] = \mathbf{1}$. We write $A \in \mathcal{F}_0$ in such a case.

(2) Suppose A is free of H but contains $\exists$. We write $A \in \mathcal{F}_1$ in such a case.

(2.1) $[\![\exists x B]\!] \equiv N \times [\![B]\!]$.

(2.2) $[\![\forall y B]\!] \equiv \{y\}[\![B]\!]$

(2.3) $[\![B \supset C]\!] \equiv [\![B]\!] \to [\![C]\!]$,

where $\mathbf{1} \to \gamma$ is identified with γ and $\beta \to \mathbf{1}$ is identified with $\mathbf{1}$.

(2.4) $[\![B \wedge C]\!] \equiv [\![B]\!] \times [\![C]\!]$ where $\mathbf{1} \times \gamma$ is identified with γ and $\beta \times \mathbf{1}$ is identified with β.

(3) Let $K(\Xi)$ be an admissible, H-free formula with a binary predicate parameter Ξ. (Ξ is not in the scope of $\exists$.) We write $K(\Xi) \in \mathcal{F}_2$ in such a case. We define $[\![K(\Xi)]\!]$ as follows.

(3.1) $[\![\Xi(i,a)]\!] \equiv \pi(\Xi\ ;\ i,a)$

(3.2) $[\![j <_I i \ \&\ \Xi(j,b)]\!] \equiv \rho[j <_I i\ ;\ \pi(\Xi\ ;\ j,\ b)]$.

(3.3) For $\forall$, $\supset$ and $\wedge$, see (2.2)~(2.4).

(4) Suppose A contains H (written as $A \in \mathcal{F}_3$) and

$$\forall i \in I \forall a\, (H(i,\ a) \equiv G\,(i,\ a,\ H[i]\ ))$$

is the axiom **TRD**(G) of $\mathbf{TRDB}_1$. $[\![G(i,\ a,\ \Xi)]\!] \equiv \eta(\Xi)$ can be defined according to (3) above.

(4.1) $[\![H(i,\ a)]\!] \equiv \mathcal{R}[i,\ a]$.

(4.2) $[\![j <_{\text{I}} i\ \&\ H(j,\ b)]\!] \equiv \rho[j <_I i\ ;\ \mathcal{R}[j,\ b]]$

(4.3) For $\forall$, $\supset$ and $\wedge$, apply (3.3), reading H for Ξ and replacing $\pi(\Xi\ ;\ i, a)$ by $\mathcal{R}[i, a]$.

Corollary 62. *(1) $[\![A]\!]$ contains a variable x (free) if and only if A contains a subformula $H\,(i(x),\ a(x))$ or $j(x) <_I i(x)\ \&\ H\,(i(x),\ b(x))$ (whose x is free in A).*

(2) $[\![A[t/x]]\!] \equiv [\![A]\!][t/x]$

(3) $[\![\forall x \exists y A]\!] \equiv \{x\}N$ if A is H- and quautifier-free.

(4) $[\![G(i, a, H[i])]\!] \equiv \eta[i/k, a/w][R(i)/\Xi]$

In order to associate a term-form with a proof, we reformulate $\mathbf{TRDB_1}$ in the natural deduction system.

Definition 63. $\mathbf{TRDB}_1$ can be formulated in terms of natural deductions as follows. (See, for example, [3]. Refer to Definition 55 for $\mathbf{TRDB}_1$.)

(a) Axioms are quantifier-free mathematical axioms and WF(I).

Some of the inference rules are listed below.

(b) $BI(R,\ A)$

$$\frac{Hyp\ 3 \quad Hyp\ 4}{A(z_0)},$$

where z_0 is an arbitrary number term. Hyp 3 is

$$\forall z\,(R(z) \supset A(z))$$

and Hyp 4 is

$$\forall z\,(\forall k A(z * k) \supset A(z))\,.$$

Notice that Hyp 1 and Hyp 2 are assumed for R.

(c) **TRD**(G) (transfinite recursive definition)

$$\frac{H(i,\ a)}{G(i,\ a,\ H[i])}\ ; \quad \frac{G(i,\ a,\ H[i])}{H(i,\ a)}$$

(d) $\forall f$

$$\frac{A}{\forall f A}\ ; \quad \frac{\forall f A}{A[t/f]}$$

Definition 64. Let Q be a proof in $\mathbf{TRDB}_1$. We associate a term-form $[\![Q]\!]$ to Q such that, if the endformula of Q is A, then $[\![Q]\!]\ :\ [\![A]\!]$. We also require the following properties for $[\![Q]\!]$.

1°. A free variable-form $X_l{}^{[\![A]\!]}$ occurs in $[\![Q]\!]$ free if and only if A is a live assumption in Q which has label l.

2°. A variable x occurs free in $[\![Q]\!]$ if and only if it does in the endformula of Q and is in H.

3°. If the end-formula of $[\![Q]\!]$ is in $\mathcal{F}_0$, then $[\![Q]\!]$ is $*$, where X^1 is identified with $*$.

Now we define $[\![Q]\!]$. (1) Q is a hypothesis A (with label l). $[\![Q]\!] \equiv X_l{}^{[\![A]\!]}$ (which we may write X^A for short).

(2) If Q is a quantifier-free axiom, then $[\![Q]\!] \equiv *$. If Q is WF(I), then put $[\![Q]\!] \equiv \mu$.

Consider subsequently the last inference J of Q. We assume a term-form (or two), say ϕ (and ψ), for the premise(s) and define a term-form for Q from it (them). The inference J and the definition of $[\![Q]\!]$ will be juxtaposed.

(3)

$$\cfrac{\begin{matrix}[A] \\ \vdots \\ B\end{matrix}}{A \supset B} \qquad \frac{\phi}{\lambda X^A.\,\phi}$$

$\lambda X^A.\,\phi$ is identified with $\phi\,[*/X^A]$ if $[\![A]\!] = \mathbf{1}$, and it is identified with $*(\equiv \phi)$ if $[\![B]\!] \equiv \mathbf{1}$.

$$\frac{A \qquad A \supset B}{B} \qquad \frac{\phi \quad \psi}{\psi\phi}$$

$\psi\phi$ is identified with ψ if $[\![A]\!] \equiv \mathbf{1}$ and with $*(\equiv \psi)$ if $[\![B]\!] \equiv \mathbf{1}$.

(4) $\wedge$

$$\frac{B \qquad C}{B \wedge C} \qquad \frac{\phi \quad \psi}{(\phi,\ \psi)}$$

$(\phi,\ \psi)$ is identified with ψ or ϕ respectively if $[\![B]\!] = \mathbf{1}$ or $[\![C]\!] = \mathbf{1}$.

$$\frac{B \wedge C}{B} \qquad \frac{\phi}{\phi 0}$$

$$\frac{B \wedge C}{C} \qquad \frac{\phi}{\phi 1}$$

(5)

$$\frac{F}{\forall y F} \qquad \frac{\phi}{\lambda y.\phi}$$

Recall that $\lambda y.\phi\ :\ \{y\}[\![\phi]\!]$. $\lambda y.\phi$ is identified with $*$ if $\forall y F \in \mathcal{F}_0$.

$$\frac{\forall y F}{F[t/y]} \qquad \frac{\phi}{\phi t}$$

ϕt is identified with $*$ if $F \in \mathcal{F}_0$.

(6)

$$\frac{F[t/x]}{\exists x F} \qquad \frac{\phi}{(t\ ,\ \phi)}.$$

$(t\ ,\ \phi)$ is identified with t if $\phi \equiv *$.

$$\frac{\exists x F \qquad \begin{array}{c}[F]\\ \vdots \\ C\end{array}}{C} \qquad \frac{\chi \qquad \psi}{\psi\,[\pi_2\chi/X^F]}$$

(7)

$$\frac{H(i,\ a)}{G\,(i,\ a,\ H[i])} \qquad \frac{\phi}{\phi}$$

$$\frac{G\,(i,\ a,\ H[i])}{H(i,\ a)} \qquad \frac{\phi}{\phi}$$

(8)

$$\frac{Hyp\ 3 \quad Hyp\ 4}{A(z_0)} \qquad \frac{\phi_3 \qquad \phi_4}{\mathcal{B}[\mathbf{b},\ \phi_3,\ \phi_4\ ;\ lg(z_0),\ z_0]}$$

b corresponds to R as in Section 1. (Read R for the T there.)

Proposition 65. $1° \sim 3°$ *in Definition 64 are observed by the definitions of* $[\![Q]\!]$.

4° *Typing of term-forms is consistent.*

Proposition 66. *A proof (without live assumptions) of a closed theorem is assigned a hyper-term (a closed term).*

Definition 67. Introduce to $\mathcal{L}$ (the language of **TRDB**) a constant c, and thus extend $\mathcal{L}$ to $\mathcal{L}'$. $[\![A]\!]$, the type-form of A, can be defined for an $\mathcal{L}'$-admissible formula A in the same way as in Definition 61. For each admissible sentence A of $\mathcal{L}'$ and each term-form $\phi\ :\ [\![A]\!]$, $\phi \models A$ (ϕ realizes A) is defined as follows (in (1) $\sim$ (3)).

(1) If $A \in \mathcal{F}_0$, then $\phi \models A$ if A is "true" in the natural interpretation of symbols.

(2) Suppose $A \in \mathcal{F}_1$.

(2.1) $\phi \models \exists x B$ if $\phi 1 \models B\,[|\phi 0|/x]$ is true, where $|\phi 0|$ is the normal form of $\phi 0$, which is a numeral. (See Lemma 54 of Section 7.)

(2.2) $\phi \models \forall y B$ if $\phi t \models B[t/y]$ for every closed t.

(2.3) $\phi \models B \supset C$ if, for every $\psi\ :\ [\![B]\!]$ such that $\psi \models B$, $\phi\psi \models C$. (If $[\![B]\!] = \mathbf{1}$, then $\phi \models B \supset C$ when the truth of B implies $\phi \models C$. Other special cases are treated similarly.)

(2.4) $\phi \models B \wedge C$ if $\phi 0 \models B$ and $\phi 1 \models C$.

(3) $\phi \models H(i,\ a)$ is defined by transfinite induction on i. Assume, for any c, $j <_I i$ and $\psi\ :\ \mathcal{R}[j,\ c]$, $\psi \models H(j,\ c)$ has been defined. If A is of the form $k <_I i \& H(k, d)$, then for any $\chi\ :\ \rho\,[k <_I i\ ;\ \mathcal{R}_0[k,\ x]]$, $\chi \models A$ is defined as follows. If $k <_I i$ is false, then $\chi \not\models A$; if $k <_I i$ is true, then $\chi \models A$ if and only if $\chi \models H(k,\ d)$. Based on these and applying (1) and (2), $\phi \models G(i,\ a,\ H[i])$ can be defined. Let $\phi \models H(i,\ a)$ be $\phi \models G\,(i,\ a,\ H[i])$.

(4) For any admissible $\mathcal{L}'$-formula A, $\phi \models A$ if $\sigma\phi \models \sigma A$ for every σ, where σq represents a substitution of closed terms for the free variables in q.

Proposition 68. *(1) Suppose* $\forall x \exists y A(x, y)$ *is a* $\prod_2^0$*-sentence (of arithmetic). Then, for every* $\phi : \{x\}N$, $\phi \models \forall x \exists y A(x, y)$ *if and only if* $* \models A(n, |\phi n|)$ *for each numeral* n. *Notice that* $|\phi n|$ *is a numeral.*

(2) If $\phi_1 \simeq \phi_2$, *then* $\phi_1 \models A$ *if and only if* $\phi_2 \models A$.

Proposition 69. *Let* Q *be a proof in* $\mathbf{TRDB}_1$ *whose endformula is* A. *Suppose* $A_1, \cdots, A_k$ *are all the live hypotheses in* Q. *For every* $\psi_1, \cdots, \psi_k$ *such that* $\psi_l \models A_l, \quad 1 \leq l \leq k$, $[\![Q]\!] \, [\psi_1/X^{A_1}, \cdots, \psi_k/X^{A_k}] \models A$.

Proof. We prove this according to Definitions 64 and 67. We quote the cases in Definition 63. If Q consists of a hypothesis A, then $\psi \models A$ trivially implies $X^A[\psi/X^A] \models A$.

(a) Q consists of WF(I). $[\![Q]\!] = \mu$ and $\mu \models$WF(I) by the definition of μ.

(b) Suppose $\phi_i \models Hyp\ i$, $i = 3, 4$. $\phi_3 \models Hyp\ 3$ means that, for every c, R(c) implies $\phi_3 c \models A(c)$. $\phi_4 \models Hyp\ 4$ means that, for every c and every χ, $\chi \models \forall k A(c * k)$ implies $\phi_4 c \chi \models A(c)$. We show that $\mathcal{B}[\mathbf{b}\ ;\ \phi_3,\ \phi_4\ ;\ m,\ f] \models A(f\lceil m)$ for each m and f.

By means of Proposition 3, $R(f\lceil m)$ holds if $m \geq \mathbf{b}(f)$. So, by $\phi_3 \models Hyp\ 3$, $app(\phi_3\ ;\ f\lceil m) \models A(f\lceil m)$ for such m. In such a case, $\mathcal{B}[\mathbf{b}\ ;\ \phi_3,\ \phi_4\ ;\ m,\ f] \simeq app(\phi_3\ ;\ f\lceil m)$, and hence $\mathcal{B}[\mathbf{b}\ ;\ \phi_3,\ \phi_4\ ;\ m,\ f] \models A(f\lceil m)$. Suppose $m < \mathbf{b}(f)$ and

$$\mathcal{B}[\mathbf{b}\ ;\ \phi_3,\ \phi_4\ ;\ m+1,\ f^*] \models A(f^*\lceil(m+1))$$

for every f^* an extension of $f\lceil m$. By $\phi_4 \models Hyp\ 4$,

$$app\,(app(\phi_4\ ;\ f\lceil m)\ ;\ \lambda k \mathcal{B}\,[\mathbf{b}\ ;\ \phi_3,\ \phi_4\ ;\ m+1,\ (f\lceil m) * k]) \models A(f\lceil m).$$

From this and (2) of Proposition 68 follows

$$\mathcal{B}[\mathbf{b}\ ;\ \phi_3,\ \phi_4\ ;\ m,\ f] \models A(f\lceil m).$$

Put

$$C(z)\ :\ \forall m \forall f\,(z = f\lceil m \supset \mathcal{B}[\mathbf{b}\ ;\ \phi_3,\ \phi_4\ ;\ m,\ f] \models A(f\lceil m)).$$

For $R(z)$ and $C(z)$, the hypotheses of the bar induction hold, and so it follows that $C(z_0)$, or $\mathcal{B}[\mathbf{b}\ ;\ \phi_3,\ \phi_4\ ;\ lg(z_0),\ z_0] \models A(z_0)$ by an informal account of the bar induction.

(c) $\phi \models H(i, a)$ if and only if $\phi \models G\,(i, a, H[i])$ by definition.

(d) Suppose $\phi \models A$. By definition, $\phi[f/y] \models A[f/y]$ for every f. $(\lambda y.\ \phi)f \models A[f/y]$, and hence $\lambda y.\ \phi \models \forall y A$. Suppose next, $\phi \models \forall y A$. By definition, $\phi f \models A[f/y]$ for every f, and in particular, for $f = |t|$.

Other cases can be dealt with similarly. Consider as an example,

$$\frac{\begin{array}{c}[A]\\ \vdots \\ B\end{array}}{A \supset B}.$$

Suppose $\phi[\psi/X, \chi/Y] \models B$ holds for every ψ such that $\psi \models A$ and appropriate χ. $\phi[\psi/X,\chi/Y] \models B$ implies $((\lambda X^A.\ \phi)[\chi/Y])\,\psi \models B$. Then, by definition, $(\lambda X^A.\ \phi)[\chi/Y] \models A \supset B$.

The necessity of Theorem 60 in Section 7 immediately follows from this.

Corollary 70. *Let* $\forall x \exists y A(x,\ y)$ *be a closed,* $\prod_2^0$*-theorem of* $\mathbf{TRDB}_1$. *Let* P *be a proof of this. Then* $[\![P]\!]\ :\ \{x\}N$, *and* $A(n,\ |[\![P]\!]n|)$ *is true for every numeral* n.

Just by comparing the terms obtained in [9] and here, we obtain the

Proposition 71. *Let* P *be a proof in* $\mathbf{TRDB}_1$. *The term-form obtained from* P *for the mr (modified realizability)-translation of the endformula of* P *and the one by the direct translation in Definition 64 are the same. (See §4 of Part III in [9].)*

References

1. H. P. Barendregt, The lambda calculus (North-Holland, Amsterdam, 1981).
2. Th. Coquand and G. Huet, Calculus of constructions, Information and Computation 76 (1988), 95-120.
3. J-Y. Girard, P. Taylor and Y. Lafont, Proofs and types (Cambridge University Press, Cambridge, 1989).
4. W. A. Howard and G. Kreisel, Transfinite induction and bar induction of types zero and one, and the role of continuity in intuitionistic analysis, J. Symbolic Logic 31 (1966), 325-358.
5. J. Lambek and P. J. Scott, Introduction to higher order categorical logic (Cambridge University Press, Cambridge, 1984).
6. Z. Luo, An extended calculus of constructions (Department of Computer Science, University of Edinburgh, 1990).
7. G. Takeuti and M. Yasugi, The ordinals of the systems of second order arithmetic with the provably $\Delta^1{}_2$-comprehension axiom and with the $\Delta^1{}_2$-comprehension axiom respectively, Japanese J. Math. 41 (1973), 1-67.
8. M. Yasugi, Construction principle and transfinite induction up to ϵ_0, J. Austral. Math. Soc. 32 (1982), 24-47.
9. M. Yasugi, Hyper-principle and the functional structure of ordinal diagrams, Comment. Math. Univ. St. Pauli 34 (1985), 227-263 (the opening part) ; 35 (1986), 1-37 (the concluding part).
10. M. Yasugi and S. Hayashi, Interpretations of transfinite recursion and parametric abstraction in types, Words, Languages and Combinatorics IIedited by M. Ito and H. Jurgensen (World Scientific Publ., Singapore), to appear.
11. J. I. Zucker, Iterated inductive definitions, trees and ordinals, Metamathematical investigations of intuitionistic arithmetic and analysis, ed. by A. S. Troelstra, Lecture Notes in Math. 344 (Springer-Verlag, Berlin 1973), 392-453.

The Non-deterministic Catch and Throw Mechanism and Its Subject Reduction Property

Hiroshi Nakano

Department of Applied Mathematics and Informatics,
Ryukoku University, Seta, Otsu, 520-21, Japan
nakano@rins.ryukoku.ac.jp

Abstract. A simple programming language and its typing system is introduced to capture the catch and throw mechanism with its non-deterministic feature. The subject reduction property of the system, which compensates for the unpleasant feature of the non-determinism, is shown.

1 Introduction

The catch and throw mechanism is a programming facility for non-local exit which plays an important role when programmers handle exceptional situations. In a previous paper [4], the author showed that the catch/throw mechanism corresponds to a variant formulation of Genzen's LJ following the Curry-Howard isomorphism in the opposite direction, and gave a realizability interpretation of the formal system by an abstract stack machine, in which the computational behavior of the mechanism was treated by a fixed evaluation strategy, and therefore the result of evaluation was unique. However, generally, the catch/throw mechanism introduces a non-determinism to evaluation processes, that is, the result of evaluation depends on the evaluation strategy. For example, let M be a term defined by

$$M = \mathbf{catch}\ u\ ((\lambda x.\, \lambda y.\, 1)\,(\mathbf{throw}\ u\ 2)\,(\mathbf{throw}\ u\ 3)).$$

There are three possible results for the evaluation of M depending on the evaluation strategy.

In this paper, we first extend the language to capture the non-deterministic feature of the catch/throw mechanism, and introduce its typing system. We next show the subject reduction property of the system.

2 A programming language with catch/throw

We first introduce a programming language based on λ-calculus. The language has the catch and throw mechanism.

2.1 Syntax

Constants and variables. We first assume the following disjoint sets of individual constants, individual variables and tag variables are given.

C_i A set of individual constants $c, d, \ldots$.
V_i A countably infinite set of individual variables $x, y, z, \ldots$.
V_t A countably infinite set of tag variables $u, v, w, \ldots$.

Tag variables are called tags.

Terms. The set of *terms* E is defined as follows:

$$\begin{aligned} E ::= \ & C_i \mid V_i \mid \mathbf{catch}\, V_t\, E \mid \mathbf{throw}\, V_t\, E \\ \mid\ & \lambda V_i.\, E \mid E\,E \mid \kappa V_t.\, E \mid E\, V_t \\ \mid\ & <E,\ E> \mid \mathbf{proj_1}\, E \mid \mathbf{proj_2}\, E \\ \mid\ & \mathbf{inj_1}\, E \mid \mathbf{inj_2}\, E \mid \mathbf{case}\, E\ V_i.E\ V_i.E\ . \end{aligned}$$

Example 1.

$$\lambda x.\, \mathbf{case}\ x\ y.(\mathbf{inj_2}\ y)\ z.(\mathbf{inj_1}\ z)$$
$$\mathbf{catch}\ u\ ((\kappa v.\, \mathbf{proj_1} <x,\ \mathbf{throw}\ v\ y>)\, u)$$

We use $M, N, \ldots$ to denote terms. The terms $\kappa V_t.E$ and $E\,V_t$ are used to denote a tag-abstraction and a tag-instantiation, respectively, c.f. [4]. Free and bound occurrences of variables are defined in the standard manner. We regard a tag variable u as bound in **catch** $u\ M$ and $\kappa u.\, M$. We also define alpha-convertibility in the standard manner where we admit renaming of bound tag variable as well as bound individual variables. Hereafter, we treat terms modulo this alpha-convertibility. A term M so represents an equivalence class of terms which are alpha-convertible to M. We denote the set of individual and tag variables occurring freely in M by $FIV(M)$ and $FTV(M)$, respectively.

Definition 1 (Substitution). Let $M, N_1, \ldots, N_n$ be terms, and let $x_1, \ldots, x_n$ be individual variables. We use $M[N_1/x_1, \ldots, N_n/x_n]$ to denote the term obtained from M by replacing all free occurrences of $x_1, \ldots, x_n$ by $N_1, \ldots, N_n$, respectively. $M[v_1/u_1, \ldots, v_n/u_n]$ is defined similarly, where $u_1, \ldots, u_n$ and $v_1, \ldots, v_n$ are tag variables.

2.2 Operational semantics

Now we define an operational semantics of the language by a set of reduction rules on terms. The non-deterministic feature of the catch/throw mechanism is introduced by the following rule.

Definition 2 ($\underset{\mathrm{t}}{\mapsto}$). A relation $\underset{\mathrm{t}}{\mapsto}$ on terms is defined as follows:

$$M[\mathbf{throw}\ u\ N/x] \underset{\mathrm{t}}{\mapsto} \mathbf{throw}\ u\ N \qquad (x \in FIV(M),\ x \not\equiv M)\,.$$

Example 2.

$$\begin{aligned}
\texttt{<}\mathbf{inj_1}\ (\mathbf{throw}\ u\ M),\ \mathbf{throw}\ v\ N\texttt{>} &\underset{t}{\mapsto} \mathbf{throw}\ u\ M \\
\texttt{<}\mathbf{inj_1}\ (\mathbf{throw}\ u\ M),\ \mathbf{throw}\ v\ N\texttt{>} &\underset{t}{\mapsto} \mathbf{throw}\ v\ N \\
\mathbf{throw}\ u\ M &\underset{t}{\not\mapsto} \mathbf{throw}\ u\ M \\
\mathbf{case}\ z\ x.(\mathbf{throw}\ u\ x)\ y.y &\underset{t}{\not\mapsto} \mathbf{throw}\ u\ x \\
\mathbf{catch}\ u\ (\mathbf{throw}\ u\ M) &\underset{t}{\not\mapsto} \mathbf{throw}\ u\ M \\
\mathbf{catch}\ v\ (\mathbf{throw}\ u\ (M\,v)) &\underset{t}{\not\mapsto} \mathbf{throw}\ u\ (M\,v)
\end{aligned}$$

The rest is defined by the following rules.

Definition 3 ($\underset{n}{\mapsto}$). A relation $\underset{n}{\mapsto}$ on terms is defined as follows:

$$\begin{aligned}
\mathbf{catch}\ u\ M &\underset{n}{\mapsto} M && (u \notin FTV(M)) \\
\mathbf{catch}\ u\ (\mathbf{throw}\ u\ M) &\underset{n}{\mapsto} M && (u \notin FTV(M)) \\
(\lambda x.\,M)\,N &\underset{n}{\mapsto} M[N/x] \\
(\kappa u.\,M)\,v &\underset{n}{\mapsto} M[v/u] \\
\mathbf{proj_1}\ \texttt{<}M,\ N\texttt{>} &\underset{n}{\mapsto} M \\
\mathbf{proj_2}\ \texttt{<}M,\ N\texttt{>} &\underset{n}{\mapsto} N \\
\mathbf{case}\ (\mathbf{inj_1}\ L)\ x.M\ y.N &\underset{n}{\mapsto} M[L/x] \\
\mathbf{case}\ (\mathbf{inj_2}\ L)\ x.M\ y.N &\underset{n}{\mapsto} N[L/y]
\end{aligned}$$

Definition 4 (Reduction rules). We define a relation, denoted by $\mapsto$, by the union of $\underset{t}{\mapsto}$ and $\underset{n}{\mapsto}$, that is,

$$M \mapsto N \quad \text{iff} \quad M \underset{t}{\mapsto} N \text{ or } M \underset{n}{\mapsto} N.$$

Definition 5 ($\rightarrow$). We define a relation, denoted by $\rightarrow$, as follows: $M \rightarrow N$ if and only if N is obtained from M by replacing an occurrence of M' in M by N' such that $M' \mapsto N'$. Let $\xrightarrow{*}$ be the transitive and reflexive closure of the relation $\rightarrow$.

Example 3. Let 1, 2 and 3 be distinct individual constants, and let M be as $M = \mathbf{catch}\ u\ ((\lambda x.\,\lambda y.\,1)\,(\mathbf{throw}\ u\ 2)\,(\mathbf{throw}\ u\ 3))$.

$$\begin{aligned}
&M \rightarrow \mathbf{catch}\ u\ ((\lambda y.\,1)\,(\mathbf{throw}\ u\ 3)) \rightarrow \mathbf{catch}\ u\ 1 \rightarrow 1 \\
&M \rightarrow \mathbf{catch}\ u\ (\mathbf{throw}\ u\ 2) \rightarrow 2 \\
&M \rightarrow \mathbf{catch}\ u\ (\mathbf{throw}\ u\ 3) \rightarrow 3
\end{aligned}$$

3 A typing system

We now introduce a typing system for the programming language.

3.1 Syntax of typing judgements

Type expressions. Type expressions of our typing system consist of atomic types, conjunctions ($A \wedge B$), disjunctions ($A \vee B$), implications ($A \supset B$) and exceptions ($A \triangleleft B$). The last one is introduced to handle the catch/throw mechanism and represents another kind of disjunction (c.f. [4]).

Individual contexts. An *individual context* is a finite mapping which assigns a type expression to each individual variable in its domain. We use $\Gamma, \Gamma', \ldots$ to denote individual contexts, and denote the domain of an individual context Γ by $Dom(\Gamma)$. Let $A_1, \ldots, A_n$ be type expressions, and $x_1, \ldots, x_n$ individual variables such that if $x_i = x_j$ then $A_i = A_j$ for any i and j. We use $\{x_1 : A_1, \ldots, x_n : A_n\}$ to denote an individual context whose domain is $\{x_1, \ldots, x_n\}$ and which assigns A_i to x_i for each i.

Tag contexts. A *tag context* is a finite mapping which assigns a pair of a type expression and a set of individual variables to each tag variable in its domain. We use $\Delta, \Delta', \ldots$ to denote tag contexts. Let $u_1, \ldots, u_n$ be tag variables. Let $B_1, \ldots, B_n$ be type expressions, and let $V_1, \ldots, V_n$ be sets of individual variables such that if $u_i = u_j$ then $B_i = B_j$ and $V_i = V_j$ for any i and j. We use $\{u_1 : B_1^{V_1}, \ldots, u_n : B_n^{V_n}\}$ to denote a tag context whose domain is $\{u_1, \ldots, u_n\}$ and which assigns the pair (B_i, V_i) to u_i for each i. We denote the first and the second components of $\Delta(u)$ by $\Delta^t(u)$ and $\Delta^v(u)$, respectively. For example, $\Delta^t(u_i) = B_i$ and $\Delta^v(u_i) = V_i$ if $\Delta = \{u_1 : B_1^{V_1}, \ldots, u_n : B_n^{V_n}\}$.

Definition 6 (Compatible contexts). Let Γ and Γ' be individual contexts. Γ is *compatible* with Γ' if and only if $\Gamma(x) = \Gamma'(x)$ for any individual variable $x \in Dom(\Gamma) \cap Dom(\Gamma')$. We denote this by $\Gamma \parallel \Gamma'$. Note that $\Gamma \cup \Gamma'$ is also an individual context if $\Gamma \parallel \Gamma'$ is. The compatibility of tag contexts is also defined as follows: Δ is *compatible* with Δ' if and only if $\Delta^t(u) = \Delta'^t(u)$ for any individual variable $u \in Dom(\Delta) \cap Dom(\Delta')$. We denote this by $\Delta \parallel \Delta'$. When Δ and Δ' are compatible, we define a new tag context $\Delta \sqcup \Delta'$ as follows.

$$(\Delta \sqcup \Delta')(u) = \begin{cases} (\Delta^t(u),\ \Delta^v(u) \cup \Delta'^v(u)) & \text{if } u \in Dom(\Delta) \cap Dom(\Delta') \\ \Delta(u) & \text{if } u \in Dom(\Delta) \text{ and } u \notin Dom(\Delta') \\ \Delta'(u) & \text{if } u \notin Dom(\Delta) \text{ and } u \in Dom(\Delta') \end{cases}$$

Note that $Dom(\Delta \sqcup \Delta') = Dom(\Delta) \cup Dom(\Delta')$.

Definition 7. Let Δ be as $\Delta = \{u_1 : B_1^{V_1}, \ldots, u_n : B_n^{V_n}\}$, and let u and v be tag variables. If $\{u, v\} \subset Dom(\Delta)$ implies $\Delta^t(u) = \Delta^t(v)$, then we define a tag context $\Delta[v/u]$ as follows.

$$\Delta[v/u] = \{u_1[v/u] : B_1^{V_1}, \ldots, u_n[v/u] : B_n^{V_n}\}.$$

We define $\Gamma[y/x]$ similarly for an individual context Γ and individual variables x and y.

Definition 8. Let V be a set of individual variables. We define a tag context $\Delta[V/\{x\}]$ as follows.

$$Dom(\Delta[V/\{x\}]) = Dom(\Delta)$$
$$\Delta[V/\{x\}]^t(u) = \Delta^t(u)$$
$$\Delta[V/\{x\}]^v(u) = \begin{cases} (\Delta^v(u) - \{x\}) \cup V & \text{if } x \in \Delta^v(u) \\ \Delta^v(u) & \text{otherwise} \end{cases}$$

Typing judgement. Let Γ and Δ be an individual context and a tag context, respectively, such that $\Delta^v(u) \subset Dom(\Gamma)$ for any $u \in Dom(\Delta)$. Let M be a term, and C a type expression. *Typing judgements* have the following form.

$$\Gamma \vdash M : C;\ \Delta$$

The intended meaning of a typing judgement $\{x_1 : A_1, \ldots, x_m : A_m\} \vdash M : C;$ $\{u_1 : B_1^{V_1}, \ldots, u_n : B_n^{V_n}\}$ is roughly that when we execute the program M supplying values of the types $A_1 \ldots A_m$ for the corresponding free variables $x_1, \ldots, x_m$ of M, it normally reduces to a value of the type C, otherwise the program throws a value of B_j with a tag u_j for some j $(1 \leq j \leq n)$, and the thrown value depends on only the individual variables which belong to V_j.

3.2 $L_{c/t}$

We denote the typing system by $L_{c/t}$, which can be considered as a natural-deduction-style reformulation of the logical system presented in [4]. We can see a more direct correspondence between proofs and programs in $L_{c/t}$.

Definition 9 (Typing rules). $L_{c/t}$ is defined by the following set of typing rules.

$$\frac{}{\Gamma \cup \{x : A\} \vdash x : A;\ \Delta}\ (var) \qquad \frac{\Gamma \vdash M : A;\ \Delta \sqcup \{u : A^V\}}{\Gamma \vdash \mathbf{catch}\ u\ M : A;\ \Delta}\ (catch)$$

$$\frac{\Gamma_1 \vdash M : E;\ \Delta}{\Gamma_1 \cup \Gamma_2 \vdash \mathbf{throw}\ u\ M : A;\ \Delta \sqcup \{u : E^{Dom(\Gamma_1)}\}}\ (throw)$$

$$\frac{\Gamma \cup \{x : A\} \vdash M : B;\ \Delta}{\Gamma \vdash \lambda x.\, M : A \supset B;\ \Delta}\ (\supset\text{-I}) \quad (x \notin \Delta^v(u) \text{ for any } u \in Dom(\Delta))$$

$$\frac{\Gamma_1 \vdash M : A \supset B;\ \Delta_1 \quad \Gamma_2 \vdash N : A;\ \Delta_2}{\Gamma_1 \cup \Gamma_2 \vdash M\, N : B;\ \Delta_1 \sqcup \Delta_2}\ (\supset\text{-E})$$

$$\frac{\Gamma \vdash M : A;\ \Delta \sqcup \{u : E^V\}}{\Gamma \vdash \kappa u.\, M : A \triangleleft E;\ \Delta}\ (\triangleleft\text{-I}) \qquad \frac{\Gamma_1 \vdash M : A \triangleleft E;\ \Delta}{\Gamma_1 \cup \Gamma_2 \vdash M\, u : A;\ \Delta \sqcup \{u : E^{Dom(\Gamma_1)}\}}\ (\triangleleft\text{-E})$$

$$\frac{\Gamma_1 \vdash M : A;\ \Delta_1 \quad \Gamma_2 \vdash N : B;\ \Delta_2}{\Gamma_1 \cup \Gamma_2 \vdash \langle M,\ N \rangle : A \wedge B;\ \Delta_1 \sqcup \Delta_2}\ (\wedge\text{-I})$$

$$\frac{\Gamma \vdash M : A \wedge B;\ \Delta}{\Gamma \vdash \mathbf{proj_1}\ M : A;\ \Delta}\ (\wedge_1\text{-E}) \qquad \frac{\Gamma \vdash M : A \wedge B;\ \Delta}{\Gamma \vdash \mathbf{proj_2}\ M : B;\ \Delta}\ (\wedge_2\text{-E})$$

$$\frac{\Gamma \vdash M : A;\ \Delta}{\Gamma \vdash \mathbf{inj_1}\ M : A \vee B;\ \Delta}\ (\vee_1\text{-I}) \qquad \frac{\Gamma \vdash M : B;\ \Delta}{\Gamma \vdash \mathbf{inj_2}\ M : A \vee B;\ \Delta}\ (\vee_2\text{-I})$$

$$\frac{\Gamma_1 \vdash L : A \vee B;\ \Delta_1 \quad \Gamma_2 \cup \{x : A\} \vdash M : C;\ \Delta_2 \quad \Gamma_3 \cup \{y : B\} \vdash N : C;\ \Delta_3}{\begin{array}{l}\Gamma_1 \cup \Gamma_2 \cup \Gamma_3 \vdash \mathbf{case}\ L\ x.M\ y.N : C;\\ \qquad \Delta_1 \sqcup \Delta_2[Dom(\Gamma_1)/\{x\}] \sqcup \Delta_3[Dom(\Gamma_1)/\{y\}]\end{array}}\ (\vee\text{-E})$$

The side condition for ($\supset$-I) is necessary to keep the system constructive. Note that the following inference rule of [4] corresponds to ($\supset$-I) of $L_{c/t}$.

$$\frac{\Gamma A \rightarrow B;}{\Gamma \rightarrow A \supset B;}\ (\rightarrow\supset)$$

A natural translation of this rule into $L_{c/t}$ would be as follows.

$$\frac{\Gamma \cup \{x : A\} \vdash M : B;\ \{\}}{\Gamma \vdash \lambda x.\, M : A \supset B;\ \{\}}\ (\supset\text{-I})'$$

As a logic, ($\supset$-I)$'$ is equivalent to ($\supset$-I) of Definition 9, but is too restrictive with respect to the variation of proofs, i.e., typed programs. For example, the following typing judgement, which is derivable in $L_{c/t}$, would not be derivable if we replaced ($\supset$-I) by ($\supset$-I)$'$.

$$\{\} \vdash \mathbf{catch}\ u\ (\lambda x.\, \mathbf{throw}\ u\ (\lambda y.\, y)) : A \supset A;\ \{\}$$

Moreover, the language would not have a subject reduction property, because

$$\{\} \vdash \mathbf{catch}\ u\ ((\lambda z.\, \lambda x.\, z)\, (\mathbf{throw}\ u\ (\lambda y.\, y))) : A \supset A;\ \{\}$$

would be still derivable, but

$$\mathbf{catch}\ u\ ((\lambda z.\, \lambda x.\, z)\, (\mathbf{throw}\ u\ (\lambda y.\, y))) \rightarrow \mathbf{catch}\ u\ (\lambda x.\, \mathbf{throw}\ u\ (\lambda y.\, y)).$$

This is the reason why we maintain the set of the relevant individual variables to each tag in tag contexts of typing judgements.

The following example of a derivation shows that the programming language does not have Church-Rosser property even if we consider only the well-typed terms. Let M be the term $\lambda x.\, \lambda f.\, \mathbf{catch}\ u\ ((\lambda y.\, x)\, (\mathbf{throw}\ u\ (f\, x)))$. The well-typed term M has two normal forms as follows.

$$M \rightarrow \lambda x.\, \lambda f.\, \mathbf{catch}\ u\ (\mathbf{throw}\ u\ (f\, x)) \rightarrow \lambda x.\, \lambda f.\, f\, x$$
$$M \rightarrow \lambda x.\, \lambda f.\, \mathbf{catch}\ u\ x \rightarrow \lambda x.\, \lambda f.\, x$$

Example 4. Let Γ be as $\Gamma = \{x:A, f:A\supset A\}$.

$$
\dfrac{\dfrac{\dfrac{\dfrac{\dfrac{}{\{y:B\}\vdash x:A;\ \{\}}\,(var)}{\{\}\vdash \lambda y.\,x:B\supset A;\ \{\}}\,(\supset\text{-I}) \qquad \dfrac{\dfrac{\dfrac{}{\Gamma\vdash f:A\supset A;\ \{\}}\,(var) \quad \dfrac{}{\Gamma\vdash x:A;\ \{\}}\,(var)}{\Gamma\vdash f\,x:A;\ \{\}}\,(\supset\text{-E})}{\Gamma\vdash \mathbf{throw}\ u\,(f\,x):B;\ \{u:A^{\{x,f\}}\}}\,(throw)}{\Gamma\vdash (\lambda y.\,x)\,(\mathbf{throw}\ u\,(f\,x)):A;\ \{u:A^{\{x,f\}}\}}\,(\supset\text{-E})}{\Gamma\vdash \mathbf{catch}\ u\,((\lambda y.\,x)\,(\mathbf{throw}\ u\,(f\,x))):A;\ \{\}}\,(catch)}{\{x:A\}\vdash \lambda f.\,\mathbf{catch}\ u\,((\lambda y.\,x)\,(\mathbf{throw}\ u\,(f\,x))):(A\supset A)\supset A;\ \{\}}\,(\supset\text{-I})}{\{\}\vdash \lambda x.\,\lambda f.\,\mathbf{catch}\ u\,((\lambda y.\,x)\,(\mathbf{throw}\ u\,(f\,x))):A\supset(A\supset A)\supset A;\ \{\}}\,(\supset\text{-I})
$$

3.3 Basic properties of $L_{c/t}$

In this subsection, we presents a some basic properties of the system as a preparation for proving the subject reduction property of $L_{c/t}$.

Proposition 10. *If $\Gamma\vdash M:C;\ \Delta$ is derivable, then $FIV(M)\subset Dom(\Gamma)$ and $FTV(M)\subset Dom(\Delta)$.*

Proof. By induction on the derivation of $\Gamma\vdash M:C;\ \Delta$. □

Definition 11. Let Δ and Δ' be tag contexts. We define a relation $\Delta\sqsubset\Delta'$ as follows. The relation $\Delta\sqsubset\Delta'$ holds if and only if

- $\Delta\parallel\Delta'$,
- $Dom(\Delta)\subset Dom(\Delta')$, and
- $\Delta^v(u)\subset\Delta'^v(u)$ for any $u\in Dom(\Delta)$.

Note that $\Delta\sqsubset(\Delta\sqcup\Delta')$ if $\Delta\parallel\Delta'$.

Definition 12. Let d be a natural number. We say a typing judgement is d-*derivable* if there exists a derivation of the judgement whose depth is less than or equal to d.

Proposition 13. *Let d be a natural number, and let $\Gamma\vdash M:C;\ \Delta$ be a d-derivable typing judgement.*

1. *If $\Gamma\subset\Gamma'$ and $\Delta\sqsubset\Delta'$, then $\Gamma'\vdash M:C;\ \Delta'$ is also d-derivable.*
2. *If $\Gamma[y/x]$ is well defined, then $\Gamma[y/x]\vdash M[y/x]:C;\ \Delta[\{y\}/\{x\}]$ is also d-derivable.*
3. *If $\Delta[v/u]$ is well defined, then $\Gamma\vdash M[v/u]:C;\ \Delta[v/u]$ is also d-derivable.*

Proof. By simultaneous inductions on d. □

Proposition 14. *Let x and u be as $x\notin FIV(M)$ and $u\notin FTV(M)$.*

1. *If $\Gamma\cup\{x:A\}\vdash M:C;\ \Delta$ is derivable, then $\Gamma\vdash M:C;\ \Delta$ is also derivable.*
2. *If $\Gamma\vdash M:C;\ \Delta\sqcup\{u:E^V\}$ is derivable, then $\Gamma\vdash M:C;\ \Delta$ is also derivable.*

Proof. Straightforward induction on the derivations. □

Proposition 15. *Let M be term, and let u be a tag variable. If $\Gamma \vdash$ **throw** u $M : C\,;\ \Delta$ is derivable, then $\Gamma \vdash$ **throw** $u\ M : A\,;\ \Delta$ is also derivable for any type A.*

Proof. Since $\Gamma \vdash$ **throw** $u\ M : C\,;\ \Delta$ is derivable, so is $\Gamma \vdash M : E\,;\ \Delta'$ for some E and Δ' such that $\Delta = \Delta' \sqcup \{u : E^{Dom(\Gamma)}\}$. Therefore, we can derive $\Gamma \vdash$ **throw** u $M : A\,;\ \Delta$ for any A by (*throw*). □

Proposition 16 (Substitution). *Let Γ_1, Γ_2, Δ_1 and Δ_2 be as $\Gamma_1 \parallel \Gamma_2$ and $\Delta_1 \parallel \Delta_2$. If $\Gamma_1 \vdash N : A\,;\ \Delta_1$ and $\Gamma_2 \cup \{x : A\} \vdash M : C\,;\ \Delta_2$ are derivable, then $\Gamma_1 \cup \Gamma_2 \vdash M[N/x] : C\,;\ \Delta_1 \sqcup \Delta_2[Dom(\Gamma_1)/\{x\}]$ is also derivable.*

Proof. By induction on the depth of the derivation of $\Gamma_2 \cup \{x : A\} \vdash M : C\,;\ \Delta_2$. Suppose that $\Gamma_1 \vdash N : A\,;\ \Delta_1$ and $\Gamma_2 \cup \{x : A\} \vdash M : C\,;\ \Delta_2$ are derivable. By cases on the last rule used in the derivation of $\Gamma_2 \cup \{x : A\} \vdash M : C\,;\ \Delta_2$.

Case 1: The last rule is (*var*). That is, $M = y$ for some individual variable y such that $\{y : C\} \subset \Gamma_2 \cup \{x : A\}$. If $M = x$, then we can derive $\Gamma_1 \cup \Gamma_2 \vdash M[N/x] : C\,; \Delta_1 \sqcup \Delta_2[Dom(\Gamma_1)/\{x\}]$ by applying Proposition 13 to the derivation of $\Gamma_1 \vdash N : A\,;\ \Delta_1$ since $M[N/x] = N$ and $C = A$ in this case. If $M \neq x$, then we can derive it by (*var*) since $M[N/x] = y$ and $\{y : C\} \subset \Gamma_2$ in this case.

Case 2: The last rule is (*catch*). In this case, $M =$ **catch** $u\ M'$ and the following judgement is derivable for some u, V and M'.

$$\Gamma_2 \cup \{x : A\} \vdash M' : C\,;\ \Delta_2 \sqcup \{u : C^V\}$$

We can assume that $u \notin Dom(\Delta_1)$ by Proposition 13. By the induction hypothesis, we have a derivation of

$$\Gamma_1 \cup \Gamma_2 \vdash M'[N/x] : C\,;\ \Delta_1 \sqcup (\Delta_2 \sqcup \{u : C^V\})[Dom(\Gamma_1)/\{x\}]. \qquad (1)$$

Since $u \notin Dom(\Delta_1)$, we get $M[N/x] =$ **catch** $u\ (M'[N/x])$. By applying (*catch*) to (1), we get $\Gamma_1 \cup \Gamma_2 \vdash M[N/x] : C\,;\ \Delta_1 \sqcup \Delta_2[Dom(\Gamma_1)/\{x\}]$.

Case 3: The last rule is (*throw*). In this case, $M =$ **throw** $u\ M'$ and the following judgement is derivable for some u, M', E, Γ_2' and Δ such that $\Gamma_2' \subset \Gamma_2 \cup \{x : A\}$ and $\Delta_2 = \Delta \sqcup \{u : E^{Dom(\Gamma_2') \cup \{x\}}\}$.

$$\Gamma_2' \vdash M' : E\,;\ \Delta$$

Let Γ be as $\Gamma = \Gamma_2' - \{x : A\}$. Note that $\Gamma \subset \Gamma_2$ and $\Gamma_2' \subset \Gamma \cup \{x : A\}$. Therefore, by Proposition 13,

$$\Gamma \cup \{x : A\} \vdash M' : E\,;\ \Delta.$$

By the induction hypothesis, we have a derivation of

$$\Gamma_1 \cup \Gamma \vdash M'[N/x] : E\,;\ \Delta_1 \sqcup \Delta[Dom(\Gamma_1)/\{x\}].$$

Since $M[N/x] = \textbf{throw}\ u\ (M'[N/x])$, by applying (*throw*),

$$\Gamma_1 \cup \Gamma \vdash M[N/x] : C\,;\ \Delta_1 \sqcup \Delta[Dom(\Gamma_1)/\{x\}] \sqcup \{u : E^{Dom(\Gamma_1 \cup \Gamma)}\}.$$

Since $\Gamma \subset \Gamma_2$, by Proposition 13 again,

$$\Gamma_1 \cup \Gamma_2 \vdash M[N/x] : C\,;\ \Delta_1 \sqcup \Delta[Dom(\Gamma_1)/\{x\}] \sqcup \{u : E^{Dom(\Gamma_1 \cup \Gamma)}\}.$$

Note that $\Delta[Dom(\Gamma_1)/\{x\}] \sqcup \{u : E^{Dom(\Gamma_1 \cup \Gamma)}\} = \Delta_2[Dom(\Gamma_1)/\{x\}]$ because $\Delta_2 = \Delta \sqcup \{u : E^{Dom(\Gamma_2') \cup \{x\}}\}$ and $x \notin Dom(\Gamma)$.

Case 4: The last rule is ($\supset$*-I*). In this case $M = \lambda y.\, M'$, $C = C_1 \supset C_2$ and the following judgement is derivable for some y, C_1, C_2 and M' such that $y \notin \Delta_2^v(u)$ for any $u \in Dom(\Delta_2)$.

$$\Gamma_2 \cup \{x : A\} \cup \{y : C_1\} \vdash M' : C_2\,;\ \Delta_2$$

We can assume that $y \notin Dom(\Gamma_1)$ by Proposition 13, and get $M'[N/x] = \lambda y.\,(M[N/x])$. By the induction hypothesis, we have a derivation of

$$\Gamma_1 \cup \Gamma_2 \cup \{y : C_1\} \vdash M'[N/x] : C_2\,;\ \Delta_1 \sqcup \Delta_2[Dom(\Gamma_1)/\{x\}]. \qquad (2)$$

Since $y \notin \Delta_2^v(u)$ for any $u \in Dom(\Delta_2)$ and $y \notin Dom(\Gamma_1)$, we get $y \notin (\Delta_1 \sqcup \Delta_2[Dom(\Gamma_1)/\{x\}])^v(u)$ for any $u \in Dom(\Delta_1 \sqcup \Delta_2[Dom(\Gamma_1)/\{x\}])$. Therefore we can derive $\Gamma_1 \cup \Gamma_2 \vdash \lambda y.\,(M'[N/x]) : C_2\,;\ \Delta_1 \sqcup \Delta_2[Dom(\Gamma_1)/\{x\}]$ by applying ($\supset$-I) to (2).

Case 5: The last rule is one of others. Similar. □

4 The subject reduction property of $L_{c/t}$

As mentioned in Section 3.2, the language does not have Church-Rosser property even if we consider only the well-typed terms. However, it has the subject reduction property, which compensates for this unpleasant feature. In this section, we show the subject reduction property of $L_{c/t}$.

Lemma 17. *If* $\Gamma \vdash M : C\,;\ \Delta$ *is derivable and* $M \underset{t}{\mapsto} \textbf{throw}\ v\ N$*, then* $\Gamma \vdash \textbf{throw}\ v\ N : C\,;\ \Delta$ *is also derivable.*

Proof. By induction on the depth of the derivation of $\Gamma \vdash M : C\,;\ \Delta$. Suppose that $\Gamma \vdash M : C\,;\ \Delta$ is derivable and $M \underset{t}{\mapsto} \textbf{throw}\ v\ N$. By Proposition 15, it is enough to show that $\Gamma \vdash \textbf{throw}\ v\ N : C'\,;\ \Delta$ is derivable for some C'. By cases according to the last rules used in the derivation.

Case 1: The last rule is (*var*). This is impossible because $M \underset{t}{\mapsto} \textbf{throw}\ v\ N$.

Case 2: The last rule is (catch). $M = \textbf{catch}\ u\ M'$ and the following judgement is derivable for some u, V and M'.

$$\Gamma \vdash M' : C\,;\ \Delta \sqcup \{u : C^V\} \tag{3}$$

We can assume that $u \notin FTV(\textbf{throw}\ v\ N)$ by Proposition 13, and get $M' = \textbf{throw}\ v\ N$ or $M' \underset{t}{\mapsto} \textbf{throw}\ v\ N$ from $M \underset{t}{\mapsto} \textbf{throw}\ v\ N$. Therefore, from (3) or the induction hypothesis on (3),

$$\Gamma \vdash \textbf{throw}\ v\ N : C\,;\ \Delta \sqcup \{u : C^V\}.$$

We get $\Gamma \vdash \textbf{throw}\ v\ N : C\,;\ \Delta$ by Proposition 14 since $u \notin FTV(\textbf{throw}\ v\ N)$.

Case 3: The last rule is (throw). In this case, $M = \textbf{throw}\ u\ M'$ and the following judgement is derivable for some u, M', E, Γ' and Δ' such that $\Gamma' \subset \Gamma$ and $\Delta = \Delta' \sqcup \{u : E^{Dom(\Gamma')}\}$.

$$\Gamma' \vdash M' : E\,;\ \Delta' \tag{4}$$

We get $M' = \textbf{throw}\ v\ N$ or $M' \underset{t}{\mapsto} \textbf{throw}\ v\ N$ from $M \underset{t}{\mapsto} \textbf{throw}\ v\ N$. Therefore, from (4) or the induction hypothesis on (4),

$$\Gamma' \vdash \textbf{throw}\ v\ N : E\,;\ \Delta'.$$

We get $\Gamma \vdash \textbf{throw}\ v\ N : E\,;\ \Delta$ by Proposition 13 since $\Gamma' \subset \Gamma$ and $\Delta' \sqsubset \Delta$.

Case 4: The last rule is ($\supset$-I). $M = \lambda x.\, M'$, $C = C_1 \supset C_2$ and the following judgement is derivable for some x, C_1, C_2 and M' such that $x \notin \Delta^v(u)$ for any $u \in Dom(\Delta)$.

$$\Gamma \cup \{x : C_1\} \vdash M' : C_2\,;\ \Delta \tag{5}$$

We can assume that $x \notin FIV(\textbf{throw}\ v\ N)$ by Proposition 13, and get $M' = \textbf{throw}\ v\ N$ or $M' \underset{t}{\mapsto} \textbf{throw}\ v\ N$ from $M \underset{t}{\mapsto} \textbf{throw}\ v\ N$. Therefore, from (5) or the induction hypothesis on (5),

$$\Gamma \cup \{x : C_1\} \vdash \textbf{throw}\ v\ N : C_2\,;\ \Delta.$$

We get $\Gamma \vdash \textbf{throw}\ v\ N : C_2\,;\ \Delta$ by Proposition 14 since $x \notin FIV(\textbf{throw}\ v\ N)$.

Case 5: The last rule is one of others. Similar to Case 2 and Case 3. □

Lemma 18. *If $\Gamma \vdash M : C\,;\ \Delta$ is derivable and $M \underset{n}{\mapsto} N$, then $\Gamma \vdash N : C\,;\ \Delta$ is also derivable.*

Proof. By induction on the depth of the derivation of $\Gamma \vdash M : C\,;\ \Delta$. □

Suppose that $\Gamma \vdash M : C\,;\ \Delta$ is derivable and $M \underset{n}{\mapsto} N$. By cases according to the form of M.

Case 1: $M = \textbf{catch}\ u\ N$ *and* $u \notin FTV(N)$. In this case, $\Gamma \vdash N : C\,; \Delta \sqcup \{u : C^V\}$ is derivable for some V. We get $\Gamma \vdash N : C\,;\ \Delta$ by Proposition 14 since $u \notin FTV(N)$.

Case 2: $M = \mathbf{catch}\ u\ (\mathbf{throw}\ u\ N)$ *and* $u \notin FTV(N)$. The following judgement is derivable for some V, Γ' and Δ' such that $\Gamma' \subset \Gamma$ and $\Delta \sqcup \{u : C^V\} = \Delta' \sqcup \{u : C^{Dom(\Gamma')}\}$.

$$\Gamma' \vdash N : C\ ;\ \Delta'$$

Since $\Gamma' \subset \Gamma$ and $\Delta' \sqsubset \Delta \sqcup \{u : C^V\}$, $\Gamma \vdash N : C\ ;\ \Delta \sqcup \{u : C^V\}$ is derivable by Proposition 13. Therefore, $\Gamma \vdash N : C\ ;\ \Delta$ is also derivable by Proposition 14 since $u \notin FTV(N)$.

Case 3: $M = (\lambda x.\, M_1)\, M_2$ *and* $N = M_1[M_2/x]$ *for some* x, M_1 *and* M_2. The following two judgements are derivable for some A and $x \notin \Delta^v(u)$ for any $u \in Dom(\Delta)$.

$$\Gamma \cup \{y : A\} \vdash M_1 : C\ ;\ \Delta \qquad (6)$$

$$\Gamma \vdash M_2 : A\ ;\ \Delta \qquad (7)$$

We get $\Gamma \vdash M_1[M_2/x] : C\ ;\ \Delta[Dom(\Gamma)/\{x\}]$ from (6) and (7) by Lemma 16, where $\Delta[Dom(\Gamma)/\{x\}] = \Delta$ since $x \notin \Delta^v(u)$ for any $u \in Dom(\Delta)$.

Case 4: $M = (\kappa u.\, M')\, v$ *and* $N = M'[v/u]$ *for some* u, v *and* M'. The following judgement is derivable for some E, Γ', Δ' and V such that $\Gamma' \subset \Gamma$ and $\Delta = \Delta' \sqcup \{v : E^{Dom(\Gamma')}\}$.

$$\Gamma' \vdash M' : C\ ;\ \Delta' \sqcup \{u : E^V\}$$

Since $\Delta' \parallel \{v : E^{Dom(\Gamma')}\}$, $\Gamma' \vdash M'[v/u] : C\ ;\ \Delta'[v/u] \cup \{v : E^V\}$ is derivable by Proposition 13. Since $\Gamma' \subset \Gamma$, by Proposition 13 again,

$$\Gamma \vdash M'[v/u] : C\ ;\ \Delta'[v/u] \cup \{v : E^V\}.$$

Since $V \subset Dom(\Gamma')$,

$$\Delta'[v/u] \sqcup \{v : E^V\} \sqsubset \Delta'[v/u] \sqcup \{v : E^{Dom(\Gamma')}\} \sqsubset \Delta' \sqcup \{v : E^{Dom(\Gamma')}\} = \Delta.$$

Therefore, $\Gamma \vdash M'[v/u] : C\ ;\ \Delta$ is derivable by Proposition 13.

Case 5: $M = \mathbf{proj}_i <M_1,\ M_2>$ *and* $N = M_i$ *for some* i $(i = 1, 2)$. Similar.

Case 6: $M = \mathbf{case}\ (\mathbf{inj}_i\, M_0)\ x_1.M_1\ x_2.M_2$ *and* $N = M_i[M_0/x_i]$ *for some* i $(i = 1, 2)$. Similar. □

Lemma 19. *If* $\Gamma \vdash M : C\ ;\ \Delta$ *is derivable and* $M \mapsto N$, *then* $\Gamma \vdash N : C\ ;\ \Delta$ *is also derivable.*

Proof. Straightforward from Lemma 17 and Lemma 18. □

Theorem 20 (Subject reduction). *If* $\Gamma \vdash M : C\ ;\ \Delta$ *is derivable and* $M \to N$, *then* $\Gamma \vdash N : C\ ;\ \Delta$ *is also derivable.*

Proof. By induction on the depth of the derivation of $\Gamma \vdash M : C\,;\ \Delta$. Suppose that $\Gamma \vdash M : C\,;\ \Delta$ is derivable and $M \rightarrow N$. If $M \mapsto N$, then trivial by Lemma 19. Therefore we can assume that $M \rightarrow N$ and $M \not\mapsto N$. By cases according to the last rules used in the derivation. A typical one is the case that the last rule is (*throw*). In this case, $M = \mathbf{throw}\ u\ M'$ and

$$\Gamma' \vdash M' : E\,;\ \Delta'$$

is derivable for some u, M', E, Γ' and Δ' such that $\Gamma' \subset \Gamma$ and $\Delta = \Delta' \sqcup \{u : E^{Dom(\Gamma')}\}$. Since $M \rightarrow N$ and $M \not\mapsto N$, $M' \rightarrow N'$ and $N = \mathbf{throw}\ u\ N'$ for some N'. Therefore, $\Gamma' \vdash N' : E\,;\ \Delta'$ is derivable by the induction hypothesis. We get $\Gamma \vdash \mathbf{throw}\ u\ N' : E\,;\ \Delta$ by applying (*throw*). The proofs for other cases are just similar. □

5 Concluding remarks

We have presented a programming language and its typing system which capture the non-deterministic feature of the catch/throw mechanism. We have shown that the system has subject reduction property, which compensates for the unpleasant feature of the non-determinism.

There remain some problems which should be considered. Two major ones are (1) semantics, especially realizability interpretations, of typing judgements, and (2) normalizability, especially strong normalizability, of well-typed terms. The subject reduction property is good news concerning these problems, but both are still open.

References

1. M. Felleisen, D. Friedman, E. Kohlbecker, and B. Duba, A syntactic theory of sequential control, Theoretical Computer Science **52**(1987) 205-237.
2. T. G. Griffin, A formulae-as-types notion of control, Conf. Rec. ACM Symp. on Principles of Programming Languages (1990) 47-58.
3. C. R. Murthy, An evaluation semantics for classical proofs, Proc. the 6th Annual IEEE Symp. on Logic in Computer Science (1991) 96-107.
4. H. Nakano, A Constructive Formalization of the Catch and Throw Mechanism, Proc. the 7th Annual IEEE Symp. on Logic in Computer Science (1992) 82-89.
5. G. D. Plotkin, Call-by-name, call-by-value and the λ-calculus, Theoretical Computer Science **1**(1975) 125-159.

Conservativeness of Λ over $\lambda\sigma$-calculus

Masahiko Sato and Yukiyoshi Kameyama

Research Institute of Electrical Communication
Tohoku University, Sendai 980, Japan
masahiko@sato.riec.tohoku.ac.jp
kam@sato.riec.tohoku.ac.jp

Abstract. Λ is a unique functional programming language which has the facility of the *encapsulated assignment*, without losing *referential transparency*. The `let`-construct in Λ can be considered as an environment, which has a close relationship to substitution in $\lambda\sigma$-calculus. This paper discusses the relationship between these two calculi; we first define a slightly modified version of Λ-calculus which adopts de Bruijn's index notation. We then define an injective map from $\lambda\sigma$-calculus to Λ, and show that the *Beta*-reduction and the σ-reductions in $\lambda\sigma$-calculus correspond to the β-reduction and `let`-reductions in Λ-calculus, respectively. Finally, we prove that, as equality theories, Λ is *conservative* over the $\lambda\sigma$-calculus.

1 Introduction

Λ is a unique functional programming language which has the facility of the *encapsulated assignment*, without losing *referential transparency* [4]. We can *assign* a value to a variable in a similar way with imperative languages. By this facility, Λ programs can be quite efficient compared with programs written in ordinary functional languages. In spite of the existence of assignment, Λ does not lose mathematically good features. Namely, it has a clear semantics, and it is referentially transparent in the sense that the equality is preserved through substitution. (See [4] for details.) We believe that Λ is a good starting point of treating assignment in a mathematically well-founded manner.

In Λ-calculus, the `let`-construct plays a fundamental role. The evaluation of the `let`-construct (`let` ((x a)) b) can be naturally considered as evaluating b under the environment $x = a$. This concept of environment is closely related to the substitution in $\lambda\sigma$-calculus in [1]. $\lambda\sigma$-calculus is an extension of λ-calculus where substitution has its own syntax, and explicitly described. $\lambda\sigma$-calculus is well founded, since it is conservative over λ-calculus.

This paper discusses the relationship between Λ-calculus and $\lambda\sigma$-calculus. First, we define a slightly modified version of Λ-calculus. The version we present in this paper adopts de Bruijn's index notation, and has a slightly extended `let`-reductions. Next, we define an injection Φ from $\lambda\sigma$-calculus to Λ-calculus. Then we show that the *Beta*-reduction and the σ-reductions in $\lambda\sigma$-calculus correspond to the β-reduction and `let`-reductions in Λ-calculus. Finally, we prove that, as equality theories, Λ is *conservative* over $\lambda\sigma$-calculus; namely, we have that $s = t$ in $\lambda\sigma$-calculus if and only if $\Phi(s) = \Phi(t)$ in Λ.

In the following, we use meta-variables t, s, u for $\lambda\sigma$-terms, θ, ϕ, χ for $\lambda\sigma$-substitutions, a, b, c for Λ-terms, n, m for natural numbers.

2 $\lambda\sigma$-calculus with de Bruijn index

We quote the untyped $\lambda\sigma$-calculus in de Bruijn's index notation from [1]. We assume that readers are familiar with de Bruijn's notation and $\lambda\sigma$-calculus. See also [1] and [3].

Definition 1 (Term t and Substitution θ).

$$t ::= 1 \mid tu \mid \lambda t \mid t[\theta]$$
$$\theta ::= \mathtt{id} \mid \uparrow \mid t \cdot \theta \mid \theta \circ \phi$$

In de Bruijn's notation, all the bound variables disappear if they are just after λ, or otherwise replaced by indices 1, 2, $\cdots$. The indices represents the number of λ-binders between the occurrence of the bound variable and the λ-binder which actually binds this occurrence. For example, the term $\lambda x.\lambda y.xy$ will be represented by $\lambda(\lambda(21))$ in this notation. The term 1 represents the first index. An index larger than 1 is represented by 1 and $\uparrow$. The terms tu and λt are as usual, except that there appears no bound variable after λ. The term $t[\theta]$ is the term t to which the substitution θ is applied.

Each substitution intuitively represents a simultaneous substitution for indices. The substitution id is the identity. The substitution $\uparrow$ is the "shift" operator, which substitutes $n + 1$ for each index n. The substitution $t \cdot \theta$ is "cons" of a term t and a substitution θ, which intuitively represents the substitution $\{1 := t, 2 := s_1, 3 := s_2, \cdots\}$ where θ means $\{1 := s_1, 2 := s_2, \cdots\}$ Finally, $\theta \circ \phi$ is the composition of two substitutions.

Definition 2 (Context C).

$$C ::= \langle\,\rangle \mid Ct \mid tC \mid \lambda C \mid C[\theta] \mid t[\Theta]$$
$$\Theta ::= \langle\,\rangle \mid C \cdot \theta \mid t \cdot \Theta \mid \Theta \circ \theta \mid \theta \circ \Theta$$

A context C has just one hole $\langle\,\rangle$. To emphasize it, we sometimes use the notation $C\langle\,\rangle$. We may replace the hole with a term t or a substitution θ in a context $C\langle\,\rangle$, which is denoted as $C\langle t\rangle$ or $C\langle\theta\rangle$.

Definition 3 (1-step reduction $\rightarrow$).

Beta	$(\lambda t)s \rightarrow t[s \cdot \mathtt{id}]$
VarID	$1[\mathtt{id}] \rightarrow 1$

VarCons	$1[t \cdot \theta] \to t$
App	$(ts)[\theta] \to (t[\theta])(s[\theta])$
Abs	$(\lambda t)[\theta] \to \lambda(t[1 \cdot (\theta \circ \uparrow)])$
Clos	$t[\theta][\phi] \to t[\theta \circ \phi]$
IdL	$\mathrm{id} \circ \theta \to \theta$
ShiftId	$\uparrow \circ\, \mathrm{id} \to \uparrow$
ShiftCons	$\uparrow \circ (t \cdot \theta) \to \theta$
Map	$(t \cdot \theta) \circ \chi \to t[\chi] \cdot (\theta \circ \chi)$
Ass	$(\theta \circ \phi) \circ \chi \to \theta \circ (\phi \circ \chi)$

Rules other than *Beta* are called σ-rules. Reduction relations for the *Beta*-rule and the σ-rules are written as $\to_B$ and $\to_\sigma$. *Beta*-reduction corresponds to the usual β-reduction in λ-calculus, but it does not actually perfom the substitution. It merely adds a new substitution $s \cdot \mathrm{id}$ to the term t. This substitution will be later resolved by σ-reductions.

Definition 4 (Reduction $\twoheadrightarrow$). The relation $\twoheadrightarrow$ is the least relation satisfying the following conditions:

1. $\twoheadrightarrow$ is reflexive and transitive.
2. $t \to s$ implies $C\langle t\rangle \twoheadrightarrow C\langle s\rangle$.
3. $\theta \to \phi$ implies $C\langle \theta\rangle \twoheadrightarrow C\langle \phi\rangle$.

The equality $=$ is the equivalence relation induced by $\twoheadrightarrow$.

Theorem 5 (Abadi et al). *The σ-reduction is confluent and terminating. The whole* $\lambda\sigma$-calculus *is confluent.*

The σ-normal form of a $\lambda\sigma$-term t is written as $\sigma(t)$.

3 Λ-calculus and plet-calculus

3.1 The Functional Programming Language Λ

Λ is a type-free functional programming language which has the facility of the *encapsulated assignment.* We can *assign* a value to a variable in a similar way with imperative languages. In spite of the existence of assignment, Λ does not lose mathematically good features. Namely, it has a clear semantics by Church-Rosser Theorem, and it is referentially transparent in the sense that the equality is preserved through substitution. In this paper, we reinforce this viewpoint by the fact that Λ is a conservative extension of $\lambda\sigma$-calculus. The terms in $\lambda\sigma$-calculus can be naturally translated into Λ, however, it is not clear that the equality is preserved through this translation, since the introduction of assignment to Λ forces us to fix evaluation order to some extent while $\lambda\sigma$-calculus allows strong reductions, which may reduce subterms inside λ, in an arbitrary context. Therefore, conservativeness of Λ is an interesting problem.

3.2 Modification to Λ-calculus

This paper adopts a modified version of Λ-calculus. In this version, we use de Bruijn's index notation rather than using variable names. Therefore, a variable is represented as a natural number.

Another modification is essential. Consider the following equation (taken from [4]):

```
(let ((x t)) (apply a b))
   = (apply (let ((x t)) a) (let ((x t)) b))
```

In this example, t, a, and b represent some terms in Λ-calculus. In a natural translation from $\lambda\sigma$-calculus, this equation is expected to hold in any context. If t does not have assignable variables, the equation (without any context) holds. However, this equation does not hold in an arbitrary context. Consider the following (incorrect) equation:

```
(lambda (y) (let ((x y)) (apply a b)))
   = (lambda (y) (apply (let ((x y)) a) (let ((x y)) b)))
```

In the original Λ-calculus, we have no way to evaluate the subterm `(let ((x y)) (apply a b))`, since `y` is not closed. From the Church-Rosser Property of the original Λ-calculus, we can show that the equation above does not hold, which means the original calculus is not conservative over $\lambda\sigma$-calculus under a natural translation. Similarly, the original Λ-calculus is not conservative over the pure λ-calculus; two equal λ-terms $\lambda y.(\lambda x.xx)y$ and $\lambda y.yy$ are translated into two Λ-terms which are not equal[1].

This example motivates our modification. We allow reductions of a term `(let ((x t) a)`, not only in the case that t is closed (and a is arbitrary), but also in the case that t and a are read-only. A read-only term is a term which does not have side-effect. Note that a read-only term a may contain assignment even if a has assignment; in this case, every variable in the assignment must be bound by `let`-construct or `lambda`-construct in a. By extending `let`-reduction in this way, we can reduce, for example, the term like:

```
(lambda (y) (let ((x y)) (apply a b)))
   → (lambda (y) (apply a_x[y] b_x[y]))
```

where $a_x[y]$ means the usual substitution if a and b are read-only. We can show that the resulting calculus still satisfies the Church-Rosser Property, and has the referential transparency. We simply call this modified version Λ, and use the term the "original" version if we mention Λ in [4].

[1] It follows that Theorem 4.6 in [4] also needs modification in the definition of Λ.

3.3 Definition of Λ-calculus

The set of N-terms is defined for each natural number N as follows.

Definition 6 (Term a_N of Λ-calculus).

$$\begin{aligned} a_N ::= &\ n \quad if\, n \geq 1 \\ |&\ \texttt{(set!}\ n\ a_N\texttt{)} \quad if\, n \leq N \\ |&\ \texttt{(let ((}a_N\texttt{))}\ b_{N+1}\texttt{)} \\ |&\ \texttt{(while}\ a_N\ b_N\ c_N\texttt{)} \\ |&\ \texttt{(if}\ a_N\ b_N\ c_N\texttt{)} \\ |&\ \texttt{nil} \\ |&\ \texttt{(null?}\ a_N\texttt{)} \\ |&\ \texttt{(pair}\ a_N\ b_N\texttt{)} \\ |&\ \texttt{(pair?}\ a_N\texttt{)} \\ |&\ \texttt{(car}\ a_N\texttt{)} \\ |&\ \texttt{(cdr}\ a_N\texttt{)} \\ |&\ \texttt{(lambda ()}\ a_1\texttt{)} \\ |&\ \texttt{(fun?}\ a_N\texttt{)} \\ |&\ \texttt{(apply}\ a_N\ b_N\texttt{)} \\ |&\ \texttt{(mu}\ a_N\texttt{)} \end{aligned}$$

Intuitively, an N-term a_N is a term whose assignable variables are less than or equal to N. We often call an N-term a term simply. The term `(set!` n a_N`)` represents assignment for the variable n to the value a_N. In order to keep referential transparency, we restrict the assignable variables to be bound by a `let`-construct or a `lambda`-construct. Term constructs such as `while`, `if`, `nil`, `pair`, `car`, `cdr`, `lambda`, and `apply` have usual meaning. Terms such as `(null?` a`)` are predicates which decide whether a is `nil` or not, and return `true` or `false`. The term `(mu` a`)` is the μ-operator which invokes a recursive call. A term which is constructed from variables, `lambda`-construct, `apply`-construct, and `let`-construct is called a *pure* term. The terms `nil`, `(pair` a_N b_N`)`, and `(lambda ()` a_N`)` are called constructor terms, and the terms `(null?` a_N`)`, `(pair?` a_N`)`, and `(fun?` a_N`)` are called recognizer terms. We also say that `nil` and `(null?` a_N`)` are of the same kind. Likewise, `(pair` a_N b_N`)` and `(pair?` a_N`)`, are of the same kind, and `(lambda ()` a_N`)` and `(fun?` a_N`)` are of the same kind. Other combinations of pairs of these terms are of the different kind.

The reduction rules of Λ-calculus are listed in the Appendix. The confluency of the original Λ-calculus is proved in [4], and the confluency of this version is proved similarly. The equality in Λ-calculus is the least equivalence relation which contains $\rightarrow$. Instead of explaining the reductions rules in detail, we give a simple example here. Readers are encouraged to read [4] for thorough understanding of the original Λ-calculus.

Example 1 (Reduction in Λ). Let t be the following term.

```
(lambda ()
   (apply
      (apply
         (lambda () (lambda () (pair 1 (pair 2 3))))
         1)
      nil))
```

If we use the notation with variable names, t is written as follows:

```
(lambda (x)
   (apply
      (apply
         (lambda (y) (lambda (z) (pair z (pair y x))))
         x)
      nil))
```

The following sequence is a reduction sequence starting from t.

```
t  →  (by Rule 12)
(lambda ()
   (apply
      (let ((1))
         (lambda () (pair 1 (pair 2 3))))
      nil))
  →  (by Rule 17)
(lambda ()
   (apply
      (let ((1))
         (lambda () (pair 1 (pair 3 3))))
      nil))
  →  (by Rule 16)
(lambda ()
   (apply
      (lambda () (pair 1 (pair 2 2)))
      nil))
  →  (by Rule 12)
(lambda ()
   (let ((nil))
      (pair 1 (pair 2 2))))
```

```
   →  (by Rule 17)
(lambda ()
   (let ((nil))
      (pair nil (pair 2 2))))
   →  (by Rule 16)
(lambda () (pair nil (pair 1 1)))
```

In this paper, we are mainly concerned with the fragment of Λ-calculus consisting of pure terms, which are sufficient for the translation from $\lambda\sigma$-calculus. The fragment is called the *pure-fragment.* The pure-fragment is closed under reduction.

In the translation given later, we will need an intermediate calculus, which we temporarily call `plet`-calculus (parallel-`let` calculus).

Definition 7 (Term a of `plet`-calculus).

$$
\begin{aligned}
a ::= {} & n \quad if\ n \geq 1 \\
\mid {} & \texttt{(let ((}a_1\texttt{) (}a_2\texttt{)} \ \cdots \ \texttt{(}a_k\texttt{))} \ b\texttt{)} \\
\mid {} & \texttt{(lambda () } a\texttt{)} \\
\mid {} & \texttt{(apply } a \ b\texttt{)}
\end{aligned}
$$

Since `plet`-calculus is solely used for the translation, we do not define reduction rules for it.

4 Translation of $\lambda\sigma$-calculus into the pure-fragment of Λ-calculus

4.1 Translation of $\lambda\sigma$-calculus into `plet`-calculus

This section presents a translation from $\lambda\sigma$-terms to `plet`-terms. We begin with an auxiliary definition.

Definition 8 (Degree $\delta(a)$). For each `plet`-term a, its degree $\delta(a)$ is a natural number defined as follows:

$$
\begin{aligned}
\delta(n) &\stackrel{\triangle}{=} n \quad if\ n \geq 1 \\
\delta(\texttt{(let ((}a_1\texttt{)} \ \cdots \ \texttt{(}a_k\texttt{))} \ b\texttt{)}) &\stackrel{\triangle}{=} max(\delta(a_1), \cdots, \delta(a_k), \delta(b) - k) \\
\delta(\texttt{(lambda () } a\texttt{)}) &\stackrel{\triangle}{=} max(1, \delta(a) - 1) \\
\delta(\texttt{(apply } a \ b\texttt{)}) &\stackrel{\triangle}{=} max(\delta(a), \delta(b))
\end{aligned}
$$

Intuitively, $\delta(a)$ is the maximum index of free variables in a. If a does not have free variables, $\delta(a)$ is defined to be 1 rather than 0.

Definition 9 (Translation $t^\dagger$). For each $\lambda\sigma$-term t, a `plet`-term a is defined as follows:

$$
\begin{aligned}
\mathtt{1}^\dagger &\triangleq \mathtt{1}\\
(ts)^\dagger &\triangleq (\mathtt{apply}\ t^\dagger\ s^\dagger)\\
(\lambda t)^\dagger &\triangleq (\mathtt{lambda}\ ()\ t^\dagger)\\
(t[\theta])^\dagger &\triangleq (\mathtt{let}\ \theta^{(\delta(t^\dagger))}\ t^\dagger)
\end{aligned}
$$

The translation for substitution $-^{(n)}$ is defined as follows.

Definition 10 (Translation $\theta^{(n)}$). For a substitution θ in $\lambda\sigma$-calculus and a natural number n ($n \geq 1$), $\theta^{(n)}$ is a list of singleton-lists of `plet`-terms defined as follows:

$$
\begin{aligned}
\mathtt{id}^{(n)} &\triangleq ((1)\ (2)\ \cdots\ (n))\\
\uparrow^{(n)} &\triangleq ((2)\ (3)\ \cdots\ (n+1))\\
(a\cdot\theta)^{(n)} &\triangleq ((a^\dagger)\ (b_1)\ (b_2)\ \cdots\ (b_k)\ (k+2))\\
&\qquad \mathit{if}\ \theta^{(n)}\ \mathit{is}\ ((b_1)\ (b_2)\ \cdots\ (b_k))\\
(\theta\circ\phi)^{(n)} &\triangleq (((\mathtt{let}\ \phi^{(m)}\ a_1))\cdots((\mathtt{let}\ \phi^{(m)}\ a_k)))\\
&\qquad \mathit{if}\ \theta^{(n)}\ \mathit{is}\ ((a_1)\ (a_2)\ \cdots\ (a_k))\\
&\qquad \mathit{and}\ m\ \mathit{is}\ \mathit{max}(\delta(a_1),\cdots,\delta(a_k)).
\end{aligned}
$$

Proposition 11. *The translation $-^\dagger$ is injective.*

Proof. First note that, for each substitution θ and natural number n, the length (as a list) of $\theta^{(n)}$ is equal to or more than n. It follows that the length of $(a\cdot\theta)^{(n)}$ is more than $n+1$, so $(a\cdot\theta)^{(n)}$ cannot be identical to $\mathtt{id}^{(n)}$ nor $\uparrow^{(n)}$. Moreover, its last element is a natural number $k+2$, and differs[2] from the last element of $(\theta\circ\phi)^{(n)}$. Hence, the images of $-^{(n)}$ for four classes of substitutions do not overlap. Using this fact, we can prove that, $t^\dagger$ and $\theta^{(n)}$ (for each n) are injective by the simultaneous induction on the complexity of the term t and the substitution θ. □

4.2 Translation from `plet`-calculus to Λ-calculus

First we define a^+ for each `plet`-term a. Intuitively, a^+ is the term a with each free variable shifted (added by one), for example,

$$(\mathtt{apply\ 3\ (lambda\ ()\ (apply\ 1\ 2))})^+$$

[2] This is the reason why we attached the seemingly meaningless term $k+2$ in the definition.

is `(apply 4 (lambda () (apply 1 3)))`. To define a^+, we need to define an auxiliary function a^+_m, which adds one for each free variable in a whose value is more than m.

Definition 12 (a^+_m).

$$n^+_m \triangleq n \quad if\ n \leq m$$

$$n^+_m \triangleq n+1 \quad if\ n > m$$

$$(\texttt{let}\ ((a_1)\ \cdots\ (a_k))\ b)^+_m \triangleq (\texttt{let}\ (((a_1)^+_m)\ \cdots\ ((a_k)^+_m))\ b)$$

$$(\texttt{lambda}\ ()\ a)^+_m \triangleq (\texttt{lambda}\ ()\ a^+_{m+1})$$

$$(\texttt{apply}\ a\ b)^+_m \triangleq (\texttt{apply}\ a^+_m\ b^+_m)$$

We simply write a^+_0 as a^+.

Definition 13 (Translation * from `plet`-calculus to Λ-calculus).

$$n^* \triangleq n$$

$$(\texttt{let}\ ()\ b)^* \triangleq (\texttt{let}\ (b^*)\ 1)$$

$$(\texttt{let}\ ((a_1)\ \cdots\ (a_{k-1})\ (a_k))\ b)^* \triangleq (\texttt{let}\ ((a_k))\ c)$$

$$if\ c\ is\ (\texttt{let}\ ((a_1{}^+)\ \cdots\ (a_{k-1}{}^+))\ b)^*$$

$$(\texttt{lambda}\ ()\ a)^* \triangleq (\texttt{lambda}\ ()\ a^*)$$

$$(\texttt{apply}\ a\ b)^* \triangleq (\texttt{apply}\ a^*\ b^*)$$

In the following, we sometimes regard `plet`-terms as pure terms in Λ-calculus (through $*$ translation).

The translation Φ from $\lambda\sigma$-calculus to the pure-fragment is defined as follows.

Definition 14 (Translation Φ from $\lambda\sigma$-calculus to Λ-calculus).

$$\Phi(t) \triangleq (t^\dagger)^*$$

Theorem 15. $-^*$ *is injective. Hence* Φ *is injective.*

Proof. Clear.

Remark. If a non-injective map were allowed as the translation Φ, part of our result (the first part of Theorem 23) would become trivial as shown below.

In $\lambda\sigma$-calculus, the set of σ-normal forms can be regarded as the set of pure λ-terms, so the map $\sigma(\ )$ can be regarded as the translation from $\lambda\sigma$-terms to pure λ-terms. We have that, $s = t$ holds if and only if $\sigma(s) = \sigma(t)$ holds. Λ-calculus is also conservative over pure λ-calculus [3]. Namely, there is a map Ψ from pure λ-terms to Λ-terms such that $a = b$ holds if and only if $\Psi(a) = \Psi(b)$ holds. Let Φ be the composition of σ and Ψ; then we have that $s = t$ holds in $\lambda\sigma$-calculus if and only if $\Phi(s) = \Phi(t)$ holds in Λ-calculus. □

[3] This claim does not hold for the original Λ-calculus, but it does hold for the modified version presented in this paper.

4.3 Properties of the translation Φ

In this section, we prove that the translation Φ preserves the equality. First we state an extension of Lemma 4.2 in [4].

Lemma 16. *Let a and b be pure N-terms for some natural number N. Then* `(let ((`a`)) `b`)` *reduces to* $b\{1 := a, 2 := 1, 3 := 2, \cdots, k := k-1\}$ *using* `let`*-rules only, where k is $\delta(b)$.*

Here $\{1 := a, 2 := 1, 3 := 2, \cdots, k := k-1\}$ denotes the simultaneous substitution. Note that a and b are not necessarily 0-terms. As was stated in Section 3.2, this lemma does not hold for the original Λ-calculus, since we cannot reduce the term `(let ((`a`)) `b`)` if a is not closed. On the contrary, the version we present in this paper satisfies this lemma, since all pure N-terms are read-only, which enables us to reduce the term `(let ((`a`)) `b`)`.

Similarly, we have the following lemma.

Lemma 17. *Let $a_1 \cdots a_k$ and b be pure N-terms, and k be $\delta(b)$. If $n \geq k$, then* `(let ((`a_1`) `$\cdots$` (`a_n`)) `b`)` *reduces to* $b\{1 := a_1, 2 := a_2, \cdots, k := a_k\}$ *using* `let`*-rules only.*

Note that, we regard `plet`-terms as Λ-terms through the translation $(\,)^*$ in Lemma 17.

These lemmata are proved by the induction on b.

Proposition 18. *For each term-reduction rule $t \rightarrow s$ in $\lambda\sigma$-calculus, $\Phi(t) = \Phi(s)$ holds in Λ-calculus. For each substitution-reduction rule $\theta \rightarrow \phi$ and a term s in $\lambda\sigma$-calculus, $\Phi(s[\theta]) = \Phi(s[\phi])$ holds in Λ-calculus.*

Proof. This proposition is proved by case analysis.

(Beta) The left hand side (LHS, in short) of *Beta* is translated into

`(apply (lambda () `$t^\dagger$`) `$s^\dagger$`)`

which β-reduces to

`(let ((`$s^\dagger$`)) `$t^\dagger$`)`

By Lemma 16, this is equal to $t^\dagger\{1 := s^\dagger, 2 := 1, 3 := 2, \cdots\}$.
The right hand side (RHS, in short) of *Beta* is translated into

`(let ((`$s^\dagger$`) (1) `$\cdots$` (`$n-1$`)) `$t^\dagger$`)`

Calculation of indexes shows that this is equal to $t^\dagger\{1 := s^\dagger, 2 := 1, 3 := 2, \cdots\}$.

(VarID) LHS is translated into `(let ((1)) 1)` which reduces to `1`. RHS is translated into `1`.

(VarCons) LHS is translated into `(let` $((t^\dagger)\cdots)$ `1)` which reduces to $t^\dagger$. RHS is translated into $t^\dagger$.

(App) Suppose $\theta^{(\delta((ts)^\dagger))}$ is $((a_1)\ \cdots\ (a_k))$.
LHS is translated into `(let` $((a_1)\ (a_2)\ \cdots\ (a_k))$ `(apply` $t^\dagger\ s^\dagger$`))`.
RHS is translated into

$$\begin{array}{l}\texttt{(apply}\\ \quad\texttt{(let}\ ((a_1)\ (a_2)\ \cdots\ (a_l))\ t^\dagger\texttt{)}\\ \quad\texttt{(let}\ ((a_1)\ (a_2)\ \cdots\ (a_m))\ s^\dagger\texttt{))}\end{array}$$

where l and m are $\delta(t^\dagger)$ and $\delta(s^\dagger)$.
By Lemma 17, `(let` $((a_1)\ \cdots\ (a_k))\ t^\dagger$`)` is equal to

$$t^\dagger\{1{:=}a_1,\cdots,l{:=}a_l\}$$

and similarly for $s^\dagger$. Hence, by Lemma 16, LHS and RHS reduce to

$$\begin{array}{l}\texttt{(apply}\ t^\dagger\{1{:=}a_1,\cdots,l{:=}a_l\}\\ \qquad\qquad s^\dagger\{1{:=}a_1,\cdots,m{:=}a_m\}\texttt{)}\end{array}$$

(Abs) Suppose $\theta^{(\delta((\lambda t)^\dagger))}$ is $((a_1)\ \cdots\ (a_k))$.
LHS is translated into `(let` $((a_1)\ \cdots\ (a_k))$ `(lambda ()` $t^\dagger$`))`. This reduces to

$$\begin{array}{l}\texttt{(lambda ()}\\ \quad t^\dagger\{2{:=}a_1\{1{:=}2,2{:=}3,\cdots\},\\ \qquad\ldots\\ \qquad k+1{:=}a_k\{1{:=}2,2{:=}3,\cdots\}\}\texttt{)}.\end{array}$$

RHS is translated into

$$\begin{array}{l}\texttt{(lambda ()}\\ \quad\texttt{(let ((1)}\\ \qquad\quad\texttt{((let ((2) (3)}\ \cdots\texttt{)}\ a_1\texttt{))}\\ \qquad\quad\ldots\\ \qquad\quad\texttt{((let ((2) (3)}\ \cdots\texttt{)}\ a_k\texttt{)))}\\ \qquad t^\dagger\texttt{))}\end{array}$$

The latter term reduces to the former by Lemma 17.

(Clos) Suppose $\theta^{(\delta(t^\dagger))}$ is $((a_1)\ \cdots\ (a_l))$, and $\phi^{(n)}$ is $((b_1)\ \cdots\ (b_k))$ where n is $max(a_1,\cdots,a_l)$.
LHS is translated into

$$\begin{array}{l}\texttt{(let}\ ((b_1)\ \cdots\ (b_k))\\ \quad\texttt{(let}\ ((a_1)\ \cdots\ (a_l))\ t^\dagger\texttt{))}\end{array}$$

RHS is translated into

$$\begin{aligned}&\texttt{(let (((let ((}b_1\texttt{)} \cdots \texttt{(}b_k\texttt{))}\ a_1\texttt{))}\\&\qquad \cdots\\&\qquad \texttt{((let ((}b_1\texttt{)} \cdots \texttt{(}b_k\texttt{))}\ a_l\texttt{)))}\\&\quad t^\dagger\texttt{)}\end{aligned}$$

LHS and RHS reduce to

$$\begin{aligned}&t^\dagger\{1\texttt{:=}a_1\{1\texttt{:=}b_1,\cdots,k\texttt{:=}b_k\},\\&\quad\cdots\\&\quad l\texttt{:=}a_l\{1\texttt{:=}b_1,\cdots,k\texttt{:=}b_k\}\}.\end{aligned}$$

(IdL) Let n be $\delta(s)$. Suppose $\theta^{(n)}$ is $\texttt{((}b_1\texttt{)} \cdots \texttt{(}b_k\texttt{))}$. Then, $s\texttt{[id}\circ\theta\texttt{]}$ is translated into

$$\begin{aligned}&\texttt{(let (((let ((}b_1\texttt{)} \cdots \texttt{(}b_k\texttt{)) 1))}\\&\qquad \cdots\\&\qquad \texttt{((let ((}b_1\texttt{)} \cdots \texttt{(}b_k\texttt{))}\ n\texttt{)))}\\&\quad s^\dagger\texttt{)}\end{aligned}$$

Since $k \geq n$, this reduces to $\texttt{(let ((}b_1\texttt{)} \cdots \texttt{(}b_n\texttt{))}\ s^\dagger\texttt{)}$ Then this term is identical to $(s\texttt{[}\theta\texttt{]})^\dagger$ by Lemma 17.

(ShiftId) Let n be $\delta(s)$. The term $s\texttt{[}\uparrow\circ\texttt{id]}$ is translated into

$$\begin{aligned}&\texttt{(let (((let ((1)} \cdots \texttt{(}n+1\texttt{)) 2))}\\&\qquad \texttt{((let ((1)} \cdots \texttt{(}n+1\texttt{)) 3))}\\&\qquad \cdots\\&\qquad \texttt{((let ((1)} \cdots \texttt{(}n+1\texttt{))}\ n+1\texttt{)))}\\&\quad s^\dagger\texttt{)}\end{aligned}$$

This reduces to $\texttt{(let ((2)} \cdots \texttt{(}n+1\texttt{))}\ s^\dagger\texttt{)}$ which is identical to $(s\texttt{[}\uparrow\texttt{]})^\dagger$.

(ShiftCons) Let n be $\delta(s)$. Suppose $\theta^{(n+1)}$ is $\texttt{((}b_1\texttt{)} \cdots \texttt{(}b_k\texttt{))}$.
Then, $s\texttt{[}\uparrow\circ(t\cdot\theta)\texttt{]}$ is translated into

$$\begin{aligned}&\texttt{(let (((let ((}t^\dagger\texttt{) (}b_1\texttt{)} \cdots \texttt{(}b_k\texttt{) (}k+2\texttt{)) 2))}\\&\qquad \texttt{((let ((}t^\dagger\texttt{) (}b_1\texttt{)} \cdots \texttt{(}b_k\texttt{) (}k+2\texttt{)) 3))}\\&\qquad \cdots\\&\qquad \texttt{((let ((}t^\dagger\texttt{) (}b_1\texttt{)} \cdots \texttt{(}b_k\texttt{) (}k+2\texttt{))}\ n+1\texttt{)))}\\&\quad s^\dagger\texttt{)}\end{aligned}$$

We also have $k \geq n+1$, and the term above reduces to

$$\texttt{(let ((}b_1\texttt{)} \cdots \texttt{(}b_n\texttt{))}\ s^\dagger\texttt{)}$$

which is equal to $(s[\theta])^\dagger$.

(Map) Let n be $\delta(s)$. Suppose $\theta^{(n)}$ is $((a_1) \cdots (a_k))$, and $\chi^{(m)}$ is $((b_1) \cdots (b_l))$ where m is $max(\delta(t), \delta(a_1), \cdots, \delta(a_k), k+2)$.
Then, $s[(t \cdot \theta) \circ \chi]$ is translated into

```
(let (((let ((b_1) ··· (b_l)) t†))
      ((let ((b_1) ··· (b_l)) a_1))
      ···
      ((let ((b_1) ··· (b_l)) a_k))
      ((let ((b_1) ··· (b_l)) k + 2)))
   s†)
```

$s[t[\chi] \cdot (\theta \circ \chi)]$ is translated into

```
(let (((let ((b_1) ··· (b_o)) t†))
      ((let ((b_1) ··· (b_q)) a_1))
      ···
      ((let ((b_1) ··· (b_q)) a_k))
      (k + 2))
   s†)
```

where $\delta(t)$ is p, $\chi^{(p)}$ is $((b_1) \cdots (b_o))$, $max(\delta(a_1), \cdots, \delta(a_k))$ is r, and $\chi^{(r)}$ is $((b_1) \cdots (b_q))$.
We have that $p \leq o \leq l$, $r \leq q \leq l$, and $n \leq k$, therefore, by Lemma 17, both of these terms are equal to

$$
\begin{aligned}
s^\dagger\{&1{:=}t^\dagger\{1{:=}b_1, \cdots, p{:=}b_p\},\\
&2{:=}a_1\{1{:=}b_1, \cdots, r{:=}b_r\},\\
&\cdots\\
&n{:=}a_n\{1{:=}b_1, \cdots, r{:=}b_r\}\}
\end{aligned}
$$

(Ass) Let n be $\delta(s)$. Suppose $\theta^{(n)}$ is $((a_1) \cdots (a_k))$, $\phi^{(o)}$ is $((b_1) \cdots (b_l))$, and $\chi^{(p)}$ is $((c_1) \cdots (c_m))$ for appropriate o and p.
Then, $s[(\theta \circ \phi) \circ \chi]$ is translated into

```
(let (((let ((c_1) ··· (c_m))
          (let ((b_1) ··· (b_l)) a_1))
      ···
      ((let ((c_1) ··· (c_m))
          (let ((b_1) ··· (b_l)) a_k)))
   s†)
```

$s[\theta \circ (\phi \circ \chi)]$ is translated into

```
(let (((let (((let ((c1) ··· (cm)) b1))
                 ...
                 ((let ((c1) ··· (cm)) bl)))
           a1))
        ...
        ((let (((let ((c1) ··· (cm)) b1))
                 ...
                 ((let ((c1) ··· (cm)) bl)))
           ak)))
   s†)
```

Both of these terms reduce to

$$s^{\dagger}\{1\!:=\!a_1\{1\!:=\!b_1\{1\!:=\!c_1,\cdots,m\!:=\!c_m\},\cdots,l\!:=\!b_l\{1\!:=\!c_1,\cdots,m\!:=\!c_m\}\},$$
$$\cdots$$
$$1\!:=\!a_k\{1\!:=\!b_1\{1\!:=\!c_1,\cdots,m\!:=\!c_m\},\cdots,l\!:=\!b_l\{1\!:=\!c_1,\cdots,m\!:=\!c_m\}\}$$

Note that, we have used only `let`-rules for proving the cases for σ-rules. Note also that, the 1-step *Beta* reduction can be simulated by the 1-step β-reduction with some `let`-rules. □

Proposition 19. *Let t and s be $\lambda\sigma$-terms. If $t = s$, then $\Phi(t) = \Phi(s)$ in* Λ-calculus.

Proof. We first prove that, the result of Proposition 18 can be extended to an arbitrary context. Namely, for a context $C\langle\,\rangle$, if $t \to s$, then $\Phi(C\langle t\rangle) = \Phi(C\langle s\rangle)$ where t and s are terms or substitutions. These are straightforward if the used reduction rule is a σ-rule. However, in the case of *Beta*-rule, there occurs a subtle point; for example, $((\lambda 2)3)[\uparrow]$ is translated into

```
(let ((2) (3) (4)) (apply (lambda () 2) 3)).
```

On the other hand, the result of applying *Beta* rule to it is $1[\uparrow]$ which is translated into `(let ((2)) 1)`. We can use Lemma 17 to overcome this difficulty, and can prove the equality of $\Phi(C\langle t\rangle)$ and $\Phi(C\langle s\rangle)$.

Finally, we can extend the result for 1-step reductions to the general case, and get the desired proposition. □

By checking the proofs, we know that, if $t = s$ is shown by σ-rules only, then $\Phi(t) = \Phi(s)$ is shown by `let`-rules only.

5 Translation of the pure-fragment into $\lambda\sigma$-calculus

We now define the reverse translation, namely the translation from the pure-fragment of Λ-calculus to $\lambda\sigma$-calculus.

Definition 20 (Translation Ψ).

$$\Psi(n) \stackrel{\triangle}{=} \texttt{1[}\uparrow^n\texttt{]}$$
$$\Psi(\texttt{(let ((}a\texttt{)) }b\texttt{))} \stackrel{\triangle}{=} \Psi(b)\texttt{[}\Psi(a)\cdot\texttt{id]}$$
$$\Psi(\texttt{(lambda () }a\texttt{))} \stackrel{\triangle}{=} \lambda\Psi(a)$$
$$\Psi(\texttt{(apply }a\ b\texttt{))} \stackrel{\triangle}{=} \Psi(a)\Psi(b)$$

In the first clause, $\texttt{1[}\uparrow^n\texttt{]}$ is n-times application of substitution, that is, $\texttt{1}\overbrace{\texttt{[}\uparrow\texttt{]}\cdots\texttt{[}\uparrow\texttt{]}}^{n}$.

Proposition 21. *We have the following;*
1. Ψ is injective.
2. Let a and b be pure N-terms in Λ. If $a = b$, then $\Psi(a) = \Psi(b)$ holds.

Proof. We first prove the theorem for the case of $a \to b$. It is proved by the induction on the derivation of $a \to b$. We only have to consider Rules 1, 3, 5, 7, 12, 16, 17, and 19.

(Rules 1, 3, 5, 7) These cases are proved easily.
(Rule 12) Suppose a is $\texttt{(apply (lambda () }c\texttt{) }d\texttt{)}$, b be $\texttt{(let ((}d'\texttt{)) }c'\texttt{)}$, $c \to c'$ and $d \to d'$. Then, $\Psi(a)$ is $(\lambda\Psi(c))\Psi(d)$, and $\Psi(b)$ is $\Psi(c')\texttt{[}\Psi(d')\cdot\texttt{id]}$. By the induction hypothesis and the *Beta* rule in $\lambda\sigma$-calculus, these terms are equal.
(Rule 16) Suppose a is $\texttt{(let ((}c\texttt{)) }d\texttt{)}$, $1 \notin FV(d)$. $d \to e$, and b is e^-. We have $\Psi(a)$ is $\Psi(d)\texttt{[}\Psi(c)\cdot\texttt{id]}$. We can show that, all the occurrences of 1 in $\Psi(d)$ are followed by one or more $\uparrow$'s, hence $\Psi(d)\texttt{[}\Psi(c)\cdot\texttt{id]}$ is equal to $\Psi(d)\{2 := 1, 3 := 2, \cdots\}$, which is again equal to $\Psi(d^-)$. We have $1 \notin FV(e)$, and, therefore, $d^- \to e^-$. By the induction hypothesis $\Psi(d^-) = \Psi(e^-)$, hence $\Psi(a) = \Psi(b)$.
(Rule 17) Suppose a is $\texttt{(let ((}c\texttt{)) }d\texttt{)}$, $\rho(d,p) = 1$, $c \to c'$, $d \to d'$, and $e \equiv d'_p[c'^+]$, b is $\texttt{(let ((}c'\texttt{)) }e\texttt{)}$. Then, $\Psi(a)$ is $\Psi(d)\texttt{[}\Psi(c)\cdot\texttt{id]}$, which is equal to $\Psi(d')\texttt{[}\Psi(c')\cdot\texttt{id]}$, by the induction hypothesis. By the induction on the term $\Psi(d')$, we have that the σ-normal forms of this term and the term $\Psi(e)\texttt{[}\Psi(c')\cdot\texttt{id]}$ are identical. Hence we have that $\Psi(a)$ and $\Psi(b)$ are σ-equal.
(Rule 19) This case is proved in a similar way as Rule 17.

We can extend the result above to the equality $a = b$. □

6 Main Theorem

This section presents the main theorem of this paper.

Proposition 22. *For each $\lambda\sigma$-term t, $\Psi(\Phi(t)) = t$ holds. Moreover, the equality is shown by the* `let`*-rules only.*

Proof. This proposition is proved by the induction on the term t. □

Theorem 23. *Let t and s be $\lambda\sigma$-terms. Then, $t = s$ holds if and only if $\Phi(t) = \Phi(s)$ holds.*

Moreover, if t is shown to be equal to s using σ-rules only, $\Phi(t)$ and $\Phi(s)$ are shown to be equal using `let`*-rules only. If t is shown to be equal to s by several times applications of the Beta-rule, $\Phi(t)$ and $\Phi(s)$ are shown to be equal by the same times applications of the β-rule, and some applications of* `let`*-rules.*

Proof. The first part follows from Propositions 19, 21 and 22. The second part follows from the remarks for these propositions. □

Remark. Theorem 23 shows that the pure-fragment of Λ-calculus and $\lambda\sigma$-calculus have a close relationship; as equality theories, Λ-calculus (the version presented in this paper) is conservative over $\lambda\sigma$-calculus.

However, we can see several differences between them. Firstly, the reduction rules do not directly correspond, namely, $t \twoheadrightarrow s$ in $\lambda\sigma$-calculus does not necessarily imply $\Phi(t) \rightarrow \Phi(s)$ in Λ-calculus. Secondly, substitutions are objects in $\lambda\sigma$-calculus, and can be directly treated, while its corresponding expression (`let` ((a)) $\langle\rangle$) is not a term in Λ-calculus. This reflects that, in Λ we only consider the environment with some term, and never treat one as an independent object. One of the design goals of Λ is to treat assignment in a mathematically well founded manner, which means we want to keep the referential transparency in our sense, and therefore, we do not separate terms and environments.

As in $\lambda\sigma$-calculus, we have a complete normal-order strategy for the reductions in Λ, which we plan to implement on a computer. □

7 Terms with Names

The results for the calculi with de Bruijn's index notation also hold for the calculi with variable-names. In this section, we briefly explain how to translate terms with variable-names between $\lambda\sigma$-calculus and Λ-calculus.

Suppose X is a list of variables. In the following, (x . X) represents the cons of the variable x and the list X. The expression (x) represents the singleton list.

Definition 24 (Term a in Λ).

$$
\begin{aligned}
a_X ::= \; & x \\
\mid \; & \texttt{(set! } x\ a\texttt{)} \quad \textit{if } x \in X \\
\mid \; & \texttt{(let ((}x\ a_X\texttt{))}\ b_{(x.X)}\texttt{)} \\
\mid \; & \texttt{(while } a_X\ b_X\ c_X\texttt{)} \\
\mid \; & \texttt{(if } a_X\ b_X\ c_X\texttt{)} \\
\mid \; & \texttt{nil} \\
\mid \; & \texttt{(null? } a_X\texttt{)} \\
\mid \; & \texttt{(pair } a_X\ b_X\texttt{)}
\end{aligned}
$$

$$
\begin{array}{l}
\mid \texttt{(pair? } a_X\texttt{)} \\
\mid \texttt{(car } a_X\texttt{)} \\
\mid \texttt{(cdr } a_X\texttt{)} \\
\mid \texttt{(lambda (}x\texttt{) } a_{(x)}\texttt{)} \\
\mid \texttt{(fun? } a_X\texttt{)} \\
\mid \texttt{(apply } a_X\ b_X\texttt{)} \\
\mid \texttt{(mu } a_X\texttt{)}
\end{array}
$$

The pure-fragment and plet-calculus are defined similarly.
We take the $\lambda\sigma$-calculus with names which does not have $\uparrow$ operator.

Definition 25 (Term t and Substitution θ in $\lambda\sigma$-calculus).

$$
\begin{array}{l}
t ::= x \mid tu \mid \lambda x.t \mid t\texttt{[}\theta\texttt{]} \\
\theta ::= \texttt{id} \mid (t/x)\cdot\theta \mid \theta\circ\phi
\end{array}
$$

Definition 26 (Translation $t^\dagger$). For each $\lambda\sigma$-term t, a plet-term a is defined as follows:

$$
\begin{aligned}
x^\dagger &\triangleq x \\
(ts)^\dagger &\triangleq \texttt{(apply } t^\dagger\ s^\dagger\texttt{)} \\
(\lambda x.t)^\dagger &\triangleq \texttt{(lambda (}x\texttt{) } t^\dagger\texttt{)} \\
(t\texttt{[}\theta\texttt{]})^\dagger &\triangleq \texttt{(let } \theta^\circ\ t^\dagger\texttt{)}
\end{aligned}
$$

Definition 27 (Translation θ°). We fix a fresh variable v. For a substitution θ in $\lambda\sigma$-calculus θ° is a list which consists of pairs of variables and plet-terms:

$$
\begin{aligned}
\texttt{id}^\circ &\triangleq \texttt{((}v\ v\texttt{))} \\
((a/x)\cdot\theta)^\circ &\triangleq \texttt{((}x\ a^\dagger\texttt{) (}x_1\ b_1\texttt{) (}x_2\ b_2\texttt{)} \cdots \texttt{(}x_k\ b_k\texttt{) (}v\ v\texttt{))} \\
&\quad \textit{if } \theta^\circ \textit{ is } \texttt{((}x_1\ b_1\texttt{) (}x_2\ b_2\texttt{)} \cdots \texttt{(}x_k\ b_k\texttt{))} \\
(\theta\circ\phi)^\circ &\triangleq \texttt{((}x_1\ \texttt{(let } \phi^\circ\ a_1\texttt{))} \\
&\quad \ldots \\
&\quad \texttt{(}x_k\ \texttt{(let } \phi^\circ\ a_k\texttt{)))} \\
&\quad \textit{if } \theta^\circ \textit{ is } \texttt{((}x_1\ a_1\texttt{) (}x_2\ a_2\texttt{)} \cdots \texttt{(}x_k\ a_k\texttt{))}
\end{aligned}
$$

The translation $*$ from plet-terms to Λ-terms are defined as in the nameless case. Let the translation $\Phi(t)$ be $(t^\dagger)^*$.

Definition 28 (Translation Ψ).

$$\Psi(x) \triangleq x$$
$$\Psi(\texttt{(let ((}x\ a\texttt{))}\ b\texttt{))} \triangleq \Psi(b)\texttt{[}(\Psi(a)/x)\cdot\texttt{id]}$$
$$\Psi(\texttt{(lambda (}x\texttt{)}\ a\texttt{))} \triangleq \lambda x.\Psi(a)$$
$$\Psi(\texttt{(apply}\ a\ b\texttt{))} \triangleq \Psi(a)\Psi(b)$$

We have the following theorem for these translations.

Theorem 29. *We have the following;*
1. *Φ and Ψ are injective.*
2. *For a $\lambda\sigma$-term t, $\Psi(\Phi(t)) = t$ holds.*
3. *Let t and s be $\lambda\sigma$-terms. Then, $t = s$ if and only if $\Phi(t) = \Phi(s)$.*

Remark. There are two versions of $\lambda\sigma$-calculus with variable names, one without the shift operator and one with the shift operator. We chose the first (naive) one here. The shift operator $\uparrow$ in the calculus with variable names refers to a variable beyond a binder; for example, the third occurrence of x in the term $\lambda x.\lambda x.(x\texttt{[}\uparrow\texttt{]})$ is bound by the first λ. The present Λ does not have such facility, and we cannot translate the latter version of $\lambda\sigma$-calculus into Λ-calculus. If we would extend Λ so that we could refer a variable beyond a binder, we would be also able to embed this calculus into Λ-calculus. □

8 Conclusion

In this paper, we have shown the rigid relationship between "explicit substitution" ($\lambda\sigma$-calculus) and our functional language Λ. We first presented a modified version of Λ so that we may reduce `let`-terms under the "read-only" condition. We used de Bruijn's index notation in this presentation. We then gave a translation from $\lambda\sigma$-calculus into the pure-fragment of Λ-calculus, and a reverse one. We proved that, through these translations, σ-rules correspond to `let`-rules, *Beta*-rule corresponds to β-rule, and finally Λ is conservative over $\lambda\sigma$-calculus. We also presented a brief sketch of translation for calculi with variable names. Together with the Church-Rosser property and the referential transparency presented in [4], our result establishes that Λ is a well-founded programming language with assignment.

As a future work, we will implement the language Λ on a computer, and develop a proof-system for Λ-programs.

Acknowledgements

We would like to thank Makoto Tatsuta and Morten Heine Sørensen for constructive comments. This work was partly supported by Grant-in-Aid for Scientific Research from the Ministry of Education, Science and Culture of Japan, No. 04235104 for the first author and No. 05780221 for the second author.

References

1. Abadi, M., L. Cardelli, P.-L. Curien, and J.-J. Levy: Explicit Substitutions, *17th Annual ACM Symp. on Principles of Programming Languages*, pp. 31-46, 1990.
2. Curien, P.-L.: Categorical Combinators, *Information and Control*, 69, pp. 188-254, 1986.
3. de Bruijn, N. G., Lambda-calculus Notation with Nameless Dummies, a Tool for Automatic Formula Manipulation, *Indag. Mat.*, 34, pp. 381-392, 1972.
4. Sato, M: A Purely Functional Language with Encapsulated Assignment, to appear in *Proc. of Second Intl Symp. on Theoretical Aspects of Computer Software*, 1994.

Appendix: Λ-calculus in de Bruijn's notation

The Appendix gives several definitions including the reduction rules of Λ in de Bruijn's index notation.

A *position* is a finite sequence of positive integers, with ϵ being the empty sequence. For instance, `121` is a position.

Each subterm in a term is specified by a position in a usual way. We use the notation t/p for the subterm of a term t at the position p. For instance,

`(apply (apply` a b`)` c`)/22` is a, and
`(apply (apply` a b`)` c`)/`ϵ is `(apply (apply` a b`)` c`)`.

For a term a and a position p, $\nu(a,p)$ intuitively means the number of surrounding binders (`let` or `lambda`) at the position p, and is defined as follows.

Definition 30.

$$\nu(\texttt{(let ((}b\texttt{))}\ c\texttt{)}, 211q) \triangleq \nu(b,q)$$
$$\nu(\texttt{(let ((}b\texttt{))}\ c\texttt{)}, 3q) \triangleq \nu(c,q)+1$$
$$\nu(\texttt{(lambda ()}\ b\texttt{)}, 3q) \triangleq \nu(b,q)+1$$
$$\nu(\texttt{(}f\ b_1\ \cdots\ b_m\texttt{)}, iq) \triangleq \nu(b_{i-1},q)\ \textit{where } f \textit{ is not } \texttt{let} \textit{ nor } \texttt{lambda},$$
$$\nu(a,p) \triangleq 0\ \textit{otherwise}$$

Suppose a/p is a variable i. This occurrence of a variable is called *bound* if $i \leq \nu(a,p)$, and *free* otherwise.

Next, we define a natural number $\rho(a,p)$ for a term a and a position p. In a term a, there may be several occurrences of a variable, and each may take a different value. We, therefore, sometimes need to know the absolute value of a variable-occurrence if we look at this occurrence from outside of a. The number $\rho(a,p)$ is defined to be $i - \nu(a,p)$ where a/p is a free occurrence of a variable in a, and i is the variable. Otherwise, $\rho(a,p)$ is undefined.

$FV(a)$ is the set of $\rho(a,p)$ where p ranges over all the free occurrences of variables in a.

Let us take an example. Let a be `(let ((2)) (pair 1 2))`. Then $\nu(a, 211)$ is 0, the occurrence at 211 of a is free, and $\rho(a, 211)$ is 2. $\nu(a, 32)$ is 1, the occurrence at 32 of a is bound, and $\rho(a, 32)$ is undefined. $\nu(a, 33)$ is 1, the occurrence at 33 of a is free, and $\rho(a, 33)$ is 1.

For a term a, two terms a^+ and a^- are the term a with each free variable added by one, and subtracted by one, respectively. For instance,

a^+ is `(let ((3)) (pair 1 3))`

a^- is `(let ((1)) (pair 1 1))`

A precise definition of a^+ is given by Definition 12.

An N-term a is called *N-closed* if $FV(a) \cap \{1, \cdots, N\} = \emptyset$. The set C_N represents the set of N-closed terms. An N-term a is called *N-read-only* if, for any subterm in the form (`set!` n b), n is bound in a. R_N represents the set of N-read-only terms.

Definition 31 (Substitution). Let a and d be terms, and p be a position. We will define a term $a_p[d]$ as follows:

- If p is ϵ, $a_p[d]$ is d.
- Otherwise,
  - if a is (`lambda ()` b),
    then $a_p[d]$ is (`lambda ()` $b_q[d^+]$) if p is $3q$, and is undefined otherwise.
  - if a is (`let` ((b)) c),
    then $a_p[d]$ is (`let` (($b_q[d]$)) c) if p is $211q$. $a_p[d]$ is (`let` ((b)) $c_q[d^+]$) if p is $3q$. $a_p[d]$ is undefined otherwise.
  - if a is (f b_1 $\cdots$ b_n) where f is not `let` nor `lambda`,
    $a_p[d]$ is (f b_1 $\cdots$ $b_{i_q}[d]$ $\cdots$ b_m) if p is jq, $2 \leq j \leq m+1$, and i is $j-1$.
  - otherwise
    $a_p[d]$ is undefined.

Substitution for multiple occurrences $a_{p_1,\cdots,p_k}[b]$ is defined to be $a_{p_1}[b]$ if $k = 1$, and $(a_{p_1}[b])_{p_2,\cdots,p_k}[b]$ if $k > 1$.

We next define the set $\Sigma_N(a)$ for each N-term a in Λ-calculus. Intuitively, if $p \in \Sigma_N(a)$, the subterm a/p should be evaluated at the next step by the `let`-reduction. Note, however, that we fix the evaluation order only for one occurrence of the `let`-construct. If other rules are applicable, or there are other `let`-constructs which do not interfere with this `let`-construct, we may evaluate other subterms than one specified by $\Sigma_N(a)$. For a position p and a set S, pS is the set $\{pq \mid q \in S\}$.

Definition 32. If $a \in C_N$, then $\Sigma_N(a)$ is $\emptyset$. Otherwise,

$$\Sigma_N(n) \triangleq \{\epsilon\}$$

$$\Sigma_N(\texttt{(let ((}a\texttt{))}\ b\texttt{)}) \triangleq \begin{cases} 3\Sigma_{N+1}(b) & \textit{if } a \in C_N, \\ 211\Sigma_N(a) \cup 3\Sigma_{N+1}(b) & \textit{if } a \in R_N \textit{ and } b \in R_{N+1}, \\ 211\Sigma_N(a) & \textit{otherwise.} \end{cases}$$

$$\Sigma_N(\texttt{(set! } n\ a\texttt{)}) \triangleq \begin{cases} \{\epsilon\} & \textit{if } a \in C_N, \\ 3\Sigma_N(a) & \textit{otherwise.} \end{cases}$$

$$\Sigma_N(\texttt{(lambda () } a\texttt{)}) \triangleq \{\epsilon\}$$

$$\Sigma_N(\texttt{(while } a\ b\ c\texttt{)}) \triangleq 2\Sigma_N(a)$$

$$\Sigma_N(\texttt{(if } a\ b\ c\texttt{)}) \triangleq 2\Sigma_N(a)$$

$$\Sigma_N(\texttt{(apply } a\ b\texttt{)}) \triangleq \begin{cases} 3\Sigma_N(b) & \textit{if } a \in C_N, \\ 2\Sigma_N(a) \cup 3\Sigma_N(b) & \textit{if } a \in R_N \textit{ and } b \in R_N, \\ 2\Sigma_N(a) & \textit{otherwise.} \end{cases}$$

$$\Sigma_N(\texttt{(pair } a\ b\texttt{)}) \triangleq \begin{cases} 3\Sigma_N(b) & \textit{if } a \in C_N, \\ 2\Sigma_N(a) \cup 3\Sigma_N(b) & \textit{if } a \in R_N \textit{ and } b \in R_N, \\ 2\Sigma_N(a) & \textit{otherwise.} \end{cases}$$

$$\Sigma_N(\texttt{(f } a\texttt{)}) \triangleq 2\Sigma_N(b) \quad \textit{where } f \textit{ is a term construct not listed above}$$

Note that, for a pure, open term a, $\Sigma_N(a)$ is not empty.

The 1-step reduction relation $\rightarrow$ in de Bruijn notation is defined as follows:

Definition 33. 1. If n is a variable (an index), then $n \rightarrow_N n$.

2. If $a \rightarrow_N d$ and s is one of `fun?`, `null?`, `pair?`, `car`, `cdr`, and `mu`, then

$$(s\ \ a) \rightarrow_N \ (s\ \ d).$$

3. If $a \rightarrow_N d$ and $b \rightarrow_N e$ and s is one of `pair`, `apply`, then

$$(s\ \ a\ \ b) \rightarrow_N \ (s\ \ d\ \ e).$$

4. If $a \rightarrow_N d$, $b \rightarrow_N e$ and $c \rightarrow_N f$ and s is `if` or `while`, then

$$(s\ \ a\ \ b\ \ c) \rightarrow_N \ (s\ \ d\ \ e\ \ f).$$

5. If $a \rightarrow_1 d$, then (`lambda` () a) $\rightarrow_N$ (`lambda` () d).

6. If $a \rightarrow_N d$, then (`set!` n a) $\rightarrow_N$ (`set!` n d).

7. If $a \rightarrow_N d$ and $b \rightarrow_{N+1} e$, then (`let` ((a)) b) $\rightarrow_N$ (`let` ((d)) e).

8. If $a \in R_N$, (`s` a) is a recognizer term of some kind, and a is a constructor term of the same kind, then (`s` a) $\rightarrow_N$ `true`.

9. If $a \in R_N$, (`s` a) is a recognizer term of some kind, and a is a constructor term of a different kind, then (`s` a) $\rightarrow_N$ `false`.

10. If $a \in R_N$, $b \in R_N$, and $a \rightarrow_N d$, then (`car` (`pair` a b)) $\rightarrow_N d$.

11. If $a \in R_N$, $b \in R_N$, and $b \rightarrow_N e$, then (`cdr` (`pair` a b)) $\rightarrow_N e$.

12. If (`lambda` () a) $\in R_N$, $b \in R_N$, $a \rightarrow_{N+1} d$ and $b \rightarrow_N e$, then

$$\texttt{(apply (lambda () } a\texttt{) } b\texttt{)} \rightarrow_N \texttt{(let ((}e\texttt{)) } d\texttt{)}.$$

13. If $a \in R_N$ and $a \rightarrow_N d$, then (`mu` a) $\rightarrow_N$ (`apply` d (`mu` d)).

14. If $b \rightarrow_N e$ then (`if true` b c) $\rightarrow_N e$.

15. If $c \rightarrow_N f$ then (`if false` b c) $\rightarrow_N f$.

16. If $a \in R_N$, $1 \notin FV(b)$, $b \in C_{N+1}$, and $b \rightarrow_{N+1} e$, then

$$\texttt{(let ((}a\texttt{)) }b\texttt{)} \rightarrow_N e^-.$$

17. If $a \rightarrow_N d$, $p \in \Sigma_{N+1}(b)$, $\rho(b,p) = 1$, $b \rightarrow_{N+1} e$, and either (i) $a \in C_N$, or (ii) $a \in R_N$ and $b \in R_{N+1}$, then $\texttt{(let ((}a\texttt{)) }b\texttt{)} \rightarrow_N \texttt{(let ((}d\texttt{)) }e_p[d^+]\texttt{)}$.

18. If $p \in \Sigma_{N+1}(b)$, $b/p \equiv \texttt{(set! }n\ f\texttt{)}$, $b \rightarrow_{N+1} e$, $e/p \equiv \texttt{(set! }n\ g\texttt{)}$, $\rho(b, p2) = 1$, and either (i) $a \in C_N$, or (ii) $a \in R_N$ and $b \in R_{N+1}$, then

$$\texttt{(let ((}a\texttt{)) }b\texttt{)} \rightarrow_N \texttt{(let ((}g^-\texttt{)) }e_p[g]\texttt{)}.$$

19. If $a \rightarrow_N d$, $p \in \Sigma_{N+1}(b)$, $b/p \equiv \texttt{(lambda () }f\texttt{)}$, $\nu(b,p) = m$, $b \rightarrow_{N+1} e$, $FV(f) \cap \{m+3, \cdots, m+2+N\} = \emptyset$, $\nu(e,p) = n$, $e/p \equiv \texttt{(lambda () }g\texttt{)}$, positions $p_1, \cdots, p_k$ are all the free occurrences in g satisfying $\rho(g, p_i) = n+2$, and either (i) $a \in C_N$, or (ii) $a \in R_N$ and $b \in R_{N+1}$, then

$$\texttt{(let ((}a\texttt{)) }b\texttt{)} \rightarrow_N \texttt{(let ((}d\texttt{)) }e_p[\texttt{(lambda ()}g_{p_1,\cdots,p_k}[d^{\overbrace{+\cdots+}^{n+2}}]\texttt{)}]\texttt{)}.$$

20. If $b \rightarrow_N e$ and $c \rightarrow_N f$, then

$$\texttt{(while true }b\ c\texttt{)} \rightarrow_N \texttt{(let ((}x\ e\texttt{)) (while }f\ e\ f\texttt{))}.$$

21. $\texttt{(while false }b\ c\texttt{)} \rightarrow_N \texttt{nil}$.

We often omit the subscript N in $\rightarrow_N$. We call the rule 12 β-rule, and the rules 16, 17, 18 and 19 `let`-rules. As in $\lambda\sigma$-calculus, β-rule just adds a new environment to a term, and does not perform substitution. Later, `let`-rules will resolve this environment and perform the substitution. In `let`-rules, we may evaluate a subterm at a position in the set $\Sigma(a)$. Rules 17 and 19 do substitution for occurrences of the variable bound by this `let`. Rule 18 is the execution of assignment. Rule 16 eliminates `let` environment if there are no occurrences of the variable bound by this `let`.

Note that `let`-rules are extended from the original Λ by the reason stated in Section 3.2.

ML with First-Class Environments and its Type Inference Algorithm

Shin-ya Nishizaki

Research Institute for Mathematical Sciences, Kyoto University,
Kitashirakawa-Oiwakecho, Kyoto, 606-01, Japan

Abstract. We present a typed λ-calculus which enables us to handle first-class environments. The syntax and the reduction are obtained by applying the idea of Curien's "explicit substitution". The type system has ML-polymorphism and a type inference algorithm which is sound and terminates.

1 Introduction

We treat various kinds of objects in programming languages. Most objects, e.g. integers or boolean values can be passed and returned between procedures. However, we cannot always use all of them in such a way. For example, procedures themselves are passed and returned between procedures in Lisp. In contrast, it is impossible to do so in BASIC. Objects which can be passed and returned between procedures, are said to be *first-class.* Many implementations ([MIT], [Lau90]) of the programming language Scheme enable us to utilize environments as first-class objects although this facility is not defined in its standardization ([RC86]). We consider the following two primitives as the principal ones:

- `(the-environment)` which returns the current environment, and
- `(eval` ⟨ *list* ⟩ ⟨ *environment* ⟩`)` which returns the result of evaluation of the expression represented by ⟨ *list* ⟩ under ⟨ *environment* ⟩.

By these primitives, we can export an environment to anywhere independently of the textual structure of a program:

```
((lambda (env) (eval '(+ x 1) env))
 (let ((x 1)) (the-environment))).
```

The expression `(+ x 1)` is not evaluated under the environment where it appears, but under the one where `(the-environment)` appears. Therefore, the result is 2.

This construct will support packaging of procedures (see [AS85]) or debugging of programs.

In order to obtain λ-calculus with first-class environments, we adopt the idea of *explicit substitution,* i.e. $\lambda\sigma$-calculus ([Cur86], [nACCL90], [Cur91], [CHL92]). Next, we would like to explain how the idea of $\lambda\sigma$-calculus is applied to first-class environments.

In the usual λ-calculus, β-reduction is considered as the fundamental mechanism of computation. An example of β-reduction is as

$$
\begin{aligned}
& (\lambda x.\, \lambda y.\, x) M_1 M_2 & (1)\\
& \xrightarrow{\beta} (\lambda y.\, x)[x{:=}M_1] M_2 & (2)\\
& \quad \equiv (\lambda y.\, M_1) M_2 & (3)\\
& \xrightarrow{\beta} \cdots. & (4)
\end{aligned}
$$

β-reduction is applied between Line (1) and Line (2). The hidden important point is that substitution operation is defined at the meta level, which means that the term in Line (2) is actually equivalent to the one in Line (3) and the description in Line (2) is nothing but an illusion at the object level. In other words, the variable reference mechanism is implemented at the meta level. This is the reason why environments do not appear anywhere in the process of β-reduction.

In contrast, substitution operation is made explicit in $\lambda\sigma$-calculus by defining them in the *object level*, what is called, *explicit substitution.* This reveals the notion of environment, which is concealed in the meta level:

$$
\begin{aligned}
& (\lambda x.\lambda y.x) M_1 M_2 & (5)\\
& \xrightarrow{\beta} ((\lambda y.x)[(M_1/x) \cdot id]) M_2 & \\
& \xrightarrow{\beta} x[(M_1/x) \cdot id][(M_2/y) \cdot id] & (6)\\
& \xrightarrow{\sigma} M_1[(M_2/y) \cdot id] & \\
& \rightarrow \cdots. &
\end{aligned}
$$

A term in Line (6) corresponds to a term written $x[x{:=}M_1, y{:=}M_2]$ in the usual λ-calculus. We notice that this term can be read as the evaluation of variable x under *environment* $(x \mapsto M_1, y \mapsto M_2)$. We here find one of the important ideas in $\lambda\sigma$-calculus: *environments as substitutions.*

From the discussion above, we know that we obtain the calculus with first-class environments from $\lambda\sigma$-calculus by merging the syntactic classes of terms and of environments. We have investigated typed lambda calculus with first-class environments and already proposed the simply typed one in the previous paper [Nis94]. In this paper, we would like to introduce a ML-polymorphic version and present two fundamental properties: one is subject reduction theorem and the other existence of a type inference algorithm.

2 ML-polymorphic Calculus ML_{env} with First-Class Environments

Before defining our calculus in detail, we recall what ML-polymorphism is.

2.1 ML-polymorphism

ML is a functional programming language equipped with a type inference facility. The first important point of ML is its *implicit* type system: we do not need to append a type information to each argument. For example, in ANSI C, we write a program as

```
int abs(int i) return (i>0) ? i : -i ;
```

where we must specify what type the argument i should be. In contrast, in ML, it is not necessary to specify types of arguments:

```
fun abs i = if i > 0 then i else ( i);
```

Instead, the type inference algorithm of ML finds the type of *i*:

```
abs : int -> int
```

And the second point is *polymorphism* which allows us to give several different types to one term. For example, in a term

$$(let\ f = \lambda x.x\ in\ (f f)\ end) \tag{7}$$

the variable f is of type $(\alpha \to \alpha) \to (\alpha \to \alpha)$ at the first occurrence in $(f f)$, and of type $\alpha \to \alpha$ at the second occurrence. These two types are derived from a polymorphic type $\forall\alpha.\alpha \to \alpha$ (also called a *type scheme*). Polymorphism appears at variables which is quantified by let-expressions. Although a term $(\lambda f.(f f))(\lambda x.x)$ is operationally equivalent to (7), the former term is untypable in ML. The syntax of ML typing can be summarized in the following:

Type Judgement	$\Gamma \vdash M : \sigma$
Monomorphic Type	$A ::= \alpha \mid (A \to B)$
Polymorphic Type	$\sigma ::= \forall\alpha_1 \cdots \forall\alpha_n.A$
Polymorphic Type Assignment	$\Gamma ::= \{x_1 : \sigma_1\} \cdots \{x_n : \sigma_n\}$.

The class of types in ML is a proper subset of the one in polymorphic typed lambda calculus System F. For example, $(\forall\alpha.(\alpha \to \alpha)) \to \forall\alpha.(\alpha \to \alpha)$ is not a type of ML. This restriction on types ensures the existence of a type inference algorithm. Since, we have aimed at finding a type inference algorithm for a typed lambda calculus with first-class environments, we adopt ML as the base type theory.

In $\Gamma \vdash M : \sigma$, type assignment Γ gives us the type information of environments where M is evaluated. Therefore, we will obtain a definition of polymorphic environment types from that of polymorphic type assignments.

2.2 Syntax of ML_{env}

Definition 1 Types of ML_{env}. Suppose that we are given three countable sets:

- a set *TypeVar* of *type variables*,

- a set *EnvTypeVar* of *environment type variables,*
- a set *TermVar* of *term variables*

and

- a mapping PVar which assigns each type variable to a finite set of term variables, called *prohibited variables*, which satisfies the condition that $\mathsf{PVar}^{-1}(\{x_1, \ldots, x_n\})$ is an infinite set for any $\{x_1, \ldots, x_n\}$.

Then, *environment monotypes E*, *monotypes A*, *polytypes σ*, and *environment polytypes Γ* are mutual-inductively defined as

[environment monotype]

$E ::= \{x_1 : A_1\} \cdots \{x_n : A_n\}\rho,$

where $n \geq 0$, $\{x_1, \ldots, x_n\} \subseteq \mathsf{PVar}(\rho)$, and $x_1, \ldots, x_n$ are distinct from each other. We do not distinguish them from sets of ordered pairs $\{x_i : A_i\}$.

[monotype]

$A ::= \alpha \mid E \mid (A \rightarrow B)$

[polytype]

$\sigma ::= \forall\alpha_1 \cdots \forall\alpha_k.A,$

where $k \geq 0$.

We assume α-equivalence on this ∀-abstraction. For example, we do not distinguish $\forall\alpha.\alpha \rightarrow \alpha$ *from* $\forall\beta.\beta \rightarrow \beta$.

[environment polytype]

$\Gamma ::= \{x_1 : \sigma_1\} \cdots \{x_n : \sigma_n\}\rho$

where $n \geq 0$, $\{x_1, \ldots, x_n\} \subseteq \mathsf{PVar}(\rho)$, and $x_1, \ldots, x_n$ are distinct from each other. We do not distinguish them from sets of ordered pairs $\{x_i : \sigma_i\}$.

From the above definition, we know the following inclusion relation:

environment polytypes
$\cup$
environment monotypes ⊂ monotypes ⊂ polytypes

We imposed the syntactic restrictions on environment mono- and environment polytypes, for the existence of a unification algorithm which derives most general unifiers. As a result, a few conditions are placed also on substitutions for environment type variables:

Definition 2 Substitution for (environment) type variables. A *substitution θ* on environment type variables and type variables is a function which maps each type variable α to a type A and each environment type variable ρ to an environment type $\overline{\{x_n : A_n\}}\rho'$ such that $\mathsf{PVar}(\rho) \cap \{x_1, \ldots, x_n\} = \emptyset, \mathsf{PVar}(\rho) \subseteq \mathsf{PVar}(\rho')$, and $\{x_1, \ldots, x_n\} \subseteq \mathsf{PVar}(\rho')$, and its *domain*

$$\mathsf{dom}(\theta) = \{\alpha \in \mathit{TypeVar} \mid \alpha^\theta \neq \alpha\} \cup \{\rho \in \mathit{EnvTypeVar} \mid \rho^\theta \neq \rho\}$$

is finite.

A substitution θ defined as above is extended uniquely to a function $\hat{f}$ on types as:

$$\begin{aligned}
\alpha^{\hat{\theta}} &= \alpha^\theta, \\
(A \to B)^{\hat{\theta}} &= A^{\hat{\theta}} \to B^{\hat{\theta}}, \\
(\{x_1 : \sigma_1\} \cdots \{x_n : \sigma_n\}\rho)^{\hat{\theta}} &= \{x_1 : \sigma_1{}^{\hat{\theta}}\} \cdots \{x_n : \sigma_n{}^{\hat{\theta}}\}\rho^\theta, \text{ and} \\
(\forall\alpha_1 \cdots \forall\alpha_k.A)^{\hat{\theta}} &= \forall\alpha_1 \cdots \forall\alpha_k.(A^{\hat{\theta}}),
\end{aligned}$$

where we assume that $(\forall\alpha_1 \cdots \forall\alpha_k.A)$ is appropriately α-converted with respect to bound type variables.

We will identify θ and $\hat{\theta}$ in the rest of this paper.

Definition 3 Restriction and Extension. Let $\mathcal{V}$ be a set of (environment) type variables and θ a substitution.

A *restriction* $\theta|_{\mathcal{V}}$ of θ on $\mathcal{V}$ is a substitution that maps $\alpha \notin \mathcal{V}$ (or $\rho \notin \mathcal{V}$) to α^θ (or ρ^θ, resp.) but $\alpha \in \mathcal{V}$ (or $\rho \in \mathcal{V}$) to α (or ρ, resp.).

θ' is an *extension* of θ, or θ is extended to θ', if $\theta = \theta'|_{\mathsf{dom}(\theta)}$.

It is easily checked that

Proposition 4. *Let E be an environment type and θ a substitution. Then, E^θ is an environment type.*

Definition 5 Raw Terms in ML_{env}. *Raw terms M* are inductively defined as

$$M ::= x \mid \lambda x.\, M \mid (MN) \mid id \mid (M/x) \cdot N \mid (M \circ N)$$

which are called a *variable*, a *lambda-abstraction*, a *function application*, an *identity environment*, an *extension*, and a *composition*, respectively.

The first three constructs are similar to the usual λ-calculus' ones, in contrast, the last three new. The identity environment id returns the current environment when it is evaluated. We can regard id as `(the-environment)` of Scheme. Extension $(M/x) \cdot N$ corresponds to the environment made by appending a new binding from x to M, to environment N. Composition $(M \circ N)$ is the result to which M evaluates in an environment N, when M is regarded as a term and N as an environment. In this case, we can regard $(M \circ N)$ as `(eval '`M N`)` of Scheme. If M is also an environment, then $(M \circ N)$ is the substitution composition, identifying an environment with a substitution.

Notation 6. We will use the following vector notation:

$$\begin{aligned}
\overline{\{x_n : A_n\}}\rho &\equiv \{x_1 : A_1\} \cdots \{x_n : A_n\}\rho, \\
\overline{\{x_n : \sigma_n\}}\rho &\equiv \{x_1 : \sigma_1\} \cdots \{x_n : \sigma_n\}\rho, \text{ and} \\
\{\overline{x_n}\} &\equiv \{x_1, \ldots, x_n\}.
\end{aligned}$$

2.3 Typing Rules of ML_{env}

Definition 7 Type Judgement and Typing Rules. We define a *type judgement* $\Gamma \vdash M : \sigma$ for an environment polytype Γ, a term M, and a polytype σ by the following rules called *typing rules* or sometimes *type inference rules.* When $\Gamma \vdash M : \sigma$ holds, we say that term M has type σ under Γ.

Typing Rules:

$$\frac{}{\{x : \sigma\}\Gamma \vdash x : \sigma}\ \mathsf{Var}_{\vdash}$$

$$\frac{\{x : A\}\Gamma \vdash M : B}{\Gamma \vdash (\lambda x.\, M) : (A \to B)}\ \mathsf{Lam}_{\vdash} \qquad \frac{\Gamma \vdash M : (A \to B) \quad \Gamma \vdash N : A}{\Gamma \vdash (MN) : B}\ \mathsf{App}_{\vdash}$$

$$\frac{}{\Gamma \vdash id : \Gamma}\ \mathsf{Id}_{\vdash}$$

$$\frac{\Gamma \vdash M : \sigma \quad \Gamma \vdash N : \Gamma'}{\Gamma \vdash (M/x) \cdot N : \{x : \sigma\}\Gamma'}\ \mathsf{Extn}_{\vdash} \qquad \frac{\Gamma \vdash N : \Gamma' \quad \Gamma' \vdash M : \sigma}{\Gamma \vdash (M \circ N) : \sigma}\ \mathsf{Comp}_{\vdash}$$

$$\frac{\Gamma \vdash M : \sigma \quad \alpha \notin \mathsf{Ftv}(\Gamma)}{\Gamma \vdash M : (\forall \alpha.\sigma)}\ \mathsf{TypeGen}_{\vdash} \qquad \frac{\Gamma \vdash M : (\forall \alpha.\sigma)}{\Gamma \vdash M : \sigma^{[\alpha \mapsto A]}}\ \mathsf{TypeInst}_{\vdash}$$

$$\frac{\Gamma \vdash M : \{x : \sigma\}\Gamma' \quad \alpha \notin \mathsf{Ftv}(\Gamma) \cup \mathsf{Ftv}(\Gamma')}{\Gamma \vdash M : \{x : \forall \alpha.\sigma\}\Gamma'}\ \mathsf{EnvGen}_{\vdash}$$

$$\frac{\Gamma \vdash M : \{x : \forall \alpha.\sigma\}\Gamma'}{\Gamma \vdash M : \{x : \sigma^{[\alpha \mapsto A]}\}\Gamma'}\ \mathsf{EnvInst}_{\vdash}$$

Readers should notice that side conditions are implicitly imposed by meta-variables in each typing rules. For example,

$$\frac{\begin{array}{c}\vdots \\ \{x : \forall \alpha.\, \alpha \to \alpha\}\rho \vdash x : \forall \alpha.\, \alpha \to \alpha\end{array}}{\rho \vdash (\lambda x.\, x) : (\forall \alpha.\, \alpha \to \alpha) \to (\forall \alpha.\, \alpha \to \alpha)}\ \mathsf{Lam}_{\vdash}$$

is a *wrong* inference since $(\forall \alpha.\alpha \to \alpha)$ is not a monotype.

$$\frac{}{\{x : \alpha\}\{x : \beta\}\rho \vdash x : \rho}\ \mathsf{Var}_{\vdash}$$

is also wrong since $\{\underline{x} : \alpha\}\{\underline{x} : \beta\}\rho$ is not valid environment polytype.

The let-expression in the usual ML is definable by the constructs for first-class environment as

$$(\mathsf{let}\ x = N\ \mathsf{in}\ M\ \mathsf{end}) \stackrel{def}{=} M \circ ((M/x) \cdot id).$$

This term is typable as

$$\frac{\dfrac{\begin{array}{c}\vdots \\ \Gamma \vdash N : \sigma\end{array} \quad \dfrac{}{\Gamma \vdash id : \Gamma}\ \mathsf{Id}_{\vdash}}{\Gamma \vdash (N/x) \cdot id : \{x : \sigma\}\Gamma}\ \mathsf{Extn}_{\vdash} \qquad \begin{array}{c}\vdots \\ \{x : \sigma\}\Gamma \vdash M : \tau\end{array}}{\Gamma \vdash (M \circ ((N/x) \cdot id)) : \tau}\ \mathsf{Comp}_{\vdash}$$

similarly to the typing in the usual ML:

$$\frac{\begin{matrix}\vdots & & \vdots \\ \Gamma \vdash N : \sigma & & \{x:\sigma\}\Gamma \vdash M : \tau\end{matrix}}{\Gamma \vdash (\mathsf{let}\ x = N\ \mathsf{in}\ M\ \mathsf{end}) : \tau}$$

This justifies our definition of let-expression from the aspect of typing. We will present its explanation from computational aspect in the next section.

We end this section with the following proposition which is easily checked.

Proposition 8. *If $\Gamma \vdash M : \sigma$ (or $\Gamma \vdash M : \Delta$), then $\Gamma^\theta \vdash M : \sigma^\theta$ (or $\Gamma^\theta \vdash M : \Delta^\theta$, respectively).*

2.4 Computation Rules of ML_{env}

In the previous work [Nis94], we give a reduction to the *simply typed* lambda calculus with first-class environments, named $\lambda_{env}^{\rightarrow}$. Actually, the reduction is not only defined for typed terms, but also for raw terms.

Definition 9 Weak Reduction. A binary relation $(-) \underset{wr}{\rightarrow} (-)$, called *weak reduction*, is inductively defined by the following rules:

[Substitution Rules]

Ass_{wr} : $(L \circ M) \circ N \underset{wr}{\rightarrow} L \circ (M \circ N)$

IdL_{wr} : $id \circ M \underset{wr}{\rightarrow} M$

IdR_{wr} : $M \circ id \underset{wr}{\rightarrow} M$

DExtn_{wr} : $((L/x) \cdot M) \circ N \underset{wr}{\rightarrow} ((L \circ N)/x) \cdot (M \circ N)$

VarRef_{wr} : $x \circ ((M/x) \cdot N) \underset{wr}{\rightarrow} M$

$\mathsf{VarSkip}_{wr}$: $y \circ ((M/x) \cdot N) \underset{wr}{\rightarrow} y \circ N$ *where* $x \not\equiv y$

DApp_{wr} : $(M_1 M_2) \circ N \underset{wr}{\rightarrow} (M_1 \circ N)(M_2 \circ N)$

[Beta Rules]

$\mathsf{Beta1}_{wr}$: $((\lambda x.\, M) \circ L)N \underset{wr}{\rightarrow} M \circ ((N/x) \cdot L)$

$\mathsf{Beta2}_{wr}$: $(\lambda x.\, M)N \underset{wr}{\rightarrow} M \circ ((N/x) \cdot id)$

[Compatibility Rules]

AppL_{wr} : $(MN) \underset{wr}{\rightarrow} (M'N)$ *if* $M \underset{wr}{\rightarrow} M'$

AppR_{wr} : $(MN) \underset{wr}{\rightarrow} (MN')$ *if* $N \underset{wr}{\rightarrow} N'$

Lam_{wr} : $(\lambda x.\, M) \underset{wr}{\rightarrow} (\lambda x.\, M')$ *if* $M \underset{wr}{\rightarrow} M'$

CompL_{wr} : $(M \circ N) \underset{wr}{\rightarrow} (M' \circ N)$ *if* $M \underset{wr}{\rightarrow} M'$

CompR_{wr} : $(M \circ N) \underset{wr}{\rightarrow} (M \circ N')$ *if* $N \underset{wr}{\rightarrow} N'$

ExtnL_{wr} : $((M/x) \cdot N) \underset{wr}{\rightarrow} ((M'/x) \cdot N)$ *if* $M \underset{wr}{\rightarrow} M'$

ExtnR_{wr} : $((M/x) \cdot N) \underset{wr}{\rightarrow} ((M/x) \cdot N')$ *if* $N \underset{wr}{\rightarrow} N'$

The readers should note that $(\lambda x.(-)) \circ (-)$ is *not* a redex in the reduction given here. This is the reason why we call this computation rule *weak reduction* (see also [CHL92]).

The above reduction is actually defined independently of type system and therefore, we obtain an untyped calculus:

Definition 10 Untyped Calculus λ_{env}. We call the system which consists of raw terms and the above reduction rules, *untyped calculus λ_{env}*.

We here mention the connection between the above system and the usual calculus *without* first-class environments, i.e. $\lambda\sigma$-calculus. Readers familiar enough with the $\lambda\sigma$-calculus should realize the following proposition:

Proposition 11. *λ_{env} is a conservative extension of $\lambda\sigma_w$([CHL92]), that is, if a term M is reduced to N in $\lambda\sigma_w$, then the term M is also reduced to N in λ_{env} under the identification of $M[\sigma]$ to $(M \circ \sigma)$.*

An example of terms not in $\lambda\sigma$-calculus but in $\lambda_{env}^{\rightarrow}$ is $L \circ ((\lambda x. M)N)$: the classes of environments and of the terms are disjoint in $\lambda\sigma$-calculus, and therefore, an environment must not be a term e.g. $(\lambda x. M)N$.

We next show two example of reduction. The first one is as follows:

$$
\begin{array}{ll}
((\lambda y. \lambda x. id)M)N & \\
\underset{wr}{\rightarrow} ((\lambda x. id) \circ ((M/y) \cdot id))N & \mathsf{Beta2}_{wr} \\
\underset{wr}{\rightarrow} id \circ ((N/x) \cdot (M/y) \cdot id) & \mathsf{Beta1}_{wr} \\
\underset{wr}{\rightarrow} (N/x) \cdot (M/y) \cdot id & \mathsf{IdL}_{wr}
\end{array}
$$

The term $((\lambda y. \lambda x. id)M)N$ in the first line corresponds to Scheme's program:

```
(((lambda (y) (lambda (x) (the-environment))) M) N).
```

The second example is more complicated:

$$
\begin{array}{ll}
(\lambda e. (y \circ e))((\lambda y. \lambda x. id)MN) & \\
\overset{*}{\underset{wr}{\rightarrow}} (\lambda e. (y \circ e))((N/x) \cdot (M/y) \cdot id) & \textit{similar to the first example} \\
\underset{wr}{\rightarrow} (y \circ e) \circ ((((N/x) \cdot (M/y) \cdot id)/e) \cdot id) & \mathsf{Beta2}_{wr} \\
\underset{wr}{\rightarrow} y \circ (e \circ ((((N/x) \cdot (M/y) \cdot id)/e) \cdot id)) & \mathsf{Ass}_{wr} \\
\underset{wr}{\rightarrow} y \circ ((N/x) \cdot (M/y) \cdot id) & \mathsf{VarRef}_{wr} \\
\underset{wr}{\rightarrow} y \circ ((M/y) \cdot id) & \mathsf{VarSkip}_{wr} \\
\underset{wr}{\rightarrow} M & \mathsf{VarRef}_{wr}
\end{array}
$$

The term $(\lambda e. (y \circ e))((\lambda y. \lambda x. id)MN)$ corresponds to the following program:

```
((lambda (e) (eval 'y e))
 (((lambda (y) (lambda (x) (the-environment))) M) N))
```

In the previous section on typing, the let-expression is defined by first-class environment's constructs presents a justification from the viewpoint of typing. In the usual λ-calculus, let-expression ($\mathsf{let}\ x = N\ \mathsf{in}\ M\ \mathsf{end}$) is equivalent to β-redex $(\lambda x.\, M)N$ as far as the evaluation of terms is concerned. Rule Beta2 means that $(\lambda x.\, M)N$ is operationally equivalent to $M \circ ((N/x) \cdot id)$. Therefore, we know the justification of the definition that ($\mathsf{let}\ x = N\ \mathsf{in}\ M\ \mathsf{end}$) $\stackrel{def}{=} M \circ ((N/x) \cdot id)$.

2.5 Fundamental Properties of ML_{env}

The goal of this section is the *subject reduction theorem*, which is the property that types of any terms are preserved during their reduction. In order to prove it, we here introduce another judgement on typing, written $\Gamma \Vdash M : A$ (see also [Gun92]). The important difference between $\vdash$- and $\Vdash$-judgement is that the derivation tree of judgement $\Gamma \Vdash M : A$ is uniquely determined by a term M. In contrast, there may exist several derivation trees of a judgement $\Gamma \vdash M : \sigma$ for a term M. Thanks to this uniqueness, we can use induction on the structure on terms, in proving propositions on $\Vdash$-judgement. The first part of this section is mainly devoted to prepare the notion of $\Vdash$-judgement and its related properties.

We first extend the notion of *generic instance* as used in the context of ML:

Definition 12 Generic Instance. A binary relation $(-) \leq (-)$ is first defined between a polytype and a monotype as

$$\forall \alpha_1 \cdots \forall \alpha_k.A \leq A^{[\alpha_1 \mapsto A_1, \ldots, \alpha_k \mapsto A_k]}.$$

Second, this binary relation is extended to one between polytypes as

$$\sigma \leq \tau \quad \Leftrightarrow \quad \sigma \leq A \textit{ for every } A \textit{ such that } \tau \leq A.$$

Third, this relation is extended also to the one between environment polytypes as

$$\{x_1 : \sigma_1\} \cdots \{x_n : \sigma_n\}\rho \leq \{x_1 : \tau_1\} \cdots \{x_n : \tau_n\}\rho \quad \Leftrightarrow \quad \sigma_1 \leq \tau_1, \ldots, \sigma_n \leq \tau_n.$$

The following three propositions are not difficult.

Proposition 13 Reflexivity and Transitivity of $\leq$-relation.
$\leq$-relation is reflexive and transitive.

Proposition 14. *Let θ be a substitution for (environment) type variables. If $\sigma \leq \tau$ ($\Gamma \leq \Delta$) then $\sigma^\theta \leq \tau^\theta$ ($\Gamma^\theta \leq \Delta^\theta$, respectively).*

Proposition 15. *If $\sigma \leq \sigma'$ and $\Gamma \vdash M : \sigma$, then we have $\Gamma \vdash M : \sigma'$ (by several applications of* $\mathsf{TypeInst}_\vdash$*).*

If $\Delta \leq \Delta'$ and $\Gamma \vdash M : \Delta$, then we have $\Gamma \vdash M : \Delta'$ (by several applications of $\mathsf{EnvInst}_\vdash$*).*

Definition 16 $\Vdash$**-judgement.** We define a ternary relation $\Gamma \Vdash M : A$ among an environment polytype Γ, a term M, and a monotype A inductively by the following rules:

$$\frac{\sigma \leq A}{\{x : \sigma\}\Gamma \Vdash x : A} \ \mathsf{Var}_{\Vdash}$$

$$\frac{\Gamma \Vdash M : (A \to B) \quad \Gamma \Vdash N : A}{\Gamma \Vdash (MN) : B} \ \mathsf{App}_{\Vdash} \qquad \frac{\{x : A\}\Gamma \Vdash M : B}{\Gamma \Vdash (\lambda x. M) : (A \to B)} \ \mathsf{Lam}_{\Vdash}$$

$$\frac{\Gamma \leq E}{\Gamma \Vdash id : E} \ \mathsf{Id}_{\Vdash}$$

$$\frac{\Gamma \Vdash M : A \quad \Gamma \Vdash N : E}{\Gamma \Vdash (M/x) \cdot N : \{x : A\}E} \ \mathsf{Extn}_{\Vdash}$$

$$\frac{\Gamma \Vdash N : E \quad \mathsf{Close}(\mathsf{Ftv}(\Gamma), E) \Vdash M : A}{\Gamma \Vdash (M \circ N) : A} \ \mathsf{Comp}_{\Vdash}$$

where Close is defined as follows.

Definition 17 Closure Operation Close**.** For a set $\mathcal{TV}$ of type variables and a monotype, $\mathsf{Close}(\mathcal{TV}, A)$ is defined as

$$\begin{aligned}
\mathsf{Close}(\mathcal{TV}, \rho) &= \rho \\
\mathsf{Close}(\mathcal{TV}, \{x : A\}E) &= \{x : \sigma\}\Gamma \\
&\quad \textit{where } \sigma = \mathsf{Close}(\mathcal{TV} \cup \mathsf{Ftv}(E), A), \textit{ and} \\
&\quad\quad\quad \Gamma = \mathsf{Close}(\mathcal{TV} \cup \mathsf{Ftv}(A), E) \\
\mathsf{Close}(\mathcal{TV}, A) &= \forall\beta_1 \cdots \forall\beta_l.A \\
&\quad \textit{where } \{\beta_1, \ldots, \beta_l\} = \mathsf{Ftv}(A) \setminus \mathcal{TV} \textit{ and} \\
&\quad A \textit{ is either a type variable or a function type.}
\end{aligned}$$

For example,

$$\begin{aligned}
&\mathsf{Close}(\emptyset, \{x : \alpha \to \gamma \to \gamma\}\{y : \alpha\}\{z : \beta \to \beta\}\rho) = \\
&\quad \{x : \alpha \to \gamma \to \gamma\}\{y : \alpha\}\{z : \forall\beta.\beta \to \beta\}\rho.
\end{aligned}$$

The following proposition is evident from the definition of operation Close:

Proposition 18. *If* $\Gamma \vdash M : \sigma$, *then* $\Gamma \vdash M : \mathsf{Close}(\mathsf{Ftv}(\Gamma), \sigma)$.

Noting the transitivity of $\leq$-relation, the following proposition is easily proved by induction on the structure of M:

Proposition 19. *If* $\Gamma \Vdash M : A$ *and* $\Gamma' \leq \Gamma$ *then* $\Gamma' \Vdash M : A$.

In order to prove Proposition 21, we will use

Proposition 20. *If* $\Gamma \Vdash M : A$, *then* $\Gamma^{[\gamma \mapsto C]} \Vdash M : A^{[\gamma \mapsto C]}$.

(This proposition's proof is in Appendix B.)

$\Vdash$-judgement is essentially equivalent to $\vdash$-judgement:

Proposition 21.
(1) If $\Gamma \Vdash M : A$, then $\Gamma \vdash M : A$ holds.
(2-1) If $\Gamma \vdash M : \sigma$ and $\sigma \leq A$, then $\Gamma' \Vdash M : A$.
(2-2) If $\Gamma \vdash M : \Gamma'$ and $\Gamma' \leq E$, then $\Gamma \Vdash M : E$.

Proof. (1): The proof is by induction on the structure of M. The cases where M is an application, a λ-abstraction, an extension, or a composition, are easy.
Case $M = id$: For some Γ and E, it holds that

$$\frac{\Gamma \leq E}{\Gamma \Vdash id : E}\ \mathsf{Id}_{\Vdash}.$$

Since $\Gamma \leq E$, we know that

$$\begin{array}{l} \overline{\Gamma \vdash id : \Gamma}\ \mathsf{Id}_{\vdash} \\ \quad \vdots\ \textit{Several applications of}\ \mathsf{EnvInst}_{\vdash} \\ \Gamma \vdash id : E \end{array}.$$

Case $M = (M_1 \circ M_2)$: For some Γ, E, and A, it holds that

$$\frac{\Gamma \Vdash M_2 : E \quad \mathsf{Close}(\mathsf{Ftv}(\Gamma), E) \Vdash M_1 : A}{\Gamma \Vdash (M_1 \circ M_2) : A}\ \mathsf{Comp}_{\Vdash}.$$

By the induction hypothesis, $\Gamma \vdash M_2 : E$ and $\mathsf{Close}(\mathsf{Ftv}(\Gamma), E) \vdash M_1 : A$. We infer $\Gamma \vdash M_2 : \mathsf{Close}(\mathsf{Ftv}(\Gamma), E)$ from the former using Rule $\mathsf{EnvInst}_{\vdash}$. Therefore, we know that $\Gamma \vdash M_1 \circ M_2 : A$.

(2-1) and (2-2): The proof is by induction on the structure of the derivation tree of $\Gamma \vdash M : \sigma$ or of $\Gamma \vdash M : \Gamma'$. We can prove easily the cases of $\mathsf{Var}_{\vdash}$, $\mathsf{Lam}_{\vdash}$, $\mathsf{App}_{\vdash}$, $\mathsf{Id}_{\vdash}$, $\mathsf{Extn}_{\vdash}$, $\mathsf{TypeInst}_{\vdash}$, or $\mathsf{EnvInst}_{\vdash}$.
Case $\mathsf{Comp}_{\vdash}$: Suppose that $M = (M_1 \circ M_2)$, $\sigma \leq A$, and

$$\frac{\Gamma \vdash M_2 : \Gamma' \quad \Gamma' \vdash M_1 : \sigma}{\Gamma \vdash M_1 \circ M_2 : \sigma}\ \mathsf{Extn}_{\vdash}.$$

By the induction hypothesis,

$$\Gamma \Vdash M_2 : E' \text{ and } \Gamma \Vdash M_1 : A,$$

where E' is a generic instance of Γ' by substituting fresh type variables for all type variables which are universally quantified. It is easy to know that $\mathsf{Close}(\mathsf{Ftv}(\Gamma), E') \leq \Gamma'$. Therefore, by Proposition 19,

$$\mathsf{Close}(\mathsf{Ftv}(\Gamma), E') \Vdash M_1 : A.$$

Using Rule $\mathsf{Comp}_{\Vdash}$, we know that $\Gamma \Vdash (M_1 \circ M_2) : A$.
Case $\mathsf{TypeGen}_{\vdash}$: Suppose that $\forall\alpha.\sigma \leq A$ and

$$\frac{\Gamma \vdash M : \sigma \quad \alpha \notin \mathsf{Ftv}(\Gamma)}{\Gamma \vdash M : (\forall\alpha.\sigma)}\ \mathsf{TypeGen}_{\vdash}.$$

$(\forall\alpha.\sigma) \leq A$ implies that there exists A' and C such that $A'^{[\alpha\mapsto C]} = A$ and $\sigma \leq A'$.

By the induction hypothesis, $\Gamma \Vdash M : A'$. By Proposition 20 and $\alpha \notin \mathsf{Ftv}(\Gamma)$, it holds that $\Gamma \Vdash M : A'^{[\alpha\mapsto C]}$, i.e. $\Gamma \Vdash M : A$.

The case of $\mathsf{EnvGen}_{\Vdash}$ is similar to this case.

Theorem 22 Subject Reduction Theorem. *Let M and M' be terms satisfying $M \underset{wr}{\rightarrow} M'$. If $\Gamma \vdash M : \sigma$ (or $\Gamma \vdash M : \Gamma'$), then $\Gamma \vdash M' : \sigma$ (or $\Gamma \vdash M' : \Gamma'$ respectively) also holds.*

This theorem is derived from the following proposition using Proposition 21:

Proposition 23 Subject Reduction Theorem for $\Vdash$-judgement. *Let M and M' be terms such that $M \underset{wr}{\rightarrow} M'$. If $\Gamma \Vdash M : A$. Then, $\Gamma \Vdash M' : A$ also holds.*

Proof. We prove this proposition by induction on the derivation which infers $M \underset{wr}{\rightarrow} M'$. The cases of the compatibility rules, which are inductive steps, are straightforward. The cases of the substitution rules or of the beta rules are checked by using Proposition 15, Proposition 19, and Proposition 21. As space is limited we show typical cases only.

Case IdR_{wr}: Suppose that $M = M_1 \circ id \underset{wr}{\rightarrow} M_1$. Then, for some Γ and some E,

$$\dfrac{\dfrac{\Gamma \leq E}{\Gamma \Vdash id : E} \quad \dfrac{\vdots}{\mathsf{Close}(\mathsf{Ftv}(\Gamma), E) \Vdash M_1 : A}}{\Gamma \Vdash M_1 \circ id : A}\ \mathsf{Comp}_{\Vdash}$$

By $\Gamma \leq \mathsf{Close}(\mathsf{Ftv}(\Gamma), E)$, $\mathsf{Close}(\mathsf{Ftv}(\Gamma), E) \Vdash M_1 : A$ and Proposition 19, we know that $\Gamma \Vdash M_1 : A$.

Case BetaI_{wr}: Suppose that $M = ((\lambda x.\, N_1) \circ N_2)L \underset{wr}{\rightarrow} N_1 \circ ((L/x) \cdot N_2)$. Then, for some Γ, E, and C,

$$\dfrac{\dfrac{\dfrac{\vdots}{\Gamma \Vdash N_2 : E} \quad \dfrac{\dfrac{\vdots}{\{x : C\}\mathsf{Close}(\mathsf{Ftv}(\Gamma), E) \Vdash N_1 : A}}{\mathsf{Close}(\mathsf{Ftv}(\Gamma), E) \Vdash \lambda x.\, N_1 : C \to A}\ \mathsf{Lam}_{\Vdash}}{\Gamma \Vdash ((\lambda x.\, N_1) \circ N_2) : C \to A}\ \mathsf{Comp}_{\Vdash} \quad \Gamma \Vdash L : C}{\Gamma \Vdash ((\lambda x.\, N_1) \circ N_2)L : C}\ \mathsf{App}_{\Vdash}$$

By Proposition 21,

$$\dfrac{\dfrac{\dfrac{\vdots}{\Gamma \vdash L : C} \quad \dfrac{\dfrac{\vdots}{\Gamma \vdash N_2 : E}}{\Gamma \vdash N_2 : \Delta}\ \mathsf{TypeGen}_{\vdash}}{\Gamma \vdash (L/x) \cdot N_2 : \{x : C\}\Delta}\ \mathsf{Extn}_{\vdash} \quad \dfrac{\vdots}{\{x : C\}\Delta \vdash N_1 : A}}{\Gamma \vdash N_1 \circ ((L/x) \cdot N_2) : A}\ \mathsf{Comp}_{\vdash}$$

where $\Delta = \mathsf{Close}(\mathsf{Ftv}(\Gamma), E)$.

3 Type Inference Algorithm for ML_{env}

In this section, we propose a *type inference algorithm* (or sometimes called a *type reconstruction* algorithm) for ML_{env}. We first present a unification algorithm on monotypes and its fundamental properties in Section 3.1 (in Appendix A in detail). Second, we propose a type inference algorithm and give its soundness and termination.

3.1 Unification

Definition 24 Unifier and Its Generality. A *unifier* θ of monotype A and B is a substitution such that $A^\theta = B^\theta$.

Let θ and η be unifiers of A and B. θ is said to be *more general than* η, if there exists a substitution η' such that $\eta = \theta\eta'$.

A unifier θ of A and B is called the *most general unifier*, or often *mgu*, if θ is more general than any other unifier of A and B.

We often call a monotype's pair, written $A \stackrel{?}{=} B$, a *monotype equation.*

There exists a unification algorithm which finds the most general unifier for a given finite set of monotype equations:

Definition 25 Unification Algorithm Unify.
Algorithm Unify
Input: $(\mathcal{E}, \mathcal{V})$,
where $\mathcal{E}$ is a finite set of monotype equations and $\mathcal{V}$ a finite set of environment type variables and type variables.
Output: a failure signal or $(\theta, \mathcal{V})$,
where θ is a substitution and $\mathcal{V}$ a set of environment type variables and type variables.
(More detailed definition is in Appendix A.)

Theorem 26 Soundness of Unify. *Given a finite set $\mathcal{E}$ of monotype equations and a set $\mathcal{V}$ of (environment) type variables, if* Unify$(\mathcal{E}, \mathcal{V})$ *succeeds and returns $(\theta, \mathcal{V}')$ as its output, then θ unifies $\mathcal{E}$.*

Theorem 27 Termination of Unify. Unify$(\mathcal{E}, \mathcal{V})$ *terminates for any $(\mathcal{E}, \mathcal{V})$.*

Theorem 28 Completeness. *Let $\mathcal{E}$ be a set of monotype equations and $\mathcal{V}$ a set of (environment) type variables. If there exists a unifier θ such that* $\mathsf{dom}(\theta) \subseteq \mathcal{V}$, *then algorithm* Unify$(\mathcal{E}, \mathcal{V})$ *succeeds. In such a case, if the output is $(\theta_0, \mathcal{V}_0)$, then $\theta_0|_{\mathcal{V}}$ is more general than any unifier η of $\mathcal{E}$ such that* $\mathsf{dom}(\eta) \subseteq \mathcal{V}$.

3.2 Type Inference Algorithm

We give a type inference algorithm to ML_{env}using the unification algorithm in the previous section.

Definition 29 Type Inference Algorithm Infer.

Algorithm Infer:
Input

$$\begin{cases} \Gamma: & \textit{an environment polytype;} \\ M: & \textit{a term;} \\ \mathcal{V}: & \textit{a set of (environment) type variables.} \end{cases}$$

Output

in success case:

$$\begin{cases} A: & \textit{a monotype;} \\ \theta: & \textit{a substitution;} \\ \mathcal{V}': & \textit{a set of (environment) type variables.} \end{cases}$$

in failure case:
a failure signal

$\mathsf{Infer}(\Gamma, x, \mathcal{V})$ =
  if $\{x : \sigma\} \in \Gamma$
  then let $(A, \mathcal{V}')$ = $\mathsf{Inst}(\sigma, \mathcal{V})$
    in $(A, \mathsf{idsubst}, \mathcal{V}')$
  else let $\overline{\{x_n : \sigma_n\}}\rho$ = Γ
    and α *and* ρ' *be more fresh than the ones in* $\mathcal{V}$
    in $(\alpha, [\rho \mapsto \{x : \alpha\}\rho'], \{\alpha, \rho'\} \cup \mathcal{V})$
$\mathsf{Infer}(\Gamma, (MN), \mathcal{V})$ =
  let $(C, \theta_1, \mathcal{V}_1)$ = $\mathsf{Infer}(\Gamma, M, \mathcal{V})$
  and $(A, \theta_2, \mathcal{V}_2)$ = $\mathsf{Infer}(\Gamma^{\theta_1}, N, \mathcal{V}_1)$
  and β *be more fresh than the ones in* $\mathcal{V}_2$
  and $(\theta, \mathcal{V}_3)$ = $\mathsf{Unify}(C^{\theta_2}, A \to \beta, \mathcal{V}_2)$
  in $(\beta^\theta, \theta_1\theta_2\theta, \mathcal{V}_3)$
$\mathsf{Infer}(\Gamma, (\lambda x.\, M), \mathcal{V})$ =
  let α *be more fresh than the ones in* $\mathcal{V}$
  and $(B, \theta, \mathcal{V}')$ = $\mathsf{Infer}(\{x : \alpha\}\Gamma, M, \mathcal{V} \cup \{\alpha\})$
  in $((\alpha^\theta \to B), \theta, \mathcal{V}')$
$\mathsf{Infer}(\Gamma, id, \mathcal{V})$ =
  let $(E, \mathcal{V}')$ = $\mathsf{Inst}(\Gamma, \mathcal{V})$
  in $(E, \mathsf{idsubst}, \mathcal{V}')$
$\mathsf{Infer}(\Gamma, (M/x) \cdot N, \mathcal{V})$=
  let $(A_1, \theta_1, \mathcal{V}_1)$ = $\mathsf{Infer}(\Gamma, M, \mathcal{V})$
  and $(A_2, \theta_2, \mathcal{V}_2)$ = $\mathsf{Infer}(\Gamma^{\theta_1}, N, \mathcal{V}_1)$
  in if A_2 *is an environment monotype* E
    then $(\{x : A_1^{\theta_2}\}E, \theta_1\theta_2, \mathcal{V}_2)$
    else if A_2 *is a type variable* α

```
            then let ρ be more fresh than the ones in V₂
                     in ({x : A₁^{θ₂[α↦ρ]}}ρ, θ₁θ₂[α ↦ ρ], V₂ ∪ {α, ρ})
        else raise a failure signal
Infer(Γ, M ∘ N, V) =
    let (A₁, θ₁, V₁) = Infer(Γ, N, V)
    in if A₁ is an environment monotype E
        then let (A₂, θ₂, V₂) = Infer(Close(Ftv(Γ^{θ₁}), E), M, V₁)
             in (A₂, θ₁θ₂, V₂)
        else if A₁ is a type variable α
             then let ρ be more fresh than the ones in V₂
                      and (A₂, θ₂, V₂) = Infer(ρ, M, V₁ ∪ {ρ})
                      in (A₂, θ₁[α ↦ ρ]θ₂, V₂)
        else (* A₁ is a function type *)
             raise a failure signal
```

where a subroutine Inst is defined as follows.
Note that a *failure signal* may occur also in unification algorithm Unify.

Algorighm Inst:
Input

$$\begin{cases} \sigma: & \text{a polytype;} \\ \mathcal{V}: & \text{a set of (environment) type variables.} \end{cases}$$

Output

$$\begin{cases} A: & \text{a monotype;} \\ \mathcal{V}': & \text{a set of (environment) type variables.} \end{cases}$$

```
Inst(∀α₁ ⋯ ∀α_k.A, V)
= let β₁, ..., β_k be more fresh than the ones in V
  in (A^{[α₁↦β₁,...,α_k↦β_k]}, {β₁, ..., β_k} ∪ V)
```

We next present two fundamental properties of this algorithm.

Theorem 30 Soundness of Infer. *If algorithm* Infer$(\Gamma, M, \mathcal{V})$ *succeeds and its result is* $(A, \theta, \mathcal{V}')$, *then* $\Gamma^\theta \vdash M : A^\theta$ *holds.*

Proof. It is enough to prove the following theorem by Proposition 21.

Lemma 31 Soundness on $\Vdash$**-judgement.** *If* Infer$(\Gamma, M, \mathcal{V})$ *succeeds and returns* $(A, \theta, \mathcal{V}')$ *as output, then* $\Gamma^\theta \Vdash M : A^\theta$ *holds.*

Proof. The proof is by induction on the structure of term M. All cases are easy and straightforward except the case when M is a composition $(L \circ N)$.

Case $M = (L \circ N)$: Suppose that Infer$(\Gamma, (L \circ N), \mathcal{V})$ succeeds. Then, we know that Infer$(\Gamma, N, \mathcal{V})$ also succeeds and the results is either $(\alpha, \theta_1, \mathcal{V}_1)$ or $(E, \theta_1, \mathcal{V}_1)$ for some α, θ_1, and $\mathcal{V}_1$.

The first case $(\alpha, \theta_1, \mathcal{V}_1)$: By the induction hypothesis, $\Gamma^{\theta_1} \Vdash N : \alpha$. In this case, it holds that $(A_2, \theta_2, \mathcal{V}_2) =$ Infer$(\rho, L, \mathcal{V}_1 \cup \{\rho\})$ for some ρ, A_2, θ_2, and $\mathcal{V}_2$. By the induction hypothesis, $\rho^{\theta_2} \Vdash L : A_2$. From Proposition 20 (with a substitution $[\alpha \mapsto \rho]\theta_2$), we know that $\Gamma^{\theta_1[\alpha\mapsto\rho]\theta_2} \Vdash N : \rho^{\theta_2}$. Then, using Rule $\mathsf{Comp}_{\Vdash}$, we have $\Gamma^{\theta_1[\alpha\mapsto\rho]\theta_2} \Vdash (L \circ N) : A_2$.

The second case $(E, \theta_1, \mathcal{V}_1)$: By the induction hypothesis, $\Gamma^{\theta_1} \Vdash N : E$. In this case, it holds that $(A_2, \theta_2, \mathcal{V}) = \mathsf{Infer}(\mathsf{Close}(\mathsf{Ftv}(\Gamma^{\theta_2}), E), L, \mathcal{V}_1)$. By the induction hypothesis, $\mathsf{Close}(\mathsf{Ftv}(\Gamma^{\theta_1}), E)^{\theta_2} \Vdash L : A_2$. Because $\mathsf{Ftv}(\mathsf{Close}(\mathsf{Ftv}(\Gamma^{\theta_1}), E)) = \mathsf{Ftv}(\Gamma^{\theta_1}) \cap \mathsf{Ftv}(E)$, we can restrict the domain of θ_2: $\mathsf{Close}(\mathsf{Ftv}(\Gamma^{\theta_1}), E)^{\theta_2'} \Vdash L : A_2$ where $\theta_2' = \theta_2|_{\mathsf{Ftv}(\Gamma^{\theta_1})\cap\mathsf{Ftv}(E^{\theta_1})}$. Noting that $\mathsf{Close}(\mathsf{Ftv}(\Gamma^{\theta_1}), E)^{\theta_2'} = \mathsf{Close}(\mathsf{Ftv}(\Gamma^{\theta_1\theta_2'}), E^{\theta_2'})$, we know that

$$\frac{\Delta \Vdash N : E' \quad \mathsf{Close}(\mathsf{Ftv}(\Delta), E') \Vdash M : A_2}{\Delta \Vdash M \circ N : A_2},$$

where $\Delta = \Gamma^{\theta_1\theta_2'}$ and $E' = E^{\theta_2'}$.

Theorem 32 Termination of Infer. *Algorithm* Infer *terminates.*

Proof. Easily proved by the induction on the size of a term given as the second argument.

We would like to finish this section with an example of type inference:

Example 1. Let us type a term

$$(ff) \circ ((\lambda f.\, id)(\lambda x.\, x)),$$

which corresponds to a Scheme program:

```
(eval '(f f) ( (lambda (f) (the-environment))
               (lambda (x) x))).
```

A trace of an execution of Infer is as follow.

$>\ \mathsf{Infer}(\rho,\ (ff)\circ((\lambda f.\, id)(\lambda x.\, x)),\ \{\rho\})$
$>>\ \mathsf{Infer}(\rho,\ ((\lambda f.\, id)(\lambda x.\, x)),\ \{\rho\})$
$>>>\ \mathsf{Infer}(\rho,\ (\lambda f.\, id),\ \{\rho\})$
$>>>>\ \mathsf{Infer}(\{f:\gamma\}\rho,\ id,\ \{\rho,\gamma\})$
$>>><\ (\{f:\gamma\}\rho,\ \mathsf{idsubst},\ \{\rho,\gamma\})$
$>><\ (\gamma \to \{f:\gamma\}\rho,\ \mathsf{idsubst},\ \{\rho,\gamma\})$
$>>>\ \mathsf{Infer}(\rho,\ (\lambda x.\, x),\ \{\rho,\gamma\})$
$>>><\ (\{x:\alpha\}\rho,\ x,\ \{\rho,\gamma,\alpha\})$
$>><\ (\alpha \to \alpha,\ \mathsf{idsubst},\ \{\rho,\gamma,\alpha\})$
$>>>\ \mathsf{Unify}(\gamma \to \{f:\gamma\}\rho,\ (\alpha\to\alpha)\to\beta,\ \{\rho,\gamma,\alpha,\beta\})$
$>><\ ([\gamma\mapsto(\alpha\to\alpha),\ \beta\to\{f:(\alpha\to\alpha)\}\rho],\ \{\rho,\gamma,\alpha,\beta\})$
$><\ (\{f:\alpha\to\alpha\}\rho,\ [\gamma\mapsto\cdots,\ \beta\mapsto\cdots],\ \{\rho,\gamma,\alpha,\beta\})$
$>>\ \mathsf{Infer}(\{f:\forall\alpha.\alpha\to\alpha\}\rho,\ (ff),\ \{\rho,\gamma,\alpha,\beta\})$
$>>>\ \mathsf{Infer}(\{f:\forall\alpha.\alpha\to\alpha\}\rho,\ f,\ \{\rho,\gamma,\alpha,\beta\})$
$>><\ (\alpha_1\to\alpha_1,\ \mathsf{idsubst},\ \{\rho,\gamma,\alpha,\beta,\alpha_1\})$
$>>>\ \mathsf{Infer}(\{f:\forall\alpha.\alpha\to\alpha\}\rho,\ f,\ \{\rho,\gamma,\alpha,\beta\})$

>>< $(\alpha_2 \to \alpha_2,\ \mathsf{idsubst},\ \{\rho, \gamma, \alpha, \beta, \alpha_1, \alpha_2\})$
>>> $\mathsf{Unify}(\alpha_1 \to \alpha_1,\ (\alpha_2 \to \alpha_2) \to \beta',\ \{\rho, \gamma, \alpha, \beta, \alpha_1, \alpha_2, \beta'\})$
>>< $([\alpha_1 \mapsto (\alpha_2 \to \alpha_2),\ \beta' \mapsto (\alpha_2 \to \alpha_2),\ \{\rho, \gamma, \alpha, \beta, \alpha_1, \alpha_2, \beta'\})$
>< $(\alpha_2 \to \alpha_2,\ [\alpha_1 \mapsto \cdots,\ \beta' \mapsto \cdots],\ \{\rho, \gamma, \alpha, \beta, \alpha_1, \alpha_2, \beta'\})$
< $(\alpha_2 \to \alpha_2,\ [\alpha_1 \mapsto \cdots,\ \beta' \mapsto \cdots],\ \{\rho, \gamma, \alpha, \beta, \alpha_1, \alpha_2, \beta'\})$

The resultant derivation tree is as follows.

$$\dfrac{\begin{array}{c}\vdots\ \Sigma_1\\ \rho \Vdash (\lambda f.\, id)(\lambda x.\, x) : \{f : \alpha \to \alpha\}\rho\end{array} \quad \begin{array}{c}\vdots\ \Sigma_2\\ \{f : \forall\alpha.\alpha \to \alpha\}\rho \Vdash (f f) : \alpha_2 \to \alpha_2\end{array}}{\rho \Vdash (f f) \circ ((\lambda f.\, id)(\lambda x.\, x)) : \alpha_2 \to \alpha_2}\ \mathsf{Comp}_{\Vdash}$$

Subtree Σ_1 is

$$\dfrac{\dfrac{\dfrac{\{f : (\alpha \to \alpha)\}\rho \leq \{f : (\alpha \to \alpha)\}\rho}{\{f : (\alpha \to \alpha)\}\rho \Vdash id : \{f : \alpha \to \alpha\}\rho}\ \mathsf{Id}_{\Vdash}}{\rho \Vdash (\lambda f.\, id) : (\alpha \to \alpha) \to \{f : \alpha \to \alpha\}\rho}\ \mathsf{Lam}_{\Vdash} \quad \dfrac{\dfrac{\alpha \leq \alpha}{\{x : \alpha\}\rho \Vdash x : \alpha}\ \mathsf{Var}_{\Vdash}}{\rho \Vdash (\lambda x.\, x) : \alpha \to \alpha}\ \mathsf{Lam}_{\Vdash}}{\rho \Vdash (\lambda f.\, id)(\lambda x.\, x) : \{f : \alpha \to \alpha\}\rho}\ \mathsf{App}_{\Vdash}\ .$$

Subtree Σ_2 is

$$\dfrac{\dfrac{\forall\alpha.\alpha \to \alpha \leq (\alpha_2 \to \alpha_2) \to (\alpha_2 \to \alpha_2)}{\{f : \forall\alpha.\alpha \to \alpha\}\rho \Vdash f : (\alpha_2 \to \alpha_2) \to (\alpha_2 \to \alpha_2)} \quad \dfrac{\forall\alpha.\alpha \to \alpha \leq \alpha_2 \to \alpha_2}{\{f : \forall\alpha.\alpha \to \alpha\}\rho \Vdash f : (\alpha_2 \to \alpha_2)}}{\{f : \forall\alpha.\alpha \to \alpha\}\rho \Vdash (f f) : \alpha_2 \to \alpha_2}\ .$$

4 Concluding Remarks

4.1 Our previous work and its results

We investigated a simply-typed lambda calculus with first-class environments, called $\lambda_{\overrightarrow{env}}$, in the previous work [Nis94]. The following definitions and results on $\lambda_{\overrightarrow{env}}$ are presented there:

Syntax, Reduction and Typing The raw terms and the weak reduction rule of $\lambda_{\overrightarrow{env}}$ are the same as the ones of ML_{env}. The typing rules of $\lambda_{\overrightarrow{env}}$ give a subsystem of ML_{env}, where types are restricted to (environment) monotypes:

$$\dfrac{}{\{x : A\}E \vdash x : A}$$

$$\dfrac{E \vdash M : A \to B \quad E \vdash N : A}{E \vdash MN : B} \qquad \dfrac{\{x : A\}E \vdash M : B}{E \vdash \lambda x.\, M : A \to B}$$

$$\dfrac{}{E \vdash id : E}$$

$$\dfrac{E \vdash N : E' \quad E' \vdash M : A}{E \vdash M \circ N : A} \qquad \dfrac{E \vdash M : A \quad E \vdash N : E'}{E \vdash (M/x) \cdot N : \{x : A\}E'}$$

Confluence We obtained confluence of weak reduction of $\lambda_{env}^{\rightarrow}$by the same method as $\lambda\sigma$-calculus', "interpretation method" (see [CHL92]).

Strong normalizability The strong normalizability is proved by the method of translation from typed terms of $\lambda_{env}^{\rightarrow}$ to typed terms of simply typed λ-calculus λ_{record} with extensible records: the strong normalizability of λ_{record} implies the one of $\lambda_{env}^{\rightarrow}$. We do not discuss strong normalizability of ML_{env}, mainly because of lack of time and space. We will surely obtain this property by a similar method.

Type inference algorithm A type inference algorithm is given to $\lambda_{env}^{\rightarrow}$and it is proved that the algorithm does not only enjoy soundness but also completeness. Unfortunately, we have not obtained completeness of ML_{env}as yet.

4.2 Reflective Functional Programming

Many researchers have studied reflective functional programming, where programmers can directly treat a current status of an evaluator in a program and can obtain a very strong expressive power ([Smi84], [WF88], [Dr88], [DF90]). In contrast to this research, our system supports only reification and reflection of environments and is limited to a certain fragment of their systems. And such a restriction helps us to study syntactical properties (e.g. confluence, strong normalizability, and type inference). This point is common to calculi with first-class continuations (e.g. [FFKD86]).

4.3 Record and Environment

We have been interested in fragments which are conservative extensions of $\lambda\sigma_w$-calculus and have studied them. There is another research direction: *discovery of powerful constructs on first-class environments.* For this purpose, results on record calculi seems to be helpful, since we can regard records as reified environments:

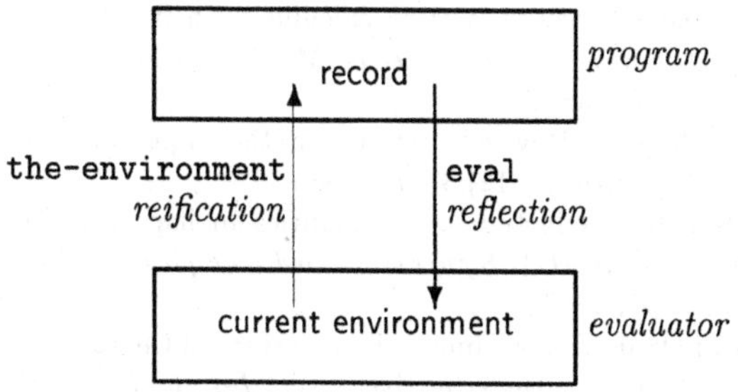

5 Acknowledgement

I am indebted to my friends, my colleagues, and my co-supervisors: Prof. Satoru Takasu and Prof. Masami Hagiya. I owe what I am to them. Thanks are due also to Prof. Pierre-Louis Curien, Prof. Atsushi Ohori, and anonymous referees for discussions, comments, and pointing out of errors in the draft.

References

[AS85] Harold Abelson and Gerald Jay Sussman. *Structure and Interpretation of Computer Programs.* The MIT Press, 1985.

[CHL92] Pierre-Louis Curien, Thérèse Hardin, and Jean-Jacques Lévy. *Confluence Properties of Weak and Strong Calculi of Explicit Substitutions.* Rapports de Recherche 1617, INRIA, February 1992.

[Cur86] Pierre-Louis Curien. Categorical combinators. *Information and Control*, 69:188–254, 1986.

[Cur91] Pierre-Louis Curien. An abstract framework for environment machines. *Theoretical Computer Science*, 82:389–402, 1991.

[DF90] Olivier Danvy and Andrzej Filinski. Abstracting control. In *Proceedings of the 1990 Conference on LISP and Functional Programming*, pages 151–160, 1990.

[Dr88] Olivier Danvy and Karoline Malmkjær. Intensions and extensions in a reflective tower. In *Proceedings of the 1988 Conference on LISP and Functional Programming*, pages 327–341, 1988.

[FFKD86] Matthias Felleisen, Daniel P. Friedman, Eugene Kohlbecker, and Bruce Duba. Reasoning with continuations. In *Proceedings of the Symposium on Logic in Computer Science*, IEEE Computer Society Press, 1986.

[Gun92] Carl A. Gunter. *Semantics of programming languages: structures and techniques.* The MIT Press, 1992.

[JM93] Lalita A. Jategaonkar and John C. Mitchell. Type inference with extended pattern matching and subtypes. *Fundamenta Informaticae*, 19:127–166, 1993.

[Lau90] Oliver Laumann. *Reference Manual for the Elk Extension Language Interpreter.* 1990.

[MIT] *MIT Scheme Reference Manual.* MIT.

[nACCL90] Martín Abadi, Luca Cardelli, Pierre-Louis Curien, and Jean-Jacques Lévy. Explicit substitutions. In *proceedings of the Seventeenth Annual ACM SIGACT-SIGPLAN Symposium on Principles of Programming Languages*, San Francisco, California, January 1990.

[Nis94] Shinya Nishizaki. Simply typed lambda calculus with first-class environments. *Publication of Research Institute for Mathematical Sciences Kyoto University*, 1994. To appear.

[RC86] J. Rees and W. Clinger. Revised^3 repord on the algorithmic language scheme. *SIGPLAN Notices*, 21(12):37–79, 1986.

[Smi84] Brian Cantwell Smith. Reflection and semantics in lisp. In *Conference Record of the 11th Annual ACM Symposium on Principles of Programming Languages*, pages 23–35, 1984.

[WF88] Mitchell Wand and Daniel P. Friedman. The mystery of the tower revealed: a nonreflective description of the reflective tower. *Lisp and Symbolic Computation*, 1:11–37, 1988.

A Unification Algorithm

In this section, we present the definition of unification algorithm referred in Section 3. This algorithm is originally proposed by Jategaonkar and Mitchell in

[JM93] and the author reformulated it in the style of transformation. If the readers interests in correctness of this algorithm, they can find its proof in [Nis94].

Definition 33 Solved Set of Monotype Equations. A monotype equation $\alpha \stackrel{?}{=} A$ (or $\rho \stackrel{?}{=} E$) is called *solved* in a set of $\mathcal{E}$ of monotype equations, if α (or ρ, resp.) does not occur anywhere else in $\mathcal{E}$. This α (or ρ resp.) is called *solved variable.* $\mathcal{E}$ is called *solved* if all its pairs are solved.

If $\mathcal{E}$ is solved, it is clear that $\mathcal{E}$ has a form:

$$\{\alpha_1 \stackrel{?}{=} A_1, \cdots, \alpha_m \stackrel{?}{=} A_m, \rho_1 \stackrel{?}{=} E_1, \cdots, \rho_n \stackrel{?}{=} E_n\},$$

where $\alpha_1, \ldots, \alpha_m, \rho_1, \ldots, \rho_m$ are distinct with each other and any α_i and ρ_j does not occur anywhere else except themselves.

Therefore, we make the following substitution from $\mathcal{E}$:

$$[\alpha_1 \mapsto A_1, \cdots, \alpha_m \mapsto A_m, \rho_1 \mapsto E_1, \cdots, \rho_n \mapsto E_n].$$

We identify this substitution to $\mathcal{E}$ itself.

Definition 34 Unification Transformer. Next, we define a transformation $(\mathcal{E}, \mathcal{V}) \Rightarrow (\mathcal{E}', \mathcal{V}')$ which maps each pair of a set $\mathcal{E}$ of monotype equations and a set $\mathcal{V}$ of variables occurring in $\mathcal{E}$, to a pair of $\mathcal{E}'$ and $\mathcal{V}'$ of the same kind respectively, as follows:

TrTvarTvar

$(\mathcal{E} \cup \{\alpha \stackrel{?}{=} \alpha\}, \mathcal{V})$
$\Rightarrow (\mathcal{E}, \mathcal{V})$

TrTvarTvar

$(\mathcal{E} \cup \{\alpha \stackrel{?}{=} A\}, \mathcal{V})$
$\Rightarrow (\mathcal{E}^{[\alpha \mapsto A]} \cup \{\alpha \stackrel{?}{=} A\}, \mathcal{V})$
where $\alpha \stackrel{?}{=} A$ is not solved in $\mathcal{E} \cup \{\alpha \stackrel{?}{=} A\}$, and $\alpha \notin \mathsf{Ftv}(A)$.

TrFunFun

$(\mathcal{E} \cup \{A \rightarrow B \stackrel{?}{=} C \rightarrow D\}, \mathcal{V})$
$\Rightarrow (\mathcal{E} \cup \{A \stackrel{?}{=} C, B \stackrel{?}{=} D\}, \mathcal{V})$

TrEvarEvar

$(\mathcal{E} \cup \{\rho \stackrel{?}{=} \rho\}, \mathcal{V})$
$\Rightarrow (\mathcal{E}, \mathcal{V})$

TrEvarEtype

$(\mathcal{E} \cup \{\rho \stackrel{?}{=} E\}, \mathcal{V})$
$\Rightarrow (\mathcal{E}^{[\rho \mapsto E]} \cup \{\rho \stackrel{?}{=} E\}, \mathcal{V})$
where $\rho \stackrel{?}{=} E$ is not solved in $\mathcal{E} \cup \{\rho \stackrel{?}{=} E\}$,
$[\rho \mapsto E]$ is a valid substitution, and $\rho \notin \mathsf{Ftv}(E)$

TrEtypeEtype1

$(\mathcal{E} \cup \{\overline{\{x_p : A_p\}}\rho \stackrel{?}{=} \overline{\{x_p : A'_p\}}\rho\}, \mathcal{V})$

$\Rightarrow (\mathcal{E} \cup \{\overline{A_p \stackrel{?}{=} A'_p}\},\ \mathcal{V})$

TrEtypeEtype2

$(\mathcal{E} \cup \{\{\overline{x_p : A_p}\}\,\{\overline{y_q : B_q}\}\rho \stackrel{?}{=} \{\overline{x_p : A'_p}\}\,\{\overline{z_r : C_r}\}\rho'\},\ \mathcal{V})$

$\Rightarrow (\mathcal{E}^\theta \cup \{\overline{A^\theta_p \stackrel{?}{=} A'^\theta_p}, \rho \stackrel{?}{=} \{\overline{z_r : C^\theta_r}\}\rho'', \rho' \stackrel{?}{=} \{\overline{y_q : B^\theta_q}\}\rho''\},\ \mathcal{V} \cup \{\rho''\})$

where $\rho \neq \rho',\quad \rho'' \notin \mathcal{V},$

$\mathsf{PVar}(\rho) \cap \{\overline{z_r}\} = \emptyset,\quad \mathsf{PVar}(\rho') \cap \{\overline{y_q}\} = \emptyset,$

$\forall k(\rho \notin \mathsf{Ftv}(C_k)),\quad \forall j(\rho' \notin \mathsf{Ftv}(B_j)),$

$\forall k(\rho \notin \mathsf{Ftv}(B_k)) \vee \forall j(\rho' \notin \mathsf{Ftv}(C_j))$, and

$\theta = [\rho \mapsto \{\overline{z_r : {C_r}^{[\rho' \mapsto \{\overline{y_q : B_q}\}\rho'']}}\}\rho'', \rho' \mapsto \{\overline{y_q : {B_q}^{[\rho \mapsto \{\overline{z_r : C_r}\}\rho'']}}\}\rho'']$

It is evident that $\mathcal{V}'$ includes every variable occurring in $\mathcal{E}'$ in any $(\mathcal{E},\ \mathcal{V}) \Rightarrow (\mathcal{E}',\ \mathcal{V}')$.

The unification algorithm Unifyis defined with the above transformation:

Definition 35 Algorithm Unify.

Algorithm Unify
Input : $(\mathcal{E}, \mathcal{V})$
Output : $(\theta, \mathcal{V}')$
or a failure signal

```
Unify(ℰ,𝒱) =
    if ℰ is solved
    then return ℰ as a substitution
    else if (ℰ,𝒱) can be transformed
         then let (ℰ,𝒱) ⇒ (ℰ',𝒱')
                  in Unify(ℰ',𝒱')
         else raise a failure signal.
```

B Proof of Proposition 20

Proof. The proof is by induction on the structure of term M. The cases except the one of composition are straightforward, noting Proposition 14.
Case $M = M_1 \circ M_2$: There exists E and A such that

$$\frac{\Gamma \Vdash M_1 : E \quad \mathsf{Close}(\mathsf{Ftv}(\Gamma), E) \Vdash M_2 : A}{\Gamma \Vdash M_1 \circ M_2 : A}\ \mathsf{Comp}_{\Vdash}. \tag{8}$$

By the induction hypothesis,

$$\Gamma^{[\gamma \mapsto C]} \Vdash M_2 : E^{[\gamma \mapsto C]} \text{ and} \tag{9}$$
$$\mathsf{Close}(\mathsf{Ftv}(\Gamma), E)^{[\gamma \mapsto C]} \Vdash M_1 : A^{[\gamma \mapsto C]}. \tag{10}$$

We next consider four subcases concerning the occurrence of γ:

Subcase $\gamma \in \mathsf{Ftv}(\Gamma)$ and $\gamma \in \mathsf{Ftv}(E)$:
Since $\mathsf{Close}(\mathsf{Ftv}(\Gamma^{[\gamma\mapsto C]}), E^{[\gamma\mapsto C]}) \leq \mathsf{Close}(\mathsf{Ftv}(\Gamma), E)^{[\gamma\mapsto C]}$, we know that

$$\mathsf{Close}(\mathsf{Ftv}(\Gamma^{[\gamma\mapsto C]}), E^{[\gamma\mapsto C]}) \Vdash M_1 : A^{[\gamma\mapsto C]} \tag{11}$$

by (10) and Proposition 19. From (9), (11), and Rule $\mathsf{Comp}_{\Vdash}$, it is inferred that

$$\Gamma^{[\gamma\mapsto C]} \Vdash (M_1 \circ M_2) : A^{[\gamma\mapsto C]}.$$

Subcase $\gamma \in \mathsf{Ftv}(\Gamma)$ and $\gamma \notin \mathsf{Ftv}(E)$: The assumption that $\gamma \notin \mathsf{Ftv}(E)$, (9) and (10) implies

$$\Gamma^{[\gamma\mapsto C]} \Vdash M_2 : E \tag{12}$$

$$\mathsf{Close}(\mathsf{Ftv}(\Gamma), E) \Vdash M_1 : A^{[\gamma\mapsto C]}. \tag{13}$$

In the left hand side of (13), we can rename the bound type variables $\mathsf{Ftv}(E) \setminus \mathsf{Ftv}(\Gamma)$. Therefore, we may assume that

$$(\mathsf{Ftv}(E) \setminus \mathsf{Ftv}(\Gamma)) \cap \mathsf{Ftv}(C) = \emptyset \tag{14}$$

without loss of generality. Then, we know that

$$\begin{aligned} &\mathsf{Close}(\mathsf{Ftv}(\Gamma^{[\gamma\mapsto C]}), E) \\ &= \mathsf{Close}(\mathsf{Ftv}(\Gamma) \cup \mathsf{Ftv}(C), E) \\ &= \mathsf{Close}(\mathsf{Ftv}(\Gamma), E) \qquad \textit{because of (14)}, \end{aligned}$$

which implies that

$$\mathsf{Close}(\mathsf{Ftv}(\Gamma^{[\gamma\mapsto C]}), E) \Vdash M_1 : A^{[\gamma\mapsto C]}. \tag{15}$$

By (12) and (15), we have

$$\Gamma^{[\gamma\mapsto C]} \Vdash M_1 \circ M_2 : A^{[\gamma\mapsto C]}.$$

Subcase $\gamma \notin \mathsf{Ftv}(\Gamma)$ and $\gamma \in \mathsf{Ftv}(E)$: From $\gamma \notin \mathsf{Ftv}(\Gamma)$, we know that γ does not occur freely in $\mathsf{Close}(\mathsf{Ftv}(\Gamma), E)$. Therefore, $\mathsf{Close}(\mathsf{Ftv}(\Gamma), E)^{[\gamma\mapsto C]} = \mathsf{Close}(\mathsf{Ftv}(\Gamma), E)$. Thus, (10) implies

$$\mathsf{Close}(\mathsf{Ftv}(\Gamma), E) \Vdash M_1 : A^{[\gamma\mapsto C]}. \tag{16}$$

By (8) and Rule $\mathsf{Comp}_{\Vdash}$, $\Gamma \Vdash M_1 \circ M_2 : A^{[\gamma\mapsto C]}$, that is, $E^{[\gamma\mapsto C]} \Vdash M_1 \circ M_2 : A^{[\gamma\mapsto C]}$.

Subcase $\gamma \notin \mathsf{Ftv}(\Gamma)$ and $\gamma \notin \mathsf{Ftv}(E)$: We know that

$$\mathsf{Close}(\mathsf{Ftv}(\Gamma), E) \Vdash M_1 : A^{[\gamma\mapsto C]} \tag{17}$$

because of $\gamma \notin \mathsf{Ftv}(E)$. By (8), (17), and Rule $\mathsf{Comp}_{\Vdash}$, $\Gamma \Vdash (M_1 \circ M_2) : A^{[\gamma\mapsto C]}$. Therefore, noting that $\gamma \notin \mathsf{Ftv}(E)$, we know that $\Gamma^{[\gamma\mapsto C]} \Vdash (M_1 \circ M_2) : A^{[\gamma\mapsto C]}$.

A Simple Proof of the Genericity Lemma

Masako Takahashi

Department of Information Science
Tokyo Institute of Technology
Ookayama, Meguro, Tokyo 152 Japan
masako@titisha.is.titech.ac.jp

Abstract. A short direct proof is given for the fundamental property of unsolvable λ-terms; if M is an unsolvable λ-term and $C[M]$ is solvable, then $C[N]$ is solvable for any λ-term N. (Here $C[\ ]$ stands for an arbitrary context.)

1. Preliminaries

A term in this note means a λ-term, which is either $x, \lambda x.M$ or MN, (where M, N are terms and x is a variable.) Unless otherwise stated, capital letters $M, N, P,...$ stand for arbitrary terms, $\mathbf{M}, \mathbf{N},...$ for (possibly null) sequences of terms, $x, y,...$ for variables, and $\mathbf{x}, \mathbf{y},...$ for (possibly null) sequences of variables. We refer to [1] as the standard text in the field.

A term of the form $\lambda\mathbf{x}.y\mathbf{M}$ (more precisely, $\lambda x_1.(\lambda x_2.(...(\lambda x_n.((...((yM_1)M_2)...)M_m))...))$ for some $n, m \geq 0$) is said to be in *head normal form* (*hnf*, for short). If a term M has a hnf (that is, $M =_\beta M'$ for a term M' in hnf), then M is called *solvable*. The following are well-known facts of solvable terms (cf.[1] 8.3.1 - 14).

(1) M is solvable if and only if $\forall P, \exists\mathbf{x}, \exists\mathbf{Q}((\lambda\mathbf{x}.M)\mathbf{Q} =_\beta P)$.
(2) $\lambda x.M$ is solvable if and only if so is M.
(3) if $M[x := N]$ is solvable then so is M.
(4) if MN is solvable then so is M.

A term in *β-normal form* (*β-nf*, for short) is recursively defined as a term of the form $\lambda\mathbf{x}.y\mathbf{M}$ where $\mathbf{M}$ is a (possibly null) sequence of terms in β-nf.

2. Propositions

First we prove a special case of the genericity lemma.

Lemma 1. Let M, N, P be terms with M unsolvable and N in β-nf. Then $P[x := M] =_\beta N$ implies $P[x := M'] =_\beta N$ for any M'.

Proof. We prove the lemma by induction on the structure of N. Suppose $P[x := M] =_\beta N$, and $N \equiv \lambda\mathbf{y}.zN_1N_2...N_n$ where $n \geq 0$ and each N_i is in β-nf. (Here, $\equiv$ denotes syntactic equality of terms.) Then since N is solvable, P is also solvable by (3) above, and hence has a hnf, say $\lambda\mathbf{u}.vP_1P_2...P_p$. Here x and v must be different. (For otherwise $P[x := M] =_\beta \lambda\mathbf{u}.M\mathbf{P}$ for some $\mathbf{P}$, and $P[x := M]$ would by (2) and (4) above be unsolvable, which contradicts our assumption.) Therefore we have $P[x := M] =_\beta \lambda\mathbf{u}.vP_1'P_2'...P_p'$ where $P_i' \equiv P_i[x := M](i = 1, 2, ..., p)$. Since $P[x := M] =_\beta N \equiv \lambda\mathbf{y}.zN_1N_2...N_n$, we know from the Church-Rosser theorem that $P_i' =_\beta N_i(i = 1, 2, ..., n)$ and $p = n$. Without loss of generality we may also assume $\mathbf{u} \equiv \mathbf{y}$ and $v \equiv z$.

If $n = 0$, then $P =_\beta \lambda\mathbf{u}.v \equiv N$. In this case, we have $P[x := M'] =_\beta (\lambda\mathbf{u}.v)[x := M'] \equiv \lambda\mathbf{u}.v \equiv N$ for any M'. If $n > 0$, then from the fact $P_i[x := M] \equiv P_i' =_\beta N_i$ and the inductive hypothesis, we get $P_i[x := M'] =_\beta N_i(i = 1, 2, ..., n)$ for any M'. In this case,

$$\begin{aligned} P[x := M'] &=_\beta (\lambda\mathbf{u}.vP_1P_2...P_n)[x := M'] \\ &\equiv \lambda\mathbf{u}.v(P_1[x := M'])(P_2[x := M'])...(P_n[x := M']) \\ &=_\beta \lambda\mathbf{y}.zN_1N_2...N_n \equiv N. \end{aligned}$$

This proves the lemma. $\square$

Lemma 2. ([1] 14.3.24. Genericity lemma) Let M be an unsolvable term, and $C[\ ]$ be a context such that $C[M]$ has a β-nf. Then $C[M] =_\beta C[M']$ for any M'.
Proof. For given M', let $\mathbf{y}$ be a sequence of all free variables in MM'. Take a new variable x (neither in $C[M]$ nor $C[M']$), and let $P \equiv C[x\mathbf{y}]$. Then since $\lambda\mathbf{y}.M$ and $\lambda\mathbf{y}.M'$ are closed terms, we have

$$P[x := \lambda\mathbf{y}.M] \equiv C[(\lambda\mathbf{y}.M)\mathbf{y}] =_\beta C[M],$$
$$P[x := \lambda\mathbf{y}.M'] \equiv C[(\lambda\mathbf{y}.M')\mathbf{y}] =_\beta C[M'].$$

The term $\lambda\mathbf{y}.M$ therefore satisfies $P[x := \lambda\mathbf{y}.M] =_\beta C[M] =_\beta N$ for some N in β-nf. Here $\lambda\mathbf{y}.M$ is unsolvable because so is M. Hence by applying lemma 1 we get $P[x := \lambda\mathbf{y}.M'] =_\beta N$, which implies $C[M] =_\beta C[M']$. □

Corollary 3. If M is unsolvable and $C[M]$ is solvable, then $C[M']$ is solvable for any M'.
Proof. Since $C[M]$ is solvable, by (1) above there exist $\mathbf{x}$ and $\mathbf{N}$ such that $(\lambda\mathbf{x}.C[M])\mathbf{N}$ has a β-nf. Then by lemma 2 (applied to the context $(\lambda\mathbf{x}.C[\ ])\mathbf{N}$), we know $(\lambda\mathbf{x}.C[M'])\mathbf{N}$ has a β-nf for any M'. This means $(\lambda\mathbf{x}.C[M'])\mathbf{N}$ is solvable, and consequently $C[M']$ is solvable. □

The proof presented provides an alternative to the conventional one which uses a topological argument on Böhm trees (cf.[1] Chapters 10 and 14).

Reference

[1] H. P. Barendregt, *The Lambda Calculus* (North-Holland 1984).

The Logic of FOL Systems: Formulated in Set Theory

Richard W. Weyhrauch and Carolyn Talcott

IBUKI and Stanford

Abstract. In this paper we use set theory to describe **FOL** systems. This restatement of the notions implicit in First Order Logic facilitates their interpretation as finite data structures. This is a crucial step toward the goal of building an artificial reasoner.

This paper is dedicated to Professor Takasu for his dedication to science and his recognition that logic is important both for program correctness and theories of reasoning.

1 The FOL Agenda

The goal of the FOL project is to provide data structures that can be used as the mind of a man-made individual–one who has an active mental life; can come to know about its world; and can reason well enough to survive by itself. Our goal/dream is to build an object that can understand and reason about the world and the details of what we present here are directed at this goal. We believe that there is an important difference in the way logic needs to be used if the goal is to build a reasoner, rather than provide a theory about what a reasoner might have done.

A formal system that is adequate for talking about reasoning is unlikely to be an adequate blueprint for building a reasoner. The understanding of this distinction is critical to understanding why we have gone to so much trouble in this paper to make distinctions that are, from the point of view of a theory of reasoning, irrelevant.

The path approach of this paper is simple–we reinterpret each of the ideas of traditional logic from the point of view of our goal. In order to get a top level view of these ideas, in this paper, we use set theory to describe the structures that interest us. This description just sets the stage. It is not the finished work, but it serves simply to "reorganize" the territory of logic. Because of its extensional nature it is inadequate for our goal. In later papers we will show how each of these structures can be realized as a data structure in the memory of a computer. On the way we will, by means of examples, show how these structures can be used, not simply as descriptions of the solutions to puzzles, but rather as containers where knowledge resides and out of which can come answers to questions about this knowledge. Once again, let us emphasize how important it is to realize that our goal is *not* to use formal systems (logic) to explain the solution to some problem, but rather, to define data structures that can contain knowledge. Once we have these structures, by understanding how they change over time, we can explain how knowledge is acquired and how such an object can use its knowledge to make accurate judgements about its environment.

As mentioned above, in this paper we set the stage by describing FOL systems as sets, but we always need to keep in mind that an important part of our final goal is to turn each of these sets into a data structure that can be embedded in the memory of a computer. An important property of real knowing agents, either biological or not, is that they consist of only a finite amount of material. This means that ultimately their reasoning capabilities and knowledge must consist of only a finite number of finite structures. Thus, one of our goals is to define FOL systems so that every idea and notion is representable as a finite structure.

From the more technical point of view, the logic of FOL systems provides a new way to formalize the notion of theory. It is more expressive than thinking of theories as sets of formulas because it permits more direct and natural formal presentations of informal theories. Formalizations in FOL systems reflect the intensional aspects of evolving theories and the FOL paradigm provides a natural explanation of classical reasoning that is both effective and finitistically acceptable. It gives an answer to the question: How do we apparently carry out classical reasoning about abstract (possibly infinite) structures with only a finite amount of physical stuff (our brains) to accomplish this activity.

New notions from the point of view of logic are: partial structures, FOL contexts, FOL systems, and inference rules as maps on contexts or systems.

Partial structures, when presented as sets, are like partial models. They function as an explicit representation of objects in the intended model and provide information about the intended models of an FOL context. Later, by realizing the functions and relations in the partial structure as continuation based computation rules, partial structures provide a mechanism for realizing the resource limited reality of actual reasoners.

FOL contexts are presentations of theories. An FOL context contains a language, a partial structure, a connection between the symbols of the language and objects of the partial structure, and a set of facts. A model of an FOL context is a classical model that extends the partial structure, satisfies the facts, and preserves the connection between symbols and objects. An FOL context is consistent if it has a model.

FOL systems are collections of FOL contexts. The notion of consistency extends naturally to FOL systems. The mechanism for reasoning is to apply rules that preserve the consistency of FOL systems. Sometimes we also consider rules that also preserve stronger constraints. The apparent weakening that results from looking at simple consistency preserving rules on FOL systems, rather than validity preserving ones, turns out to be one of the major strengths of the FOL paradigm.

2 The Structure of FOL Systems

The definition of FOL systems proceeds by first defining FOL contexts, the basic building blocks of our theory, and then collecting them together to form FOL systems.

2.1 Similarity Type

A *similarity type* (sometimes called a *signature*), is a triple

$$\tau = \langle p, q, \alpha \rangle$$

where $p = \langle p_1, \ldots, p_k \rangle$ and $q = \langle q_1, \ldots, q_l \rangle$ are finite sequences of positive integers whose lengths are k and l respectively and where α is an ordinal.

Given two similarity types

$$\tau = \langle p, q, \alpha \rangle$$

and

$$\tau' = \langle p', q', \gamma \rangle$$

we say τ *is extended by* τ' or τ' *extends* τ and write $\tau \preceq \tau'$ if

1) $k \leq k'$, and for $1 \leq i \leq k$, $p_i = p'_i$
2) $l \leq l'$, and for $1 \leq i \leq l$, $q_i = q'_i$
3) $\alpha \leq \gamma$.

2.2 First order languages

We start with a set of symbols for constructing languages. We say $\mathcal{L}_\tau$ is a *first order language of type* τ if

$$\mathcal{L}_\tau = \langle \langle r_1, \ldots, r_k \rangle, \langle f_1, \ldots, f_l \rangle, \langle c_\beta \rangle_{1 \leq \beta < \alpha} \rangle$$

where all the r_i, f_i and c_i are distinct symbols and by virtue of their appearance in $\mathcal{L}_\tau$:

(i) r_i is called a relation symbol of p_i arguments for $1 \leq i \leq k$;
(ii) f_i is called a function symbol of q_i arguments for $1 \leq i \leq l$;
(iii) c_i is called an individual constant symbol for $1 \leq i < \alpha$.

By the *symbols* of $\mathcal{L}_\tau$ we mean the set

$$\{r_1, \ldots, r_k, f_1, \ldots, f_l, c_\beta\}_{1 \leq \beta < \alpha}.$$

Terms and *formulae* of $\mathcal{L}_\tau$ are built up in the usual way from a countable set of individual variable symbols, *Var*, a countable set of individual parameter symbols, *Par*, the sentential connectives, $\wedge$ (and), $\vee$ (or), $\Rightarrow$ (implies), $\Leftrightarrow$ (equivalant), $\neg$ (not), and the quantifiers, $\forall$ (universal), and $\exists$ (existential) and $=$ (equal) (see Prawitz [4]). We say that e is an *expression* of (the language) $\mathcal{L}_\tau$, when e is either a term or a formula of $\mathcal{L}_\tau$.

Given two first order languages

$$\mathcal{L}_\tau = \langle\langle r_1, \ldots, r_k\rangle, \langle f_1, \ldots, f_l\rangle, \langle c_\beta\rangle_{1\leq\beta<\alpha}\rangle,$$

$$\mathcal{L}'_{\tau'} = \langle\langle r'_1, \ldots, r'_{k'}\rangle, \langle f'_1, \ldots, f'_{l'}\rangle, \langle c'_\beta\rangle_{1\leq\beta<\gamma}\rangle$$

we say $\mathcal{L}_\tau$ *is extended by* $\mathcal{L}'_{\tau'}$ or $\mathcal{L}'_{\tau'}$ *extends* $\mathcal{L}_\tau$ and write $\mathcal{L}_\tau \preceq \mathcal{L}'_{\tau'}$ if $\tau \preceq \tau'$, and corresponding symbols are the same, i.e.:

(i) $r_i = r'_i$ for $1 \leq i \leq k$;

(ii) $f_i = f'_i$ for $1 \leq i \leq l$;

(iii) $c_\beta = c'_\beta$ for $1 \leq \beta < \alpha$.

2.3 Partial structures

By a *partial structure of type* τ we mean a structure

$$\mathcal{M}_\tau = \langle M, \langle R_1, ..., R_k\rangle, \langle F_1, ..., F_l\rangle, \langle m_\beta\rangle_{1\leq\beta<\alpha}\rangle$$

where

(i) $R_i = \langle \underline{R}_i, \overline{R}_i\rangle$, $\underline{R}_i, \overline{R}_i \subset M^{p_i}$, and $\underline{R}_i \cap \overline{R}_i = \emptyset$ for $1 \leq i \leq k$

(ii) $F_i = \langle \phi_i, M_i\rangle$ where $M_i \subset M^{q_i}$ and $\phi_i : M_i \mapsto M \cup \{*\}$ for $1 \leq i \leq l$

(iii) $m_i \in M \cup \{*\}$ for $1 \leq i < \alpha$.

where $*$ is not in M. We call elements of M *values* and elements of $M \cup \{*\}$ *answers*.[1] When $\mathcal{M}_\tau$ is used as an interpretation of a first order language of the same similarity type $\underline{R}_i$ ($\overline{R}_i$) consists of those p_i-tuples of M which will be assigned the truth value *False*(*True*) in the interpretation of the relation symbol r_i. A partial structure does not necessarily assign a truth value to every tuple. We define $\mathrm{Dom}(F_i) = M_i$ and $\mathrm{Fun}(F_i) = \phi_i$. Each ϕ_i determines an answer for each tuple in M_i, but only provides an answer for every q_i-tuple of arguments if $M_i = M^{q_i}$. Unlike the ordinary definition of model we allow $*$ in the list of meanings for individual constant symbols. This will allow us to construct contexts that contain names for things even though the context itself cannot determine what things they name. The exact technical meaning of $*$ will be further elaborated below.

We call $\mathcal{M}_\tau$ a *total structure* if

(i) $M \neq \emptyset$

[1] Note that M could be empty. This should be interpreted as meaning that we simply can't recognize any elements of M, not that the intended domain is empty.

(ii) $\underline{R}_i \cup \overline{R}_i = M^{p_i}$ for $1 \leq i \leq k$;
(iii) $\phi_i : M^{q_i} \mapsto M$, (thus $M_i = M^{q_i}$) for $1 \leq i \leq l$;
(iv) $m_i \in M$ for $1 \leq i < \alpha$.
Given two partial structures

$$\mathcal{M}_\tau = \langle M, \langle R_1, \ldots, R_k \rangle, \langle F_1, \ldots, F_l \rangle, \langle m_\beta \rangle_{1 \leq \beta < \alpha} \rangle,$$
$$\mathcal{M}'_{\tau'} = \langle M', \langle R'_1, \ldots, R'_{k'} \rangle, \langle F'_1, \ldots, F'_{l'} \rangle, \langle m'_\beta \rangle_{1 \leq \beta < \gamma} \rangle$$

we say $\mathcal{M}_\tau$ *is extended by* $\mathcal{M}'_{\tau'}$ or $\mathcal{M}'_{\tau'}$ *extends* $\mathcal{M}_\tau$ and write $\mathcal{M}_\tau \preceq \mathcal{M}'_{\tau'}$ if
(i) $M \subseteq M'$,
(ii) $\underline{R}_i \subseteq \underline{R}'_i$ and $\overline{R}_i \subseteq \overline{R}'_i$ for $1 \leq i \leq k$,
(iii) $\mathrm{Dom}(F_i) \subseteq \mathrm{Dom}(F'_i)$,
(iv) if $\langle a_1, \ldots, a_{q_i} \rangle \in \mathrm{Dom}(F_i)$ and $\mathrm{Fun}(F_i)(a_1, \ldots, a_{q_i}) = a \in M$, then $\mathrm{Fun}(F'_i)(a_1, \ldots, a_{q_i}) = a$ for $1 \leq i \leq l$,
(v) if $m'_\beta = *$ or $m_\beta \neq *$, then $m_\beta = m'_\beta$ for $1 \leq \beta < \alpha$.

The empty partial structure of similarity type τ, is the structure

$$\mathcal{M}^{\emptyset}_\tau = \langle \emptyset, \langle R_1, ..., R_k \rangle, \langle F_1, ..., F_l \rangle, \langle m_\beta \rangle_{1 \leq \beta < \alpha} \rangle$$

where
(i) $R_i = \langle \underline{R}_i, \overline{R}_i \rangle$ with $\underline{R}_i = \overline{R}_i = \emptyset$, for $1 \leq i \leq k$,
(ii) $F_i = \langle \phi_i, M_i \rangle$ with $M_i = \emptyset$ for $1 \leq i \leq l$, and
(iii) $m_i = *$ for $1 \leq i < \alpha$.

The relation $\preceq$ defines a partial order on partial structures. For a fixed similarity type, τ, $\mathcal{M}^{\emptyset}_\tau$ is the least element, and for a fixed M the maximal structures of this order are the total structures, i.e. the models of $\mathcal{L}_\tau$ with domain M.

A *language/partial structure pair (L/P pair) of type* τ is a pair

$$\mathcal{P}_\tau = \langle \mathcal{L}_\tau, \mathcal{M}_\tau \rangle.$$

We say an expression is a term (formula) of $\mathcal{P}_\tau$ if it is a term (formula) of $\mathcal{L}_\tau$.

2.4 Values and Satisfaction

Suppose t is a term of $\mathcal{P}_\tau$. If t is the individual constant c_β, then

$$val[\mathcal{P}_\tau](c_\beta) = m_\beta.$$

Note that this value may be $*$. If t is of the form $f_i(t_1, \ldots, t_{q_i})$, and if $val[\mathcal{P}_\tau](t_j) = a_i$ for $1 \leq j \leq q_i$, then

$$val[\mathcal{P}_\tau](t) = \begin{cases} \phi_i(a_1, \ldots, a_{q_i})) & \text{if } \langle a_1, \ldots, a_{q_i} \rangle \in M_i \\ * & \text{otherwise.} \end{cases}$$

Since $M_i \subset M^{q_i}$ if any of $val[\mathcal{P}_\tau](t_1), \ldots, val[\mathcal{P}_\tau](t_{q_i})$ are $*$ then the value of $val[\mathcal{P}_\tau](t)$ is also $*$.

If A is an atomic well-formed formula of the form $r_i(t_1, \ldots, t_{p_i})$, then

$$sat[\mathcal{P}_\tau](A) = \begin{cases} True & \text{if } \langle val[\mathcal{P}_\tau](t_1), \ldots, val[\mathcal{P}_\tau](t_{p_i})\rangle \in \overline{R}_i \\ False & \text{if } \langle val[\mathcal{P}_\tau](t_1), \ldots, val[\mathcal{P}_\tau](t_{p_i})\rangle \in \underline{R}_i \\ * & \text{otherwise.} \end{cases}$$

Since both $\underline{R}_i$ and $\overline{R}_i$ are subsets of M^{p_i} if any of the

$$val[\mathcal{P}_\tau](t_1), \ldots, val[\mathcal{P}_\tau](t_{p_i})$$

are $*$ then the value of $sat[\mathcal{P}_\tau](A)$ is also $*$.

The definition of $sat[\mathcal{P}_\tau]$ for the propositional connectives uses the following tables.

p	$\neg p$
t	f
$*$	$*$
f	t

$\wedge$	t	$*$	f
t	t	$*$	f
$*$	$*$	$*$	f
f	f	f	f

$\vee$	t	$*$	f
t	t	t	t
$*$	t	$*$	$*$
f	t	$*$	f

$\supset$	t	$*$	f
t	t	$*$	f
$*$	t	$*$	$*$
f	t	t	t

$\equiv$	t	$*$	f
t	t	$*$	f
$*$	$*$	$*$	$*$
f	f	$*$	t

These tables look like the Kleene strong 3-valued logic [3], but we will provide a different interpretation below. Our interpretation is closer to that found in Feferman's [1]. $*$ can be read as "I don't know". In all cases $sat[\mathcal{P}_\tau](w) = *$ if w is a quantified formula.

We have written $sat[\mathcal{P}_\tau](w)$ and $val[\mathcal{P}_\tau](t)$ rather than $sat(\mathcal{P}_\tau, w)$ and $val(\mathcal{P}_\tau, t)$ to point out that *val* and *sat* are uniform in $\mathcal{P}_\tau$. This uniformity assures that *val* and *sat* are computable relative to $\mathcal{P}_\tau$. We restrict the domain of $sat[\mathcal{P}_\tau]$ and $val[\mathcal{P}_\tau]$ to be expressions of $\mathcal{P}_\tau$.

Reflection: We stop here to look at the remarks that we have just made, because, the fact that they make sense demonstrates the need for our reasoner to have incomplete theories of the world. We have just written that the domains of $sat[\mathcal{P}_\tau]$ and $val[\mathcal{P}_\tau]$ are restrictions, but, what is interesting is that we have not said restrictions of what. To be more concrete, suppose we imagine that we were reading this paper to our artificial reasoner. What would its "theory" of this paper contain? First, we have implicitly assumed that we do not need to fully understand the values of $sat[\mathcal{P}_\tau]$ and $val[\mathcal{P}_\tau]$ everywhere, but only where we expect to "look". Second, in normal discourse this assumption makes sense. This implies that our reasoner must have a semantically coherent idea (i.e., theory) of what we are presently discussing without knowing anything more about the domain.

Our point is that in order to make sense out of our current lack of complete information about the domain of these functions, we need exactly the kind of partial characterization of a "function" provided by the logic of FOL. That is, we know what the values of $sat[\mathcal{P}_\tau](e)$ and $val[\mathcal{P}_\tau](e)$ are when e is in the language of $\mathcal{P}_\tau$ and we do not need to know (or even think about) what they mean on other things. FOL allows for the possibility that these functions have useful values for other arguments but, since we aren't interested in them, our understanding, up to this point, has meaning, even if these values can never be specified. This demonstrates the sense in which $*$ is just a result of *val*—not the interpretation of an expression of $\mathcal{P}_\tau$.

2.5 The meaning of $*$

The usual formulation of model theory assumes that every individual constant has an assigned interpretation. In our formulation, we use $*$ to allow for the possibility of having an individual constant for which we do not have this information.

We carry this interpretation of $*$ into our definition of *val* and *sat*. Because we are considering only *partial* structures it is reasonable that we should not be able to determine what the "meanings" of some expressions of $\mathcal{L}_\tau$ are. Thus a reasonable reading of $*$ is "I don't know".

The important thing to understand about our interpretation of $*$ is that it is **not** to be thought of as a third truth value or as an arbitrary value which is taken by functions when they would have otherwise been "partial functions". The correct way of thinking about this is as follows:

If $val[\mathcal{P}_\tau](t) = *$ for some term t then we admit that the function *val* together with the structure $\mathcal{P}_\tau$ is simply not strong enough to find a value for t. We still imagine that t could be interpreted by perhaps some stronger *val* or in some extension of $\mathcal{P}_\tau$, but these are not the tools we have available.

The same interpretation is to be given to *sat*. We simply refuse to become immobilized if we do not have the tools to determine the truth or falsity of some sentence with respect to some partial structure. Instead we do what any mature function would do and admit defeat (by outputting $*$) once we decide the we cannot get an answer.

Reflection: Remember our goal is to build a reasoner. Thus, we eventually need to consider the case where even if the context is strong enough to determine an answer, our reasoner may lack the resources to finish some computation. The semantics of FOL systems will need to be robust under fatigue and laziness. The solution to this problem will be provided later by a more intensional look at FOL systems.

The above definition of *sat* may at first seem too weak. There are at least two complaints you might have. One is that a notion of satisfiability that does not decide **any** quantified formulas can not be very useful. To this we can only say: read on and judge later. As a matter of philosophical interest we might realize that the usual finitist position doesn't allow for the infinite searches implicit in deciding these sentences either.

Secondly, you might say that even if we don't allow such infinite searches we might still do better than we have. For example, we might be able to determine the truth of some existential sentences because we may know the interpretations of some constants. Our answer to this is simple—yes, sometimes we can do better, but what we propose will turn out to be enough. More important, is to recognize that this is an instance of the principle of *tolerance*. That is, nothing in the presentation below depends on the details the choice we have made as to *when* to stop looking for a value. If you want to work harder to determine the value of *sat* then that is fine. On the other hand, if you want to be lazy and simply return $*$ for the value of all terms, that is also an acceptable definition of *val*.

> *The important thing is not that you get a value (in M) but that that you can stop computing (that is, return $*$) whenever you choose.*

Of course, the phrase "stop computing" can not be explained using the extensional descriptions of FOL contexts given in this paper.

2.6 Facts

A *fact* in a language contains a formula of that language along with its associated dependencies. For the extensional formulation of this paper, dependencies can be thought of as lists of formulas. That is, a fact is analogous to a single conclusion sequent (cf. [2] p. 82, [4]). The usual definition of a theory in logic is a deductively closed, and therefore infinite, set of facts. In FOL contexts we drop the requirement of deductive closure. By not requiring a set of facts to be deductively closed, in FOL, as opposed to the classical notion of theory, we can distinguish between a set of facts and the set of consequences of these facts. Since mechanization will preclude our having an infinite set "in hand" we will be particularly interested in finite lists of facts.

2.7 FOL Contexts: The Notion of Theory as Structure

Informally a *theory* is a partial explanation of some aspect of the world. It is about some collection of objects; it has its own jargon (vocabulary) for describing the objects and the notions we have about them; and it provides facts about the objects expressed in this jargon. It is a *partial explanation* because in general not all questions that can be posed in the language can be determined on the basis of the theory.

The notion of a theory construed as a particular kind of structure is the central theme of the FOL philosophy. We call these structures FOL contexts. We claim that FOL contexts are the appropriate building block for giving a general explanation of both reasoning and cognition. An FOL context of type τ is a structure with three parts: a language $\mathcal{L}_T$; a partial structure, $\mathcal{M}_T$, containing some objects the language is talking about; and a list, $\mathcal{F}$, of facts.

$$C_T = \langle\langle \mathcal{L}_T, \mathcal{M}_T\rangle, \mathcal{F}\rangle.$$

We will usually write this more informally as $C = \langle \mathcal{L}, \mathcal{M}, \mathcal{F}\rangle$ or as $C = \langle \mathcal{P}, \mathcal{F}\rangle$ where $\mathcal{P} = \langle \mathcal{L}, \mathcal{M}\rangle$. We say a fact F is in C if F is an element of $\mathcal{F}$. In the following we often simply use the term *context* to mean an FOL context.

A context $C = \langle \mathcal{L}, \mathcal{M}, \mathcal{F}\rangle$ is said to be *consistent* (or *satisfiable*) if there is a total structure $\mathcal{M}'$ where $\mathcal{M} \preceq \mathcal{M}'$ and all the facts of $\mathcal{F}$ are classically true in $\mathcal{M}'$. Note that the notion of consistency is not changed if, in the above definition, we require $\mathcal{M}'$ to have the same similarity type as $\mathcal{M}$.

We call the context C a *traditional context* if $\mathcal{M}$ is the empty partial structure. Thus a traditional context has the form of a first-order axiom system.

2.8 Rules of inference

A function on contexts is said to be *consistency preserving* if it maps consistent contexts onto consistent contexts. We call such a consistency preserving map a *rule of inference.* A special case are maps that preserve the set of models. We call such a map a *valid rule of inference.*

Notice that traditional rules of inference used in the setting of FOL contexts give rise to consistency preserving maps on traditional contexts that leave the language constant, extend the list of facts, and are valid rules of inference. The facts of a context are not deductively closed. FOL contexts and rules of inference allow us to distinguish between the notion of *a fact of a context*, namely those facts which actually appear in the context, and *a consequence of a context*, which are those facts which could appear in some successor of a context after the application of some number of validity preserving rules of inference.

At first, it might seem that simply preserving the consistency of a context is a notion that is too weak to be interesting. However, taking this view, many ideas can be formulated in a natural way that are hard to understand when you take the usual view that the only interesting rules are the valid ones. Interesting consistency preserving maps on contexts arises when we look at formalizing the *activity* of reasoning. Consider the following: language additions are always consistency preserving; introducing definitions changes both language and facts; adding skolem functions changes both the language and the facts; most proofs of conservative extension results can be reinterpreted as proofs that certain maps on contexts are consistency preserving; and forgetting facts is another useful operation that cannot be formulated in the traditional setting. Other examples of consistency preserving operations on contexts are: making interpretations of one theory in another; modeling reasoning as an activity that takes place over time; and realizing various meta-theoretic results, such as interpreting the fundamental theorem of projective geometry (the duality of points and lines) as a rule for adding duals of existing facts.

There are many natural interpretations of other mappings. Consider contexts C whose language only contains individual constants and whose set of facts is empty. Logicians might call these contexts interpretations, computer scientists might call them memories or environments and mathematicians might say they are finite functions. Notice that **any** map from one of these structures to another is consistency preserving.

2.9 FOL Systems

An FOL system, S, is a finite sequence of FOL contexts, written:

$$\mathcal{S} = [\![\mathcal{C}_1, \ldots, \mathcal{C}_n]\!].$$

For any i, $1 \leq i \leq n$ we say that the context $\mathcal{C}_i$ is in $\mathcal{S}$. An FOL system is consistent if all the contexts it contains are consistent. We say ρ is a *consistency preserving map* on FOL systems if ρ maps consistent FOL systems to consistent FOL systems. We will also call these maps *rules of inference*. Let

$$\rho : [\![\mathcal{C}_1, \ldots, \mathcal{C}_n]\!] \mapsto [\![\mathcal{C}'_1, \ldots, \mathcal{C}'_m]\!]$$

be a rule of inference. Sometimes we will want to put additional constraints on these maps, that is, there is some additional properties P that ρ should preserve.

$$P([\![\mathcal{C}_1, \ldots, \mathcal{C}_n]\!]) \Rightarrow P(\rho([\![\mathcal{C}_1, \ldots, \mathcal{C}_n]\!])$$

One obvious idea is to fix a set of rules of inference and then ask what properties of systems are preserved by these rules. An even more important idea is to fix a property P and ask what rules preserve P. Such a P represents a class of systems, and the allowed rules tell you the ways in which a system can evolve. Many problems of philosophy, cognitive science, and artificial intelligence can be formulated as an appropriate choice of a property P and a set of P-preserving rules of inference. Some examples are simple theories (mathematical and common sense), meta theoretic reasoning, states of knowledge that change over time, the use of more than one modal operator at a time, non-monotonic principles of reasoning, etc.

3 Examples

We now give two examples of how the above "reorganization" of ordinary logic improves our ability to naturally formalize the activity of reasoning. The first is an inference rule that provides access to the semantic information available in an FOL context. The second is the description of an FOL context for an extension of Peano arithmetic that illustrates many of the subtle distinctions that are available.

3.1 Semantic evaluation rule

By having partial structures as part of contexts we can examine semantic information as part of a deduction. A simple example of an inference rule that uses semantic information is *Srule*. *Srule* takes a context and a term or a formula in the language of that context. It either tries to find a constant whose value is the same as that of the term (using *val*), or the truth value of the formula (using *sat*). If it succeeds, the result is added to the context. Otherwise the context is unchanged. If $\mathcal{C} = \langle \mathcal{P}, \mathcal{F} \rangle$, and e is a term or formula of $\mathcal{C}$, then

$$Srule(\mathcal{C}, e) = \langle \mathcal{P}, \mathcal{F} \circ Sval[\mathcal{P}](e) \rangle$$

where $Sval[\mathcal{P}](e)$ is defined as follows. If t is a term of $\mathcal{C}$, then

$$Sval[\mathcal{P}](t) = \begin{cases} \langle t = c_\beta \rangle & \text{if } val[\mathcal{P}](t) = m_\beta \neq * \\ \langle\, \rangle & \text{otherwise.} \end{cases}$$

If w is a formula of $\mathcal{C}$, then

$$Sval[\mathcal{P}]w = \begin{cases} \langle w \rangle & \text{if } sat[\mathcal{P}](w) = True \\ \langle \neg w \rangle & \text{if } sat[\mathcal{P}](w) = False \\ \langle\, \rangle & \text{if } sat[\mathcal{P}](w) = * \end{cases}$$

Note that *Srule* is a valid inference rule.

3.2 An FOL Context for Peano Arithmetic

We illustrate the construction of an FOL context by showing one way to formalize a variant of Peano arithmetic. We call this context PA^+. The similarity type of PA^+ is

$$\tau_{PA^+} = \langle \langle 2 \rangle, \langle 2, 1, 1 \rangle, \omega \rangle.$$

In this similarity type $p = \langle 2 \rangle$, $p_1 = 2$, $q = \langle 2, 1, 1 \rangle$, $q_1 = 2$, $q_2 = 1$, $q_3 = 1$, and $\alpha = \omega$.

The language of PA^+ is

$$\mathcal{L}_{PA^+} = \langle \langle < \rangle, \langle \times, s, p \rangle, \langle \overline{n} \rangle_{0 \leq n < \omega} \rangle.$$

If instead we had defined $\mathcal{L}_{PA^+}$ as

$$\mathcal{L}_{PA^+} = \langle \langle < \rangle, \langle \times, p, s \rangle, \langle \overline{n} \rangle_{0 \leq n < \omega} \rangle.$$

by switching the order of s and p then, from our intensional point of view, this is a different language of type τ_{PA^+}, which happens to contain the same symbols as $\mathcal{L}_{PA^+}$. The similarity type tells us that $<$ is a binary relation symbol, $\times$, s, and p are function symbols with $\times$ taking two arguments, and s and p taking only taking one. We write $\overline{n}$ for the nth numeral.

In order to illustrate some important points we define a weak partial structure of similarity type τ_{PA^+}. Let $\mathcal{N}$ be the set of non-negative integers and +1 the successor function on $\mathcal{N}$.

$$\mathcal{M}_{PA^+} = \langle \mathcal{N}, \langle\langle R_< \rangle, \langle M_*, M_s, M_* \rangle, \langle *, 1, 2, *, \ldots, *, \ldots \rangle\rangle.$$

where

$R_< = \langle \underline{R}_<, \overline{R}_< \rangle$

$\underline{R}_< = \{\langle 3, 1 \rangle\}$

$\overline{R}_< = \{\langle 1, 2 \rangle\}$

$M_s = \langle +1, \mathcal{N} \rangle$

$M_* = \langle \emptyset, \emptyset \rangle$

The domain of the partial structure is the set $\mathcal{N}$. There is only one relation $R_< = \langle \underline{R}_<, \overline{R}_< \rangle$. Looking at $\underline{R}_<$ and $\overline{R}_<$ we see that the *only* thing we know about "less than" is: 3 "less than" 1 is false and 1 "less than" 2 is true.

When written in parallel lines, the L/P pair $\mathcal{P}_{PA^+}$ associating the language $\mathcal{L}_{PA^+}$ with the partial $\mathcal{M}_{PA^+}$ structure looks like

$$\begin{array}{llllllllll} \langle\ \langle\ \ < & \rangle, \langle \times, & s, & p\ \rangle, & \langle \overline{0}, & \overline{1}, & \overline{2}, & \overline{3}, \ldots, & \overline{n}, \ldots \rangle\ \rangle \\ \langle \mathcal{N}\ \langle\{\langle 3,1\rangle\},\{\langle 1,2\rangle\}\rangle, & \langle M_*, & M_s, & M_* \rangle, & \langle *, & 1, & 2, & *, \ldots, & *, \ldots \rangle\ \rangle \end{array}$$

Thus context PA^+ is

$$PA^+ = \langle \mathcal{P}_{PA^+}, \mathcal{F}_{PA^+} \rangle = \langle \mathcal{L}_{PA^+}, \mathcal{M}_{PA^+}, \mathcal{F}_{PA^+} \rangle$$

where $\mathcal{F}_{PA^+}$ is some set of facts (possibly empty) expressed in $\mathcal{L}_{PA^+}$ which we leave unspecified for now. Although this choice of context may seem a little bizarre, it illustrates several important points about FOL contexts in a familiar setting. First let us look at valuation and satisfaction in our L/P pair for Peano Arithmetic.

(v.1)) $val[\mathcal{P}_{PA^+}](\overline{1}) = 1$

(v.2) $val[\mathcal{P}_{PA^+}](\overline{0}) = *$ because there is no interpretation for $\overline{0}$

(v.3) $val[\mathcal{P}_{PA^+}](s(s(\overline{1}))) = 3$

(v.4) $val[\mathcal{P}_{PA^+}](p(\overline{2})) = *$ because there is no interpretation for p

(v.5) $val[\mathcal{P}_{PA^+}](\overline{1} \times \overline{2}) = *$ because there is no interpretation for $\times$

(s.1) $sat[\mathcal{P}_{PA^+}](\overline{1} < \overline{1}) = *$ because there is no information about the pair $\langle 1, 1 \rangle$ contianed in $R_<$.

(s.2) $sat[\mathcal{P}_{PA^+}](\overline{1} < \overline{2}) = \mathit{True}$

(s.3) $sat[\mathcal{P}_{PA^+}](\overline{3} < \overline{1}) = *$ because there is no interpretation for $\overline{3}$.

(s.4) $sat[\mathcal{P}_{PA^+}](s(\overline{2}) < \overline{1}) = \mathit{False}$ even though there is no name for 3, since $val[\mathcal{P}_{PA^+}](s(\overline{2})) = 3$ we have $\langle val[\mathcal{P}_{PA^+}](s(\overline{2})), val[\mathcal{P}_{PA^+}](\overline{1}) \rangle \in \underline{R}_<$.

Now we consider application of the semantic evaluation inference rules. The following are some examples.

(sv.1) $Sval[\mathcal{P}_{PA^+}](\overline{1}) = \langle \overline{1} = \overline{1} \rangle$

(sv.2) $Sval[\mathcal{P}_{PA^+}](\overline{0}) = \langle\ \rangle$
(sv.3) $Sval[\mathcal{P}_{PA^+}](s(\overline{1})) = \langle s(\overline{1}) = \overline{2}\rangle$, but $Sval[\mathcal{P}_{PA^+}](s(s(\overline{1}))) = \langle\ \rangle$ since $val[\mathcal{P}_{PA^+}](s(s(\overline{1})))$ gives an value that doesn't have an associated individual constant;

(ss.1) $Sval[\mathcal{P}_{PA^+}](\overline{1} < \overline{1}) = \langle\ \rangle$
(ss.2) $Sval[\mathcal{P}_{PA^+}](\overline{3} < \overline{1}) = \langle\ \rangle$
(ss.3) $Sval[\mathcal{P}_{PA^+}](s(\overline{2}) < \overline{1}) = \langle \neg(s(\overline{2}) < \overline{1})\rangle$

A more aggressive rule for accessing semantic information is *semantic simplification*. This rule tries to simplify subterms if simplification of the full term fails. In this case we would have $Sval[\mathcal{P}_{PA^+}](s(s(\overline{1}))) = \langle s(s(\overline{1})) = s(\overline{2})\rangle$.

The partialness of FOL contexts allows us to have a multitude of different choices for representing Peano Arithmetic. Even fixing the language and axioms there are many interesting choices for the partial structure. These include a partial structure in which all function and relation symbols are total, a partial structure that uses finite precision arithmetic (for example + on FIXNUMs), semantic representation of numbers base 10 with the usual grade school plus and times tables and rules for addition and multiplication using carrying.

4 Conclusion

In this paper we presented a description of the logic of FOL in set theory. Our purpose is to generalize the ideas of first order logic and model theoretic semantics in a way that can take into account both the partial nature and the dynamic quality of the actual activity of reasoning. At first glance it might not seem radically different from the traditional formalizations of logic, but in fact, we have taken great care in the choice of notions and the details of their generalizations so that we can later directly replace these notions with their more intensional counterparts. First order languages, that is, infinite sets of formulas, have been replaced by finite structures for which there is a uniform way of recognizing well formed expressions. Models have been replaced by partial structures that can correctly represent our incomplete understanding of a subject and, given a reasonable notion of computation, can be interpreted as a set of programs and data objects. Theories, which are traditionally a deductively closed infinite set of formulas, have been replaced by FOL contexts which contain a finite sets of facts. New facts can then be added to FOL contexts using our generalization of rule of inference.

In the next paper in this series we will reinterpret each "set" mentioned in this paper, by a "recognizer" described in some computation theory. A recognizer, r, is a function that, for any object, x, either says "yes", "no", or "I don't know". In this sense a recognizer, unlike a characteristic function, partially determines a set, S: if $r(x)$ is yes, then x is in S; and if $r(x)$ is no, then x is not in S. We use recognizers because *every* set has a recursively realizable recognizer–and this, of course, is not true for characteristic functions. The notions underlying the theory presented in this paper then can be reconstructed from recognizers. Further we will show that all of the functions and relations mentioned in this paper can be constructed uniformly from a finite set of computable recognizers which we will explicitly present. The uniformity guarantees that we can construct computable recognizers for all of the functions and relations mentioned in this paper.

With the reduction of classical theories to FOL systems we realize two goals at the same time. In the large, FOL systems themselves can be thought of as structures that know and that can learn over time. In the small FOL systems can be used to axiomatize specific problem domains. By using these two aspects of FOL systems together, we have the seeds of an artificial mind.

Acknowledgments. This research was partially supported by DARPA contract NAG2-703, NSF grants CCR-8917606 and CCR-8915663, and by IBUKI.

References

1. S. Feferman. Non-extensional type-free theories of partial operations and classifications, i. In J. Diller and G. H. Müller, editors, *Proof theory symposium, Kiel 1974*, number 500 in Lecture notes in mathematics, pages 73–118. Springer, Berlin, 1975.
2. G. Gentzen. *The Collected Papers of Gerhard Gentzen.* North-Holland, 1969.
3. S. C. Kleene. *Introduction to metamathematics.* North-Holland, Amsterdam, 1952.
4. D. Prawitz. *Natural Deduction: A Proof-theoretical Study.* Almquist and Wiksell, 1965.

Well-Ordering of Algebras and Kruskal's Theorem

Ryu Hasegawa

LIENS, 45 rue d'Ulm, 75230 Paris Cedex 05, France
RIMS, Kyoto University, Sakyo-ku, Kyoto, 606 Japan

Abstract. We define well-partial-orderings on abstract algebras and give their order types. For every ordinal in an initial segment of the Bachmann hierarchy there is one and only one (up to isomorphism) algebra giving the ordinal as order type. As a corollary, we show Kruskal-type theorems for various structures are equivalent to well-orderedness of certain ordinals.

1 Introduction

The main theorem we prove in this paper is that the class of algebras yields a system of ordinal notations. Before making the assertion precise, we enumerate the consequences derived from the theorem: (1) we give the order types of well-partial-orders on abstract algebras; (2) Kruskal-type theorems for abstract algebras are shown to be equivalent to well-orderedness of ordinals; (3) we calculate the order types of lexicographic path orderings for abstract algebras.

The notion of well-partial-order (and generally well-quasi-order) began to appear around 1950 in the literature, for example, by Erdös and Rado, and Higman. After the celebrated work by Higman [20], this simple notion has found a large number of applications in the fields of algebras, combinatorics, mathematical logic, and computer science. One of the most elegant is Kruskal's theorem [23,28], asserting the class of finite trees is a well-partial-order with respect to the topological embedding. In the 80's, the theorem and its extension due to Friedman were used to prove the graph minor theorem by Robertson and Seymour [32] in combinatorics, and to give independence results for strong segments of second order arithmetic [14,36] in mathematical logic, and to give useful methods to prove the termination of programs [8] in computer science.

We define a class of (abstract) algebras and partial orders (called embeddings) on them. The class of algebras is generated from an empty set and singletons by disjoint sum $+$, direct product $\times$, and the least fixpoint without nested recursion. The embedding on each algebra is defined as the divisibility ordering by Higman [20]. It is not hard to see that the embeddings are well-partial-orders.

A well-partial-order is by definition a partially ordered set that has no infinite bad sequences (See Section 2 for definition). Therefore the collection of all finite bad sequences of the well-partial-order makes a well-founded tree. Important among the properties of the well-partial-orderings is the order type, which is by definition simply the order type of the associated well-founded tree of all bad sequences. In section 2, we give two other characterizations of the order type. The one is the least ordinal reifying the well-partial-ordering, and the other is the greatest ordinal of linearizations. The reification proves well-partial-orderedness from well-orderedness, and conversely the linearization proves well-orderedness from well-partial-orderedness. Therefore knowing the order type, we may prove well-partial-orderedness from well-orderedness of the order type, and vice versa.

The substantial part of this paper is devoted to calculating the order types of the well-partial-orders of the algebra embeddings. The result is interesting in its own right. The following is our main theorem:

> *The map assigning the order type to each algebra is a bijection from the class of algebras to an initial segment of the class of ordinals.*

The initial segment is the class of ordinals up to $\varphi(\Omega^\omega, 0)$ in Bachmann hierarchy. Given two algebras, the order types of the embeddings on them are always different unless they have an isomorphism determined by simple rules. Furthermore for each ordinal α less than $\varphi(\Omega^\omega, 0)$ there is a (unique up to isomorphism) algebra whose embedding gives the order type α.

From this theorem several consequences are derived. The most immediate is that one may regard the class of algebras as a system of ordinal notations. This system has some new features in comparison with the traditional systems. Notably every notation has a meaning in our system. For example, consider the ordinal Γ_0, which has a meaning as the least strongly critical ordinal [17]. But what has a meaning is the ordinal itself, not the notation assigned to it. So the notations assigned to Γ_0 differ in one system to others. In Bachmann hierarchy it is denoted by $\varphi(\Omega, 0)$; in Buchholz notation [3] $\psi_0 \Omega^\Omega$, etc. In our system, it is denoted by $\mu X.\, 2X^2 + 1$, which is because the order type of the algebra $\mu X.\, 2X^2 + 1$ is Γ_0. There is still freedom of notations since $\mu X.\, 2X^2 + 1$ is not a unique notation for the algebra. However what is important is that we find an entity, other than the class of ordinals, naturally having a well-order thereon.

Another consequence is that we establish the equivalence of well-partial-orderedness of the algebra embeddings and well-orderedness of the ordinals that are the order types of the embeddings. The merit of this equivalence is apparent if one is concerned with proof theory. After a work of Gentzen on first order arithmetic, it is well-known that well-orderedness of large ordinals is independent from logical systems, especially fragments of second order arithmetic. For example, the ordinal ϵ_0 is independent from system ACA_0, which is a conservative extension of Peano arithmetic. Therefore our main theorem implies that well-partial-orderedness of the embedding on the algebra $\mu X.\, X^2 + 1$ of binary trees is independent from ACA_0. In other words, Kruskal's theorem for binary trees is unprovable in system ACA_0. Several results are found in Section 6.

For the calculation of lower bounds of order types of algebra embeddings, we use a version of recursive path ordering, which is a family of well-orderings most often used to prove the terminations of term rewriting systems. We associate a well-ordering called Ackermann ordering to each algebra. The ordering may be regarded as a lexicographic path ordering if we view the algebra as the collection of terms. We give the order types of the orderings in Section 6. The order types are greater than those of the recursive path orderings that are defined using multiset orderings.

2 Preliminaries

In this section, we give definitions for well-partial-orders and classic results.

A *partial order* is a set endowed with a binary relation $\trianglelefteq$ that is reflexive, transitive and anti-symmetric. A *total order* is a partial order where every two elements a, b are comparable; namely, one of $a \trianglelefteq b$ and $b \trianglelefteq a$ holds. A *bad sequence* in a partial order A is a sequence $\langle a_0, \ldots, a_n(, \ldots)\rangle$ (finite or infinite) of members of A satisfying $\forall i < j.\, a_i \ntrianglelefteq a_j$.

2.1 Definition

A *well-partial-order* is a partial order that has no infinite bad sequences. □

The order-reflecting maps are important as morphisms of well-partial-orders, since they send bad sequences to bad sequences. Here a map $f : A \to B$ of partial orders reflects order if and only if $f(a) \trianglelefteq_B f(a')$ implies $a \trianglelefteq_A a'$ for all a, a' of A. As an immediate consequence, every order-reflecting map reflects also the property of being a well-partial-order, namely the following holds:

2.2 Proposition

If $f : A \to B$ is an order-reflecting map of partial-orders and B is a well-partial-order, then A is a well-partial-order. □

Among well-partial-orders the following two are well-known. The one is Higman embedding on finite lists of members of a partial order and the other is the (homeomorphic) tree embedding of finite trees. First we give the definitions of these embeddings.

2.3 Definition

Let $\langle A, \prec\rangle$ be a partial order and A^* the set of finite lists of members of A.

The *Higman embedding* $\trianglelefteq_{hig}$ is a partial order on A^* defined as follows: $\langle a_0, \ldots, a_{m-1}\rangle \trianglelefteq_{hig} \langle a'_0, \ldots, a'_{n-1}\rangle$ if and only if there is a strictly monotonic map $f : m \to n$ such that $a_i \prec a'_{f(i)}$ for all $i < m$. □

A finite *ordered* tree is a finite tree with root where for each node there is a linear order on the set of immediate successors. A finite *non-ordered* tree is a finite tree with root without orders on immediate successors. We denote a finite ordered tree t by $t\langle t/0, \ldots, t/(n-1)\rangle$ where $t/0, \ldots, t/(n-1)$ are the immediate successors of the root in this order. As for non-ordered trees, we use the notation $t\{t/0, \ldots, t/(n-1)\}$.

2.4 Definition

The *tree embedding* $\trianglelefteq_T$ is a partial order on the set T of finite ordered trees, the order defined as follows: $t\langle t/0, \ldots, t/(m-1)\rangle \trianglelefteq_T t'\langle t'/0, \ldots, t'/(n-1)\rangle$ if and only if either

(i) $t \trianglelefteq_T t'/j$ for some $j < n$; or

(ii) there is a strictly monotonic function $f : m \to n$ such that $t/i \trianglelefteq_T t/f(i)$ for all $i < m$. □

If the node degree is fixed (e.g. binary trees) the assertion (ii) is replaced simply by that $t/i \trianglelefteq_T t'/i$ for all $i < m$. The tree embedding is also defined for non-ordered finite trees by imposing the condition that f is injection in place that f is strictly monotonic. The following two theorems assert that the Higman embedding and the tree embedding are well-partial-orders.

2.5 Theorem

(i) (Higman's Lemma) If A is a well-partial-order, then A^* is a well-partial-order with respect to the Higman embedding.

(ii) (Kruskal's Theorem) The set of finite ordered trees is a well-partial-order with respect to the tree embedding. □

Vazsonyi's conjecture was well-partial-orderedness for non-ordered trees, but Kruskal indeed proved the theorem for ordered trees and derived Vazsonyi's conjecture from that [23]. For a simpler proof by Nash-Williams using the so-called minimal bad sequence argument, we refer the reader to [28,17,36]. The proof is worth comment in two respects; it uses a non-constructive argument in an essential way, and also an impredicative argument. In fact, to formalize the proof one needs a fragment of second order arithmetic having Π^1_1-comprehension axiom or its substitute, e.g. bar induction on recursive well-founded relation.

2.6 Notation

Bad(A) denotes the tree of all finite bad sequences of a given partial order A. □

The tree *Bad*(A) is well-founded if and only if A is a well-partial-order. So the structure of the well-founded tree *Bad*(A) has a lot of information on the structure of well-partial-order A. In particular, the order type $|$*Bad*$(A)|$ of the well-founded tree is of great importance. Let T be a well-founded tree. We assign an ordinal $|\sigma|$ to each node σ by the following definition:

$$|\sigma| = \sup\{|\sigma'| + 1 \mid \sigma' \text{ is an immediate successor of } \sigma\}.$$

Then the order type $|T|$ of well-founded tree T is defined by the ordinal $|\langle\ \rangle|$ assigned to the root $\langle\ \rangle$ of T.

2.7 Definition

The *order type* of a well-partial-order A is the order type $|Bad(A)|$ of the well-founded tree $Bad(A)$. □

Note that well-orderedness of $|T|$ is equivalent to well-foundedness of T. Hence well-orderedness of the tree $|Bad(A)|$ is equivalent to well-partial-orderedness of A. It is difficult, however, to calculate the ordinal $|Bad(A)|$ concretely. The main techniques are the reification [37] and the linearization, where the reification gives upper bounds and the linearization lower bounds.

2.8 Definition

Let A be a partial order and α an ordinal.

A *reification* of A by α is a map $r : Bad(A) \to \alpha + 1$ satisfying $\sigma \subset \tau \Rightarrow r(\sigma) > r(\tau)$. (Notation: $\sigma \subset \tau$ denotes that the sequence σ is a proper initial segment of τ.) □

It is immediate to see that if a partial order A has a reification by an ordinal α, then $WO(\alpha)$ implies $Wpo(A)$. An example of reification is the assignment $|\cdot|$ given above. In fact, by recursion on the well-founded tree $Bad(A)$, we can show that the reification $|\cdot|$ is the least one: if r is a reification then $|\sigma| < r(\sigma)$ for every node σ of $|Bad(A)|$. Namely the following proposition holds.

2.9 Proposition

If a partial order A has a reification by an ordinal α, then $|Bad(A)| \leq \alpha$. □

Here for the inequality $\leq$, we cannot drop the equality. The assignment $|\cdot|$ gives a reification by the ordinal $|Bad(A)|$. This proposition shows that reifications provide upper bounds of $|Bad(A)|$. As for lower bounds, they are obtained by linearizations.

2.10 Definition

Let $\langle A, \trianglelefteq\rangle$ be a partial order.

A *linearization* of A is a total order $\sqsubseteq$ on A finer than $\trianglelefteq$, namely, the total order $\sqsubseteq$ for which $a \trianglelefteq a' \Rightarrow a \sqsubseteq a'$ holds. □

If $\langle A, \sqsubseteq\rangle$ is a linearization of a well-partial-order $\langle A, \trianglelefteq\rangle$, then $\langle A, \sqsubseteq\rangle$ becomes a well-order. It is this property that was used in [8] to prove that the simplification ordering terminates. The following proposition asserts that the linearization gives lower bounds of the order types of well-partial-orders.

2.11 Proposition
If a well-partial-order A has a linearization of order type α, then $\alpha \leq Bad(A)$.

(*Proof*) Let T be the well-founded tree of finite descending sequences with respect to the total order given by the linearization. Then $T \subseteq Bad(A)$ and so $\alpha = |T| \leq |Bad(A)|$. $\square$

In this proposition, we cannot omit the equality of $\leq$, In fact, the following is proved in [7]. Let $|Lin(A)|$ be the ordinal

$$\sup\{|\langle A, \sqsubseteq\rangle| \ : \ \langle A, \sqsubseteq\rangle \text{ is a linearization}\}.$$

De Jongh and Parikh proved that there is a linearization of order type $|Lin(A)|$. In other words, sup can be replaced by max. We can show that $|Lin(A)|$ is equal to $|Bad(A)|$, and so there is a linearization of order type $|Bad(A)|$.

Therefore if one finds an ordinal α giving both reification and linearization, then the order type $|Bad(A)|$ of well-partial-order A turns out to be equal to the ordinal α. In addition, well-partial-orderedness of A is equivalent to well-orderedness of α in the logic necessary to prove the reification and the linearization.

In order to calculate the order types of well-partial-orders, we need some ordinal notations. In later sections, we will use the class of algebras as a system of ordinal notations. We will compare the system with the Bachmann hierarchy. We refer the reader to [18] for definitions and basic properties of Bachmann hierarchy. $\langle\varphi(\alpha, \text{-})\rangle$ denotes the family of normal functions in the hierarchy. We use also the family $\langle\overline{\varphi}(\alpha, \text{-})\rangle$ modified so that $\overline{\varphi}(\text{-}, \text{-})$ becomes one-to-one. We use $\oplus$ for the natural sum of ordinals and $\otimes$ for the natural product. For the definition, see [37]. Therein we can find also the definition of additively indecomposable ordinals and multiplicatively indecomposable ordinals.

3 Discontinuity of Higman Embeddings

In this section we give an analysis of Higman embedding from the calculation of order types. The results in this section will be derived from more general theorems in later sections. A strange property of Higman embedding, however, leads us to what we want to prove later. The anomaly we show here is that, whereas the definition of Higman embedding is completely uniform on the base partial order, the order type of Higman embedding is not continuous on the order type of the base well-partial-order.

For Higman's lemma, proofs without using the minimal bad sequence argument were known to many researchers [34,37,27,31,6]. Schütte and Simpson gave a reification of Higman's embedding [34,37]. They proved that if the base partial order A is a well-partial-order and has a reification by ordinal α, then the Higman embedding has a reification $\omega^{\omega^{\alpha+1}}$. By a closer inspection, however, we see that this last ordinal is not the least reification ordinal in most cases.

We give the exact order types for Higman embedding by analyzing the proof by Schütte and Simpson. We show the order types are $\omega^{\omega^{\alpha}}$ in some cases, and $\omega^{\omega^{\alpha+1}}$ in the other. If the reification ordinal of the base partial order is of the form $\epsilon_\gamma+n$, epsilon number plus a finite number, then the order type of Higman embedding must be $\omega^{\omega^{\alpha+1}}$; otherwise $\omega^{\omega^{\alpha}}$ (if α is finite, then $\omega^{\omega^{-1+\alpha}}$). This means that the order types of Higman embedding fills all multiplicatively indecomposable ordinals *except* epsilon numbers. Therefore there are no well-partial-orders whose Higman embedding yields an epsilon number as the order type.

This observation is our start point. In later sections, we show these gaps at epsilon numbers are filled with other structures (binary trees, etc.). In fact, we show more: every ordinal up to $\varphi(\Omega^\omega, 0)$ in Bachmann hierarchy is filled up with a structure (called an *algebra*), and furthermore there is no superposition, namely, every ordinal is filled up with a unique algebra. The Higman embedding has gaps at all epsilon numbers, and these gaps are filled with other algebras. For example, the ordinal ϵ_0 is with the algebra of binary trees.

The following is a sketch of the reification of Higman embedding given in [37]. We prove the following theorem.

3.1 Theorem

If A is a well-partial-order of order type α, then Higman embedding on A^* has the order type of the following:

$$\begin{cases} \omega^{\omega^{\alpha-1}} & \text{if } \alpha = n \text{ finite} \\ \omega^{\omega^{\alpha}} & \text{if } \alpha = \beta + n \text{ where } \beta \text{ is a limit, not an epsilon number} \\ \omega^{\omega^{\alpha+1}} & \text{if } \alpha = \beta + n \text{ where } \beta \text{ is a limit, an epsilon number} \end{cases} \quad \Box$$

3.2 Notation

$s, s_1, \ldots$ for members of A
$S, S_1, \ldots$ for members of $Bad(A)$
$\sigma, \sigma_1, \ldots$ for members of A^*
$\Sigma, \Sigma_1, \ldots$ for members of $Bad(A^*)$ □

For a partial order $\langle A, \trianglelefteq \rangle$ and $s \in A$,

$$A_s =_{def} \{t \in A \mid s \ntrianglelefteq t\};$$

and for $S \in Bad(A)$,

$$A_S =_{def} \{t \in A \mid S\,\hat{}\,\langle t \rangle \in Bad(A)\}.$$

Note that for the sequence $\langle s \rangle$ of length one, $A_s = A_{\langle s \rangle}$ holds. To each $\Sigma \in Bad(A^*)$, we associate a set of the form $\coprod_i \prod_j B_{ij}$ (finite disjoint union of finite product) where the summand $\prod_j B_{ij}$ is of the form

$$(A_{S_1})^* \times A_{S'_1} \times (A_{S_2})^* \times A_{S'_2} \times \cdots \times A_{S'_{m-1}} \times (A_{S_m})^* \qquad (m \geq 1),$$

as well as a one-to-one map $h_\Sigma : (A^*)_\Sigma \hookrightarrow \coprod_i \prod_j B_{ij}$. If the bad sequence Σ is extended to $\Sigma\hat{}\langle\sigma\rangle$ where $\sigma \in (A^*)_\Sigma$, a new set $\coprod_i \prod_j B'_{ij}$ is defined by decomposing the summand such that $h_\Sigma(\sigma) \in \prod_j B_{i_0 j}$ into a disjoint sum as in Figure 1. There we suppose

$$\begin{aligned} h_\Sigma(\sigma) = {} & \langle \sigma_1, s_{n_1}, \sigma_2, s_{n_2}, \ldots, s_{n_{m-1}}, \sigma_m \rangle \\ & \in (A_{S_1})^* \times A_{S'_1} \times (A_{S_2})^* \times A_{S'_2} \times \cdots \times A_{S'_{m-1}} \times (A_{S_m})^*. \end{aligned}$$

and after the decomposition, the product $\times$ is distributed over the disjoint sum $+$ in order to maintain the form of $\coprod_i \prod_j B_{ij}$.

$$\begin{array}{lllllll}
((A_{S_1})^*)_{\sigma_1} & \times A_{S'_1} & \times (A_{S_2})^* & \times A_{S'_2} & \times \cdots \times & A_{S'_{m-1}} & \times (A_{S_m})^* \\
+ (A_{S_1})^* & \times (A_{S'_1})_{s_{n_1}} & \times (A_{S_2})^* & \times A_{S'_2} & \times \cdots \times & A_{S'_{m-1}} & \times (A_{S_m})^* \\
+ (A_{S_1})^* & \times A_{S'_1} & \times ((A_{S_2})^*)_{\sigma_2} & \times A_{S'_2} & \times \cdots \times & A_{S'_{m-1}} & \times (A_{S_m})^* \\
+ (A_{S_1})^* & \times A_{S'_1} & \times (A_{S_2})^* & \times (A_{S'_2})_{s_{n_2}} & \times \cdots \times & A_{S'_{m-1}} & \times (A_{S_m})^* \\
\vdots & & & & & & \\
+ (A_{S_1})^* & \times A_{S'_1} & \times (A_{S_2})^* & \times A_{S'_2} & \times \cdots \times & (A_{S'_{m-1}})_{s_{n_{m-1}}} & \times (A_{S_m})^* \\
+ (A_{S_1})^* & \times A_{S'_1} & \times (A_{S_2})^* & \times A_{S'_2} & \times \cdots \times & A_{S'_{m-1}} & \times ((A_{S_m})^*)_{\sigma_m}
\end{array}$$

where (with an abuse of notation), for $\sigma_i = \langle s_{n_{i-1}+1}, s_{n_{i-1}+2}, \ldots, s_{n_i-1} \rangle$,

$$\begin{aligned}
((A_{S_i})^*)_{\sigma_i} = {} & \\
& (A_{S_i\hat{}\langle s_{n_{i-1}+1}\rangle})^* \\
& + (A_{S_i\hat{}\langle s_{n_{i-1}+1}\rangle})^* \times A_{S_i} \times (A_{S_i\hat{}\langle s_{n_{i-1}+2}\rangle})^* \\
& \vdots \\
& + (A_{S_i\hat{}\langle s_{n_{i-1}+1}\rangle})^* \times A_{S_i} \times (A_{S_i\hat{}\langle s_{n_{i-1}+2}\rangle})^* \times \cdots \times A_{S_i} \times (A_{S_i\hat{}\langle s_{n_i-1}\rangle})^*
\end{aligned}$$

Figure 1

The reification given in [37] is as follows. Suppose the base well-partial-order has a reification $|\ | : Bad(A) \to \alpha+1$. Let $(A^*)\breve{}_\Sigma$ denote the set $\coprod_i \prod_j B_{ij}$ associated to $\Sigma \in Bad(A)$. If we find an ordinal assignment $|(A^*)\breve{}_\Sigma|$ to each $(A^*)\breve{}_\Sigma$ so that $|(A^*)\breve{}_\Sigma| > |(A^*)\breve{}_{\Sigma\hat{}\langle\sigma\rangle}|$ then the required reification is obtained by the mapping $\Sigma \mapsto |(A^*)\breve{}_\Sigma|$. The assignment satisfying this condition is given as follows: for each $(A^*)\breve{}_\Sigma = \coprod_i \prod_j B_{ij}$ we assign an ordinal by $|(A^*)\breve{}_\Sigma| = \bigoplus_i \bigotimes_j |B_{ij}|$ where $\oplus$ is a natural sum and $\otimes$ is a natural product. Further, to each multiplicand B_{ij} is assigned an ordinal according to whether B_{ij} has the form A_S or $(A_S)^*$ by the following equation:

$$|B_{ij}| = \begin{cases} \omega^{\omega^{|S|}} & \text{if } B_{ij} \text{ is } A_S \\ \omega^{\omega^{|S|+1}} & \text{if } B_{ij} \text{ is } (A_S)^*. \end{cases}$$

$|(A^*)^{\vee}_{\Sigma}| > |(A^*)^{\vee}_{\Sigma\hat{}\langle\sigma\rangle}|$ is easily checked using the fact that the ordinals of the form ω^{ω^x} are multiplicatively indecomposable.

It is possible, however, to assign smaller ordinals. All that is required for the assignment is that $|A_S|$ is additively indecomposable, $|(A_S)^*|$ is multiplicatively indecomposable, and $|A_S| < |(A_S)^*|$. Therefore we can assign $\omega^{|S|}$ to A_S and $\omega^{\omega^{|S|}}$ to $(A_S)^*$ *unless* $|S|$ is an epsilon number, in which case $|A_S| < |(A_S)^*|$ fails. To handle this case, define an ordinal function $(\ )^{\dagger}$ by the following:

$$\alpha^{\dagger} = \begin{cases} \alpha - 1 & \text{if } \alpha \text{ is finite} \\ \alpha & \text{if } \alpha = \beta + n \text{ and } \beta \text{ is a limit, not an epsilon number} \\ \alpha + 1 & \text{if } \alpha = \beta + n \text{ and } \beta \text{ is a limit, an epsilon number.} \end{cases}$$

This function $(\ )^{\dagger}$ simply skips all epsilon numbers. Then a new assignment to the multiplicands B_{ij} is given by the equation

$$|B_{ij}| = \begin{cases} \omega^{|S|^{\dagger}} & \text{if } B_{ij} \text{ is } A_S \\ \omega^{\omega^{|S|^{\dagger}}} & \text{if } B_{ij} \text{ is } (A_S)^*. \end{cases}$$

3.3 Lemma

The mapping $\Sigma \mapsto |(A^*)^{\vee}_{\Sigma}|$ yields a reification $Bad(A^*) \to \omega^{\omega^{\alpha^{\dagger}}} + 1$ where α is the order type of the base well-partial-order A. □

In turn, to show that these ordinals $\omega^{\omega^{\alpha^{\dagger}}}$ are exactly the order types of Higman embedding, we must give linearizations yielding the same ordinals as those of reifications. If the order type of the base well-partial-order is not of the form $\epsilon_\gamma + n$, then the required linearization is given by the recursive path ordering on monadic terms (kachinuki ordering) [24,33,26]. The *kachinuki ordering* is a linear ordering $\sqsubset$ on the set A^* of finite lists of a linear order A, the order $\sqsubset$ defined as follows: $\langle s_0, \ldots, s_{m-1}\rangle \sqsubset \langle t_0, \ldots, t_{n-1}\rangle$ if and only if one of the following holds:

(o) $m = 0$ and $n > 0$
(i) $s_0 = t_0$, $\langle s_1, \ldots\rangle \sqsubset \langle t_1, \ldots\rangle$
(ii) $s_0 \prec t_0$, $\langle s_1, \ldots\rangle \sqsubset \langle t_0, \ldots\rangle$
(iii) $s_0 \succ t_0$, $\langle s_0, \ldots\rangle \sqsubseteq \langle t_1, \ldots\rangle$

In (iii), $\succeq$ denotes $\succ \cup =$ and likewise for $\sqsubseteq$. By calculation, one can show that the order type of kachinuki ordering is the ordinal $\omega^{\omega^{-1+\alpha}}$ [33]. Hence, except the case $\alpha = \epsilon_\gamma + n$, the kachinuki ordering gives the same ordinal $\omega^{\omega^{\alpha^{\dagger}}}$ as the one given by the reification. For the exceptional case, we must create another linearization providing the maximum order type. If the order type α of the base well-partial-order is an epsilon number ϵ_γ, then the following ordering $\sqsubset'$ gives the required linearization: for $\sigma, \tau \in A^*$, the order relations $\sigma \sqsubset' \tau$ holds if and only if either $|\sigma| < |\tau|$ or both $|\sigma| = |\tau|$ and σ is smaller than τ by lexicographic ordering, where $|\sigma|$ denotes the length of the sequence σ. Then the order type of $\sqsubset'$ is $(\epsilon_\gamma)^\omega = \omega^{\omega^{\epsilon_\gamma + 1}}$. For the case $\alpha = \epsilon_\gamma + n + 1$ $(n \geq 0)$, by induction , we may assume there is an order isomorphism $|\cdot|_n$ from $(A \backslash \{m_A\})^*$

to $\omega^{\omega^{\epsilon_\gamma+n+1}}$, where m_A is the largest element of the linear order A. Then the sequence $\sigma = \langle \sigma_1, m_A, \ldots, \sigma_{k-1}, m_A, \sigma_k \rangle$ of A^* is carried to

$$|\sigma|_{n+1} = (\omega^{\omega^{\epsilon_\gamma+n+1}})^{k-1} \cdot |\sigma_1|_n + \cdots + (\omega^{\omega^{\epsilon_\gamma+n+1}}) \cdot |\sigma_{k-1}|_n + |\sigma_k|_n,$$

giving the order isomorphism from A^* to $\omega^{\omega^{\epsilon_\gamma+n+2}}$. Therefore the following lemma holds.

3.4 Lemma
Higman embedding on A^* has a linearization of order type $\omega^{\omega^{\alpha^\dagger}}$ where α is the order type of the base well-partial-order A. □

Theorem 3.1 is an immediate consequence of Lemmata 3.3 and 3.4. From this observation, we see that the order types $|Bad(A^*)|$ of Higman embedding has gaps at epsilon numbers as well as all ordinals that are not multiplicatively indecomposable. In the following sections, we show how these gaps are filled by other algebras uniquely.

4 Algebra Embedding

In his seminal paper [20], Higman studied the divisibility ordering on abstract algebras, and showed minimal algebras are well-partial-orders if the set of operators is ordered by a well-partial-ordering. In particular, if the number of operators is finite, the divisibility orderings are always well-partial-orders. Higman embedding is a special case of this general observation.

Our definition of algebras is almost on the same line of the minimal algebras. We include the disjoint sum and the direct product to the definition of algebras. Moreover we allow a set of generators, if the set itself is an algebra. In short, the class of algebras is the smallest class generated from empty sets and singletons by the disjoint sum $+$, the direct product $\times$, and the least fixpoint operator μ using one algebra variable.

Following the definition of algebras and their terms, we will define a partial ordering on each algebra, called an *algebra embedding.* This partial order is exactly the divisibility ordering of Higman. So every algebra embedding turns out to be a well-partial-order [5,20]. Our goal is to calculate the order type of these algebra embeddings. From this calculation, one unexpected property is shown: for each ordinal less than $\varphi(\Omega^\omega, 0)$, there is an algebra giving the ordinal as the order type. In addition, such an algebra is unique up to isomorphism (Theorem 6.19). In Section 5, we give the upper bounds of the order types by providing reifications, and in Section 6, the lower bounds by linearizations.

4.1 Definition
Algebras are generated by the following rules:

$$\emptyset \qquad i:1 \qquad X$$

$$\frac{A \quad B}{A+B} \qquad \frac{A \quad B}{A \times B} \qquad \frac{A}{\mu X.\,A.}$$

Here i is the identifier of the singleton, and we impose on $A+B$ and $A \times B$ the condition that all identifiers occurring in them are distinct. X is the only one algebra variable. This means in our setting only single recursion is allowed □

The intended meaning of the connectives defining algebras should be almost clear. For example, $i : 1$ is a singleton containing a unique i. We have only one algebra variable X, and so it is impossible to define a many sorted algebra with mutual recursion. The extension to this direction allows us more complicated structures as the tree embedding with gap condition, and will be handled in a forthcoming paper.

If all occurrences of the variable X are within the scopes of μ-operators, then the algebra is called *closed*; otherwise *open*. Note that though we have only single recursion, there is no restriction to use an algebra already constructed as a part of another algebra, e.g., $\mu X.\,X \times (\mu X.\,X + (i:1)) + (i':1)$.

4.2 Definition

Let A be an algebra.

t is a *term* of sort A iff $t : A$ is derived by the following rules:

$$i:1$$

$$\frac{a:A}{\iota a : A+B} \qquad \frac{b:B}{\iota' b : A+B}$$

$$\frac{a:A \quad b:B}{\langle a,b\rangle : A \times B}$$

$$\frac{a:\eta A}{\gamma a : \mu X.A} \qquad (\eta \text{ is the substitution } [(\mu X.\,A)/X]).$$

To be precise, the first rule should be written $i : (i : 1)$. Namely i is a unique element of the singleton algebra $i : 1$. ι and ι' are injections associated to each pair of algebras A and B. $\langle\cdot,\cdot\rangle$ is a pairing function associated to each pair of algebras A and B. And γ is the constructor associated to each initial algebra $\mu X.\,A$. □

4.3 Remark

In the last rule, the substitution ηA should be done without renaming of identifiers. For example, if A is $X + (i:1)$, the substitution ηA yields $(\mu X.\,X + (i:1)) + (i:1)$. This last is not an algebra in an exact sense, since there are common identifiers i therein. For simplicity, we call such objects also algebras. □

We omit identifiers of singletons 1 if the distinction of the occurrences are clear from the context.

4.4 Remark
If A is an initial algebra of the form $\mu X.\, C_1 X^{n_1} + \dots C_p X^{n_p}$ with closed algebras $C_1, \dots, C_p$, then A is isomorphic to the set of terms generated by the following BNF:

$$a \quad ::= \quad \mathtt{const}_1(c_1, \overbrace{a, \dots, a}^{n_1 \text{ copies}}) \quad | \quad \cdots \quad | \quad \mathtt{const}_p(c_p, \overbrace{a, \dots, a}^{n_p \text{ copies}})$$

$$(c_i \text{ is a term of sort } C_i)$$

where $\mathtt{const}_k$ is any symbol uniquely associated to the algebra A and the summand. To see the isomorphism, identify $\mathtt{const}_k(c_k, a_1, \dots, a_{n_k})$ with $\gamma \circ \iota_k \langle c_k, a_1, \dots, a_{n_k} \rangle$ where γ is the constructor associated to A and ι_k is the k-th injection of $C_k A^{n_k}$ to $C_1 A^{n_1} + \dots + C_k A^{n_k} + \dots + C_p A^{n_p}$. □

4.5 Example
(i) Natural numbers $N = \mu X.\, X + 1$. The terms of sort N are generated by the BNF n ::= $\mathtt{succ}(n) \mid \mathtt{zero}$.

(ii) Finite lists of A, $A^* = \mu X.\, AX + 1$. The terms are generated by the rule $l ::= \mathtt{push}(a, l) \mid \mathtt{emp}$ where $a : A$.

(iii) Finite lists of A entailed with B, $A^*B = \mu X.\, AX + B$. The terms are generated by the rule $l ::= \mathtt{push'}(a, l) \mid \mathtt{tail}(b)$ where $a : A$ and $b : B$. The terms of this sort may be written in the form $\langle a_1, \dots, a_k; b \rangle$ $(k \geq 0)$.

(iv) Binary trees $B = \mu X.\, X^2 + 1$. The terms are generated by the rule $t ::= \mathtt{cons}(t, t) \mid \mathtt{nil}$ □

4.6 Notation
Let s and t be two term, not necessarily of the same sort.

$s \subseteq t$ denotes that s is a subterm of t in a usual sense. s may be equal to t. We write $s \subset t$ if s is a proper subterm of t. □

Next we define an embedding on each algebra A. The properties of this embedding are the center of our interest. Among the rules in the following definition, the projection rule is important and makes the embedding correspond to the divisibility ordering of [20]. Other congruence rules are generally required to partially ordered algebras [20,16] (in [16] this property of preserving order is called isotony; also antitony occurs in ordered algebraic structures).

4.7 Definition
The *embedding* $\trianglelefteq_A$ is a binary relation (in fact, a partial order) on the set of terms of an algebra A given by one projection rule and five congruence rules as follows:

(*projection*)

$$\frac{a \trianglelefteq_A a'^{\circ}}{a \trianglelefteq_A a'} \quad \text{if } a'^{\circ} \text{ is a proper subterm of } a' \text{ (i.e., } a'^{\circ} \subset a'\text{) having sort } A.$$

(*congruence*)

$$i \trianglelefteq_1 i$$

$$\frac{a \trianglelefteq_A a'}{\iota a \trianglelefteq_{A+B} \iota a'} \qquad \frac{b \trianglelefteq_B b'}{\iota' b \trianglelefteq_{A+B} \iota' b'}$$

$$\frac{a \trianglelefteq_A a' \qquad b \trianglelefteq_B b'}{\langle a, b\rangle \trianglelefteq_{A\times B} \langle a', b'\rangle}$$

$$\frac{b \trianglelefteq_{B[A]} b'}{\gamma b \trianglelefteq_A \gamma b'} \quad \text{where } A = \mu X.\, B[X]. \qquad \square$$

4.8 Remark

The reason we imposed the condition that the identifiers of singletons should all be distinct is as follows: the intended meaning of $A + B$ is a disjoint sum of two partial orders A and B. Therefore the terms of A and the terms of B are incomparable. Consider an algebra $C = (\mu X.\, X + 1) + 1$, which should be a disjoint sum of the set of natural numbers and a singleton. If we suppose, however, two singletons therein have the same term i, then $\iota'(i)$ and $\iota \circ \gamma \circ \iota'(i)$ are both terms of C, where i in the first term comes from the last 1 of C, and i in the second from the first 1. By the projection rule of the embedding,

$$\iota'(i) \quad \trianglelefteq_C \quad \iota \circ \gamma \circ \iota'(i).$$

Hence two summands $\mu X.\, X + 1$ and 1 of C are not disjoint, contradicting the intended meaning. Therefore we force the identifiers of singletons to be all distinct (even if we omit the identifiers for simplicity). $\square$

4.9 Example

(i) The embedding on the algebra N of natural numbers is the linear order on natural numbers

$$\texttt{zero} \quad \trianglelefteq_N \quad \texttt{succ(zero)} \quad \trianglelefteq_N \quad \texttt{succ(succ(zero))} \quad \trianglelefteq_N \quad \cdots$$

(ii) The embedding on the algebra A^* of finite lists of A is exactly the same as Higman embedding (Definition 2.3).

(iii) The embedding on the algebra B of binary trees is exactly the tree embedding on binary trees (Definition 2.4 and the remark that follows). $\square$

In the theory of well-partial-order, order-reflecting maps play an important role as mentioned in Section 2. Since the algebra embedding is defined using subterms, we need the reflection of the property of being subterms in order to show some naturally arising maps are order-reflecting. The following definition of anti-createdness is the formalization of the reflection for subterms.

4.10 Definition
Let $A[X], B[X]$ be algebras with a free variable X, and C, D closed algebras (or in general arbitrary sets). Suppose g is a function from C to D and f a function from $A[C]$ to $B[D]$.

f anti-creates subterms with respect to g if and only if

$$\forall a : A[C]\ \forall d : D \text{ such that } d \subset fa\ \exists c : C \quad \begin{array}{ccc} c & \overset{g}{\mapsto} & d \\ \cap & & \cap \\ a & \underset{f}{\mapsto} & fa. \end{array}$$

In other words, there are no new created subterms $d \subset fa$ other than the images of some subterms $c \subset a$. □

4.11 Remark
We may be interested in the case that f and g are partial functions. The definition of anti-createdness works if we force the quantifiers $\forall a$ and $\exists c$ to range over the domains of the partial functions. □

We can extend the algebras by adjoining a class of sets as atomic sorts. We should regard the elements of the sets as atomic terms, which have no proper subterms. By this extension, every open algebra $A[X]$ may be naturally regarded as an endofunctor on the category **Set** of small sets. We can immediately prove that $A[f]$ anti-creates subterms with respect to every function f.

We are interested especially in the anti-createdness of the following two special cases:

(i) Let $A[X]$ and $B[X]$ be two open algebras and f_X a natural transformation from $A[X]$ to $B[X]$. We say the transformation f_X *anti-creates subterms* if functions f_X anti-create subterms with respect to identity functions id_X for all sets X.

(ii) Let C and D be initial algebras and f a function from C to D. We say f *anti-creates subterms* if f anti-creates subterms with respect to f itself.

The following proposition and corollary are the principal result with regard to order-reflecting maps. Namely natural transformations between open algebras induce order-reflecting maps of initial algebras, provided the natural transformations anti-create subterms.

4.12 Proposition
Let $f_X : A[X] \to B[X]$ be a natural transformation between two open algebras.

If f_X anti-creates subterms and the function f_X for each X reflects order, then the natural transformation f_X induces a function $f^\mu : \mu X.A[X] \to \mu X.B[X]$ that anti-creates subterms and reflects order.

(Proof) The value $f^\mu(\gamma a)$ is defined by $\gamma(B[f^\mu](f_{\mu X.A}(a)))$ by induction on the construction of γa. The anti-createdness is necessary to show that f^μ reflects order. □

The condition imposed on f_X is stronger than necessary. All we need is that $f_{\mu X.\,A}$ exists, reflects order and anti-creates subterms with respect to $id_{\mu X.\,A}$. However, the following corollary requires a further condition, which is derived from the hypothesis that f_X is a natural transformation.

4.13 Corollary

Let f_X be a natural transformation from an open algebra $A[X]$ to an open algebra $B[X]$.

If f_X is a natural isomorphism where both f_X and its inverse f_X^{-1} anti-create subterms and reflect order, then f^μ is an isomorphism where both f^μ and its inverse anti-create subterms and reflect order. □

From this corollary, we know that if a natural transformation and its inverse between two open algebras reflect order and anti-create subterms, then the isomorphism is applicable even within the scope of μ-operators. In the following we give such isomorphisms.

4.14 Lemma

The following are natural isomorphisms such that both the isomorphisms and their inverses reflect order and anti-create subterms.

$$(A+B)+C \xrightarrow{\simeq} A+(B+C)$$
$$(A\times B)\times C \xrightarrow{\simeq} A\times(B\times C)$$
$$A+B \xrightarrow{\simeq} B+A$$
$$A\times B \xrightarrow{\simeq} B\times A$$
$$\emptyset + A \xrightarrow{\simeq} A \qquad \emptyset\times A \xrightarrow{\simeq} \emptyset$$
$$1\times A \xrightarrow{\simeq} A$$
$$A(B+C) \xrightarrow{\simeq} AB+AC$$
$$\mu X.\,A \xrightarrow{\simeq} A \qquad \textit{whenever } A \textit{ does not contain free } X$$
$$\mu X.\,A \xrightarrow{\simeq} \emptyset \qquad \textit{whenever } A[X:=\emptyset] \xrightarrow{\simeq} \emptyset$$
$$\mu X.\,XA_1+\cdots+XA_n+B \xrightarrow{\simeq} (\mu X.\,XA_1+\cdots XA_n+1)B$$
$$\textit{where } A_1,\ldots,A_n, \textit{ and } B \textit{ are closed algebras}$$
□

The last isomorphism becomes easier to see if we write it $\mu X.\,XA+B \xrightarrow{\simeq} (\mu X.\,XA+1)B$ with $A = A_1+\cdots+A_n$. The left hand side is the algebra of finite lists of A entailed with B (Example 4.5 (iii)). The terms of this algebra can be written in the form $\langle a_1,\ldots,a_m;b\rangle$. Then the operation $\langle a_1,\ldots,a_m;b\rangle \mapsto \langle\langle a_1,\ldots,a_m\rangle,b\rangle$ yields an isomorphism from $\mu X.\,XA+B$ to the direct product

$(\mu X.XA+1)B$ of the algebra $A^* = \mu X.XA+1$ of finite lists of A and the algebra B. The rule $\mu X.A \xrightarrow{\simeq} \emptyset$ should be clear if one sees that $\emptyset$ is the least fixpoint of the operator $A[X]$ if $A[\emptyset] \cong \emptyset$.

We view the isomorphisms in the previous lemma as rewriting rules from the left hand sides to the right, except first four isomorphisms that assert associativity and commutativity for disjoint sum and direct product. So the rewriting rules are up to associativity and commutativity of $+$ and $\times$. We stress once more those isomorphisms remain valid even within the scopes of μ-operators.

4.15 Definition

A *normal form* of an algebra A is an algebra that is isomorphic to A by the isomorphisms in the previous lemma, and that has no redex if one views the isomorphisms as rewriting rules (up to associativity and commutativity of $+$ and $\times$). □

4.16 Lemma

The rewriting rules are confluent and strongly terminating. Therefore every algebra has a unique normal form. In addition, the function yielding a normal form for each algebra is primitive recursive. □

An algebra is in normal form if and only if it has the form $\coprod_i \prod_j B_{ij}$ where each B_{ij} is an initial algebra in normal form. Note that the rewriting rules are given in a form of normal conditional rewriting [11] due to the side condition $A[\emptyset] \xrightarrow{\simeq} \emptyset$ of the rule $\mu X.A[X] \xrightarrow{\simeq} \emptyset$. It is possible, however, to check the voidness of the algebra independently from the reductions. Therefore the rewriting rules may be presented as a system of usual term rewriting (though associativity and commutativity of disjoint sum and direct product are still manipulated implicitly). Then the reduction can be carried out along with the construction of algebras. Hence the primitive recursiveness of the function inducing the normal forms is almost evident.

Every initial algebra is isomorphic to an algebra written in the form of polynomials $\mu X.X^n C_n + \cdots XC_1 + C_0$ where each C_i is a closed algebra. Note that, however, in normal form the monomial $X^i(D+D')$ should be decomposed into $X^iD + X^iD'$.

4.17 Remark

In Corollary 6.20, we will show that the above isomorphisms completely determine the equivalence of algebras with respect to the morphisms respecting the embeddings. Therefore the equivalence is primitive recursively decidable by the comparison of normal forms. □

5 Reification of Algebra Embedding

In this section, we give a reification for the embedding relations $\trianglelefteq_A$ of each algebra A. The crucial idea is to use the class of algebras itself as a system of ordinal notations. To this end, we provide a well-ordering with the class of algebras and associate a descending sequence of algebras with each bad sequence of an algebra A. We give also the order isomorphism from the well-ordering of the algebras to the segment of Bachmann hierarchy up to $\varphi(\Omega^\omega, 0)$.

The reification to be given shows that well-partial-orderedness of each algebra reduces to well-orderedness of some associated ordinal. The reduction is carried out in a weak fragment of second order arithmetic, e.g. in system RCA_0 [15, 35,38], even intuitionistically. Therefore if one has an elementary proof of well-orderedness of the associated ordinal, then also well-partial-orderedness of the algebra is proved in an elementary method (we do not single out which is more elementary). Furthermore if the proof of well-ordering is constructive, so is the proof of the well-partial-orderedness.

5.1 Notation

Let A be a partial order and a an element of A.

A_a denotes the the suborder $\{x \in A \mid a \not\trianglelefteq_A x\}$ of A. $\square$

Given a bad sequence $\langle a_0, a_1, \ldots \rangle$ of a partial order A, we associate a sequence $A, A_{\langle a_0 \rangle}, A_{\langle a_0, a_1 \rangle}, \ldots$ of suborders of A. Here the suborder A_σ is defined for every finite sequence σ of members of A by

$$\begin{aligned} A_{\langle\, \rangle} &= A \\ A_{\sigma ^\frown \langle a \rangle} &= (A_\sigma)_a \end{aligned}$$

(see Figure 2). Then the sequence $A_{\langle\, \rangle}, A_{\langle a_0 \rangle}, A_{\langle a_0, a_1 \rangle}, \ldots$ are decreasing with respect to the strict inclusion $\supset$ of sets. Therefore the following observation follows:

> A partial order A is a well-partial-order if and only if the decreasing sequence $A_{\langle\, \rangle}, A_{\langle a_0 \rangle}, A_{\langle a_0, a_1 \rangle}, \ldots$ associated to each bad sequence $\langle a_0, a_1, \ldots \rangle$ eventually terminates after finite steps.

5.2 Proposition

(i) $1_i = \emptyset$

(ii) $(A+B)_{\iota a} = A_a + B$, *and* $(A+B)_{\iota b} = A + B_b$.

(iii) $(A \times B)_{\langle a,b \rangle} = (A_a \times B) \cup (A \times B_b)$.

(iv) $A_a = \gamma(B[A_a])_b$ *where* $A = \mu X.\, B[X]$ *and* $a = \gamma b$. *Here the suborder* $\gamma(B[A_a])_b$ *of* A *is defined by* $\{\gamma b' : A \mid b' \in (B[A])_b$ *and* $\forall a'^{\circ} \subset \gamma b'.\, a' : A \Rightarrow a'^{\circ} \in A_a\}$. $\square$

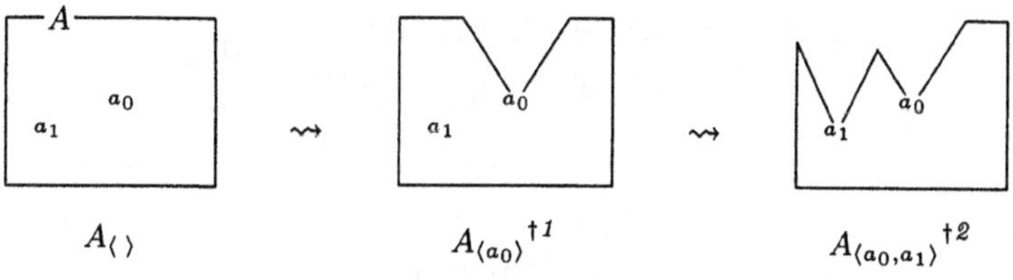

†*1*: a_0 is not in $A_{\langle a_0\rangle}$. †*2*: Neither a_0 nor a_1 is in $A_{\langle a_0,a_1\rangle}$.

Figure 2

The meaning of (iv) may be clearer if one observes that A_a is a least fixpoint of the operator $X \mapsto (B[X])_b$ in the complete lattice of all subsets of A. What we next do is to translate the above suborders A_a to algebras $A^{\vee}_a$. As seen below, the translation is simple: disjoint sum to disjoint sum, direct product to direct product, least fixpoint to least fixpoint. The only point to remark is that union is translated to disjoint sum.

5.3 Definition

An algebra $A^{\vee}_a$ is associated to each algebra A in normal form and a term a of sort A by the following definition:

(i) $1^{\vee}_i = \emptyset$.

(ii) $(A+B)^{\vee}_{\iota a} = A^{\vee}_a + B$
$(A+B)^{\vee}_{\iota' b} = A + B^{\vee}_b$

(iii) $(A \times B)^{\vee}_{\langle a,b\rangle} = A^{\vee}_a \times B + A \times B^{\vee}_b$

(iv) $(\mu X.\, B[X])^{\vee}_{\gamma b} = \mu X.\,(B[X])^{\vee}_b$ where $(B[X])^{\vee}_b$ is carried out in such a way that if $X^{\vee}_{a^\circ}$ is encountered for some a° in the process of calculation, then it is replaced by $A^{\vee}_{a^\circ}$ (see Example below). □

5.4 Example

(i) Let B be the algebra $\mu X.\, X^2+1$ of binary trees and $\mathbf{cons}(t/0, t/1)$ a term of sort B (see Example 4.5 (iv)).

$$\begin{aligned} B^{\vee}_{\mathbf{cons}(t/0,t/1)} &= \mu X.\,(X^2+1)^{\vee}_{\iota\langle t/0,t/1\rangle} \\ &= \mu X.\,(X^2)^{\vee}_{\langle t/0,t/1\rangle}+1 \\ &= \mu X.\, XB^{\vee}_{t/1} + B^{\vee}_{t/0}X + 1 \\ &= (B^{\vee}_{t/0} + B^{\vee}_{t/1})^* \end{aligned}$$

Observe that $X^{\vee}_{t/0}$ and $X^{\vee}_{t/1}$ are replaced by $B^{\vee}_{t/0}$ and $B^{\vee}_{t/1}$ respectively.

(ii) Let A^* be the algebra $\mu X.\, AX+1$ of finite lists of A and $\langle a_0, a_1 \ldots, a_{n-1}\rangle$ a term of sort A^*.

$$
\begin{aligned}
(A^*)\check{}_{\langle a_0,\ldots,a_{n-1}\rangle} &= \mu X.\, A\check{}_{a_0} X + A(A^*)\check{}_{\langle a_1,\ldots a_{n-1}\rangle} + 1 \\
&\cong (A\check{}_{a_0})^* + (A\check{}_{a_0})^* A(A^*)\check{}_{\langle a_1,\ldots a_{n-1}\rangle} \\
&\vdots \\
&\cong (A\check{}_{a_0})^* \\
&\quad + (A\check{}_{a_0})^* A(A\check{}_{a_1})^* \\
&\quad + \cdots \\
&\quad + (A\check{}_{a_0})^* A(A\check{}_{a_1})^* A \cdots A(A\check{}_{a_{n-1}})^*
\end{aligned}
$$

If we replace $(A\check{}_{a_i})^*$ by $(A_{a_i})^*$ then this becomes equal to $((A_{S_i})^*)_{\sigma_i}$ in Figure 1 by transformation $A_{S_i} \mapsto A$ and $\sigma_i \mapsto \langle a_0, \ldots, a_{n-1}\rangle$. By applying this repeatedly, the definition of $(A^*)\check{}_{\Sigma}$ given in Section 3 due to Simpson [37] (where Σ is a bad sequence of terms of sort A^*) turns out to be equal to the one in this section. □

The following lemma is almost evident, but the most important for the reification.

5.5 Lemma
Let A be an algebra in normal form and a a term of sort A.

There is a $\trianglelefteq$-reflecting map (thus injection) $f_a : A_a \rightarrowtail A\check{}_a$.

(*Proof*) Induction on the construction of a. Prove at the same time if A is written $B[C]$ for some algebra $B[X]$ and C, then f_a anti-creates subterms with respect to id_C. For the case A is an initial algebra $\mu X.\, B[X]$, the following observation is used: supposed $a = \gamma b$ where $b : B[A]$, the map $f_b : (B[A])_b \to (B[A])\check{}_b = B\check{}_b[A]$ is also a map from $(B[A_a])_b$ to $B\check{}_b[A_a]$ by anti-createdness. □

Recall that the transformation of A_a into $A\check{}_a$ changes union to disjoint sum. Hence even if $a' \trianglelefteq a'$ holds in A_a it is not necessarily the case that $f_a(a') \trianglelefteq f_a(a'')$ in $A\check{}_a$ since they may lie in different summands. So f_a reflects embedding but does not preserve it.

5.6 Remark

(i) Since union is transformed to disjoint sum, if the union has a non-void meet then f_a must choose summands for the terms in the meet. If we are concerned with constructive logic, we require the canonical choice of summands. The designing of the canonical choice is possible since $a' \in A_a$ is a primitive recursive predicate in A, a and a'.

(ii) If we are concerned with Reverse Mathematics, the lemma should be proved in a fragment of second order arithmetic that is as weak as possible. The lemma proves by induction that f_a anti-creates subterms and reflects embeddings. These two notions are formalized by Π^0_1-formulas, and therefore the lemma is provable in the most basic system RCA_0, since this system has Σ_1^0-induction that induces Π_1^0-induction. □

5.7 Corollary
Let A be an algebra in normal form and $\langle a_0, a_1, \ldots, a_{n-1}\rangle$ a bad sequence of A. There is a $\trianglelefteq$-reflecting injection

$$A_{\langle a_0,\ldots,a_{n-1}\rangle} \rightarrowtail A^{\check{}}_{\langle a_0,\ldots,a_{n-1}\rangle}.$$

Here

$$\begin{aligned} A_{\langle a_0,\ldots,a_{n-1}\rangle} &= (\cdots((A_{a_0})_{a_1})\cdots)_{a_{n-1}} \\ A^{\check{}}_{\langle a_0,\ldots,a_{n-1}\rangle} &= (\cdots((A^{\check{}}_{a_0})^{\check{}}_{a_1})\cdots)^{\check{}}_{a_{n-1}}. \end{aligned}$$

In the right hand side of the second equation, for example, a_1 is identified with its image under $f_{a_0} : A_{a_0} \to A^{\check{}}_{a_0}$. □

By this corollary, we can associate to each bad sequence $\langle a_0, a_1, \ldots\rangle$ of an algebra A a sequence of algebras, $A, A^{\check{}}_{\langle a_0\rangle}, A^{\check{}}_{\langle a_0,a_1\rangle}, \ldots$. Therefore showing A is a well-partial-order is equivalent to saying that all sequences $A, A^{\check{}}_{\langle a_0\rangle}, A^{\check{}}_{\langle a_0,a_1\rangle}, \ldots$ associated to bad sequences of A eventually terminate after finite steps. This last is proved by providing a well-ordering with the class of algebras so that the sequences are strictly decreasing.

The basic idea is to regard the expressions of algebras as finite trees. Suppose given a closed algebra in normal form. If the algebra is of the form $A_0+A_1+\cdots+A_{n-1}$, then it is regarded as a tree $+\{A_0, A_1, \ldots, A_{n-1}\}$ having n immediate successors $A_0, A_1, \ldots, A_{n-1}$ of the root, and labeled by $+$ on the root node. Likewise for $A_0 \times A_1 \times \cdots \times A_{n-1}$. If the algebra is an initial algebra equivalent to $\mu X. X^n A_n + \cdots + XA_1 + A_0$ (if there are many homogeneous monomials $X^iC + \cdots + X^iC'$ then identify it with a single monomial $X^i(C + \cdots C')$), then it is regarded as a tree $\mu\langle A_n, \ldots, A_1, A_0\rangle$ labeled by μ on the root. Note that for the nodes labeled by $+$ or $\times$ there are no orders on immediate successors, while for the nodes labeled by μ there are orders. Following the recursive path ordering with status [25,21], we define a well-order on the class of algebras incorporating both multiset path ordering and lexicographic path ordering depending on the labels on the nodes. The precedence order of the labels is $\emptyset \prec 1 \prec + \prec \times \prec \mu$.

In the following definition, the term *subalgebra* is used to denote the subexpressions of algebras (like subterms), not the subalgebra in the theory of universal algebra. We need multiset ordering $<^\circ$ on multisets [10] and lexicographic ordering $<^*$ on finite lists of variable lengths. This last ordering is defined as follows: $\langle a_m, \ldots, a_1, a_0\rangle <^* \langle a'_n, \ldots, a'_1, a'_0\rangle$ if and only if either (i) $m < n$; or (ii) $m = n$ and there is $j \le m$ such that $a_m = a'_m$, $a_{m-1} = a'_{m-1}$, ..., $a_{j+1} = a'_{j+1}$ and $a_j < a'_j$. This ordering corresponds to $<_r$ in [11].

5.8 Definition
Let A, B be closed algebras regarded as finite trees by the procedure mentioned

above. Suppose $\alpha, \beta \in \{\emptyset, 1, +, \times, \mu\}$ are the labels on the roots of A, B respectively. The set of labels has the precedence order $\emptyset \prec 1 \prec + \prec \times \prec \mu$.

The binary relation $A < B$ is defined by the following:

(i) $A < B$ if there is a proper subalgebra B° of B such that $A \leq B^\circ$. Here $A \leq B$ means $A < B$ or $A = B$.

(ii) $A < B$ if $\alpha \prec \beta$ and for all proper subalgebra A°, it holds that $A^\circ < B$.

(iii) $A < B$ if $\alpha = \beta$ and one of the following is the case:

(a) The label α is either $+$ or $\times$, and $\{A_0, A_1, \ldots, A_{m-1}\} <^\circ \{B_0, B_1, \ldots, B_{n-1}\}$ by multiset ordering, where A_i, B_j are immediate successors of the root of the trees A, B respectively.

(b) The label α is μ, and $\langle A_m, \ldots, A_1, A_0\rangle <^* \langle B_n, \ldots, B_1, B_0\rangle$ by lexicographic ordering, where A_i, B_j are immediate successors of the root of the trees A, B respectively.

(iv) $A < B$ holds only when one of (i) through (iii) applies. □

Another view for $\langle A_m, \ldots, A_0\rangle <^* \langle B_n, \ldots, B_0\rangle$ is to regard X as greater than all closed algebras and compare $X^m A_m + \cdots + A_0$ and $X^n B_n + \cdots + B_0$. This approach has an advantage that there is no need to transform initial algebras to the form $\mu X. X^n C_n + \cdots + C_0$. The following proposition is proved by the usual argument that derives a contradiction assuming there is a minimal infinite descending sequence.

5.9 Proposition

The binary relation $<$ is a well-order on the class of algebras in normal form. Let us denote by $|A|$ the ordinal corresponding to an algebra A. □

5.10 Proposition

If A is an algebra in normal form, then $A^{\check{}}_a < A$ for every $a : A$. □

The proof is easy by definition of $A^{\check{}}_a$. We remark that if A is not in normal form then this proposition does not necessarily hold. For example, consider $A = 2 \times 3$. Then $A^{\check{}}_a = 1 \times 3 + 2 \times 2 = 7 > 6$ for all $a : A$.

Recall that we associated a sequence $A, A^{\check{}}_{\langle a_0\rangle}, A^{\check{}}_{\langle a_0, a_1\rangle}, \ldots$ of algebras to each bad sequence $\langle a_0, a_1, \ldots\rangle$ of A. By the last proposition, we have the decreasing sequence $A > A^{\check{}}_{\langle a_0\rangle} > A^{\check{}}_{\langle a_0, a_1\rangle} > \cdots$. This sequence must be finite since the order $<$ is a well-order on the class of algebras in normal form by Proposition 5.9. Therefore the mapping $\langle a_0, \ldots, a_{n-1}\rangle \mapsto |A^{\check{}}_{\langle a_0, \ldots, a_{n-1}\rangle}|$ yields a reification of the partial order A by the ordinal $|A|$. This observation leads us to the following theorem, which is a main theorem of this section.

5.11 Theorem

Every algebra is a well-partial-order with respect to the embedding $\trianglelefteq_A$ *and the order type* $|Bad(A)|$ *of the well-partial-order is upper bounded by the ordinal* $|A|$. □

5.12 Remark

The argument used in this section is quite elementary except the proof that the order $<$ on the class of algebras is a well-order. So the reduction of well-partial-orderedness of an algebra A to well-orderedness of the ordinal $|A|$ is proved in system RCA_0, even intuitionistically (see Remark 5.6). □

In order to compare the upper bound $|A|$ of the algebra embedding with a traditional ordinal notation, we give an order isomorphism from the class of algebras in normal form to an initial segment of Bachmann hierarchy. We refer the reader to [18] for a comprehensive definition of Bachmann hierarchy. The family of normal functions of the hierarchy is denoted by $\langle\varphi_\alpha(\text{-})\rangle$ where α ranges over all ordinals less than $\epsilon_{\Omega+1}$ (Ω is the first regular ordinal greater than ω). For our purpose, it suffices to consider the indices α up to Ω^ω. We choose as the base normal function $\varphi_0(\text{-})$ the enumeration ω^{ω^x} of multiplicatively indecomposable ordinals. This choice is because our definition of algebras has connectives $+$ and also $\times$, and so every ordinal between consecutive multiplicatively indecomposable ordinals is constructed in terms of these two connectives. The family $\langle\overline{\varphi}_\alpha\rangle$ is a modification of the hierarchy so that ordinals have unique notations [18]. The reader might observe that the recursion relation of $\overline{\varphi}$ [18] has the same outlook as the lexicographic path ordering (also the ordinal function ϑ in [30] has the same relation). We first employ an auxiliary ordinal function $\overline{\mu}$ from Ω^ω to Ω^ω in order to make the description easier.

5.13 Definition

The function $\overline{\mu}$ is a map from Ω^ω to Ω^ω, the map defined as in Figure 3. There $\alpha < \Omega^\omega$ is supposed to be in Cantor normal form $\Omega^n\alpha_n + \cdots + \Omega\alpha_1 + \alpha_0$ to base Ω. □

Note that if every coefficient α_i of the Cantor normal form is less than $\varphi(\Omega^\omega, 0)$ then $\overline{\mu}(\alpha)$ is also less than $\varphi(\Omega^\omega, 0)$. The definition of $\overline{\mu}$ may appear complicated, but it is a kind of adjustment for the case $\alpha < \Omega^2$. An order isomorphism of the class of algebras into an initial segment of Bachmann hierarchy up to $\varphi(\Omega^\omega, 0)$ is defined as follows:

5.14 Proposition

By the following equations, the class of algebras in normal form becomes order isomorphic to the ordinal $\varphi(\Omega^\omega, 0)$.

$$|\emptyset| \quad = \quad 0$$

Cantor Normal Form of α	Value of $\overline{\mu}(\alpha)$
$\alpha < \Omega$	α
$\alpha = \Omega\alpha_1 + \alpha_0$	$\overline{\varphi}(0, -1+\alpha_1) \otimes (1+\alpha_0)$
$\alpha = \Omega^2 + \Omega\alpha_1 + \alpha_0$	$\overline{\varphi}(1+\alpha_1, \alpha_0)$
$\alpha = \Omega^2\alpha_2 + \Omega\alpha_1 + \alpha_0 \ (\alpha_2 > 1)$	$\overline{\varphi}(\Omega(-1+\alpha_2) + \alpha_1, \alpha_0)$
$\alpha \geq \Omega^3$	$\overline{\varphi}(\Omega^{n-1}\alpha_n + \cdots + \Omega\alpha_2 + \alpha_1, \alpha_0)$

Figure 3

$$\begin{array}{lcll} |1| & = & 1 & \\ |A+B| & = & |A| \oplus |B| & \textit{(natural sum)} \\ |A \times B| & = & |A| \otimes |B| & \textit{(natural product)} \\ \multicolumn{4}{l}{|\mu X.\, X^n C_n + \cdots + XC_1 + C_0|} \\ & = & \overline{\mu}(\Omega^n|C_n| + \cdots + \Omega|C_1| + (-1+|C_0|)) & \square \end{array}$$

6 Linearization of Algebra Embeddings

In the last section, the upper bounds of order types of algebra embeddings are given by the well-ordering on the class of algebras. Namely for each algebra A the order type of $Bad(A)$ is upper bounded by $|A|$, which is the ordinal corresponding to A in the well-ordering of the class of algebras.
The lower bounds of well-partial-orders are given by linearizations, as seen in Preliminaries. In this section, we give a uniform way to linearize the algebra embeddings, called Ackermann orderings. We show for almost all algebras A an Ackermann ordering gives a linearization of order type $|A|$. For exceptional cases, a modification of the Ackermann ordering yields the order type $|A|$. Therefore the ordinals $|A|$ are lower bounds of algebra embeddings as well as their upper bounds. So we derive that the order type of embedding of an algebra A is exactly the ordinal $|A|$.
Ackermann orderings on algebras depend on the orders of summands and multiplicands. That is to say, if one exchanges the order of summands from $A + B$ to $B + A$ then the associated Ackermann orderings are in general different, and likewise for $A \times B$. Given an algebra, therefore, there are several associated Ackermann orderings according to the permutations of summands and multiplicands.

6.1 Convention

In this section, $+$ and $\times$ are non-commutative unless otherwise mentioned. $\square$

6.2 Definition

Let A be a closed algebra where the order of summands and multiplicands is fixed.

The *Ackermann ordering* on A is the binary relation $<_A$ between terms of A defined as follows:

(i) $A = \emptyset$ or 1.
$<_A$ is void.

(ii) $A = B + C$.
$a <_A a'$ if and only if one of
(1) $a = \iota b$ and $a' = \iota' c$;
(2) $a = \iota b, a' = \iota b'$ and $b <_B b'$;
(3) $a = \iota' c, a' = \iota' c'$ and $c <_C c'$.

(iii) $A = B \times C$.
$\langle b, c\rangle <_A \langle b', c'\rangle$ if and only if either
(1) $c <_C c'$;
(2) $c = c'$ and $b <_B b'$.

(iv) $A = \mu X.\, C[X]$.
$\gamma c <_A \gamma c'$ (where $c, c' : C[A]$) if and only if either
(1) $\gamma c \leq_A a'$ for some proper subterm $a' : A$ of $\gamma c'$. Here $\leq_A$ is $<_A$ or $=$.
(2) $c <_{C[A]} c'$ and $a <_A \gamma c'$ for all proper subterm $a : A$ of γc. □

6.3 Notation
We write *Ack*(A) if we emphasize that we are concerned with the Ackermann ordering on an algebra A. □

Our definition of Ackermann ordering is based on the same idea of the orderings in [1,11,22]. Note that the Ackermann ordering associated to a direct product algebra $A \times B$ is the lexicographic ordering, but it compares from right to left in the reverse order to the usual lexicographic ordering. This choice is in order to accommodate our ordering to the traditional ordinal notations.

6.4 Proposition
The reflexive closure $\leq_A$ of Ackermann ordering $<_A$ is a total order and is a linearization of the algebra embedding $\trianglelefteq_A$, that is,

$$a \trianglelefteq_A a' \quad \Rightarrow \quad a \leq_A a'. \quad \square$$

It is convenient to introduce an alternative way to construct initial algebras. This is for reducing the number of exceptional cases in the argument below. The difference is that we assume the existence of the least element.

6.5 Definition
$\tilde{\mu}X.\, B[X]$ is an alternative form of an initial algebra whose terms are generated by the following rules (where $A = \tilde{\mu}X.\, B[X]$):

$$0_A : A \qquad \frac{b : B[A]}{\gamma b : A}$$

where 0_A is a constant term associated to each (occurrence of) the algebra A and γ is the associated constructor.

The Ackermann ordering on $A = \tilde{\mu}X. B[X]$ is defined as follows: $a <_A a'$ if and only if either

(i) $a = 0_A$ and $a' \neq 0_A$ (i.e., 0_A is the least element)
(ii) $a \leq_A a'^{\circ}$ for some proper subterm a'° of a' having sort A.
(iii) $a = \gamma b$, $a' = \gamma b'$, $b <_{B[A]} b'$ and $a^{\circ} < a'$ for all proper subterm a° of a having sort A. □

The initial algebra $\tilde{\mu}X. B[X]$ is translated to the former notation by $\tilde{\mu}X. B[X] = \mu X. 1 + B[X]$. It is easy to see these two are order isomorphic with respect to the associated Ackermann orderings.

The following are a set of isomorphisms respecting Ackermann orderings. There we say a morphism $f : A \to B$ preserves Ackermann orderings if it satisfies $a <_A a' \Rightarrow f(a) <_B f(a')$. As in the case of algebra embeddings, we regard those isomorphisms as rewriting rules from left to right.

6.6 Proposition
The following nine natural transformations are isomorphisms where both the isomorphisms and their inverses preserve Ackermann orderings.

$$\begin{array}{lll}
\emptyset + A & \xrightarrow{\simeq} & A \\
A + \emptyset & \xrightarrow{\simeq} & A \\
\emptyset \times A & \xrightarrow{\simeq} & \emptyset \\
A \times \emptyset & \xrightarrow{\simeq} & \emptyset \\
1 \times A & \xrightarrow{\simeq} & A \\
A \times 1 & \xrightarrow{\simeq} & A \\
A(B + C) & \xrightarrow{\simeq} & AB + AC \\
\tilde{\mu}X. A & \xrightarrow{\simeq} & 1 + A \qquad \textit{whenever } A \textit{ is closed} \\
\tilde{\mu}X.B[X] + C & & \\
& \xrightarrow{\simeq} & (\tilde{\mu}X. B[X]) + (\tilde{\mu}X. B^1[X])C \\
& & \qquad \textit{if } B[X] \textit{ is of degree } 1 \textit{ and } C \textit{ is closed.}
\end{array}$$

In the last transformation $B^1[X]$ *is obtained from* $B[X]$ *by erasing all constant summands. For example, if* $B[X] = F + DXE + F' + D'XE'$ *then* $B^1[X] = DXE + D'XE'$. □

Note that $(A + B)C$ is not isomorphic to $AC + BC$. Also there is no need for the rule $\tilde{\mu}X. B[X] \xrightarrow{\simeq} \emptyset$ since $\tilde{\mu}X. B[X]$ is always non-empty.

Next we calculate the order types of Ackermann orderings. It suffices to consider the algebras having no redices for the rewriting rules in the previous proposition. The full exposition is lengthy. So we will be content with a brief description how the calculation is carried out. The first thing is to associate to each closed algebra A a sequence that is strictly increasing and unbounded with respect to the Ackermann ordering $<_A$. Later we will give the ordinals corresponding to the components of the sequence so that the supremum of those ordinals provide the order types of $<_A$.

6.7 Definition

Let A be a closed algebra having no redices for the rewriting rules defined by the previous proposition.

A sequence $\langle a[n]\rangle_{n\in\omega}$ is associated to A by the following definition (we follow the convention that $\langle c[n]\rangle_{n\in\omega}$ is the sequence associated to C, etc.):

(o) $\emptyset$ and 1 have no associated sequences.

(i) For a disjoint sum algebra $A = B + C$,

$$a[n] \;=\; \iota'(c[n])$$

(ii) For a product algebra $A = B \times C$,

$$a[n] = \langle 0_B, c[n]\rangle \qquad \text{where } 0_B \text{ denotes the least element of } B.$$

(iii) For an initial algebra, the sequence is manipulated by the following four cases (a) through (d).

(a) If A is of the form $\tilde{\mu}X.\,B[X] + C[X]\cdot D$ ($C[X]$ may be void), then

$$\begin{aligned} a[0] &= 0_A \\ a[n+1] &= \gamma^D\langle 0_{C[A]}, d[n]\rangle \end{aligned}$$

where $\gamma^D : C[A]\cdot D \to A$ is the composition of the constructor γ preceded by the injection from $C[A]\cdot D$ to $B[A] + C[A]\cdot D$.

(b) If A is of the form $\tilde{\mu}X.\,B[X] + C[X]\cdot X$ ($C[X]$ may be void), then

$$\begin{aligned} a[0] &= 0_A \\ a[n+1] &= \gamma^X\langle 0_{C[A]}, a[n]\rangle \qquad \text{where } \gamma^X : C[A]\cdot A \to A. \end{aligned}$$

(c) If A is of the form $\tilde{\mu}X.\,B[X] + C[X]\cdot D + E + 1$ ($C[X]$ must contain X),

$$\begin{aligned} a[0] &= \gamma^1(i) \qquad \text{where } \gamma^1 : 1 \to A \\ a[n+1] &= \gamma^D\langle c_0, d[n]\rangle \end{aligned}$$

where $c_0 : C[A]$ is defined as follows: if $C[A] = C_1 \times \cdots \times C_n$ then the i-th component of c_0 is the least element 0_{C_i} for all C_i except the leftmost occurrence of A, for which the component is set $a[0]$. Namely if $C[X] = C_1 \cdots X \cdots C_n$ where the designated X is the leftmost occurrence of X, then c_0 is put $\langle 0_{C_1}, \ldots, a[0], \ldots, 0_{C_n}\rangle$ where the component $a[0]$ corresponds to the occurrence of X. The component $a[0]$ in the definition of $a[n+1]$ ensures $a[0] <_A a[n+1]$.

(d) If A is of the form $\tilde{\mu}X.\,B[X] + C[X] \cdot X + E + 1$ ($C[X]$ may be void),

$$\begin{aligned} a[0] &= \gamma^1(i) \\ a[n+1] &= \gamma^X\langle 0_{C[A]}, a[n]\rangle \quad \Box \end{aligned}$$

6.8 Proposition
Let A be a closed algebra with the associated sequence $\langle a[n]\rangle_{n\in\omega}$.

The sequence $\langle a[n]\rangle_{n\in\omega}$ is strictly increasing and unbounded with respect to Ackermann ordering $<_A$. $\Box$

In the above we associate a sequence of terms to each closed algebra A. In the following we associate a sequence of algebras to each closed algebra A. The proposition after the definition shows that these two sequences are related intimately.

6.9 Definition
Let A be a closed algebra having no redices for the rewriting rules defined in Proposition 6.6.

The *fundamental sequence* $\langle A\hat{}_n\rangle_{n\in\omega}$ is a sequence of closed algebras associated to each A as follows (the cases correspond to those in the Definition 6.7):

(o) $\emptyset$ and 1 has no fundamental sequences.

(i) $\begin{aligned} A &= B + C \\ A\hat{}_n &= B + C\hat{}_n \end{aligned}$

(ii) $\begin{aligned} A &= B \times C \\ A\hat{}_n &= B \times C\hat{}_n \end{aligned}$

(iii) A is an initial algebra.

(a) $\begin{aligned} A &= \tilde{\mu}X.\,B + CD \\ A\hat{}_0 &= \emptyset \\ A\hat{}_{n+1} &= \tilde{\mu}X.\,B + CD\hat{}_n \end{aligned}$

(b) $\begin{aligned} A &= \tilde{\mu}X.\,B + CX \\ A\hat{}_0 &= \emptyset \\ A\hat{}_{n+1} &= \tilde{\mu}X.\,B + CA\hat{}_n \end{aligned}$

(c) $\begin{aligned} A &= \tilde{\mu}X.\,B + CD + E + 1 \\ A\hat{}_0 &= \tilde{\mu}X.\,B + CD + E \\ A\hat{}_{n+1} &= \tilde{\mu}X.\,B + CD\hat{}_n + A\hat{}_0 + 1 \end{aligned}$

(d) $\begin{aligned} A &= \tilde{\mu}X.\,B + CX + E + 1 \\ A\hat{}_0 &= \tilde{\mu}X.\,B + CX + E \\ A\hat{}_1 &= \tilde{\mu}X.\,B + CA\hat{}_0 + 1 \\ A\hat{}_{n+2} &= \tilde{\mu}X.\,B + CA\hat{}_{n+1} \end{aligned}$ $\Box$

For an algebra A and a term a of sort A, let $A_{<a}$ denote the suborder $\{x : A \mid x <_A a\}$ of A.

6.10 Proposition

(i) $Ack(A_{<a[n]})$ *is order isomorphic to* $Ack(A\hat{_n})$.

(ii) $Ack(A)$ *is order isomorphic to* $\sup_{n\in\omega}(Ack(A\hat{_n}))$. □

(i) is proved by giving morphisms preserving Ackermann orderings from $A_{<a[n]}$ to $A\hat{_n}$, and from $A\hat{_n}$ to $A_{<a[n]}$. (ii) is an immediate consequence of (i) since the sequence $\langle a[n]\rangle_{n\in\omega}$ is unbounded. This assertion (ii) allows us to calculate the order type of Ackermann ordering $Ack(A)$ from the smaller order types of $Ack(A\hat{_n})$.

6.11 Definition

The function $\mu : \Omega^\omega \to \Omega^\omega$ has the same definition as $\overline{\mu}$ of Definition 5.13 except that all $\overline{\varphi}$ therein is replaced by φ and that $\mu(\Omega\alpha_1+\alpha_0) = \varphi(0, -1+\alpha_1)\times(1+\alpha_0)$ (natural product is replaced by ordinary product). □

Now we provide the order type $A^\star$ of Ackermann ordering $Ack(A)$. In the following, we say an initial algebra $\tilde{\mu}X.\,B[X]$ has *degree n* if the largest number of X in a single summand of $B[X]$ is n (an analogy of the degrees of polynomials). The *rightmost multiplicand* of $\coprod_{i=1}^{m}\prod_{j=1}^{n_i} B_{ij}$ where B_{ij} is not decomposable any more to the form of a product, is the multiplicand $B_{m\,n_m}$.

6.12 Definition

Let A be a closed algebra. Without loss of generality we assume A has no redices for the rewriting rules given in Proposition 6.6.

An ordinal $A^\star$ is associated to each A by the following

(o) $\emptyset^\star = 0,\quad 1^\star = 1,\quad X^\star = \Omega.$

(i) $(A+B)^\star = A^\star + B^\star.$

(ii) $(A\times B)^\star = A^\star \times B^\star.$

(iii) In case A is an initial algebra,

(a) If $A = \tilde{\mu}X.\,B[X] + C$ is of degree 2 or more (C may be void), let α be the least ordinal satisfying $\max({D_i}^\star) < \mu(B^\star + \alpha)$ where D_i ranges over all proper subalgebras of $\tilde{\mu}X.\,B[X]$ other than the rightmost multiplicand of $B[X]$. Then $A^\star = \mu(B^\star + \alpha + C^\star)$.

(b) If A has degree 1, it has the form $A = \tilde{\mu}X.\,B[X] + E + DXC$ ending with a summand of degree 1 (E may be void), since we assumed A has no redices. Let α be the least ordinal fulfilling $\max\{(\tilde{\mu}X.\,B^1[X])^\star, D^\star\} < \omega^{\omega^{\alpha+1}}$ where $B^1[X]$ is obtained from $B[X]$ by erasing all constant summands (see Proposition 6.6). If $(\tilde{\mu}X.\,B[X])^\star$ and $E^\star$ are both less than $\omega^{\omega^{\alpha+1}}$ then

$$A^\star = \omega^{\omega^{\alpha+C^\star}};$$

otherwise

$$\text{if } C = 1 \text{ then } A^\star = \omega^{\delta+1}$$
$$\text{else } A^\star = \omega^{\omega^{\gamma+C^\star}}$$

where

$$\omega^\delta \leq \max\{(\tilde{\mu}X.\, B[X])^\star, E^\star\} < \omega^{\delta+1}$$
$$\omega^{\omega^\gamma} \leq \max\{(\tilde{\mu}X.\, B[X])^\star, E^\star\} < \omega^{\omega^{\gamma+1}} \quad \square$$

Note that the disjoint sum and the direct product are mapped to the ordinal sum $+$ and the ordinal product $\times$ and in addition the variable X to Ω. Therefore if an initial algebra contains the summand of the form $\cdots C \cdot X \cdots$ where C is closed, this C disappears in $\mu((B[X])^\star)$ since $C^\star \cdot \Omega = \Omega$. Likewise if two summands occur as $D[X] + E[X]$ and the degree of $D[X]$ is smaller than that of $E[X]$ then the entire $D[X]$ disappears. However the closed algebra C or the closed algebras in $D[X]$ may be too large to ignore them. The ordinals α, γ and δ occurring in the definition above reflect this effect of closed algebras that would simply be ignored if there were no adjusting ordinals α, γ, δ.

6.13 Remark

The definition of $A^\star$ is quite complicated when A is an initial algebra, especially, of degree 1. However if one is interested in the algebras of the form $A = \tilde{\mu}X.\, X^n C_n + \cdots + X C_1 + C_0$, then the associated ordinal $A^\star$ has the simple form $\mu(\Omega^n {C_n}^\star + \cdots + \Omega {C_1}^\star + {C_0}^\star)$. $\square$

The following theorem shows that $A^\star$ is exactly the order type $|Ack(A)|$ of Ackermann ordering on A.

6.14 Theorem

$|Ack(A)| = A^\star$ *for every closed algebra* A *having no redices for the rewriting rules given in Proposition 6.6.*

(*Proof*) Prove that $(\hat{A_n})^\star$ converges to $A^\star$. Therefore by transfinite induction for $A^\star$ we can prove $|Ack(A)| = A^\star$ by (ii) of Proposition 6.10. $\square$

The order types of the recursive path ordering (the multiset path ordering) seem to be folkloric. If the set of labels is well-ordered by order type α, the associated multiset path ordering is order isomorphic to $\varphi(\alpha, 0)$ in Feferman-Schütte notation [9]. The order types of lexicographic path orderings were seldom mentioned in the literature. Some partial results are found in [29,11]. From the previous theorem, we know that the order types of the lexicographic path orderings are much greater than the corresponding multiset path orderings.

Recall that Ackermann orderings are linearizations of algebra embeddings. So we have a lower bound for the order type of $Bad(A)$. Consider an initial algebra A of the form $\tilde{\mu}X.\, X^n C_n + \cdots + X C_1 + C_0$. Then the order type $|Bad(A)|$ of the algebra A is upper bounded by $\overline{\mu}(\Omega^n|C_n| + \cdots + \Omega|C_1| + |C_0|)$ by Theorem 5.11 and lower bounded by $\mu(\Omega^n C_n{}^\star + \cdots + \Omega C_1{}^\star + C_0{}^\star)$ by Theorem 6.14. If we assume as the induction hypothesis $|C_i| = C_i{}^\star$, then the difference of the upper bound and the lower bound is only the difference of $\overline{\mu}$ and μ, which comes from the one of $\overline{\varphi}$ and φ. By the recursion relation in [18] we can single out when $\overline{\mu}$ and μ coincide and when they are different as in the following.

In the following proposition, the *lowermost coefficient* of an ordinal $\beta < \Omega^\omega$ means, if we let $\Omega^n\gamma_n + \cdots + \Omega\gamma_1 + \gamma_0$ be a Cantor normal form of β to base Ω, the non-zero ordinal γ_k such that $\gamma_i = 0$ for all $i < k$.

6.15 Proposition

Let $\beta = \beta_0 + m$ be an ordinal less than Ω^ω where β_0 is a limit and m is finite. If $\beta \geq \Omega^2$ then

$$\overline{\mu}(\beta) = \begin{cases} \mu(\beta+1) & \text{if the lowermost coefficient of } \beta_0 \text{ is equal to } \mu(\beta_0) \\ \mu(\beta) & \text{otherwise.} \end{cases}$$

If $\beta = \Omega\gamma$ and $\gamma = \gamma_0 + m$ where γ_0 is a limit and m is finite, then

$$\overline{\mu}(\beta) = \begin{cases} \mu(\Omega(\gamma+1)) & \text{if } \gamma_0 = \mu(\beta) \\ \mu(\beta) & \text{otherwise} \end{cases} \qquad \Box$$

Therefore $A^\star \neq |A|$ happens only when either

(i) A is of the form $\tilde{\mu}X.\, X^n C_n + \cdots + X^k C_k + m$ ($n \geq 2$, $k \geq 0$ and m is finite) and $C_k{}^\star = \mu(\Omega^n C_n{}^\star + \cdots + \Omega^k C_k{}^\star)$. Then $|A| = \mu(\Omega^n C_n{}^\star + \cdots + \Omega^k C_k{}^\star + 1 + m)$.

(ii) A is of the form $\tilde{\mu}X.\, X(C_1 + m)$ (m is finite) and $C_1{}^\star = \mu(\Omega \cdot C_1{}^\star)$. In this case, $|A| = \mu(\Omega(C_1{}^\star + 1 + m))$.

In these cases, we must find other linearizations yielding the same ordinals as the upper bounds $|A|$. The most difficult is to manipulate the case $k \geq 1$ of (i).

6.16 Lemma

Let A be an initial algebra of the form $\tilde{\mu}X.\, B[X] + X^k C + D$ (degree 2 or more, $k \geq 1$, C, D are closed, and $B[X]$ may be void).

If $A^\star = C^\star$ there is a linearization of the embedding $\trianglelefteq_A$ such that the order type of the linearization is $\mu(B^\star + \Omega^k C^\star + 1 + D^\star)$.

(*Proof*) Put $A' = \tilde{\mu}X.\, C + B[X] + X^k C + D$, whose Ackermann ordering has order type $\mu(B^\star + \Omega^k C^\star + 1 + D^\star)$. There is a bijection $f : A \to A'$ such that if $a \trianglelefteq_A a'$ then $f(a) \leq_{A'} f(a')$. The inverse image of f gives the required linearization. $\Box$

The case (i) above is handled by this lemma if $k \geq 1$. That is to say, the linearization of the lemma applied to the algebra $A = \tilde{\mu}X.\, X^n C_n + \cdots + X^k C_k + m$ provides the order type $\mu(\Omega^n C_n{}^\star + \cdots \Omega^k C_k{}^\star + 1 + m) = |A|$ as required. If $k = 0$, we simply exchange the order of the summand as $A' = \tilde{\mu}X.\, C_0 + \Omega^n C_n + \cdots + m$. Then the Ackermann ordering of A' gives a linearization of A with order type $|A|$ by Theorem 6.14. For the case (ii), we consider the algebra $A'' = \tilde{\mu}X.\, C_1 X + Xm$. The Ackermann ordering on A'' is the linearization of A with order type $|A|$. Therefore we have the following theorem and corollary as the main results of this section.

6.17 Theorem
Let A be a closed algebra in normal form in the sense of Section 4.

There is a linearization of the embedding $\trianglelefteq_A$ such that the order type of the linearization is equal to $|A|$. □

6.18 Corollary
For each closed algebra A, the embedding $\trianglelefteq_A$ is a well-partial-order whose order type $|Bad(A)|$ is equal to $|A|$ (where A is assumed to be reduced to a normal form without loss of generality). □

So the order types $|Bad(A)|$ of algebra embeddings are given effectively by $|A|$. Recall that the mapping $|\cdot|$ is a bijection up to isomorphism respecting embeddings into the class of ordinals. Hence we have the following theorem, which is the main achievement of this paper.

6.19 Theorem
The mapping $A \mapsto |Bad(A)|$ is a bijection from the class of algebras (up to isomorphism) onto an initial segment of ordinals up to $\varphi(\Omega^\omega, 0)$. □

In other words, for each ordinal less than $\varphi(\Omega^\omega, 0)$ there is an algebra whose order type is equal to the ordinal, and furthermore such an algebra is unique up to embedding-reflecting isomorphism. We also note that the isomorphism of algebras is primitive recursively decidable:

6.20 Corollary
The following is primitive recursively decidable: given two closed algebras, determine whether they are isomorphic with respect to embedding-reflecting morphisms.

(*Proof*) If the normal forms of two algebras are distinct, then they have different order types and thus cannot be isomorphic. The reduction to normal forms is primitive recursive (Lemma 4.16). □

We give several examples of the order types $|A| = |Bad(A)|$ of algebras. For the second and the fourth, we can find announcements in [7].

$$
\begin{array}{lll}
|\mu X.\, X+1| & = \omega & \\
|\mu X.\, X^2+1| & = \epsilon_0 & \\
|\mu X.\, X^2+XN+1| & = \varphi(\omega,0) & \text{where } N \text{ is } \mu X.\, X+1 \\
|\mu X.\, X^2 2+1| & = \Gamma_0 & \\
|\mu X.\, X^{n+1}+1| & = \varphi(\Omega^n,0) & \text{where } n \geq 2
\end{array}
$$

Also the result in Section 3 follows since $|\mu X.\, AX + 1|$ is equal to $\omega^{\omega^{-1+|A|+1}}$ if $|A|$ is of the form $\epsilon_\gamma + n$, epsilon number plus finite number; and equal to $\omega^{\omega^{-1+|A|}}$ otherwise.

The merit of reducing well-partial-orderedness to well-orderedness becomes apparent when proof theory is combined. After a famous work of Gentzen, ordinal numbers are known to be useful to measure the strength of logical systems. The *proof theoretical ordinal* $|T|$ of a logical system T is the least ordinal α such that well-orderedness of α is not provable in T [3]. The following are known.

$$
\begin{array}{lll}
|\mathrm{ACA}_0| & = \epsilon_0 & \\
|\Sigma^1_1\text{-}\mathrm{DC}_0| & = \varphi(\omega,0) & [4] \\
|\mathrm{ATR}_0| & = \Gamma_0 & [15]
\end{array}
$$

These systems are fragments of second order arithmetic, assuming as basic axioms the comprehension axiom for recursive formulas and the induction axiom (not the induction scheme; the subscript $(\text{-})_0$ comes from this restriction on the induction). This basic system is called RCA_0. System ACA_0 has in addition a comprehension axiom for arithmetical formulas [35,38]. This system is a conservative extension of Peano arithmetic. The proof theoretical ordinal ϵ_0 follows from this fact. System Σ^1_1-DC_0 has the dependent choice axiom for Σ^1_1-formulas [4]. System ATR_0 has the axiom asserting the existence of Turing jumps along any recursive well-ordering [15,35,38].

Therefore well-partial-orderedness of the algebra $\mu X.\, X^2+1$ of binary trees is non-provable in system ACA_0, but provable in any stronger system having a greater proof theoretical ordinal, e.g., Σ^1_1-DC_0, ACA, ACA_0 + Π^1_1-Reflection. Likewise well-partial-orderedness of embedding on $\mu X.\, X^2 + XN + 1$ is non-provable in Σ^1_1-DC_0 and well-partial-orderedness of embedding on $\mu X.\, X^2 2 + 1$ is independent from ATR_0, while they are provable in any stronger systems than Σ^1_1-DC_0 and ATR_0 (respectively) having greater proof theoretical ordinals.

Another immediate consequence of our main results is that we can use the class of algebras as an ordinal notation up to $\varphi(\Omega^\omega, 0)$. This ordinal notation has some new features in comparison with traditional ordinal notations; (i) every ordinal notation has a meaning. For example, $\mu X.\, X^2 + 1$ denotes the ordinal ϵ_0 since the order type of the corresponding algebra embedding is equal to ϵ_0; (ii) every notation can be encoded by a Π^1_1-formulas. As is well-known, non-iterated inductive definitions on arithmetical formulas are simulated by the comprehension axiom for Π^1_1 formulas without set parameters [12]. (iii) our system of notations provides an alternative description for Bachmann hierarchy. The Bachmann hierarchy is defined by the Bachmann collection, which is sensitive to the choice of fundamental sequences for limit ordinals. Our theorem shows the hierarchy can admit a definition without using the fundamental sequences. The Feferman-Aczel notation θ [2] also arose for giving the system of notations not depending on fundamental sequences [13].

One might say the obtained notation is up to $\varphi(\Omega^\omega, 0)$ (smaller than Howard ordinal $\varphi(\epsilon_{\Omega+1}, 0)$) and is too weak to analyze impredicative logical system. However we hope to show in a forthcoming paper this bound can be extended to $\theta\Omega_\omega 0 = |\Pi^1_1\text{-CA}_0|$ by allowing mutual recursions.

7 Embedding on Finite Trees

We turn to finite ordered trees, the nodes of which have outdegrees finite but without upper bounds on the number. The set of finite ordered trees is defined naturally if we use a subsidiary sort F (forest), which should be the sort of finite lists of trees. The following rules generate finite ordered trees t and forests f (see Figure 4):

$$\begin{array}{lll} t & ::= & \texttt{span}(f) \\ f & ::= & \texttt{nil} \mid \texttt{cons}(t, f) \end{array}$$

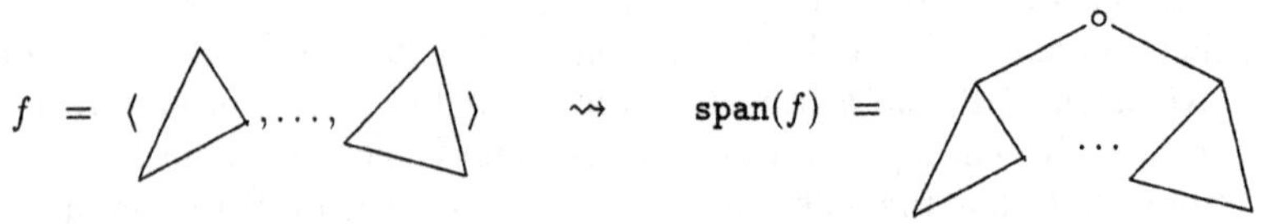

Figure 4

In other words, the algebra T of finite ordered trees is a solution of system of equations

$$\begin{array}{lll} T & = & F \\ F & = & 1 + T \cdot F. \end{array}$$

The algebra T is not definable in the sense of Definition 4.1 since it uses a subsidiary sort F and mutual recursion. In the form of μ-operators, the algebra T is written $\mu X.(\mu Y.1 + XY)$ where two variables X and Y are in the scope of μY. Recall that the algebra in the sense of Definition 4.1 admits only one variable.

Allowing a finite number of sort variables, we can define more complicated structures and we need higher ordinals to reify them. We leave the extension to this direction to a forthcoming paper, and here are content with an analysis of the algebra T of finite ordered trees, which is important and the simplest (in a precise sense; the algebra T yields the least order type among those algebras requiring mutual recursion to define).

Finite trees in T are represented using a unary node **span**, a binary node **cons** and a 0-ary node **nil**. T should be different, however, from the algebra $\mu X.\, X^2 + X + 1$ that has the same family of nodes. The difference arises from the different notions of subterms. Suppose given a tree $t = t\langle t/0, \ldots, t/(n-1)\rangle$ (represented by **span**, **cons** and **nil**). For the notion of subtrees (subterms of sort T), there are few problems: every t/i is a subtree of t and every subtree of t/i is a subtree of t. The problem lies in the sort F of forests. Let $f = \langle t/0, \ldots, t/(n-1)\rangle$ be a forest. The term f is represented by **cons** and **nil** as

$$\mathbf{cons}(t/0, \ldots \mathbf{cons}(t/(n-1), \mathbf{nil}) \ldots)$$

If we follow the idea in Section 4 that subterms are simply subexpressions, then $\langle t/1, \ldots, t/(n-1)\rangle$, $\langle t/2, \ldots, t/(n-1)\rangle$ etc. are sub-forests of f. There are, however, other subterms of sort F hidden in each t/i. If t/i is of the form $u\langle u/0, \ldots, u/(p-1)\rangle$, the forest $\langle u/0, \ldots, u/(p-1)\rangle$ is a subexpression of $\langle t/0, \ldots, t/i, \ldots, t/(n-1)\rangle$. But if we admitted this as subterms (recall that algebra embeddings are defined using subterms), then the embedding on the algebra T would be different with the tree embedding given in Definition 2.4. For example, consider two trees s and t in Figure 5. s does not embed into t

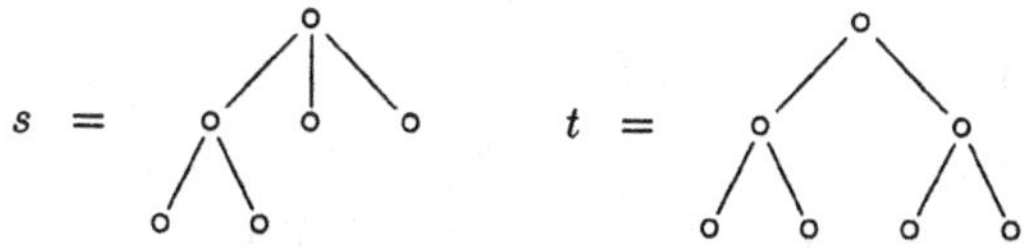

Figure 5

by tree embedding since t has no nodes of outdegree 3. If one admits all subexpressions of sort F as sub-forests, then s embeds into t, as in the following: Consider two forests $\langle \circ, \circ\rangle$ and $\langle \mathbf{span}\langle \circ, \circ\rangle\rangle$, where $\circ$ stands for $\mathbf{span}(\mathbf{nil})$. Since the first is a subexpression of the second, we have $\langle \circ, \circ\rangle \trianglelefteq_F \langle \mathbf{span}\langle \circ, \circ\rangle\rangle$ by the projection rule of algebra embeddings. Then one can derive $\langle \mathbf{span}\langle \circ, \circ\rangle, \circ, \circ\rangle \trianglelefteq_F \langle \mathbf{span}\langle \circ, \circ\rangle, \mathbf{span}\langle \circ, \circ\rangle\rangle$ and then $\mathbf{span}\langle \mathbf{span}\langle \circ, \circ\rangle, \circ, \circ\rangle \trianglelefteq_T \mathbf{span}\langle \mathbf{span}\langle \circ, \circ\rangle, \mathbf{span}\langle \circ, \circ\rangle\rangle$ by congruence rules. The last means $s \trianglelefteq_T t$ and thus the embedding on T is undesirably not equal to the tree embedding.

This dilemma is settled simply by rejecting that $\langle \circ, \circ\rangle$ is a subterm of $\langle \mathbf{span}\langle \circ, \circ\rangle\rangle$. In general, if $f = \langle t/0, \ldots, t/n-1\rangle$ is a term of sort F, then the subterms of f having sort F are only $\langle t/1, \ldots, t/n-1\rangle$, $\langle t/2, \ldots, t/n-1\rangle$ etc., and never look inside of the already formed tree t/i. In the form of inference rules, a is a subterm of b (where a, b are terms of sort T or F) if and only if the relation $a \subseteq b$ is derived by the following rules:

$a \subseteq a$ for every term a

$$\frac{a \subseteq f}{a \subseteq \texttt{cons}(t, f)} \quad t : T \text{ and } f : F$$

$$\frac{a \subseteq f}{a \subseteq \texttt{span}(f)} \quad f : F$$

Note that there is no rule inferring from $a \subseteq \texttt{cons}(t, f)$ from $a \subseteq t$. Then the embeddings associated to the algebras T and F are defined in the same way as in Definition 4.7. One has only to read $a'^{\circ} \subseteq a$ the relation derived by the above rules. It is easy to see that $\trianglelefteq_T$ is the tree embedding on finite ordered trees and $\trianglelefteq_F$ is the Higman embedding induced from the tree embedding.

We give a reification of the tree embedding by the ordinal $\varphi(\Omega^\omega, 0)$. Recall that this ordinal is the supremum of the order types of all (single recursive) algebras. We associate to each bad sequence of finite ordered trees a descending sequence of algebras. The reification technique given in Section 5 works completely as well. To $F[X] = \mu Y.\, 1 + XY$ and $f = \gamma_F(a) : F[T]$ where $a : 1 + TF$, an algebra $F^{\smile}_f[X]$ is associated by $F^{\smile}_f[X] = \mu Y.\, (1 + XY)^{\smile}_a$ where all $X^{\smile}_s$ is replaced by $T^{\smile}_s$ and all $Y^{\smile}_g$ by $F^{\smile}_g[X]$. Moreover to $T = \mu X.\, F[X]$ and $t = \gamma_T(f)$, an algebra $T^{\smile}_t$ is associated by $T^{\smile}_t = \mu X.\, F^{\smile}_f[X]$ where each $X^{\smile}_s$ is replaced by $T^{\smile}_s$.

7.1 Example

Let $t : T$ be $\texttt{span}\langle t/0, \ldots, t/n-1\rangle$.

$$\begin{aligned}
T^{\smile}_t &= \mu X.\, F^{\smile}_{\langle t/0,\ldots,t/n-1\rangle}[X] \\
&= \mu X.\, (\mu Y.\, 1 + T^{\smile}_{t/0} Y + X \cdot F^{\smile}_{\langle t/1,\ldots,t/n-1\rangle}[X]) \\
&\cong \mu X.\, (T^{\smile}_{t/0})^*(1 + X \cdot F^{\smile}_{\langle t/1,\ldots,t/n-1\rangle}[X]) \\
&\;\;\vdots \\
&\cong \mu X.\, (T^{\smile}_{t/0})^* + X(T^{\smile}_{t/0})^*(T^{\smile}_{t/1})^* + \cdots + X^{n-1}(T^{\smile}_{t/0})^* \cdots (T^{\smile}_{t/n-1})^*
\end{aligned}$$

Note that $T^{\smile}_t$ is a single recursive algebra. □

We can show that there is an embedding-reflecting injection $T_t \rightarrowtail T^{\smile}_t$ for all $t : T$ as in Lemma 5.5. Hence to each bad sequence $\langle t/0, t/1, \ldots\rangle$ of terms of sort T we can associate a descending sequence $T^{\smile}_{\langle t/0\rangle}, T^{\smile}_{\langle t/0,t/1\rangle}, \cdots$ of algebras. Therefore well-orderedness of the relation $<$ on the class of algebras, which is equivalent to well-orderedness of $\varphi(\Omega^\omega, 0)$, shows that the tree embedding is well-partial-ordered.

Conversely well-partial-orderedness of $\trianglelefteq_T$ implies well-orderedness of $\varphi(\Omega^\omega, 0)$. To see this, note that $\varphi(\Omega^\omega, 0)$ is the supremum of $\varphi(\Omega^n, 0)$ $(n < \omega)$ and $\varphi(\Omega^n, 0)$ is the order type of well-partial-order on the algebra $\mu X.\, X^{n+1} + 1$ of $(n+1)$-ary trees for $n \geq 2$. There is an embedding-reflecting map from $\mu X.\, X^{n+1} + 1$ to T as easily seen. Hence $Wpo(T)$ implies $Wpo(\mu X.\, X^{n+1} + 1)$ for all n, which in turn implies well-orderedness of $\varphi(\Omega^\omega, 0)$.

7.2 Theorem

Well-partial-orderedness of the tree embedding on finite ordered trees is equivalent to well-orderedness of the ordinal $\varphi(\Omega^{\omega}, 0)$. □

This theorem is first proved by Rathjen and Weiermann [30] for non-ordered trees. We do not claim our method is essentially different with theirs. We include our method here hoping that the the reader might feel the argument is simpler and having an intention to provide a guide to more general arguments for mutual recursion.

We also give a brief description for another result on finite trees, which already appeared in the literature but can be simplified by our method. In [19], Gupta proved that well-partial-orderedness of the tree minor relation is equivalent to well-orderedness of the ordinal ϵ_0. The method in [19] is to associate regular expressions to trees and ordinals to regular expressions so that bad sequences with respect to the tree minor yield descending sequences of ordinals less than ϵ_0.

A finite non-ordered tree is a *minor* of another if and only if the former is obtained from the latter by several applications of edge deletion and edge contraction. We write $s \trianglelefteq_m t$ if s is a tree minor of t (equal to the relation $\triangleleft_{m^r}$ in [19]). This is the graph minor relation applied on rooted trees but respecting the orientation on the edges (rooted trees may be regarded as oriented graphs where the orientations on the edges are from roots to leaves).

In the above, we modified the notion of subterms to obtain the tree embedding as the embedding on the algebra T. In Figure 5, we observed that if the notion of subterms is not modified then s embeds into t undesirably. However the reader might notice that s is a minor of t by contracting the rightmost edge from the root of t (s, t are ordered trees here). In fact, if we add the omitted rule of subterms

$$\frac{a \subseteq t}{a \subseteq \mathtt{cons}(t, f)} \qquad t : T \text{ and } f : F$$

then a finite ordered tree s embeds into t by the algebra embedding $\trianglelefteq_T$ if and only if s is obtained from t by several applications of two rewriting rules in Figure 6. Observe that the rule (i) is the combination of a single application of edge contraction and several applications of edge deletion, and the rule (ii) is a consequence of several applications of edge deletions. So fixing in some canonical way the order on the sets of immediate successors of all nodes in order to transform non-ordered trees to ordered trees, we easily see $s \trianglelefteq_T t$ (with the added rule above for subterms) implies $s \trianglelefteq_m t$. Therefore $Wpo(\trianglelefteq_m)$ implies $Wpo(\trianglelefteq_T)$.

On the other hand, the rules in Figure 6 correspond exactly the algebra embedding on $B = \mu X. X^2 + 1$ of binary trees by the transformation $s \mapsto s^\flat$ from B to T in Figure 7. Hence $Wpo(\trianglelefteq_B)$ implies $Wpo(\trianglelefteq_T)$ and so in turn $Wpo(\trianglelefteq_m)$. Since

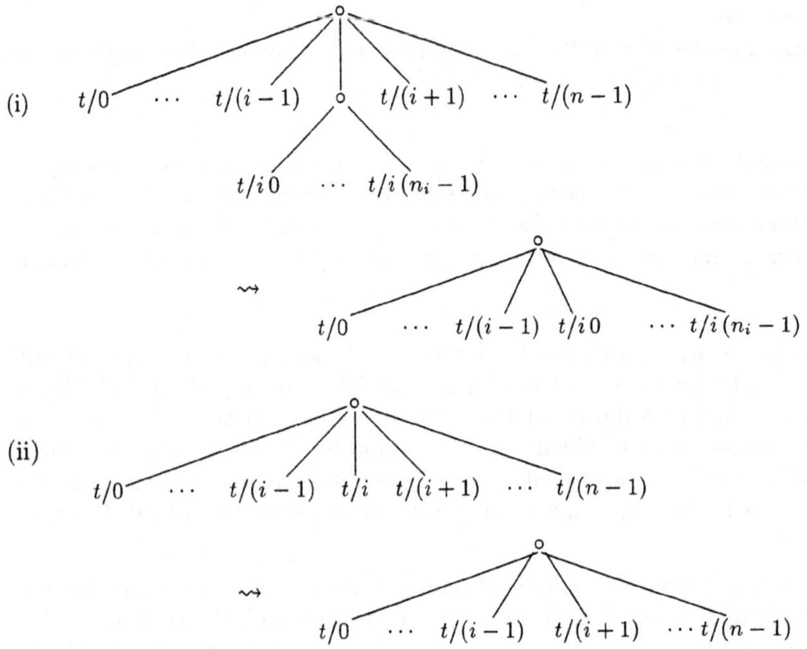

Figure 6

Theorem 5.11 shows the algebra B is reified by the ordinal ϵ_0, we finally have the proof that well-orderedness of ϵ_0 implies well-partial-orderedness of the tree minor relation. The converse is easier. Therefore we have the following theorem first proved by Gupta [19].

7.3 Theorem
Well-partial-orderedness of the tree minor is equivalent to well-orderedness of the ordinal ϵ_0 □

So it is independent from system ACA_0 that the set of finite non-ordered trees is well-partial-ordered with respect to the tree minor relation. In addition, since the argument is formalizable in intuitionistic logic, we have a constructive proof of the fact that the tree minor is a well-partial-ordered, from a constructive proof of well-orderedness of ϵ_0 (See [19]).

Acknowledgements: I am indebted to Adam Cichon, Nachum Dershowitz, Laurence Puel, Kazuyuki Tanaka, and Mariko Yasugi for fruitful discussions

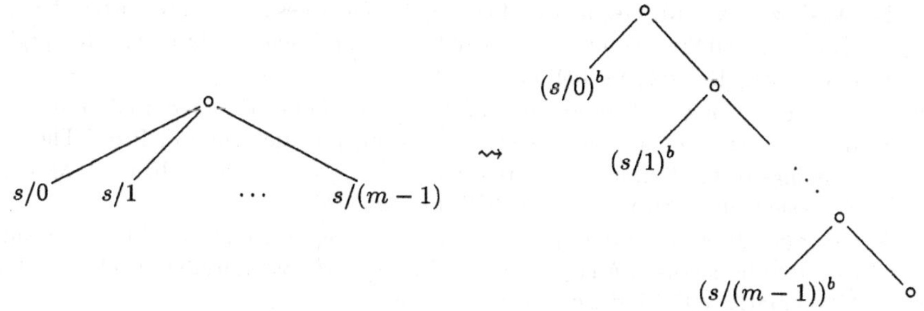

Figure 7

and their pertinence answering to my questions. I am grateful for Yoji Akama to make me notice the work of Rathjen and Weiermann. Most of this work was done during the visit to LIENS in the years 1992/93. I want to express special thanks to Pierre-Louis Curien.

References

1. W. Ackermann, Konstruktiver Aufbau eines Abschnitts der zweiten Cantorschen Zahlenklasse, Math. Z. 53 (1951) 403–413.
2. W. Buchholz, Normalfunktionen und konstruktive Systeme von Ordinalzahlen, in: Proof Theory Symposion, Kiel 1974, J. Miller, G. H. Müller eds., Lecture Notes in Mathematics 500, (Springer, 1975) pp.4–25.
3. W. Buchholz and K. Schütte, Proof Theory of Impredicative Subsystems of Analysis, (Bibliopolis, 1988).
4. A. Cantini, On the relation between choice and comprehension principles in second order arithmetic, J. Symb. Logic 51 (1986) 360–373.
5. P. M. Cohn, Universal Algebra, Revised edition, (D. Reidel, 1981).
6. T. Coquand, A proof of Higman's lemma by structural induction, manuscript, April 1993, Chalmers University, Göteborg, Sweden, 4 pages.
7. D. H. J. de Jongh and R. Parikh, Well-partial orderings and hierarchies, Indag. Math. 39 (1977) 195–207.
8. N. Dershowitz, Orderings for term-rewriting systems, Theoretical Computer Science 17 (1982) 279–301.
9. N. Dershowitz, Trees, ordinals and termination, in: TAPSOFT '93: Theory and Practice of Software Development, Orsay, France, 1993, M.-C. Gaudel, J.-P. Jouannaud eds., Lecture Notes in Computer Science 668 (Springer, 1993) pp. 243–250.
10. N. Dershowitz and Z. Manna, Proving termination with multiset orderings, Comm. ACM (1979) 465–476.

11. N. Dershowitz and M. Okada, Proof theoretic techniques for term rewriting theory, in: Third Annual Symposium on Logic in Computer Science, July 1988, Edinburgh, Scotland, (IEEE, 1988) pp.104–111.
12. S. Feferman, Formal theories for transfinite iterations of generalized inductive definitions and some subsystems of analysis, in: Intuitionism and Proof Theory, Proceedings of the Summer Conference at Buffalo N.Y. 1968, A, Kino, J. Myhill, R. E. Vesley eds., (North-Holland 1970) pp. 303–326.
13. S. Feferman, Preface: how we get from there to here, in: Iterated Inductive Definitions and Subsystems of Analysis: Recent Proof-Theoretical Studies, Lecture Notes in Mathematics 897 (Springer, 1981) pp.1–15.
14. H. Friedman, N. Robertson and P. Seymour, The metamathematics of the graph minor theorem, in: Contemporary Mathematics, Vol. 65, Logic and Combinatorics, Aug 1985, (AMS, 1987) pp.229–261.
15. H. Friedman, K. McAloon and S. Simpson, A finite combinatorial principle which is equivalent to the 1-consistency of predicative analysis, in: Patras Logic Symposion, G. Metakides ed., (North-Holland, 1982) pp. 197-230.
16. L. Fuchs, Partially Ordered Algebraic Systems, (Pengamon Press, 1963).
17. J. H. Gallier, What's so special about Kruskal's theorem and the ordinal Γ_0? A survey of some results in proof theory, Ann. Pure Appl Logic 53 (1991) 199–260.
18. H. Gerber, An extension of Schütte's klammersymbols, Math. Ann. 174 (1967) 203–216.
19. A. Gupta, A constructive proof that tree are well-quasi-ordered under minors (detailed abstract), in: Logical Foundations of Computer Science - Tver '92, A. Nerode, M. Taitslin eds., Tver, Russia, July 1992, Lecture Notes in Computer Science 620, (Springer, 1992) pp. 174–185.
20. G. Higman, Ordering by divisibility in abstract algebras, Proc. London. Math. Soc. Third Series 2 (1952) 326–336.
21. J.-P. Jouannaud and M. Okada, Satisfiability of systems of ordinal notations with the subterm property is decidable, preprint.
22. S. Kamin and J.-J. Lévy, Attempts for generalizing the recursive path orderings, handwritten notes, Feb. 1980, 26pp.
23. J. B. Kruskal, Well-quasi-ordering, the tree theorem, and Vazsonyi's conjecture, Trans. Am. Math. Soc. 95 (1960) 210–225.
24. P. Lescanne, Two implementations of the recursive path ordering on monadic terms, Proc. 19th Allerton House Conference on Communication, Control and Computing, (University of Illinois Press, 1981) pp. 634–643.
25. P. Lescanne, Uniform termination of term rewriting systems, recursive decomposition ordering with status, in: Ninth Colloquium on Trees in Algebra and Programming, March 1984, Bordeaux, France, B. Courcelle ed., (Cambridge University Press, 1984) pp. 181–194.
26. U. Martin and E. Scott, The order types of termination orderings on monadic terms, strings and multisets, Proc. Eighth Annual IEEE Symposium on Logic in Computer Science, June 1992, Montreal, Canada, (IEEE, 1993) pp. 356–363.
27. C. R. Murthy and J. R. Russell, A constructive proof of Higman's lemma, in: Proceedings of the Fifth Annual Symposium on Logic in Computer Science, (IEEE, 1990) pp. 257–267.
28. C. St. J. A. Nash-Williams, On well-quasi-ordering finite trees, Proc. Camb. Philos. Soc. 59 (1963) 833–835.

29. M. Okada and A. Steele, Ordering structures and the Knuth-Bendix completion algorithm, in: Proceedings of the Allerton Conference on Communication, Control and Computing, Monticello, IL, 1988.

30. M. Rathjen and A. Weiermann, Proof-theoretic investigations on Kruskal's theorem, Ann. Pure Appl. Logic 60 (1993) 49–88.

31. F. Richman and G. Stolzenberg, Well-quasi-ordered sets, Adv. Math 97 (1993) 145–153.

32. N. Robertson and P. D. Seymour, Graph minors IV. Tree-width and well-quasi-ordering, J. Comb. Th. Series B 48 (1990) 227–254.

33. K. Sakai, Knuth-Bendix algorithm for Thue system based on kachinuki ordering, ICOT Technical Memorandum: TM-0087, ICOT, Institute for New Generation Computer Technology, Dec. 1984

34. K. Schütte and S. G. Simpson, Ein in der reinen Zahlentheorie unbeweisbarer Satz über endliche Folgen von natürlichen Zahlen, Arch. Math. Logik Grundlagenforsch 25 (1985) 75–89.

35. S. G. Simpson, Reverse mathematics, in: Recursion Theory, A. Nerode, R. A. Shore, eds., Proceedings of Symposia in Pure Mathematics, Volume 42 (AMS, 1985) pp. 461–471.

36. S. G. Simpson, Nonprovability of certain combinatorial properties of finite trees, in: Harvey Friedman's research on the foundations of mathematics, L. A. Harrington, M. D. Morley, A. Scedrov, S. G. Simpson, eds., (North-Holland, 1985) pp. 87–117.

37. S. G. Simpson, Ordinal numbers and the Hilbert basis theorem, J. Symbolic Logic 53 (1988) 961–974.

38. K. Tanaka, Reverse mathematics and subsystems of second-order arithmetic, Sugaku Expositions 5 (1992) 213–234.

On Locomorphism in Analytical Equivalence Theory*

Shigeru Igarashi, Tetsuya Mizutani, Takashi Tsuji and Chiharu Hosono

Institute of Information Science, University of Tsukuba
Tsukuba, JAPAN 305

Abstract. A ν-definable act is a program, logical and procedural at the same time, and also it is very close to a specification. Its semantics called the analytic semantics is given in a completely logical manner. The concept of homomorphism between acts called locomorphism, which is a generalization of equivalence, is introduced. A necessary and sufficient condition for whether or not there exists a morphism between two acts, one parallel and the other sequential, is presented, and some examples are studied.

1 Introduction

A *ν-definable act*, ν-act or act for short, is obtained from a logical formula by means of ν-conversion so that acts and formulas are related closely to each other. An act is a program, which is both logical and procedural, and can be regarded almost as a specification depending on the point of view and on the style [3,4,5,11]. The semantics of acts is given both simply and precisely on the basis of logic and formal mathematics. This enables us to give a method to verify even a system of parallel programs in a uniform way. Incidentally there are two main interpretations of acts, one called 'oncer' and the other 'eternal', the latter of which will be applied in the present paper.

We consider that the verification of programs is reduced to the equivalence of programs. A program is *equivalent* to another if the output values of their corresponding variables coincide whenever the input values do. Equivalence ascertains that a program has the same properties as those of the other already verified program [2]. Therefore it will be desirable for us to generalize the concept of equivalence, especially, for parallel programs involving nondeterminism. For this purpose we consider the *loci* of programs. A locus is a function from rational numbers representing time to the program states, which are functions from the set of variables to values, namely, data. In this paper, we will consider the concept of function *locomorphism* [12,13] defined from the set of loci of a program to that of another program. The properties of an already verified program are conveyed to other programs via locomorphisms.

* This work was supported in part by the Grant-in-Aid for the Scientific Research of Ministry of Education, Science and Culture (No. 05302011) and also by Fuji Xerox.

Related to this work, many systems to verify parallel programs have been proposed. Well-known systems include temporal logic [6,7,9,14], TCSP [1,8], Petri net [15], event structures [8], CCS [10] and so on.

The definition of acts and their semantics are given in the next section. In section 3 the locomorphism is introduced, and a necessary and sufficient condition whether a locomorphism exists or not between two acts, one parallel and the other sequential, is presented. In section 4 some examples of locomorphisms will be shown. Further discussions will be found in section 5.

2 The ν-Conversion

Among higher type languages that enable us to define various data types and to analyze parallel programs, formal real analysis FA [17] is chosen as the original theory of mathematics, because of transparency and capability of developing contemporary real analysis, which is a conservative extension of arithmetic developed on the logical system LK and can be regarded as a "typed LK" with arithmetic, and whose objects are typed abstracts (sets intuitively) starting from rational numbers. (We will use non-arithmetical abstracts, as well as the arithmetical ones permitted in the original FA.) We think that we must deal with at least rational numbers both as time values and as data. They are necessary for the former in analysis of parallel programs and for the latter in numerical programs. We prefer totally ordered time to partially ordered time, especially for the theoretical foundations, since the latter has to be always mapped onto the former both practically and theoretically. The formal semantics will be called *analytic semantics.*

Definition 1. Let x, y, z, ... be metavariables denoting free variables. A word of the form νx is called a *qualitative*, and for any formula A, an expression obtained from A by substituting at least one qualitative in place of free variables is called a *ν-definable act.* □

Among many interpretations of acts, we adopt here the interpretation called the *cosmos* defined by the *predicate of action* which is introduced below. Hereafter, the variable t is assumed to represent time, and for each free variable x, a higer type variable $\hat{x}$ is introduced, where $\hat{x}(t)$ represents the value of x at time t. A sequence of variables $\langle \hat{x}_1, \ldots, \hat{x}_n \rangle$ is denoted by $\hat{\boldsymbol{x}}$ and $\hat{\boldsymbol{x}}(t)$ will be written as $\boldsymbol{x}(t)$ when there is no confusion.

Definition 2. The formula

$$\forall t \forall \epsilon > 0((\exists y A[\hat{\boldsymbol{x}}(t), \boldsymbol{y}, t] \supset \exists \delta > 0(\delta < \epsilon \wedge A[\hat{\boldsymbol{x}}(t), \hat{\boldsymbol{x}}(t+\delta), t]))$$

$$\wedge(\forall \delta \geq 0(\delta < \epsilon \supset \neg \exists \boldsymbol{y} A[\hat{\boldsymbol{x}}(t+\delta), \boldsymbol{y}, t+\delta]) \supset \hat{\boldsymbol{x}}(t) = \hat{\boldsymbol{x}}(t+\epsilon))) \ ,$$

abbreviated by $Pa(A, \hat{\boldsymbol{x}})$, is called the *predicate of action*, where $A[\boldsymbol{x}, \nu \boldsymbol{x}, t]$ is an act, and $\hat{\boldsymbol{x}}$ defined by it is called a *locus* of A. □

The cosmos is given solely by the predicate. Since the interpretation of every program is defined by the predicate, analytic semantics is simpler than many other verification systems (eg. denotational semantics [16]).

The notion of loci, characterized by theorem 5 below, is a generalization of that of execution sequences of programs. And it must be noted that acts are interpreted on some model and not treated formally in the strict sense. From now on, we adopt nonnegative rational numbers as time values.

Definition 3. A set of rational numbers is said to be *discrete* if and only if there exists a positive δ and it holds that $|x - y| > \delta$ for arbitrary distinct elements x, y of it. □

Notation 4. The set of all nonnegative rational numbers and that of all natural numbers are denoted by $Q^{\geq 0}$ and N, respectively. For a strictly increasing sequence $(u_k)_{k \in V}$ of $Q^{\geq 0}$, where V is the set N or an initial segment of N, and its greatest element, if exists, is denoted by λ, a left continuous step function f such that

$$f(u) = \begin{cases} y_0 & \text{if } 0 \leq u \leq u_0, \\ y_{k+1} & \text{if } u_k < u \leq u_{k+1}, \\ y_\lambda & \text{if } u_\lambda < u \text{ (if } V \text{ is finite)} \end{cases}$$

may be denoted by $\theta((u_k, y_k)_{k \in V})$. □

Theorem 5. *Let A be an act such that the set $S = \{t | \exists \boldsymbol{y} A[\hat{\boldsymbol{x}}(t), \boldsymbol{y}, t]\}$ is discrete for any locus $\hat{\boldsymbol{x}}$ of A, every element of which is denoted by t_k in increasing order so that $0 \leq t_k < t_{k+1}$ $(k \geq 0)$. Then for each locus $\hat{\boldsymbol{x}}$, it holds that $A[\hat{\boldsymbol{x}}(t_k), \hat{\boldsymbol{x}}(t_{k+1}), t_k]$ for any $k < \lambda$ and $\hat{\boldsymbol{x}}$ is the step function $\theta((t_k, \hat{\boldsymbol{x}}(t_k))_{k \in V})$, where V is N (and λ is infinite for convenience' sake) if S is infinite, and $V = \{0, \ldots, \lambda\}$ and t_λ is arbitrary one greater than $t_{\lambda-1}$ if S has λ elements.*

Proof. Assume that $t_k < t < t_{k+1}$ and $\epsilon = t_{k+1} - t$ in $Pa(A, \hat{\boldsymbol{x}})$, then we have $\hat{\boldsymbol{x}}(t) = \hat{\boldsymbol{x}}(t_{k+1})$. In a similar manner, we have $\hat{\boldsymbol{x}}(t) = \hat{\boldsymbol{x}}(t_0)$ for $0 \leq t < t_0$, and $\hat{\boldsymbol{x}}(t) = \hat{\boldsymbol{x}}(t_\lambda)$ for $t > t_\lambda$ if S is finite.

If $t = t_k$ for $k < \lambda$ on the other hand, then there exists $\boldsymbol{y}$ such that $A[\hat{\boldsymbol{x}}(t_k), \boldsymbol{y}, t_k]$. Thus, for any positive ϵ there exists δ such that $0 < \delta < \epsilon$ and $A[\hat{\boldsymbol{x}}(t_k), \hat{\boldsymbol{x}}(t_k + \delta), t_k]$. Hence, we have $A[\hat{\boldsymbol{x}}(t_k), \hat{\boldsymbol{x}}(t_{k+1}), t_k]$ for any $k < \lambda$. □

Proofs that are evident will be omitted hereafter.

Definition 6. An act $A[\boldsymbol{x}, \nu\boldsymbol{x}, t]$, or a formula $A[\boldsymbol{x}, \boldsymbol{y}, t]$, is said to be *doable* or *actable* on $\boldsymbol{x}$ at t if and only if $A[\boldsymbol{x}, \boldsymbol{y}, t]$ holds for some $\boldsymbol{y}$. Otherwise, A is said to be *unactable* on $\boldsymbol{x}$ at t. If we are not interested in $\boldsymbol{x}$ or t, it will be omitted. □

Proposition 7. *Let $(t_k, \boldsymbol{x}_k)_{k \in V}$ be a sequence satisfying that $A[\boldsymbol{x}_k, \boldsymbol{x}_{k+1}, t_k]$ holds for each $k < \lambda$ and A is unactable on any $\boldsymbol{x}$ at any t distinct form every t_k $(k < \lambda)$. Then $\hat{\boldsymbol{x}} = \theta((t_k, \boldsymbol{x}_k)_{k \in V})$ is a locus of A.* □

Definition 8. A sequence which satisfies the condition of proposition 7 is called a *trace* of A. □

Example 1. Let us consider the following puzzle:

"There are two bottles. One can contain 10 l and the other, 3 l. There is a big barrel containing enough water. Then measure off 5 l of water from the barrel using only these bottles."

The following expression, abbreviated by $M[x, y, \nu x, \nu y]$, is an act which satisfies the specification of the puzzle.

$$N(t) \wedge x \neq 5 \ \wedge$$
$$(0 \leq \nu x \leq 10 \wedge (\nu y = 0 \vee \nu y = 3) \wedge (\nu x = x \vee \nu x + \nu y = x + y)$$
$$\vee \ 0 \leq \nu y \leq 3 \wedge (\nu x = 0 \vee \nu x = 10) \wedge (\nu y = y \vee \nu x + \nu y = x + y)),$$

where x and y represent the contents of the 10 l and 3 l bottles, respectively, and $N(t)$ means that t is a natural number.

This act performs nondeterministically, i.e., there are infinitely many loci. Among which traces of two loci are illustrated below. The first one is

$$(\langle t_k, x_k, y_k \rangle)_{k \in \{0,\ldots,12\}} =$$
$$(\langle 0,0,0\rangle, \langle 1,0,3\rangle, \langle 2,3,0\rangle, \langle 3,3,3\rangle, \langle 4,6,0\rangle,$$
$$\langle 5,6,3\rangle, \langle 6,9,0\rangle, \langle 7,9,3\rangle, \langle 8,10,2\rangle, \langle 9,0,2\rangle,$$
$$\langle 10,2,0\rangle, \langle 11,2,3\rangle, \langle 12,5,0\rangle) \ .$$

Another trace is that

$$(\langle t_k, x_k, y_k \rangle)_{k \in N} =$$
$$(\langle 0,0,0\rangle, \langle 1,0,3\rangle, \langle 2,0,0\rangle, \langle 3,0,3\rangle, \langle 4,0,0\rangle,$$
$$\langle 5,0,3\rangle, \langle 6,0,0\rangle, \ldots),$$

which is infinite.

It is noted that we get a correct answer if the act performs as the former. □

We shall introduce in section 3 a more convenient concept similar to traces, but used with a restricted form of acts.

It is usually supposed that actions in the cosmos keep values of the variables unchanged as long as possible in accordance with a certain optimization strategy called the *principle of the least action*, a typical strategy of which is given by the following definition.

Definition 9. Let $\boldsymbol{x}$ be a sequence of variables $\langle x_1, \ldots, x_n \rangle$. For a given act $A[\boldsymbol{x}, \nu\boldsymbol{x}, t]$, the act $A^{\#}[\boldsymbol{x}, \nu\boldsymbol{x}, t]$ defined by

$$\forall \boldsymbol{x} \forall \boldsymbol{y} \forall t (A^{\#}[\boldsymbol{x}, \boldsymbol{y}, t] \equiv \exists \boldsymbol{z}(\ ^{-}A[\boldsymbol{x}, \boldsymbol{z}, t] \wedge \boldsymbol{x} \neq \boldsymbol{z}) \wedge \ ^{-}A[\boldsymbol{x}, \boldsymbol{y}, t])$$

is called the *sharping* of A, where ^{-}A is the act ^{n}A defined by induction as follows:

$$^{1}A \equiv A \wedge (\exists y_2 \ldots \exists y_n A_{y_1}[x_1] \supset x_1 = y_1),$$
$$^{2}A \equiv A \wedge \ ^{1}A \wedge (\exists y_1 \exists y_3 \ldots \exists y_n \ ^{1}A_{y_2}[x_2] \supset x_2 = y_2),$$
$$\ldots$$
$$^{n}A \equiv A \wedge {}^{1}A \wedge \ldots \wedge {}^{n-1}A \wedge (\exists y_1 \exists y_2 \ldots \exists y_{n-1} \ {}^{n-1}A_{y_n}[x_n] \supset x_n = y_n) \ .$$

□

The sharping of A satisfies the principle of the least action.

Example 2. If an act $A[x_1, x_2; \nu x_1, \nu x_2]$ is $x_1 > 0 \supset \nu x_2 = x_2 - 1$, then ^{-}A and $A^{\#}$ are as follows.

$$^{-}A[x_1, x_2; \nu x_1, \nu x_2] \equiv (x_1 > 0 \supset \nu x_2 = x_2 - 1) \wedge (x_1 \leq 0 \supset \nu x_2 = x_2) \wedge \nu x_1 = x_1 \ .$$

$$A^{\#}[x_1, x_2; \nu x_1, \nu x_2] \equiv x_1 > 0 \wedge \nu x_1 = x_1 \wedge \nu x_2 = x_2 - 1 \ .$$

□

The sharping oprerator is used for the sake of convenience. As shown in the above example on the other hand, the sharped act has less nondeterminism. Hence, when we want to express a fully nondeterministic act, the operator is not used.

3 The Locomorphism

Definition 10. If A and B are two acts on the data domains D and D', respectively, and $\langle \psi, \pi \rangle$ is a pair of functions with ψ from D to D' and π from $Q^{\geq 0}$ to $Q^{\geq 0}$, then *an act A restricted by a precondition p is locomorphic to an act B w. r. t.* $\langle \psi, \pi \rangle$, abbreviated by $\langle \psi, \pi \rangle : A|p \to B$, if and only if 0 is a fixed point of π, π diverges and it is monotonic, namely,

$$(a) \ \pi(0) = 0, \forall t \exists u (\pi(u) > t) \text{ and } \forall t \forall u (t < u \supset \pi(t) \leq \pi(u)),$$

and there exists a locus $\hat{\boldsymbol{y}}$ of B for any locus $\hat{\boldsymbol{x}}$ of A and $\hat{\boldsymbol{y}}(\pi(t)) = \psi(\hat{\boldsymbol{x}}(t))$ for any t if $p[\hat{\boldsymbol{x}}(0)]$, namely,

$$(b) \ \forall \hat{\boldsymbol{x}} \exists \hat{\boldsymbol{y}} (Pa(A, \hat{\boldsymbol{x}}) \wedge p[\hat{\boldsymbol{x}}(0)] \supset Pa(B, \hat{\boldsymbol{y}}) \wedge \forall t (\hat{\boldsymbol{y}}(\pi(t)) = \psi(\hat{\boldsymbol{x}}(t)))) \ .$$

It must be noted that the image locus $\hat{\boldsymbol{y}}$ is not necessary unique.

The precondition p induces the initial condition of the variables $\boldsymbol{x}$ of A. In case where $p[\boldsymbol{x}]$ is true for all $\boldsymbol{x}$, A is simply said to be *locomorphic to B w. r. t.* $\langle \psi, \pi \rangle$ and is abbreviated to $\langle \psi, \pi \rangle : A \to B$. □

Example 3. Here are two examples of locomorphisms among acts for the solution to the puzzle in example 1. The first one is from the following act M_1 to M in example 1. The act M_1 is as follows:

$$M_1[z, \nu z] :: N(t) \wedge z \neq 5 \wedge \nu z = z + 3 \ \mathbf{mod} \ 10 \ .$$

This act performs deterministically, and its trace is

$$(\langle t_k, z_k \rangle)_{k \in \{0,\ldots,5\}} = (\langle 0,0 \rangle, \langle 1,3 \rangle, \langle 2,6 \rangle, \langle 3,9 \rangle, \langle 4,2 \rangle, \langle 5,5 \rangle),$$

when an initial value of z is 0.

It is easy to see that the act M_1 restricted by $z(0) = 0$ is locomorphic to M w. r. t. $\langle \psi_1, \pi_1 \rangle$, where $\psi_1 : z \mapsto \langle x, y \rangle$ is such that $\langle x, y \rangle = \langle z, 0 \rangle$ and $\pi_1 : Q^{\geq 0} \to Q^{\geq 0}$ is such that $\pi_1(t) = 4t$.

For the second, it is easy to see that the following ALGOL-like program with parallel assignment statements represents a solution to the puzzle:

$$
\begin{array}{l}
\textbf{while } z \neq 5 \textbf{ do begin} \\
\qquad w := 3; \\
\qquad \textbf{if } z + w > 10 \textbf{ then } \langle z, w \rangle := \langle 0, z + w - 10 \rangle; \\
\qquad \langle z, w \rangle := \langle z + w, 0 \rangle \\
\textbf{end};
\end{array}
$$

This program is translated to $M_2^{\#}$, where $M_2[z, w, l, \nu z, \nu w, \nu l]$ is

$$
\begin{array}{l}
N(t) \wedge (\ l = 0 \wedge z \neq 5 \wedge \nu l = 1 \\
\qquad \vee\, l = 1 \wedge \nu w = 3 \wedge \nu l = 2 \\
\qquad \vee\, l = 2 \wedge (z + w > 10 \supset \langle \nu z, \nu w \rangle = \langle 0, z + w - 10 \rangle) \wedge \nu l = 3 \\
\qquad \vee\, l = 3 \wedge \langle \nu z, \nu w \rangle = \langle z + w, 0 \rangle \wedge \nu l = 0),
\end{array}
$$

using the stage variable l. It is easy to see that $M_2^{\#}$ is equivalent to

$$
\begin{array}{l}
N(t) \wedge (\ l = 0 \wedge z \neq 5 \wedge \langle \nu z, \nu w \rangle = \langle z, w \rangle \wedge \nu l = 1 \\
\qquad \vee\, l = 1 \wedge \langle \nu z, \nu w \rangle = \langle z, 3 \rangle \wedge \nu l = 2 \\
\qquad \vee\, l = 2 \wedge (z + w > 10 \wedge \langle \nu z, \nu w \rangle = \langle 0, z + w - 10 \rangle \\
\qquad\quad \vee z + w \leq 10 \wedge \langle \nu z, \nu w \rangle = \langle z, w \rangle) \wedge \nu l = 3 \\
\qquad \vee\, l = 3 \wedge \langle \nu z, \nu w \rangle = \langle z + w, 0 \rangle \wedge \nu l = 0)\ .
\end{array}
$$

This is also a deterministic act, and the pair of functions $\langle \psi_2, \pi_2 \rangle$ such that the function $\psi_2 : \langle z, w, l \rangle \mapsto \langle x, y \rangle$ is defined by $\langle x, y \rangle = \langle z, w \rangle$ and π_2 is by $\pi_2(t) = 2t$ is a locomorphism from $M_2^{\#}$ to M. □

Example 3'. When the bottles and the goal of the puzzle are doubled in size, the act for the solution corresponding to M_1 is the following: $N(t) \wedge v \neq 10 \wedge \nu v = v{+}6 \textbf{ mod } 20$, which gives a trivial example that the function ψ or its component is not the identity. □

For two formulas p_I and p_O, the expression $p_I\{A\}p_O$ means that for any locus $\hat{x}$ of A, if $p_I[\hat{x}(0)]$ then $p_O[\hat{x}(\infty)]$, where $p[\infty]$ is $\exists t \forall u > t.p[u]$, i.e., p_I and p_O are considered to be a precondition and postcondition of A, respectively. Let $q_I[z]$ and $q_O[z]$ be $p_I[\psi(z)]$ and $p_O[\psi(z)]$, respectively. Then the following propositions, i.e. the preservations of specifications, are immediately obtained from the locomorphism.

Proposition 11. *If $\langle \psi, \pi \rangle : A|p_I \to B$ and $q_I\{B\}q_O$, then $p_I\{A\}p_O$.* □

Proposition 12. *If $\langle \psi, \pi \rangle : A|p_I \to B$ and $p_I\{A\}p_O$, then for any initial value z_0 of B such that $q_I[z_0]$, there exists a locus $\hat{z}$ of B such that $\hat{z}(0) = z_0$ and $q_O[\hat{z}(\infty)]$.* □

It must be noted that the postconditions p_O and q_O may be obtained as the termination conditions given from the program text.

Now we show a necessary and sufficient condition for whether a locomorphism exists between acts representing programs. Firstly, we introduce some notations and definitions.

Notation 13. For a formula $R[\boldsymbol{x}, \boldsymbol{y}]$, $R^{\sim}[\boldsymbol{x}, \boldsymbol{y}]$ is the following:

$$R[\boldsymbol{x}, \boldsymbol{y}] \vee \neg \exists \boldsymbol{y} R[\boldsymbol{x}, \boldsymbol{y}] \wedge \boldsymbol{x} = \boldsymbol{y}$$

and $R^n[\boldsymbol{x}, \boldsymbol{y}]$ is defined by induction as follows:

$$R^0[\boldsymbol{x}, \boldsymbol{y}] \equiv \boldsymbol{x} = \boldsymbol{y}$$

$$\text{and } R^n[\boldsymbol{x}, \boldsymbol{y}] \equiv \exists \boldsymbol{z}(R^{n-1}[\boldsymbol{x}, \boldsymbol{z}] \wedge R[\boldsymbol{z}, \boldsymbol{y}]) \text{ for } n \geq 1 \ .$$

□

For an act $R[\boldsymbol{x}, \nu\boldsymbol{x}]$, $R^{\sim}[\boldsymbol{x}, \nu\boldsymbol{x}]$ is actable at any time and its behavior is the same as the original act except for the actability. The act $R^n[\boldsymbol{x}, \nu\boldsymbol{x}]$ induces n-step execution of the original act.

Definition 14. Let $R_1, \ldots, R_m$ be acts, none of which contains the time variable t. Let a_i $(1 \leq i \leq m)$ be a formula, called a *spur* of R_i, such that the set $\{t | a_i(t)\}$ is nonnegative, discrete and infinite and in which both $\boldsymbol{x}$ and $\nu\boldsymbol{x}$ do not occur. Let $[m]$ be the set $\{1, \ldots, m\}$. Then a system of parallel programs $(R_i)_{i \in [m]}$ with spurs $(a_i)_{i \in [m]}$ is denoted by

$$a_1(t) \uparrow R_1[\boldsymbol{x}, \nu\boldsymbol{x}] \parallel \ldots \parallel a_m(t) \uparrow R_m[\boldsymbol{x}, \nu\boldsymbol{x}],$$

which is defined by the act of the form

$$(c) \ \ ((a_1(t) \wedge \exists \boldsymbol{y} R_1[\boldsymbol{x}, \boldsymbol{y}] \supset R_1[\boldsymbol{x}, \nu\boldsymbol{x}]) \wedge \ldots \wedge (a_m(t) \wedge \exists \boldsymbol{y} R_m[\boldsymbol{x}, \boldsymbol{y}] \supset R_m[\boldsymbol{x}, \nu\boldsymbol{x}]))^{\#} \ .$$

□

It must be noted that a spur is a generalization of a scheduler.

The program system expresses a multi-CPU with simultaneous executions of processes (cf. temporal logic).

As for expression of parallel programs, the sharping operator is used for the sake of convenience. It saves us from writing a complex and complicated act shown as above. On the other hand, the expression of programs with spurs for sequential but nondeterministic processes is simple as follows.

For an act T in which t does not occur, an act of the form $b(t) \wedge T[\boldsymbol{z}, \nu\boldsymbol{z}]$, where the formula b has the same conditions as those of the spur a_i, is an act representing a sequential program T with a spur b. Here, T does not have the sharping operator since we want to express nondeterministic sequential processes (See example 6).

In order to investigate loci of parallel program systems, and to prove theorems of the locomorphism, the notion of "quasi-traces" is introduced, which is similar to that of traces but more convenient.

Notation 15. Two strictly increasing sequences $(\delta_k)_{k\in N}$ and $(\gamma_k)_{k\in N}$ consist of all elements in $\{t|a_1(t)\vee\ldots\vee a_m(t)\}$ and $\{t|b(t)\}$, respectively. The set $\{i|a_i(\delta_k)\}$ is denoted by S_k for each k. □

Intuitively, δ_k means the k-th time at which at least one process of P_1 is scheduled and γ_k does that of P_2. The set S_k is all processes of P_1 scheduled at time δ_k.

Proposition 16. *Let P be an act representing a parallel program system with a scheduler $(a_i)_{i\in[m]}$. For each locus $\hat{x}$ of P, there exists an infinite sequence $(\delta_k, \hat{x}_k)_{k\in N}$ such that $\hat{x} = \theta((\delta_k, x_k)_{k\in N})$.* □

Definition 17. For a parallel program P, a sequence given by proposition 16 is called a *quasi-trace* of the act. When we are not interested in time value δ_k, we call $(x_k)_{k\in N}$ a *quasi-trace* of P. A quasi-trace of an act representing a sequential program is defined in a similar manner. □

Now we show a necessary and sufficient condition that a locomorphism exists between a parallel program system and a sequential program.

Definition 18. For a sequence $(R_i)_{i\in[m]}$ of acts, $R_S{}^\dagger[x, y]$ is the formula

$$\bigwedge_{i\in S}(\exists y R_i[x, y] \supset R_i[x, y]),$$

where S is a nonempty subset of $[m]$. □

Hereafter, P_1 denotes an act representing a system of m parallel programs $(R_i)_{i\in[m]}$ with spurs $(a_i)_{i\in[m]}$, P_2 one representing a sequential program T with a spur b, and x and z are the sequences of variables of P_1 and P_2 on the data domains D and D', respectively.

Note 19. For a locus $\hat{z}$ of P_2, if T is unactable on $\hat{z}(t)$ at some t, then the values of $\hat{z}$ are unchanged after t, so that T is unactable also on $\hat{z}(u)$ for any u greater than t.

Note 20. The formula $R_{S_k}^{\dagger\#}$ expresses the action of P_1 at k-th scheduled time δ_k. A sequence $(\delta_k, x_k)_{k\in N}$, satisfying $R_{S_k}{}^{\dagger\#\sim}[x_k, x_{k+1}]$, is a quasi-trace of P_1 because $P_1[x, y, t]$ is equivalent to $R_{S_k}{}^{\dagger\#}[x, y]$ if $t = \delta_k$, and false otherwise. In a similar manner, a sequence $(\gamma_k, z_k)_{k\in N}$ satisfying $T^\sim[z_k, z_{k+1}]$ is a quasi-trace of P_2.

Theorem 21. *Let a function ψ from D to D' and a formula U_0 be given. For each combination of spurs $a_1, \ldots, a_m$ and b, there exists a function π such that $\langle\psi, \pi\rangle : P_1|U_0 \to P_2$ if U_k defined by (i) and ψ satisfy (ii) below, where S_k is defined in notation 15. The converse also holds, i.e., if $\langle\psi, \pi\rangle : P_1|U_0 \to P_2$ then (i) and (ii) hold for some $(U_k)_{k\in N}$.*

$$(i)\ U_{k+1}[y] \equiv \exists x(U_k[x] \wedge R_{S_k}{}^{\dagger\#\sim}[x, y])\ \text{every}\ k \in N,$$

$$(ii)\ \forall x\forall y(U_k[x] \wedge R_{S_k}{}^{\dagger\#\sim}[x, y] \supset T^{\sim n_k}[\psi(x), \psi(y)])\ \text{every}\ k \in N,$$

where n_k is some natural number depending solely on k, and $\sum_{k=0}^{\infty} n_k = \infty$.

Proof. ($\Leftarrow$) Let the function π be defined by

$$\pi(t) = \begin{cases} 0 & \text{if } 0 \le t \le \delta_0, \\ \gamma_{sum(k)} & \text{if } \delta_k < t \le \delta_{k+1}, \end{cases}$$

where $sum(k)$ is an abbreviation of $\sum_{j=0}^{k} n_j$. It is easy to see that the function π satisfies the condition (a).

Assume that $\hat{\boldsymbol{x}}$ is any locus of P_1 such that $U_0[\hat{\boldsymbol{x}}(0)]$ and $(\delta_k, \boldsymbol{x}_k)_{k\in N}$ is its quasi-trace. $U_k[\boldsymbol{x}_k]$ and $R_{S_k}{}^{\dagger\#\sim}[\boldsymbol{x}_k, \boldsymbol{x}_{k+1}]$ for each k follow from (i). Let us show that for any initial segment $\langle \boldsymbol{x}_0, \boldsymbol{x}_1, \ldots, \boldsymbol{x}_{l+1}\rangle$ of $(\boldsymbol{x}_k)_{k\in N}$ there exists an initial segment $\langle \boldsymbol{z}_0, \boldsymbol{z}_1, \ldots, \boldsymbol{z}_{sum(l)}\rangle$ of a quasi-trace of P_2 satisfying $\psi(\boldsymbol{x}_0) = \boldsymbol{z}_0$ and $\psi(\boldsymbol{x}_{k+1}) = \boldsymbol{z}_{sum(k)}$ by induction on the length of $\langle \boldsymbol{x}_0, \boldsymbol{x}_1, \ldots, \boldsymbol{x}_{l+1}\rangle$.

First, in case where the length is 1, $\langle \psi(\boldsymbol{x}_0)\rangle$ is an initial segment of a quasi-trace of P_2 since any values of suitable types can be initial values of P_2.

Next, let us assume that $\langle \boldsymbol{z}_0, \boldsymbol{z}_1, \ldots, \boldsymbol{z}_{sum(l)}\rangle$ is an initial segment of a quasi-trace of P_2, and that $\psi(\boldsymbol{x}_{l+1}) = \boldsymbol{z}_{sum(l)}$. From (ii), $(T^{\sim})^{n_{l+1}}[\psi(\boldsymbol{x}_{l+1}), \psi(\boldsymbol{x}_{l+2})]$ holds, so that there exist $n_{l+1} - 1$ elements $\langle \boldsymbol{z}_{sum(l)+1}, \ldots, \boldsymbol{z}_{sum(l)+n_{l+1}-1}\rangle$ and $\langle \boldsymbol{z}_0, \boldsymbol{z}_1, \ldots, \boldsymbol{z}_{sum(l)}, \boldsymbol{z}_{sum(l)+1}, \ldots, \boldsymbol{z}_{sum(l)+n_{l+1}-1}, \psi(\boldsymbol{x}_{l+2})\rangle$ is also an initial segment.

Therefore, it is concluded by induction that for any quasi-trace $(\boldsymbol{x}_k)_{k\in N}$ of P_1 with the initial condition $U_0[\boldsymbol{x}_0]$, there exists a quasi-trace $(\boldsymbol{z}_k)_{k\in N}$ of P_2 and $\psi(\boldsymbol{x}_{k+1}) = \boldsymbol{z}_{sum(k)}$ for each $k \ge -1$. Hence, the step function $\hat{\boldsymbol{z}} = \theta((\delta_k, \boldsymbol{z}_k)_{k\in N})$ is a locus of P_2 and it holds that $\psi(\hat{\boldsymbol{x}}(t)) = \hat{\boldsymbol{z}}(\pi(t))$.

($\Rightarrow$) It is easy to show from (i) that, for any $\boldsymbol{w}$ satisfying $U_k[\boldsymbol{w}]$, there exists a locus $\hat{\boldsymbol{x}}$ of P_1 such that $U_0[\hat{\boldsymbol{x}}(0)]$ and $\hat{\boldsymbol{x}}(\delta_k) = \boldsymbol{w}$. Let $\hat{\boldsymbol{x}}$ be such locus and $\hat{\boldsymbol{z}}$ be the image of it by the locomorphism, then it holds that $R_{S_k}{}^{\dagger\#\sim}[\hat{\boldsymbol{x}}(\delta_k), \hat{\boldsymbol{x}}(\delta_{k+1})]$. Following the locomorphism, $\psi(\hat{\boldsymbol{x}}(\delta_k)) = \hat{\boldsymbol{z}}(\pi(\delta_k))$ and $\psi(\hat{\boldsymbol{x}}(\delta_{k+1})) = \hat{\boldsymbol{z}}(\pi(\delta_{k+1}))$ hold. Let the time γ_{r_k} be the first time such that $b(\gamma_{r_k})$ holds after $\pi(\delta_k)$, and let the time $\gamma_{r_{k+1}}$ satisfy the analogous conditions, i.e., it is the first time after $\pi(\delta_{k+1})$ that $b(\gamma_{r_{k+1}})$ is true. Then $(T^{\sim})^{n_k}[\hat{\boldsymbol{z}}(\gamma_{r_k}), \hat{\boldsymbol{z}}(\gamma_{r_{k+1}})]$ holds where n_k is $r_{k+1} - r_k$, n_k depends on only $(a_i)_{i\in[m]}$, b and π, and it is independent from the choice of $\boldsymbol{w}$. Next, we show that $sum(\infty)$ tends to infinity. Assume $sum(\infty) < \infty$. Then n_j is 0 for any j greater than some k, which implies $\pi(\delta_j) = \gamma_{r_j} = \gamma_{r_k} = \pi(\delta_k)$, which contradicts (a). Hence, $sum(\infty)$ tends to infinity. □

Note 22. As shown in example 4 below, the formula U_k may be given by the parameter k in practice.

Note 23. The sufficient condition of theorem 21 is still correct without changing the proof even if the definition (i) is replaced by

$$\forall \boldsymbol{x} \forall \boldsymbol{y} (U_k[\boldsymbol{x}] \wedge R_{S_k}{}^{\dagger\#\sim}[\boldsymbol{x}, \boldsymbol{y}] \supset U_{k+1}[\boldsymbol{y}]) .$$

Hence, the following corollary also holds.

Corollary 24. *For each combination of spurs $a_1, \ldots, a_m$ and b, there exists a function π and $\langle\psi, \pi\rangle : P_1|U \to P_2$ if a formula U and a function ψ from D to D' satisfy (i′) and (ii′) below for each nonempty subset S of $[m]$.*

$$(i')\ \forall \boldsymbol{x} \forall \boldsymbol{y}(U[\boldsymbol{x}] \wedge R_S{}^{\dagger\#}[\boldsymbol{x}, \boldsymbol{y}] \supset U[\boldsymbol{y}])\ .\ (initiality)$$

$$(ii')\ \forall \boldsymbol{x} \forall \boldsymbol{y}(U[\boldsymbol{x}] \wedge R_S{}^{\dagger\#\sim}[\boldsymbol{x}, \boldsymbol{y}] \supset T^{\sim n_S}[\psi(\boldsymbol{x}), \psi(\boldsymbol{y})]),\ (continuability)$$

where n_S is a natural number depending solely on S, and $\sum_{k=0}^{\infty} n_{S_k} = \infty$. □

Remark. If $n_S \geq 1$ every S, the last condition can be omitted.

The following theorem for two sequential programs also holds, and the proof is similar to that of theorem 21.

Theorem 25. *Let P_1 be a sequential program T_1 with a spur a and P_2 be T_2 with b. Let D_1 and D_2 be data domains of P_1 and P_2, respectively. Let a formula U_0 be given. Then for each combination of spurs a and b, there exists a function π such that $\langle\psi, \pi\rangle : P_1|U_0 \to P_2$ if and only if a sequence of formulas $(U_k)_{k\in N}$ defined by the definition obtained (i) by replacing $R_{S_k}{}^{\dagger\#}$ by T_1 and a function ψ from D_1 to D_2 satisfy the condition obtained by replacing $R_{S_k}{}^{\dagger\#}$ by T_1 and T by T_2 in (ii).* □

It must be noted that corollary 24 for two sequential programs also holds if its conditions are modified similarly to theorem 25.

4 Examples

Example 4. Let us assume that the domain of every variable is the set N. Consider the following 2 acts, each of which computes n^2 or m^2, respectively:

$$P_1 :: a(t) \wedge T_1[n, i, s; \nu n, \nu i, \nu s], \quad \text{and}$$

$$P_2 :: b(t) \wedge T_2[m, r, u, j, l; \nu m, \nu r, \nu u, \nu j, \nu l],$$

where $T_1[n, i, s; \nu n, \nu i, \nu s]$ is $(i < n \wedge \nu i = i+1 \wedge \nu s = s+n)^{\#}$, and $T_2[m, r, u, j, l; \nu m, \nu r, \nu u, \nu j, \nu l]$ is

$$\begin{array}{ll}(& l = 0 \wedge r < m \wedge \nu l = 1 \\ \vee & l = 1 \wedge \nu r = r + 1 \wedge \nu l = 2 \\ \vee & l = 2 \wedge (j \leq 2r - 1 \wedge \nu j = j + 1 \wedge \nu u = u + 1 \\ & \qquad \vee\ j > 2r - 1 \wedge \nu j = 1 \wedge \nu l = 0))^{\#}\ .\end{array}$$

The original programs are as follows:
P_1:

```
while i < n do begin
      i := i + 1;
      s := s + n
end;
```

and P_2:

while $r < m$ **do begin**
  $r := r + 1$;
  while $j \leq 2r - 1$ **do begin**
    $j := j + 1$;
    $u := u + 1$
  end;
  $j := 1$
end .

Let the formula $U_0[n, i, s]$ be given by $\langle i, s \rangle = \langle 0, 0 \rangle$ and the function ψ : $\langle n, i, s \rangle \mapsto \langle m, r, u, j, l \rangle$ be defined by $\langle m, r, u, j, l \rangle = \langle n, i, i^2, 1, 0 \rangle$.

Assertion 26. ${T_2}^{2r+4}[m, r, u, 1, 0; m, r + 1, u + 2r + 1, 1, 0]$ holds if $r < m$.

Proof. If $r < m$, it is easy to show that (1) ${T_2}^2[m, r, u, 1, 0; m, r + 1, u, 1, 2]$. Assume r' is a positive natural number. Then it is trivial that $T_2[m, r', u, j, 2; m, r', u + 1, j + 1, 2]$ if $j \leq 2r' - 1$, so that, repeating $2r' - 1$ times, we have ${T_2}^{2r'-1}[m, r', u, 1, 2; m, r', u+2r'-1, 2r', 2]$. Hence, it holds that (2) ${T_2}^{2r'}[m, r', u, 1, 2; m, r', u + 2r' - 1, 1, 0]$ because $T_2[m, r', u', 2r', 2; m, r', u', 1, 0]$ for any u'. Putting $r' = r + 1$ in (2) and from (1), the conclusion holds. □

Now we show $\langle \psi, \pi \rangle : P_1 | U_0 \rightarrow P_2$ for some π by theorem 25 taking $2k + 4$ as n_k. By (i), the sequence of formulas $(U_k)_{k \in N}$ is given by $U_k[n, k, s] \equiv k \leq n \wedge \langle i, s \rangle = \langle k, k \cdot n \rangle \vee i > n \wedge \langle i, s \rangle = \langle n, n^2 \rangle$.

If $k < n$, $U_k[n, i, s]$ and ${T_1}^{\sim}[n, i, s; n', i', s']$, then $\langle i, s \rangle = \langle k, k \cdot n \rangle$ and $\langle n', i', s' \rangle = \langle n, k+1, (k+1) \cdot n \rangle$, so that, $\psi(n, i, s)$ is $\langle n, k, k^2, 1, 0 \rangle$ and $\psi(n', i', s')$ is $\langle n, k+1, (k+1)^2, 1, 0 \rangle$. Hence, ${T_2}^{2k+4}[\psi(n, k, s), \psi(n', k', s')]$ holds by assertion 26.

On the other hand, assume that $k \geq n$. Then i is n by U_k and hence T_2 is unactable. Since T_1 is also unactable on $\psi(n, n, s)$, the condition (ii) holds.

Therefore, $\langle \psi, \pi \rangle : P_1 | U_0 \rightarrow P_2$ for some π. □

Example 5. Consider the following 2 acts P_1 and P_2, each of which computes $n!$:

$$P_1 :: a(t) \wedge T_1[x, y; \nu x, \nu y],$$

$$P_2 :: b(t) \wedge T_2[z, w; \nu z, \nu w],$$

where $T_1[x, y; x', y']$ is $x \geq 1 \wedge x' = x - 1 \wedge y' = x \cdot y$ and $T_2[z, w; z', w']$ is $z \leq n \wedge z' = z + 1 \wedge w' = z \cdot w$, respectively.

Let the functions $\psi_1 : \langle x, y \rangle \mapsto \langle z, w \rangle$ and $\psi_2 : \langle z, w \rangle \mapsto \langle x, y \rangle$ be such that $\langle z, w \rangle = \langle n - x + 1,\ p_1 \cdot (n - x)! \rangle$ and $\langle x, y \rangle = \langle n - z + 1,\ p_2/(n - z + 1)! \rangle$, respectively, with parameters p_1, p_2, and let $U[x, y]$ be $N(x) \wedge N(y) \wedge x \leq n + 1$. Then it holds trivially that $U[x, y]$ and $T_1[x, y; x', y']$ imply $U[x', y']$, and it does also that $U[z, w]$ and $T_2[z, w; z', w']$ imply $U[z', w']$. Furthermore, we can derive that $U[x, y] \wedge {T_1}^{\sim}[x, y, x', y'] \supset {T_2}^{\sim}[\psi_1(x, y), \psi_1(x', y')]$ and that $U[z, w] \wedge {T_2}^{\sim}[z, w, z', w'] \supset {T_1}^{\sim}[\psi_2(z, w), \psi_2(z', w')]$. Hence, by corollary 24 (for two sequential programs), there exist two functions π_1, π_2 and $\langle \psi_1, \pi_1 \rangle : P_1 | U \rightarrow P_2$ and $\langle \psi_2, \pi_2 \rangle : P_2 | U \rightarrow P_1$. □

Example 6. Let α be a variable that is an array elements $\alpha(1), \ldots, \alpha(n)$, each with value either 0 or 1, and both $\alpha(0)$ and $\alpha(n+1)$ with the value 1. The acts P_1 and P_2 are the following, each of which checks whether $\alpha(i) = 1$ for all i in $[n]$ or not:

$$P_1 :: a_1(t) \uparrow R_1[x, y; \nu x, \nu y] \parallel a_2(t) \uparrow R_2[x, y; \nu x, \nu y]$$

and

$$P_2 :: b(t) \wedge T[v, W; \nu v, \nu W],$$

where

$$R_1[x, y; x', y'] :: \alpha(x) \cdot \alpha(y) = 1 \wedge x' < y \wedge x' = x + 1,$$

$$R_2[x, y; x', y'] :: \alpha(x) \cdot \alpha(y) = 1 \wedge x < y' \wedge y' = y - 1$$

and

$$T[v, W; v', W'] :: v = 1 \wedge \exists z (z \in \{1, \ldots, n\} - W \wedge \langle v', W' \rangle = \langle \alpha(z), W + \{z\} \rangle),$$

respectively. Now, let us assume that the function $\psi : \langle x, y \rangle \mapsto \langle v, W \rangle$ is given by

$$v = \alpha(x) \cdot \alpha(y),$$

and

$$W = \begin{cases} \{1, \ldots, x-1\} \cup \{y, \ldots, n\} & \text{if } \alpha(x) = \alpha(y) = 0, \\ \{1, \ldots, x\} \cup \{y, \ldots, n\} & \text{otherwise,} \end{cases}$$

and the formula $U[x, y]$ is also given by

$$N(x) \wedge N(y) \wedge 0 \leq x \leq y \leq n + 1 \wedge \alpha(x) \in \{0, 1\} \wedge \alpha(y) \in \{0, 1\} .$$

Note that we assume only $U[x(0), y(0)]$ here for the purpose of illustration although P_1 would be executed with a pair of initial values $\langle x(0), y(0) \rangle = \langle 0, n+1 \rangle$ in practice.

By definition 9, $R_{\{1\}}{}^{\dagger\#}$, $R_{\{2\}}{}^{\dagger\#}$ and $R_{\{1,2\}}{}^{\dagger\#}$ are as follows:

$$R_{\{1\}}{}^{\dagger\#}[x, y; x', y'] \equiv \alpha(x) \cdot \alpha(y) = 1 \wedge x' < y \wedge \langle x', y' \rangle = \langle x + 1, y \rangle,$$

$$R_{\{2\}}{}^{\dagger\#}[x, y; x', y'] \equiv \alpha(x) \cdot \alpha(y) = 1 \wedge x < y' \wedge \langle x', y' \rangle = \langle x, y - 1 \rangle \text{ and}$$

$$R_{\{1,2\}}{}^{\dagger\#}[x, y; x', y'] \equiv \alpha(x) \cdot \alpha(y) = 1 \wedge x < y' \wedge \langle x', y' \rangle = \langle x + 1, y - 1 \rangle .$$

Now we show $\langle \psi, \pi \rangle : P_1 | U \to P_2$ using corollary 24. First, (i') is shown.

Assertion 27. It holds that $U[x, y]$ and $R_S{}^{\dagger\#}[x, y; x', y']$ imply $U[x', y']$ for $S = \{1\}, \{2\}, \{1, 2\}$.

Proof. Case where $S = \{1\}$. Assume that $U[x, y]$ and $R_{\{1\}}{}^{\dagger\#}[x, y; x', y']$. It holds that $0 \leq x' \leq y' \leq n+1$ from $0 \leq x$, $x' = x+1$, $x' < y$, $y \leq n+1$ and $y' = y$. $N(x')$ and $N(y')$ are trivial. Further, $\alpha(x')$, $\alpha(y') \in \{0, 1\}$ since α is not changed and indices x' and y' lie between 0 and $n+1$. Hence, $U[x', y']$ holds.

The proofs of the other cases are similar. □

Next a trivial part is (ii') is shown.

Assertion 28. If $R_S{}^{\dagger\#}$ is unactable on $\langle x, y\rangle$, then T is also unactable on $\psi(x, y)$.

Proof. Consider the case where $S = \{1\}$ and assume that $R_S{}^{\dagger\#}$ is unactable on $\langle x, y\rangle$. Then $x+1 \geq y$ or $\alpha(x) \cdot \alpha(y) \neq 1$, which implies $(\psi(x, y))_W = \{1, \ldots, n\}$ or $(\psi(x, y))_v \neq 1$. Thus, T is also unactable on $\psi(x, y)$. Other cases are similar. □

Assertion 29. It holds that $\langle \psi, \pi\rangle : P_1|U \to P_2$ for any combination of spurs a_1, a_2 and b.

Proof. By corollary 24, assertions 27 and 28, it is sufficient to prove that the following condition holds for $S = \{1\}, \{2\}, \{1, 2\}$:

$$(1)\ U[x, y] \wedge R_S{}^{\dagger\#}[x, y; x', y'] \supset T^{\sim n_S}[\psi(x, y); \psi(x', y')],$$

where $n_{\{1\}} = n_{\{2\}} = 1$ and $n_{\{1,2\}} = 2$. Hereafter, $\{1, \ldots, n\} - (\psi(x, y))_W$ is denoted by $\overline{(\psi(x, y))_W}$.

Assume that $U[x, y]$ and $R_{\{1\}}{}^{\dagger\#}[x, y; x', y']$ hold. Since $\alpha(x) \cdot \alpha(y) = 1$, we have $(\psi(x, y))_v = 1$ and $(\psi(x', y'))_v = \alpha(x+1)$. Since $\overline{(\psi(x, y))_W}$, namely $\{x+1, \ldots, y-1\}$, is nonempty from $x+1 < y$, we choose $x+1$ for z in T and then it holds that $(\psi(x, y))_W + \{x+1\} = (\psi(x', y'))_W$. Hence, $T[\psi(x, y), \psi(x', y')]$ holds.

The formula (1) in case where $S = \{2\}$ is proved in a similar manner.

Let us assume that $U[x, y]$ and $R_{\{1,2\}}{}^{\dagger\#}[x, y; x', y']$. Trivial, $(\psi(x, y))_v = 1$. The assumption implies that $\overline{(\psi(x, y))_W}$ is nonempty, so that both $x+1$ and $y-1$ are elements of the set. Let us consider 2 cases where $x+1 \neq y-1$ and $x+1 = y-1$.

Case 1: $x+1 \neq y-1$. Since $x+1 < y$, the case implies $x+1 < y-1$. We investigate the following 3 cases: $\alpha(x+1) = 1$, $\alpha(y-1) = 1$ and $\alpha(x+1) = \alpha(y-1) = 0$.

(1a) $\alpha(x+1) = 1$. Since $T[\psi(x, y); \alpha(x+1), \{1, \ldots, x+1\} \cup \{y, \ldots, n\}]$ and $T[\alpha(x+1), \{1, \ldots, x+1\} \cup \{y, \ldots, n\}; \psi(x', y')]$ hold, we have $T^2[\psi(x, y); \psi(x', y')]$, which implies (1).

(1b) $\alpha(y-1) = 1$. Similarly to the case (1a), both $T[\psi(x, y);\ \alpha(y-1), \{1, \ldots, x\} \cup \{y-1, \ldots, n\}]$ and $T[\alpha(y-1), \{1, \ldots, x\} \cup \{y-1, \ldots, n\}; \psi(x', y')]$ hold, so that we have $T^2[\psi(x, y); \psi(x', y')]$.

(1c) $\alpha(x+1) = \alpha(y-1) = 0$. Since $\psi(x', y') = \langle \alpha(y-1), \{1, \ldots, x\} \cup \{y-1, \ldots, n\}\rangle$, $T[\psi(x,y); \psi(x',y')]$ is shown in a similar manner to the case (1b). Moreover, since $\alpha(y-1) = 0$, T is unactable on $\psi(x',y')$, whence $T^{\sim}[\psi(x',y'); \psi(x',y')]$. Thus, it holds that $T[\psi(x,y); \psi(x',y')] \wedge T^{\sim}[\psi(x',y'); \psi(x',y')]$, i.e., $(T^{\sim})^2[\psi(x,y); \psi(x',y')]$.

Case 2: $x+1 = y-1$. In this case, $\overline{(\psi(x,y))_W}$ is the singleton set $\{x+1\}$ and it holds that $\psi(x',y') = \langle \alpha(x+1), \{1, \ldots, n\}\rangle$. Hence, $T[\psi(x,y); \psi(x',y')]$ holds. Also T is unactable on $\psi(x',y')$ because $\overline{(\psi(x',y'))_W}$ is empty. Thus, in a similar manner to case (1c), we have $(T^{\sim})^2[\psi(x,y); \psi(x',y')]$, which implies (1). □

The termination condition of P_1 is defined by $\alpha(x) \cdot \alpha(y) \neq 1 \vee x+1 \geq y$, and that of P_2 is $v \neq 1 \vee \{1, \ldots, n\} - W = \emptyset$. From proposition 11 , the following facts are obtained.

Assertion 30. If P_2 terminates, then P_1 also does. □

Assertion 31. If $\langle v, W\rangle = \langle 1, \emptyset\rangle$ $\{P_2\}$ $v = \prod_{i=1}^{n} \alpha(i)$, then $\langle x, y\rangle = \langle 0, n+1\rangle$ $\{P_1\}$ $\alpha(x) \cdot \alpha(y) = \prod_{i=1}^{n} \alpha(i)$. □

Assertion 31 says the following.

Let both P_1 and P_2 start with the expected values. Then that P_1 finds $\alpha(i) = 0$ for some i and either $\alpha(x)$ or $\alpha(y)$ is 0 for the output values $\langle x, y\rangle$ is derived from that P_2 also finds $\alpha(i) = 0$ and the output value of v is 0.

5 Discussion

We have introduced the concept of locomorphism and have given useful theorems to derive it. Locomorphism is an extension of "homomorphism" of programs and one of their "simulation" discussed by McCarthy, Milner, etc., in late 1960's. There can be some relationship between the locomorphism and the "refinement" discussed by Lamport [7]. We can verify specifications of a parallel program if we investigate the images of the locomorphism. We can also investigate relationships between two parallel program systems if we verify those between corresponding "image" programs.

To investigate the related works, Petri nets and event structures do not treat the change of program variables. Therefore actual programs are not easily verified in these system. Comparing them, locomorphism deals with the change of values of variables directly, hence the behavior of programs is esasily investigated. Manna and Milner's system [9] has an idea similar to ν-conversion, but it is too complicated to verify parallel programs. On the other hand, equivalence and locomorphism are either impossible to define on temporal logic, or difficult if possible.

Although we assumed a spur to be infinite for simplicity, Theorem 21 in section 3 holds even if they are finite but large enough for processors to execute, so that in fact, conditions (i) and (ii) are still sufficient to derive the locomorphism in example 6 if each spur has at least n elements.

References

1. Hoare, C. A. R.: *Communicating Sequential Processes*, Prentice-Hall International, 1985.
2. Igarashi, S.: An axiomatic approach to the equivalence problems of algorithms with applications, *Rep. Comp. Centre Univ. Tokyo*, **1** (1968), pp. 1-101.
3. Igarashi, S.: The ν-conversion and an analytic semantics, in R. E. A. Mason (ed.), *Inf. Proc. 83*, Elsevier Science Publishers B.V., IFIP (1983), pp. 769-774.
4. Igarashi, S., Mizutani, T. and Tsuji, T.: An analytical semantics of parallel program processes represented by ν-conversion., *TENSOR, N. S.*, **45** (1987), pp. 222-228.
5. Igarashi, S., Mizutani, T. and Tsuji, T.: Specifications of parallel program processes in analytical semantics., *TENSOR, N. S.*, **45** (1987), pp. 240-244.
6. Kröger, F.: *Temporal logic of programs*, Springer-Verlag, 1987.
7. Lamport, L.: What good is temporal logic?, in R. E. A. Mason (ed.), *Inf. Proc. 83*, Elsevier Science Publishers B.V., IFIP (1983), pp. 657-668.
8. Loogen, R. and Goltz, U.: Modelling nondeterministic concurrent processes with event structures, *Fundamenta Informaticae*, **XIV** (1991), pp. 39-74.
9. Manna, Z. and Pnueli, A.: Completing the temporal picture, *Theor. Comp. Sci*, **83** (1991), pp. 97-130.
10. Milner, R.:*Communication and Concurrency*, Prentice-Hall International, 1989.
11. Mizutani, T., Hosono, C. and Igarashi, S.: Verification of programs using ν-definable acts, *Computer Software*, **2**, (1985), pp. 529-538 (in Japanese).
12. Mizutani, T.: An analytical equivalence theory of programs with applications., *Ph. D. thesis*, Univ. Tsukuba, 1987.
13. Mizutani, T., Igarashi, S. and Tsuji, T.: An analytical equivalence theory of computer programs, in A. Días, J. Echevererría and A. Ibarra (eds.), *International symposium on structures in mathematical theories* (1990), pp. 199-204.
14. Moszkowski, B. C.: *Executing Temporal Logic Programs*, Cambridge Univ. Press, 1986.
15. Olderog, E. -R.: Correctness of concurrent processes, *Theor. Comp. Sci.*, **80** (1991), pp. 263-288.
16. Soundararajan, N.: Denotational semantics of CSP, *Theor. Comp. Sci.*, **33** (1984), pp. 279-304.
17. Takeuti, G.: *Two applications of logic to mathematics*, Princeton University Press, 1978.

Analysis of a Software/Hardware System by Tense Arithmetic

Kohji TOMITA[1], Takashi TSUJI[2] and Shigeru IGARASHI[2]

[1] Mechanical Engineering Laboratory, AIST, MITI
Namiki 1–2, Tsukuba 305 JAPAN
[2] Institute of Information Science, University of Tsukuba
Tennoudai 1–1, Tsukuba 305 JAPAN

Abstract. In this paper we analyze a program of a software/hardware system using explicit rational time. The analysis is based on ν-conversion, which interprets programs with rational time, and tense arithmetic. As a typical example we adopt a kind of bounded buffer problem, in which a producer sends data to a consumer with a bounded buffer, but the producer cannot examine status of the buffer. How to send data as fast as possible without overflowing the buffer is a problem. Properties of a program of the system are analyzed and safety conditions that the buffer does not overflow are obtained.

1 Introduction

Many systems to describe and reason about properties of parallel programs have been proposed. Most of them are based on one of the following three methods. The first is Hoare logic [4] extended for parallel programs [16,17,2]. The second is temporal logic [13,12]. The third is process algebra such as CSP [6], CCS [14,15], and so on.

As for treatment of explicit time, most of these systems do not treat it a priori. But treatment of the explicit time is indispensable to describe and reason about properties of parallel programs, especially in cases for describing executions that wait for some prescribed time, or re-sending of data due to communication errors. Thus, for that purpose, they must be extended. Calculus of duration [1] and a system by Pnueli and Harel [20] are examples of extension of temporal logic. But formulas in temporal logic are rather intended for excluding explicit time from their representations. Time dependent properties are expressed using temporal operators. Thus such extensions do not seem to be suited well. Moreover many of such systems assume interleaving execution of parallel processes.

On the other hand, ν-conversion [7] deals with explicit rational time by using one special variable t which represents time in an interpretation named cosmos. Allowing the time variable, many properties can be expressed in quite a natural manner.

ν-conversion converts formulas of mathematical theory into ν-definable acts (or ν-acts, acts). A ν-act can be regarded as a generalized program, and its semantics is defined on formal logic. Using ν-conversion, we can describe, analyze and verify properties of programs rigorously and uniformly.

Moreover a system based on ν-conversion has the following advantages. First, it can prove axioms and inference rules of other systems, so that it is more general than others [7]. Second, it treats ν-acts, which are quite general representation of programs in some sense. By deciding on translation rules from programming languages to ν-acts, analysis or verification of different programming languages can be accomplished uniformly. Thus the system based on ν-conversion does not depend on a so called programming language. An example of translation of programs in CSP [5] to ν-acts is presented in [3]. Moreover, equivalence of programs, called locomorphism, has been introduced, and a verification method based on locomorphism has been developed [18,19]. Finally an interpreter which executes (a significant subset of) ν-acts as programs has been implemented [11].

In this paper we study a typical example of parallel programs using explicit rational time, used to show that ν-conversion enables natural and rigorous analysis of such programs. It is a typical example, and a similar method can be applied to other parallel programs.

Moreover, the analysis are performed within the language of tense arithmetic [10], by introducing 'explicit' or concrete time terms in order to 'readably' cope with the problem discussed.

The example we use in this paper is a variation of a bounded buffer problem, and we call it a real time problem on programs. The program is composed of two processes: one is a producer and the other is a consumer. The consumer process has a bounded buffer but the producer process can not examine whether the buffer is full or not. The problem is to send data as fast as possible without overflowing the buffer in such a configuration. For that purpose, the producer process has to know the processing time of data by the consumer process. Such situation can occur in one-way communications or in the case where communication time is so large that examination of the buffer is not practical. But such situation has not been analyzed enough.

In section 2 we give some definitions concerning ν-conversion. In section 3 we describe tense arithmetic. In section 4 we show the rational time problem in detail. In section 5 we analyze the program using ν-conversion and derive two safety conditions. In section 6 we analyze it using tense arithmetic. In section 7 we conclude the paper.

2 ν-Conversion

In this section, we give some definitions concerning ν-conversion [7] necessary for this paper.

Definition 1. Let T be a system of mathematical theory (e.g. FA [22]), $T(L)$ be the language of T, and $x, y, z, \ldots$ be metavariables representing free variables of $L(T)$. We call νx a *qualitative*. For any formula A of $L(T)$, an expression obtained by substituting at least one qualitative in place of free variables in A is called *ν-definable act* (or simply ν-act or act). This operation is called ν-conversion.

Hereafter, [ ] following a formula represents an occurrence or a substitution.

ν-acts have several interpretations. The simplest one is the primary interpretation or 'oncer' interpretation. Intuitively, under this interpretation, $A[\boldsymbol{x}, \nu\boldsymbol{x}]$ represents an action which changes the present state to a new state so that the new value of $\boldsymbol{x}$ is represented by $\nu\boldsymbol{x}$, where a state is an assignment of values to free variables, and $\boldsymbol{x}$ is an abbriviation of $x_1, \ldots, x_n$. More precisely it is defined as follows:

Definition 2. Let M be a model of $L(T)$, $L(M)$ be a language which is obtained by extending $L(T)$ so that names of all elements of the universe of M are included as constants. We denote that a formula F of $L(M)$ is true in M under an assignment σ by $\sigma \models F$. The *primary interpretation* of $A[\boldsymbol{x}, \nu\boldsymbol{x}]$ in M is as follows.

Let σ be the present state.

- If $\sigma \models \exists\boldsymbol{y}A[\boldsymbol{x}, \boldsymbol{y}]$ then A is said to be *actable*. In this case, an element $\boldsymbol{\xi}$ of the universe which satisfies $\sigma \models A[\boldsymbol{x}, \boldsymbol{\xi}]$ is chosen. Then the next state is an assignment which is obtained from σ by changing the assignment of $\boldsymbol{x}$ to $\boldsymbol{\xi}$.
- If $\sigma \models \neg\exists\boldsymbol{y}A[\boldsymbol{x}, \boldsymbol{y}]$ then A is said to be *unactable*. In this case the next state does not exist.

For example, an act $\nu x = y \;\&\; \nu y = x$ swaps the values of variables x and y under this interpretation, and an act $c \;\&\; A \vee \neg c \;\&\; B$ corresponds to a conditional statement "**if** c **then** A^* **else** B^*", where A^* and B^* are programs corresponding to A and B, respectively.

Another interpretation, called *cosmos*, is given by the *predicate of action*.

Definition 3. The predicate of action, $Pa(A, \hat{\boldsymbol{x}})$, is the following:

$$\begin{aligned}
&\forall t\ \forall\varepsilon>0\ ((\exists \boldsymbol{y}\ A[\hat{\boldsymbol{x}}(t), \boldsymbol{y}, t] \\
&\qquad\qquad \supset\ \exists\delta>0\ (\delta < \varepsilon \;\&\; A[\hat{\boldsymbol{x}}(t), \hat{\boldsymbol{x}}(t+\delta), t])) \\
&\quad \&\ (\forall\delta\geq 0\ (\delta < \varepsilon\ \supset\ \neg\exists \boldsymbol{y}\ A[\hat{\boldsymbol{x}}(t+\delta), \boldsymbol{y}, t+\delta]) \\
&\qquad\qquad \supset\ \hat{\boldsymbol{x}}(t) = \hat{\boldsymbol{x}}(t+\varepsilon)))\ .
\end{aligned}$$

$\hat{\boldsymbol{x}}$ is a sequence of higher order variables corresponding to $\boldsymbol{x}$, and $\hat{\boldsymbol{x}}(t)$ means values of variables $\boldsymbol{x}$ at time t. We denote $\hat{\boldsymbol{x}}(t)$ simply by $\boldsymbol{x}(t)$ when there is no possibility of confusion. The variable t is a special variable representing time and its domain is the set of nonnegative rationals. We call a value of $\hat{\boldsymbol{x}}$ satisfing $Pa(A, \hat{\boldsymbol{x}})$ a *locus* of variables $\boldsymbol{x}$ of act A.

Intuitively, this predicate means that an act is executed, under the oncer interpretation, in an infinitesimal time interval when actable, and that the values of variables are kept unchanged during the act is unactable.

If the set of t satisfying $\exists\boldsymbol{y}A[\hat{\boldsymbol{x}}(t), \boldsymbol{y}, t]$ is discrete, then $\hat{\boldsymbol{x}}$ is a step function continuous to the left.

In this paper we assume acts are interpreted by the predicate of action. Moreover, we assume that values of variables are kept as far as possible. It is called the *least action principle.* An act $A^{\#}$, defined later, obtained from A is similar to A but it preserves the values of variables as far as possible under some decided order of variables, so that the least action principle is satisfied. In addition, the values of variables change when it acts. Thus change of value means that an action must have occurred.

Definition 4. For a formula $A[\boldsymbol{x}, \boldsymbol{y}]$, $A^{\#}$ is defined as follows. We define $\bar{A}$ by $\bar{A} \equiv A^n$, where

$$\begin{aligned}
A^1 &\equiv A \,\&\, (\exists y_2 \cdots \exists y_n A_{y_1}[x_1] \supset x_1 = y_1), \\
A^2 &\equiv A \,\&\, A^1 \wedge (\exists y_1 \exists y_3 \cdots \exists y_n {A^1}_{y_2}[x_2] \supset x_2 = y_2), \\
&\cdots \\
A^n &\equiv A \,\&\, A^1 \,\&\, \cdots \,\&\, A^{n-1} \,\&\, (\exists y_1 \cdots \exists y_{n-1} {A^{n-1}}_{y_n}[x_n] \supset x_n = y_n) \,.
\end{aligned}$$

We define $A^{\#}[\boldsymbol{x}, \nu\boldsymbol{x}]$ for A by $\forall\boldsymbol{x}\forall\boldsymbol{y}(A^{\#}[\boldsymbol{x}, \boldsymbol{y}] \equiv \exists\boldsymbol{z}(\bar{A}[\boldsymbol{x}, \boldsymbol{z}] \,\&\, \boldsymbol{z} \neq \boldsymbol{x}) \,\&\, \bar{A}[\boldsymbol{x}, \boldsymbol{y}])$.

In the definition, $\bar{A}$ is equivalent to A except that the values of the maximum number of the leftward variables among $x_1, \ldots, x_n$ are preserved whenever permitted.

For an act $R[\boldsymbol{x}, \nu\boldsymbol{x}, t]$ and a unary predicate a, $(a(t) \supset R)^{\#}$ is an act which is obtained from R by restricting the time when it is actable so that R acts only at the time when $a(t)$ holds. Such $a(t)$ is called a *spur* for R, if the set of t satisfying $a(t)$ is discrete.

Usually we suppose that an act R represents an essential algorithm (which corresponds to a usual program) not containing scheduling information. Besides the interpretation of $(a(t) \supset R[\boldsymbol{x}, \nu\boldsymbol{x}, t])^{\#}$ by Pa corresponds to the execution of act R under a scheduler $a(t)$. Thus, it is often the case that an act interpreted by Pa includes an abstract execution system such as a scheduler.

Definition 5. $a(t) \uparrow R \parallel b(t) \uparrow S$ is defined as follows:

$$\begin{aligned}
&((a(t) \,\&\, \exists\boldsymbol{y}R[\boldsymbol{x}, \boldsymbol{y}, t] \supset R[\boldsymbol{x}, \nu\boldsymbol{x}, t]) \\
&\,\&\, (b(t) \,\&\, \exists\boldsymbol{y}S[\boldsymbol{x}, \boldsymbol{y}, t] \supset S[\boldsymbol{x}, \nu\boldsymbol{x}, t]))^{\#} \,.
\end{aligned}$$

Intuitively, it represents an act which executes acts R and S concurrently under spurs $a(t)$ and $b(t)$ respectively and satisfies the least action principle. The interpretation corresponds to an execution of a parallel program composed of two processes: one process corresponds to R and is executed when $a(t)$ holds, and the other process corresponds to S and is executed when $b(t)$ holds.

We can treat programs using explicit rational time in a natural and uniform manner in the system based on the ν-conversion. In order to prove some property P of a program, it is sufficient to prove that any locus of the program (more precisely, an act corresponding to it) interpreted by Pa satisfies P. In the case of a program which contains explicit time, the program contains the variable t representing time, and we must represent values of variables at different times. Even in such cases, we can treat them uniformly.

3 Tense Arithmetic

Tense arithmetic is based on rational number theory, and deals with time as a rational value. It is a generalization of the usual first-order predicate calculus with certain modification of terms so as to include *time terms* of the form either (i)$e\rfloor A$, (ii)$e;A$ or (iii)$\uparrow A$, where A is a logical formula and e is a (time) term. The expression $e\rfloor A$ means intuitively the infimum of the set of times when A holds, at or after the time represented by e. If the set is empty then $e\rfloor A = e-1$, and if the infimum does not exist as a rational value then $e\rfloor A = e-2$. The expressions $\uparrow A$ and $e;A$ mean intuitively the infimum of the set of times when A holds, after an observation time (or a current time), and after e, repectively. Thus $\uparrow$*true* means the currnt time, where *true* denotes the ever true predicate constant.

The axiom for $e\rfloor A$ is given by

$$\begin{aligned}&\exists x.B[x] \mathbin{\&} \exists q(I[q,B] \mathbin{\&} e\rfloor A = q)\\ \vee\ &\exists x.B[x] \mathbin{\&} \neg\exists q.I[q,B] \mathbin{\&} e\rfloor A = e-2\\ \vee\ &\neg\exists x.B[x] \mathbin{\&} e\rfloor A = e-1\ ,\end{aligned}$$

where

$$\begin{aligned}B[x] &\equiv e \le x \mathbin{\&} A_x\ ,\\ I[y,F] &\equiv L[y,F] \mathbin{\&} \forall z(L[z,F] \supset z \le y)\ ,\\ L[y,F] &\equiv \forall z(F[z] \supset y \le z)\ ,\\ A_x &\equiv x\rfloor A = x\\ &\quad \mathbin{\&} (\exists\varepsilon(\varepsilon > 0 \mathbin{\&} \forall\delta(0 < \delta \le \varepsilon \supset x+\delta\rfloor A \ne x+\delta))\\ &\qquad \vee(\exists\varepsilon(\varepsilon > 0 \mathbin{\&} \forall\delta(0 < \delta \le \varepsilon \supset x+\delta\rfloor A = x+\delta)) \mathbin{\&} x\rfloor\neg A \ne x))\ .\end{aligned}$$

Intuitively, $I[y,F]$ and $L[y,F]$ mean that y is the infimum and a lower bound of the set $\{x \mid F[x]\}$, and if the truth value of A is a step function of time, A_x means that A is true at time x.

$e;A$ is given in a similar manner to $e\rfloor A$ except that $e < x \mathbin{\&} A_x$ is used instead of $B[x]$. $\uparrow A$ is defined by $\uparrow A = \uparrow$*true*$;A$.

Let T be a (first-order) mathematical theory. We add new predicate constants called *spurs* $\alpha, \beta, \gamma, \ldots$ to the language of T, so that we obtain an extended theory $T(\alpha,\beta,\gamma,\ldots)$ adding a few axioms described later on.

A spur intuitively means a drive, control, or scheduler for parallel processes. For instance, suppose $P_1 /\!/ P_2$ stands for the concurrent programs P_1 and P_2. We associate two distinct spurs α and β with them, and assume that P_1 is moved 1 step by each α; and similarly for P_2, by each β.

In accordance with the general framework for interpretation described below, a spur α as a predicate constant will be sent on to a discrete set of rationals (as time) denoted by S_α. Thus P_1 will move 1 step further consecutively at

$t = 1.1, 1.2, 1.3$ if and only if $\{1.1, 1.2, 1.3\} \subseteq S_\alpha$ and $\{\gamma \mid 1.1 < \gamma < 1.2 \text{ or } 1.2 < \gamma < 1.3\} \cap S_\alpha = \emptyset$.

Standard abbreviations

1. $A_1; \cdots; A_n$ abbreviates $\uparrow A_1; \cdots; A_n$ for $n \geq 2$.
2. (post condition). $e\{A\}$ abbreviates that $e; A = e$ holds. Intuitively it means that A holds just after the time expressed by e.
3. (possibility). $\uparrow true \leq \uparrow A$ clearly means $\diamond A$ in the conventional temporal logic, and the latter can be regarded as an abbreviation.
4. α^{n+1} abbreviates $\alpha^n; \alpha$, where α^1 denotes α.
5. $\Delta(e, A)$ abbreviates $e; A - e$, i.e. an interval until A holds after the time expressed by e.

Example

We give a simple example here. Let P be a program $x := x+1$ which increments a variable x under an initial condition $x = 0$ and α be a spur of P such that $S_\alpha = \{1.1, 1.4, 1.6, 1.9\}$. Then the following hold at time 0:

$$\begin{array}{lll} \uparrow(x=2) = 1.4, & \uparrow(x=2); \alpha = 1.6, & \uparrow(x=2); \alpha; \alpha = 1.9, \\ (x=2); \alpha^2\{x=4\}, & \uparrow(x=5) = -1\ , & \end{array}$$

and at time 1.5,

$$\uparrow(x=1) = 0.5, \quad \uparrow(x=2) = 1.5, \quad \uparrow(x=3) = 1.6\ .$$

4 Software/Hardware System

Consider the case in which a computer generates data and transmits them to a terminal. In this case, the computer and the terminal can each be regarded as one process. Thus the overall system composed of the computer and the terminal is one parallel program system. Therefore it is clear that problems of parallel programs may occur in this case.

One of the problems, which has actually occurred, is the following: the terminal has a bounded buffer. It can store some data but the computer cannot examine whether the buffer is full or not. Under that configuration, how the computer can transmit data to the terminal as fast as possible is a problem. We call it a real time problem on programs.

On the actual problem, the computer was HITAC M170 and the terminal was Tektronix 4025. The computer transmits a sequence of vector commands to the terminal. The terminal interprets each command and generates a vector corresponding to the command, and then it displays the vector on the graphic screen. It takes some time to generate vectors. Moreover it takes an enormous time to clear the screen comparing to other commands.

If the computer sends data too fast without waiting for the terminal to display, then the buffer will overflow. On the other hand, if the computer waits too long, the user will succeed to display on the screen, but execution time becomes very large and he has to wait for an unreasonably long time. Thus it is necessary to find how to transmit data as fast as possible without overflowing the buffer.

The problem stated above is old, but such situations can occur even today in the case where the examination of the buffer is impossible (because of one-way communication) or in the case where the examination is not practical (because of long distance such as interplanetary communication, or low communication speed).

Here we simplify the problem so that each data value has the same size. Then the following program represents an essential part of the behavior of the computer:

P_0 : $\nu s = c \;\&\; \nu u = \mathit{clock} - c$;
P_1 : **loop**
    compute$(x + 1)$;
P_2 :   **if** $s \geq c$ **then**
      begin
P_2' : $\mathit{wait}(s \dot{-} (\mathit{clock} - u))$;
P_2'' : $\nu s = 0 \;\&\; \nu u = \mathit{clock}$
      end;
P_3 : $\nu x = x + 1 \;\&\; \nu w[\nu x] = \chi_{x+1} \;\&\; \nu s = s + f(\chi_{x+1})$
  end;

Program 1

The following program represents an expected behavior of the terminal:

Q_1 : **loop**
    if $x > y$ **then**
Q_2 : $\nu y = y + 1 \;\&\; \mathit{display}(w[\nu y])$
  end;

Program 2

The initial conditions are $x = 0 \;\&\; y = 0$.

Here, P_1, P_2, etc. are labels used in section 6. *clock* is the current time, and in the case of ν-conversion, it simply means the time variable t.

In these programs, w is an array representing the buffer of the terminal, and $w[i]$ represents ith data of w. Variables x and y are indices of the array elements used by the computer and by the terminal, respectively.

The size of the buffer is finite (we denote it by N), but we assume that the size of w is infinite for simplicity so that $x - y$ represents the number of data in the buffer.

compute$(x+1)$ represents a part which computes the $(x+1)$st data value χ_{x+1}, and *wait*(v) represents delaying its execution by time v. *display*$(w[y])$ represents a part whose function is to display data on the screen.

A function g is considered to represent time which is necessary to display vectors to the screen. Hence in Program 2, if the value of $w[y]$ is χ, then it takes time $g(\chi)$ for the terminal to process χ. A function f in the first program estimates the function g.

An assignment statement $\nu w[\nu x] = \chi_{x+1}$ is intended for communication, i.e. the computer transmits data χ_{x+1} to the terminal by executing it. We assume that it takes a constant time e_0 for each communication.

We denote the time from the beginning of the $(i-1)$st communication, i.e. the execution of $\nu w[\nu x] = \chi_{x+1}$, to the beginning of the next execution or the execution of *wait* by $h(i)$ for $i > 1$. $h(1)$ is the time from the beginning of *compute*$(x+1)$ when $x = 0$ to the beginning of the execution of the first communication. Intuitively $h(i)$ means a sum of the time necessary for computing χ_i and waiting due to scheduling, channel waiting and so on.

In the actual problem, the program ran successfully even when the value of f is 0 for almost all elements except for some data, e.g. screen clear command. But the reason why the program worked was unclear at that time.

5 Analysis by ν-Conversion

In this section, we analyze the program using ν-conversion and consider conditions that the buffer does not overflow.

Let W and R be ν-acts corresponding to program 1 and program 2 respectively. There will be many translations. Here we give only R as follows:

$$x > y \ \& \ v < t \ \& \ \nu y = y + 1 \ \& \ \nu v = t + g(w[y+1]) \ ,$$

where $\hat{y}(0) = 0$ and $\hat{v}(0) = 0$. In this translation, the *display* command simply waits during the time necessary for displaying its argument. For W (and also $h(i)$), we assume a standard translation (see appendix A).

Then we consider a locus of ν-act

$$a(t) \uparrow W \ || \ b(t - e_0) \uparrow R[t - e_0]$$

interpreted by the predicate of action. We use $b(t - e_0)$ as a spur of $R[t - e_0]$, because it is a simple manner to express that it takes time e_0 in communication. The condition that the buffer does not overflow can be represented by

$$\hat{x}(t) \leq \hat{y}(t) + N \qquad (1)$$

for any t.

Definition 6. $\Delta_a(t)$ and $\Delta_b(t)$ are defined as follows:

$$\Delta_a(t) = \min\{d \mid d > 0 \;\&\; a(t+d)\} \; ,$$
$$\Delta_b(t) = \min\{d \mid d > 0 \;\&\; b(t+d-e_0)\} \; .$$

Intuitively $\Delta_a(t)$ and $\Delta_b(t)$ are time intervals until a and b hold after t, respectively.

The behavior of act W is not affected by R, so we firstly consider only W and define t_k which is the time to send kth data. For that purpose we define T_m and X_m which intuitively represent the time when the computer sends the next data after it finishes mth waiting and the value of variable x at that time, respectively.

Definition 7. T_m and X_m are defined inductively as follows:

1. $T_0 = a_0 + h(1), X_0 = 0$, where a_0 satisfies $a(a_0) \;\&\; \forall t(a(t) \supset t \geq a_0)$.
2. If there exists $n(> X_m)$ such that

$$\sum_{i=X_m+1}^{n-1} f(\chi_i) < c \leq \sum_{i=X_m+1}^{n} f(\chi_i) \; ,$$

then

$$T_{m+1} = T_m + E_{X_m+1,n} + \Delta_a(T_m + E_{X_m+1,n}) \; ,$$
$$X_{m+1} = n \; ,$$

for the least such n, where

$$E_{m,n} = \max\left\{\sum_{i=m}^{n} f(\chi_i), \; \sum_{i=m+1}^{n+1} h(i)\right\} \; .$$

Otherwise $T_{m+1} = \infty, X_{m+1} = \infty$, and $T_M, X_M (M > m+1)$ are undefined.

Definition 8. t_k is defined as follows for $k > 0$:

$$t_k = T_m + \sum_{i=X_m+2}^{k} h(i)$$

for m which satisfies $X_m < k \leq X_{m+1}$.

Then $T_m \leq t_k < T_{m+1}$ clearly holds.

Next, we consider R and define t'_k which is the time that the terminal reads kth data from the buffer.

Definition 9. t'_k is defined as follows for $k > 0$:

$$t'_1 = t_1 + \Delta_b(t_1) \; ,$$
$$t'_k = \max\{t_k + \Delta_b(t_k), \; t'_{k-1} + g(\chi_{k-1}) + \Delta_b(t'_{k-1} + g(\chi_{k-1}))\}, \text{ for } k > 1 \; .$$

Then we define T'_j and X'_j which represent the time that the computer sends the next data after the buffer becomes empty for the jth time and the value of variable x (and thus y), respectively.

Definition 10. T'_j and X'_j are defined inductively as follows:

1. $T'_0 = t_1$ and $X'_0 = X_0$ $(= 0)$.
2. If there exists $n(> X'_j)$ which satisfies

$$t'_{n+1} = t_{n+1} + \Delta_b(t_{n+1}) ,$$

then

$$T'_{j+1} = t_{n+1}, \quad X'_{j+1} = n,$$

for the least such n. Otherwise $T'_{j+1} = \infty, X'_{j+1} = \infty$, and $T'_J, X'_J (J > j+1)$ are undefined.

Then

$$t'_k = T'_j + \Delta_b(T'_j) + \sum_{i=X'_j+1}^{k-1} (g(\chi_i) + \Delta_b(t'_i + g(\chi_i)))$$

holds clearly for j which satisfies $X'_j < k \leq X'_{j+1}$.

The next lemma guarantees that the definitions of t_k and t'_k suit our intention.

Lemma. *t_k and t'_k satisfy the following for any $k(> 0)$:*

$$\hat{x}(t_k) = k - 1 \ \& \ \hat{x}(t_k + 0) = k,$$
$$\hat{y}(t'_k) = k - 1 \ \& \ \hat{y}(t'_k + 0) = k,$$

where $A[t + 0]$ abbreviates for

$$\forall \varepsilon \exists \delta (\varepsilon > 0 \supset 0 < \delta < \varepsilon \ \& \ A[t + \delta]) .$$

Proposition. *A necessary and sufficient condition that the buffer does not overflow, i.e.* (1) *holds for any t, is that*

$$t'_k \leq t_{k+N} \tag{2}$$

holds for any $k(> 0)$.

Proof. From the facts that $\hat{x}$ and $\hat{y}$ are increasing functions (see Appendix B) and $\hat{y}$ is left continuous, (1) is equivalent to $\hat{x}(t'_k) \leq \hat{y}(t'_k) + N$ for any $k(> 0)$, which is equivalent to $t_{\hat{x}(t'_k)+1} \leq t_{k+N}$. Because $t_{\hat{x}(t'_k)} < t'_k \leq t_{\hat{x}(t'_k)+1}$, it is equivalent to (2). □

Corollary. *A necessary and sufficient condition that the buffer does not overflow is that*

$$T_m - T'_j + \sum_{i=X_m+2}^{k+N} h(i) - \sum_{i=X'_j+1}^{k-1} g(\chi_i) - \Delta_b(T'_j) - \sum_{i=X'_j+1}^{k-1} \Delta_b(t'_i + g(\chi_i)) \geq 0$$

holds for any j, m *such that* $X_m < k + N \leq X_{m+1}, X'_j < k \leq X'_{j+1}$ *for any* $k(> 0)$.

There are many loci which satisfy this condition. Here we consider safety conditions in two cases, one is that the computer is fast enough and the other is that it is slow.

Case 1. Firstly, we assume that the computer is fast enough, more precisely

$$\max h(i) < \min g(\chi_i) \tag{3}$$

holds. In this case, we can easily show that $\forall j \exists i T'_j = T_i$ (see appendix C). Intuitively, it means that the buffer becomes empty only when the computer is waiting. Let $T'_j = T_\ell$. Moreover we assume that the computer waits when it sends more than N data, more precisely

$$N \cdot \min f(\chi_i) \geq c \tag{4}$$

holds. Then we can obtain $k < X_m$, therefore, for n which satisfies $X_n < k \leq X_{n+1}$,

$$\begin{aligned} t_{k+N} - t'_k = \\ & \sum_{j=\ell}^{n-1} \left(E_{X_j+1,X_{j+1}} + \Delta_a(T_j + E_{X_j+1,X_{j+1}}) - \sum_{i=X_j+1}^{X_{j+1}} (g(\chi_i) + \Delta_b(t'_i + g(\chi_i))) \right) \\ & + E_{X_n+1,X_{n+1}} + \Delta_a(T_n + E_{X_n+1,X_{n+1}}) - \sum_{i=X_n+1}^{k-1} (g(\chi_i) + \Delta_b(t'_i + g(\chi_i))) \\ & + \sum_{j=X_{n+1}+1}^{X_{m-1}} (E_{X_j+1,X_{j+1}} + \Delta_a(T_j + E_{X_j+1,X_{j+1}})) + \sum_{i=X_m+2}^{k+N} h(i) - \Delta_b(T'_j) \,. \end{aligned}$$

Clearly it is sufficient that

$$E_{X_j+1,X_{j+1}} \geq \sum_{i=X_j+1}^{X_{j+1}} (g(\chi_i) + d_\beta)$$

holds in addition to condition (4), where $d_\beta = \max \Delta_b(t)$. Intuitively it means that the time of computation of data by the computer is larger than the time necessary for graphic display. Especially, it holds when

$$f(\chi_i) \geq g(\chi_i) + d_\beta \tag{5}$$

is satisfied.

Consequently we obtain the following proposition.

Proposition. *A sufficient condition that the buffer does not overflow is* (4) and (5) when the computer is fast enough, i.e. (3) holds.

The condition corresponds to the normal design of the program: while sending at most N data the computer waits for more than the time necessary for displaying them.

Case 2. Next, we consider another case, i.e. the computer is slow enough. More precisely, we assume the following two conditions:

$$\text{if } g(\chi_i) \geq c \text{ then } i = 1 \text{ and } f(\chi_1) \geq g(\chi_1) \;, \tag{6}$$
$$\text{if } g(\chi_i) < c \text{ then } g(\chi_i) + d_\beta \leq h(i) \;. \tag{7}$$

Intuitively these conditions mean that clearing the screen can be executed only once at the beginning of the program, and that the computation time of any data except the clear command is larger than the display time of it.

In this case, $t'_k - t_k \leq g_m + d_\beta$ holds for any $k(>0)$, where $g_m = \max\{g(\chi_i) \mid g(\chi_i) < c\}$ (see appendix D). Thus we obtain the following proposition.

Proposition. *When the computer is slow enough, i.e.* (6) and (7) hold, the buffer does not overflow if

$$N \cdot \min h(i) \geq g_m \tag{8}$$

holds.

Proof. $t'_{k+N} - t'_k \geq t_k + N \cdot \min h(i) - t'_k \geq N \cdot \min h(i) - (g_m + \Delta_b) \geq 0.$ □

The reason why the buffer did not overflow in the actual problem seems to be that it was similar to the second case. Of course the condition that we have sent only finite sequence of commands also affected the actual problem . It seems somewhat strange that the computer is slow compared to graphic output. It is because computation time involves waiting time for scheduling and the channel. Due to methods of scheduling or buffering, the computer has to wait too long and thus computation time can become large.

6 Analysis by Tense Arithmetic

In this section we represent and analyze the program using tense arithmetic. More precisely, analogues of definitions in section 5 such as t_k and t'_k are obtained from the specification of the program using representations in tense arithmetic, and a similar analysis is performed in usual mathematics.

At first, to express the delay of communication e_0 explicitly, we use an additional variable x' instead of x in Program 2. x' varies in accordance with x except that it is delayed for e_0 so that $x' - y$ represents the number of data in the buffer. Thus we can simply denote the overflowing state by $x' - y > N$.

Then let α and β be spurs of Program 1 and Program 2, respectively.

Assuming a frame axiom, specification of the program is given as follows:

(i) $\diamond\alpha,\ \diamond\beta$,

(ii) $P_0 \,\&\, \neg\alpha \,\&\, \uparrow\alpha = \theta \supset \uparrow\alpha\{P_1 \,\&\, s = c \,\&\, u = \theta - c\}$,

(iii) $P_1 \,\&\, \neg\alpha \,\&\, \uparrow\alpha\{P_2\}$,

(iv) $P_2 \,\&\, \neg\alpha \,\&\, \uparrow\alpha\{s < c \,\&\, P_3 \vee s \geq c \,\&\, P_2'\}$,

(v) $P_2' \,\&\, \neg\alpha \,\&\, \uparrow\alpha = \theta \supset$

$$\uparrow\alpha\{P_2'' \,\&\, s \dot{-} (\theta - t) \leq \uparrow\alpha - \uparrow true\} ,$$

(vi) $P_2'' \,\&\, \neg\alpha \,\&\, \uparrow\alpha = \theta \supset \uparrow\alpha\{P_3 \,\&\, s = 0 \,\&\, u = \theta\}$,

(vii) $P_3 \,\&\, \neg\alpha \,\&\, x = \xi - 1 \,\&\, s = \zeta \supset$

$$\uparrow\alpha\{P_1 \,\&\, x = \xi \,\&\, w[\xi] = \chi(\xi) \,\&\, s = \zeta + f(\chi(\xi))\} ,$$

(viii) $Q_1 \,\&\, \neg\beta \supset \uparrow\beta\{x' \leq y \,\&\, Q_1 \vee x' > y \,\&\, Q_2\}$,

(ix) $Q_2 \,\&\, \neg\beta \,\&\, y = \eta - 1 \supset$

$$\uparrow\beta\{Q_1 \,\&\, y = \eta \,\&\, g(w[y]) \leq \uparrow\beta - \uparrow true\} ,$$

(x) $\neg\alpha \,\&\, x = \xi \supset (\uparrow true + e_0)\{x' = \xi\}$.

(i) means that both α and β hold eventually. Behavior of Program 1 is described by formulas from (ii) to (vii). In (v), $\uparrow\alpha - \uparrow true$ means the time interval from the current time until α holds next time. (viii) and (ix) are descriptions of Program 2. (x) represents the delay e_0 between x and x'.

A part of an execution of the program is given as follows:

$$
\begin{array}{ll}
 & \{x = 0 \,\&\, y = 0 \,\&\, P_0\} \\
\alpha \Rightarrow & \text{at } P_0; \alpha \\
 & \quad \text{let } T_s \text{ be } P_0; \alpha, \\
 & \{P_1 \,\&\, s = c \,\&\, t = T_s - c\} \\
\alpha \Rightarrow & \text{at } P_1; \alpha = P_0; \alpha^2 \\
 & \{P_2\} \\
\alpha \Rightarrow & \text{at } P_2; \alpha = P_0; \alpha^3 \\
 & \{P_2'\} \\
\alpha \Rightarrow & \text{at } P_2'; \alpha = P_0; \alpha^4 \\
 & \quad \text{let } H_1 \text{ be } P_2'; \alpha, \\
 & \{P_2'' \,\&\, s = 0 \,\&\, u = H_1\} \\
\alpha \Rightarrow & \text{at } P_2''; \alpha = P_0; \alpha^5 \\
 & \quad \text{let } T_0 \text{ be } P_2''; \alpha, \\
 & \{P_3 \,\&\, s = 0 \,\&\, t = T_0\} \\
\alpha \Rightarrow & \text{at } P_0; \alpha^6 \\
 & \{P_1 \,\&\, x = 1 \,\&\, w[1] = \chi(1) \,\&\, s = f(\chi(1))\} \\
\cdots ,
\end{array}
$$

where the notation "$\alpha \Rightarrow$" represents the state just after the spur α occurs.

Thus, for example, the time that the computer sends the first data can be written as $P_0;\alpha^6$.

Now definitions are given as follows.

Definition 11. $h^*(i)$ is defined as follows:

$$\begin{aligned} h^*(1) &= \Delta(P_0;\alpha,\alpha^5)\ , \\ h^*(i) &= \min\{\uparrow(x=i-1\ \&\ P_2'),\ (x=i-1\ \&\ P_3);\alpha\} \\ &\quad -(x=i-2\ \&\ P_3);\alpha, \qquad \text{for } i>1\ . \end{aligned}$$

Definition 12. T_m^* and X_m^* are defined inductively as follows:

1. $T_0^* = P_0;\alpha + h(1), X_0^* = 0$.
2. If there exists $n(> X_m^*)$ which satisfies

$$\sum_{i=X_m^*+1}^{n-1} f(\chi_i) < c \leq \sum_{i=X_m^*+1}^{n} f(\chi_i),$$

then

$$\begin{aligned} T_{m+1}^* &= (T_m^* + E_{X_m^*+1,n}^*);\alpha^2, \\ X_{m+1}^* &= n\ , \end{aligned}$$

for the least such n, where

$$E_{m,n}^* = \max\left\{\sum_{i=m}^{n} f(\chi_i),\ \sum_{i=m+1}^{n+1} h^*(i)\right\}.$$

Otherwise $T_{m+1}^* = \infty, X_{m+1}^* = \infty$, and $T_M^*, X_M^*(M > m+1)$ are undefined.

Definition 13. t_k^* is defined as follows for $k > 0$:

$$t_k^* = T_m^* + \sum_{i=X_m^*+2}^{k} h^*(i)$$

for m which satisfies $X_m^* < k \leq X_{m+1}^*$.

Definition 14. $t_k'^*$ is defined as follows for $k > 0$:

$$\begin{aligned} t_1'^* &= (t_1^* + e_0);\beta\ , \\ t_k'^* &= \max\{(t_k^* + e_0);\beta,\ (t_{k-1}'^* + g(\chi_{k-1}));\beta\}, \qquad \text{for } k>1\ . \end{aligned}$$

Definition 15. $T_j'^*$ and $X_j'^*$ are defined inductively as follows:

1. $T_0'^* = t_1$ and $X_0'^* = X_0^* (= 0)$.
2. If there exists $n(> X_j'^*)$ which satisfies

$$t_{n+1}'^* = (t_{n+1}^* + e_0); \beta$$

then

$$T_{j+1}'^* = t_{n+1}^* + e_0 \ ,$$
$$X_{j+1}'^* = n \ ,$$

for the least such n. Otherwise $T_{j+1}'^* = \infty$, $X_{j+1}'^* = \infty$, and $T_J'^*, X_J'^* (J > j+1)$ are undefined.

Then

$$t_k'^* = T_j'^*; \beta + \sum_{i=X_j'^*+1}^{k-1} (g(\chi_i) + \Delta(t_i'^* + g(\chi_i), \beta))$$

holds clearly for j which satisfies $X_j'^* < k \leq X_{j+1}'^*$.

A necessary and sufficient condition that the buffer does not overflow, i.e. $\uparrow(x' - y > N) = \infty$, is equivalent to that

$$t_k'^* \leq t_{k+N}^* + e_0$$

holds for any $k(> 0)$.

Therefore the following two propositions are obtained.

Proposition. *When the computer is fast enough, i.e.* (3) *holds, a sufficient condition that the buffer does not overflow is* (4) *and*

$$f(\chi_i) \geq g(\chi_i) + d_\beta^* \ ,$$

where $d_\beta^* = \max\{d \mid d = \Delta(t_i'^* + g(\chi_i), \beta) \vee d = \Delta(T_j'^*, \beta)\}$.

Proof. Because $\forall j \exists i (T_j'^* = T_i^* + e_0)$ holds, it is sufficient that (4) and

$$E_{X_j^*+1, X_{j+1}^*}^* \geq \sum_{i=X_j^*+1}^{X_{j+1}^*} (g(\chi_i) + d_\beta^*)$$

hold. □

Proposition. *When the computer is slow enough, i.e.* (6) *and* (7) *hold,* the buffer does not overflow if

$$N \cdot \min h^*(i) \geq g_m$$

holds.

Proof. Because $t_k' - t_k \leq g_m + d_\beta^*$ holds for any $k(> 0)$, the proof is similar. □

7 Conclusions

We have analyzed a program of a typical example of software/hardware systems using explicit rational time, and have obtained two safety conditions. From a relation between values of variables, another relation between times, which is equivalent to the former, has been obtained and simplified in two cases. Using the ν-conversion, the analysis was quite natural, because we treated rational time explicitly. Though it is difficult in many other systems such as temporal logic, ν-conversion enables it by using a time variable. It is an important point for understandability. Further, the analysis was rigorous, and proofs of safety conditions can be also accomplished formally on FA. Moreover, the analysis was performed in the language of tense arithmetic. In that analysis, terms used in the analysis by ν-conversion were introduced naturally, and it made the analysis easier. The example was typical of programs using explicit rational time, so similar methods can be applied to other programs. But since proofs might be long and complicated, computer assistance and some supporting theorems will be necessary hereafter.

Acknowledgements

The authors would like to thank Dr. Hosono and Mr. Shirogane for their useful suggestions and comments.

References

1. Chaochen, Z., Hoare, C. A. R. and Ravn, P.: A Calculus of Durations, *Inf. Process. Lett.*, Vol. 40, pp.269–276 (1991).
2. Cousot, P.: Methods and Logics for Proving Programs, J. van Leeuwen, ed., *Handbook of Theoretical Computer Science* (1990).
3. Gao, T., Hosono, C. and Yamanaka, K.: An Analytic Semantics of CSP, *Fundamenta Informaticae*, Vol. 15, No. 2, pp.107–122 (1991).
4. Hoare, C. A. R.: An Axiomatic Basis for Computer Programming, *Comm. ACM*, Vol. 12, No. 10, pp.576–580,583 (1969).
5. Hoare, C. A. R.: Communicating Sequential Processes, *Comm. ACM*, Vol. 21, No. 8, pp.666–677 (1978).
6. Hoare, C. A. R.: *Communicating Sequential Processes*, Prentice-Hall International (1985).
7. Igarashi, S.: The ν-conversion and an Analytic Semantics, R. E. A. Mason, ed., *Inf. Proc.*, IFIP, Elsevier Science Publishers B. V.(North-Holland), pp.769–774 (1983).
8. Igarashi, S., Mizutani, T. and Tsuji, T.: An Analytical Semantics of Parallel Program Processes Represented by ν-conversion, *TENSOR, N. S.* Vol. 45, pp.222–228 (1987).
9. Igarashi, S., Mizutani, T. and Tsuji, T.: Specifications of Parallel Program Processes in Analytical Semantics, *TENSOR, N. S.* Vol. 45, pp.240–244 (1987).
10. Igarashi, S., Tsuji, T., Mizutani, T. and Haraguchi, T.: Experiments on Computerized Piano Accompaniment, *Proceedings of the 1993 International Computer Music Conference*, pp.415–417 (1993).

11. Ikeda Y.: *An interpreter of the higher typed logical programming language NU*, Ph.D. Thesis, University of Tsukuba (in Japanese) (1993).
12. Kröger, F.: *Temporal Logic of Programs*, Springer-Verlag (1987).
13. Lamport, L.: What Good is Temporal Logic?, R. E. A. Mason, ed., *Inf. Proc.*, IFIP, Elsevier Science Publishers B. V.(North-Holland), pp.657–668 (1983).
14. Milner, R.: *A Calculus of Communicating Systems*, LNCS 92, Springer-Verlag (1980).
15. Milner, R.: *Communication and Concurrency*, Prentice-Hall (1989).
16. Owicki, S. and Gries, D.: Verifying Properties of Parallel Programs: An Axiomatic Approach, *Comm. ACM*, Vol. 19, No. 5, pp.279–285 (1976).
17. Owicki, S. and Gries, D.: An Axiomatic Proof Technique for Parallel Programs I: *Acta Inf.*, Vol. 6, pp.319–340 (1976).
18. Mizutani, T: *An analytical equivalence theory of programs with applications*, Ph.D. Thesis, University of Tsukuba (1987).
19. Mizutani, T., Igarashi, S. and Tsuji, T.: An Analytical Equivalence Theory of Computer Programs, A. Díez, J. Echeverría and A. Ibarra, eds., *Structures in Mathematical Theories*, Reports of the San Sebastian International Symposium, pp.199–204 (1990).
20. Pnueli, A. and Harel, E.: Applications of temporal logic to the specification of real time systems, M. Joseph, ed., *Proc. Symp. Formal Techn. in Real-Time and Fault-Tolerant Systems*, Lecture Notes in Computer Science 331, pp.84–98 (1988).
21. Shoenfield, J. R.: *Mathematical Logic*, Addison-Wesley (1967).
22. Takeuti, G.: *Two Applications of Logic to Mathematics*, Iwanami Shoten, Publishers and Princeton University Press (1978).
23. Tomita, K., Tsuji, T. and Igarashi, S.: An Analysis of a Real Time Problem Using ν-Conversion and Its Safety Conditions, *Transactions of Information Processing Society of Japan*, Vol.34, No.5, pp.1099–1106 (In Japanese) (1993).

Appendix A

We assume that act W is as follows:

$$\begin{aligned}
&\ell = 0 \,\&\, \nu s = c \,\&\, \nu u = t - c \,\&\, \nu\ell = 1 \\
\vee\, &\ell = 1 \,\&\, C \\
\vee\, &\ell = 2 \,\&\, s \geq c \,\&\, \nu v' = t + (s \mathbin{\dot{-}} (t - u)) \,\&\, \nu\ell = 3 \\
\vee\, &\ell = 3 \,\&\, t > v' \,\& \\
&\qquad\qquad \nu x = x + 1 \,\&\, \nu w[\nu x] = \chi_{x+1} \,\&\, \nu s = f(\chi_{x+1}) \,\&\, \nu u = t \,\&\, \nu\ell = 1 \\
\vee\, &\ell = 2 \,\&\, s < c \,\&\, \nu x = x + 1 \,\&\, \nu w[\nu x] = \chi_{x+1} \,\&\, \nu s = s + f(\chi_{x+1}) \,\&\, \nu\ell = 1
\end{aligned}$$

and the initial conditions are $\hat{\ell}(0) = 0$ and $\hat{x}(0) = 0$. In the act, ℓ is a label variable, and C is a part to compute the $(x+1)$st data χ_{x+1}, and after computing, it changes the value of ℓ from 1 to 2.

In this case, $h(i)$ is written as follows: $h(1) = \max\{t \mid \hat{x}(t) = 0 \,\&\, \hat{\ell}(t) = 2\} - a_0$, where a_0 satisfies $a(a_0) \,\&\, \forall t(a(t) \supset t \leq a_0)$, and $h(i) = \max\{t \mid \hat{x}(t) = i - 1 \,\&\, \hat{\ell}(t) = 3\} - \max\{t \mid \hat{x}(t) = i - 2\}$ for $i > 1$.

Appendix B

We are to prove that $\hat{y}$ is a monotonic increasing function which satisfies $Pa(a(t) \uparrow W \parallel b(t-e_0) \uparrow R, \hat{\boldsymbol{x}})$, but we consider the case in which only R is executed for simplicity. Intuitively it can be justified because act W does not affect the variable y. But formally a similar proof is necessary.

Let R' be $(b(t)\ \&\ \exists y R[\boldsymbol{x}, \boldsymbol{y}, t] \supset R[\boldsymbol{x}, \nu\boldsymbol{x}, t])^{\#}$. From the difinition of #,

$$R' \equiv b(t)\ \&\ x > y\ \&\ v < t\ \&$$
$$\nu x = x\ \&\ \nu y = y + 1\ \&\ \nu v = t + g(w[y])\ .$$

For any $\hat{\boldsymbol{x}}$ such that $Pa(R', \hat{\boldsymbol{x}})$, if R' is actable at time t, more precisely, if $\exists \boldsymbol{y} R'[\hat{\boldsymbol{x}}(t), \boldsymbol{y}, t]$ then $R'[\hat{\boldsymbol{x}}(t), \hat{\boldsymbol{x}}(t{+}0), t]$ from the definition of Pa. Hence $\hat{y}(t{+}0) = \hat{y}(t) + 1$.

If $\forall \delta \geq 0(\delta < \varepsilon \supset \neg\exists \boldsymbol{y} R'[\hat{\boldsymbol{x}}(t+\delta), \boldsymbol{y}, t+\delta])$, i.e. if it is unactable from time t to time $t+\varepsilon$, then clearly $\hat{\boldsymbol{x}}(t) = \hat{\boldsymbol{x}}(t+\varepsilon)$ holds and thus $\hat{y}(t) = \hat{y}(t+\varepsilon)$. Therefore $\hat{y}$ is increasing.

It can be shown easily by existence of a locomorphism from $a(t) \uparrow W \parallel b(t) \uparrow R$ to $\mathbf{N}(t)\ \&\ \nu y = \nu y + 1$, where $\mathbf{N}$ is a predicate indicating natural numbers.

Appendix C

Proposition. *If* (3) *holds then* $\forall j \exists i T'_j = T_i$ *holds.*

Proof. The proof is by mathematical induction on j. Clearly $T'_0 = t_1 = T_0$ holds for $j = 0$. Suppose it holds for $j = \ell$ and let $T'_\ell = T_i$. We can assume $T'_{\ell+1} = t_m$ for some m. Then $t_{m-1} + g(\chi_{m-1}) < t_m$ holds because $t_{m-1} + g(\chi_{m-1}) < t'_{m-1} + g(\chi_{m-1}) \leq t_m$. The latter inequality is due to the facts that $t'_{m-1} + g(\chi_{m-1}) + \Delta_b(t'_{m-1} + g(\chi_{m-1})) \leq t_m + \Delta_b(t_m)$, and that for any t and u, $t + \Delta_b(t) \leq u + \Delta_b(u)$ implies $t \leq u$. If m cannot be written as the form $m = X_n + 1$, then $t_m = t_{m-1} + h(m)$, thus $h(m) > g(\chi_{m-1})$ which contradicts $\max h(i) < \min g(\chi_i)$. Therefore $m = X_n + 1$ for some n and $T'_{\ell+1} = t_{X_n+1} = T_n$. □

Appendix D

Proposition. *If* (6) *and* (7) *hold, then* $t'_k - t_k \leq g_m + d_\beta$ *holds for any* $k(>0)$.

Proof. At first we prove $t'_{k+1} - t_k \leq g_m + 2d_\beta$ for any $k(>0)$. Let $X'_j < k \leq X'_{j+1}$. The proof is by mathematical induction on k. If $k = X'_j + 1$, then $t'_{k+1} - t_k = \Delta_b(t_k) + g(\chi_k) + \Delta_b(t_k + g(\chi_k)) \leq g_m + 2d_\beta$. Suppose it holds for $k = X'_j + i$. Then $t'_{k+2} - t_{k+1} \leq t'_{k+1} + g(\chi_{k+1}) + \Delta_b(t'_{k+1} + g(\chi_{k+1})) - (t_k + h(k+1)) \leq g_m + 2d_\beta$.

If $k = 1$, clearly $t'_1 - t_1 = \Delta_b(t_1) + g(\chi_1) \leq g_m + d_\beta$ holds. If $k > 1$, $t'_k - t_k \leq t'_k - (t_{k-1} + h(k)) \leq t'_k - t_{k-1} - d_\beta \leq g_m + d_\beta$. □

The Essence of Program Transformation by Partial Evaluation and Driving*

Neil D. Jones

DIKU, University of Copenhagen
Universitetsparken 1, DK-2100 Copenhagen, Denmark
neil@diku.dk

Abstract. An abstract framework is developed to describe program transformation by *specializing* a given program to a restricted set of inputs. Particular cases include partial evaluation [19] and Turchin's more powerful "driving" transformation [33]. Such automatic program speedups have been seen to give quite signifcant speedups in practical applications.
This paper's aims are similar to those of [18]: better to understand the fundamental mathematical phenomena that make such speedups possible. The current paper is more complete than [18], since it precisely formulates correctness of code generation; and more powerful, since it includes program optimizations not achievable by simple partial evaluation. Moreover, for the first time it puts Turchin's driving methodology on a solid semantic foundation which is not tied to any particular programming language or data structure.

This paper is dedicated to Satoru Takasu with thanks for good advice early in my career on how to do research, and for insight into how to see the essential part of a new problem.

1 Introduction

1.1 History

Automatic program specialization evolved independently at several different times and places [13,31,33,5,11,20]. In recent years partial evaluation has received much attention ([19,6], and several conferences), and work has been done on other automatic transformations including Wadler's well-known *deforestation* [36,7,26].

Many of these active research themes were anticipated in the 1970's by Valentin Turchin in Moscow [29,30] in his research on *supercompilation* (= supervised compilation), and experiments were made with implementations. Examples include program optimization both by deforestation and by partial evaluation; the use and significance of self-application for generating compilers and

* This work was supported in part by the Danish Natural Science Research Council (DART project) and by an Esprit Basic Research Action (Semantique).

other program generators; and the use of grammars as a tool in program transformation [31,32,17]. Recent works on driving and supercompilation include [?,14,15,27,24,22,1].

1.2 Goals

The purpose of this paper is to formulate the essential concepts of supercompilation in an abstract and language-independent way. For simplicity we treat only imperative programs, and intentionally do not make explicit the nature of either commands or the store, except as needed for examples.

At the core of supercompilation is the program transformation called *driving* (Russian "progonka"). In principle driving is stronger than both deforestation and partial evaluation [27,36,12,19], and an example will be given to show this (the pattern matching example at the end of the paper). On the other hand, driving has taken longer to come into practical use than either deforestation or partial evaluation, for several reasons.

First, the greater strength of driving makes it correspondingly harder to tame; cause and effect are less easily understood than in deforestation and partial evaluation, and in fact it is only in the latter case that self-application has been achieved on practical applications. Second, the first papers were in Russian, and they and later ones used a computer language Refal[2] unfamiliar to western readers. Finally, the presentation style of the supercompilation papers is unfamiliar, using examples and sketches of algorithms rather than mathematical formulations of the basic ideas, and avoiding even set theory for philosophical reasons [34].

We hope the abstract framework will lead to greater practical exploitation of the principles underlying supercompilation (stronger program transformations, more automatic systems, new languages), and a better understanding in principle of the difficult problem of ensuring termination of program transformation.

1.3 Preliminary definitions

First, a quite abstract definition of an imperative program is given, as a state transition system. In our opinion the essence of the "driving" concept is more clearly exposed at this level. Later, a more intuitive flow chart formalism will be used for examples, and to clarify the problem of code generation.

Definition 1. An *abstract program* is a quadruple $\pi = (P, S, \rightarrow, p_0)$ where $p_0 \in P$ and $\rightarrow \subseteq (P \times S) \times (P \times S)$. Terminology: P is the set of *program points*, S is the set of *stores*, $\rightarrow$ is the *transition relation*, and p_0 is the *initial program point*. We write $\rightarrow$ in infix notation, e.g. $(p, s) \rightarrow (p', s')$ instead of $((p, s), (p', s')) \in \rightarrow$. A *state* is a pair $(p, s) \in P \times S$.

[2] Refal is essentially a language of Markov algorithms extended with variables. A program is a sequence of rewrite rules, used to transform data in the form of associative and possibly nested symbol strings. In contrast with most pattern matching languages, most general unifiers do not always exist.

A store such as [X↦ 1:2:[], Y ↦ 2:(4:5):[]] usually maps program variables to their values. A program point may be a flow chart node, or can be thought of as a label in a program.

Definition 2. $p \in P$ is *one-way* if $(p, s_1) \to (p', s')$ and $(p, s_2) \to (p'', s'')$ imply $p' = p''$, i.e. there is at most one p' with $(p, \_) \to (p', \_)$. State (p, s) is *terminal* if $(p, s) \to (p', s')$ holds for no (p', s'). The abstract program π is *deterministic* if for all states (p, s), $(p, s) \to (p', s')$ and $(p, s) \to (p'', s'')$ imply $p' = p''$ and $s' = s''$.

Definition 3. A *computation* (from $s_0 \in S$) is a finite or infinite sequence

$$(p_0, s_0) \to (p_1, s_1) \to (p_2, s_2) \to \ldots$$

Notation: subsets of S will be indicated by overlines, so $\overline{s} \subseteq S$. Given this, and defining $\to^*$ to be the reflexive transitive closure of $\to$, the *input/output relation* that π defines on $\overline{s}_0 \subseteq S$ is

$$IO(\pi, \overline{s}_0) = \{(s_0, s_t) \mid s_0 \in \overline{s}_0, (p_0, s_0) \to^* (p_t, s_t), \text{ and } (p_t, s_t) \text{ is terminal}\}$$

More concretely, programs can be given by flow charts whose edges are labeled by commands. These are interpreted by a *command semantics*:

$$\mathcal{C}[\![\_]\!] : Command \to (S \stackrel{partial}{\longrightarrow} S)$$

where *Command* and S are unspecified sets (but S = the set of stores as above).

Definition 4. A *flow chart* is a rooted, edge-labeled directed graph $F = (P, E, p_0)$ where $p_0 \in P$ and $E \subseteq P \times Command \times P$ (the *edges* of F). We write $p \stackrel{C}{\Rightarrow} p'$ whenever $(p, C, p') \in E$.

If $p \stackrel{C}{\Rightarrow} p'$ then C denotes a store transformation, e.g. C could be an assignment statement changing a variable's value. The formulation includes tests too: the domain of partial function $\mathcal{C}[\![C]\!]$ is the set of stores which cause transition from program point p to p'. For example, command "`if odd(X) goto`" might label that edge, corresponding to "`p: if odd(X) then goto p'`" in concrete syntax.

Definition 5. The *program denoted by F* is $\pi^F = (P, S, \to, p_0)$, where

$$(p, s) \to (p', s') \text{ if and only if } s' = \mathcal{C}[\![C]\!]s \text{ for some } p \stackrel{C}{\Rightarrow} p'$$

2 Driven programs, without store transformations

A major use of driving (and partial evaluation) is for *program specialization.* For simplicity we begin with a rather weak form of driving that does not modify the store, and give a stronger version in the next section.

Given partial information about a program's inputs (represented by a subset $\overline{s}_0 \subseteq S$ of all possible stores), driving transforms program π into another program π_d that is equivalent to π on any initial store $s_0 \in \overline{s}_0$. The goal is efficiency: once π_d has been constructed, local optimizations of transition chain compression and reduced code generation can yield a much faster program than π, as seen in [18,19] and many others.

A useful principle is to begin by saying *what* is to be done, as simply as possible, before giving constructions and algorithms saying *how* it can be accomplished. We thus first define what it means for a program π_d to be a "driven" form of program π, and defer the question of how to perform driving to Section 4.

Intuitively π_d is an "exploded" form of π in which any of π's program points p may have several annotated versions $(p, \overline{s}_1), (p, \overline{s}_2), \ldots$. Each $\overline{s}_i$ is a set of stores, required always to contain the current store in any computation by π_d.

Computations by π_d (state sequences) will be in a one-to-one correspondence with those of π, so nothing may seem to have been gained (and something lost, since π_d may be bigger than π). However, if control ever reaches an annotated program point $(p, \overline{s})$ in π_d, then the current runtime store *must lie in* $\overline{s}$. For example, $\overline{s}$ could be the set of all stores such that the value of variable X is always even.

This information is *the source of all improvements gained by partial evaluation or driving.* Its use is to optimize π_d by generating equivalent but more efficient code exploiting the information given by $\overline{s}$. In particular some computations may be elided altogether, since their effect can be achieved by using the $\overline{s}$ at transformation time; and knowledge of $\overline{s}$ often allows a much more economical representation of the stores $s \in \overline{s}$.

2.1 Abstract formulation

Definition 6. Given program $\pi = (P, S, \rightarrow, p_0)$, program $\pi_d = (P_d, S, \rightarrow_d, (p_0, \overline{s}_0))$ is an $\overline{s}_0$-*driven form* of π if $P_d \subseteq P \times \mathcal{P}(S)$ and π_d satisfies the following conditions.

1. $((p, \overline{s}), s) \rightarrow_d ((p', \overline{s}'), s')$ and $s \in \overline{s}$ imply $(p, s) \rightarrow (p', s')$. *soundness*
2. $(p, \overline{s}) \in P_d$, $(p, s) \rightarrow (p', s')$, and $s \in \overline{s}$ imply that there exists $\overline{s}'$ such that $((p, \overline{s}), s) \rightarrow_d ((p', \overline{s}'), s')$ *completeness*
3. $((p, \overline{s}), s) \rightarrow_d ((p', \overline{s}'), s')$ and $s \in \overline{s}$ imply $s' \in \overline{s}'$ *invariance* of $s \in \overline{s}$.

To begin with, $P_d \subseteq P \times \mathcal{P}(S)$, so a program point of π_d is a pair $(p, \overline{s})$ where $\overline{s} \subseteq S$ is a set of stores. The *soundness* condition says that π_d can do *only* the store transformations that π can do. The *completeness* condition says that for any driven program point $(p, \overline{s})$ of π_d, any store transformation that π can do from p on stores $s \in \overline{s}$ can also be done by π_d.

Programs may in principle be infinite, but in practice we are only interested in finite ones.

The significance of store sets. The invariance of $s \in \overline{s}$ in a transition $((p, \overline{s}), s) \rightarrow_d ((p', \overline{s}'), s')$ expresses a form of *information propagation* carried out at program transformation time [14,15].

One can think of a store set as a predicate describing variable value relationships, e.g. "X is even" or "$X = Y + 1 \wedge Z < Y$". Store sets could thus be manipulated in the form of logical formulas.

This view has much in common with regarding statements as forward or backward *predicate transformers*, as used by Dijkstra and many others for proving programs correct [10]. Further, a store set $\overline{s}$ that annotates a program point p corresponds to an *invariant*, i.e. a relationship among variable values that holds whenever control reaches point $(p, \overline{s})$ in the transformed program.

Instead of formulas, one could describe store sets using a set of *abstract values* Σ, using for example a function $\gamma : \Sigma \rightarrow \mathcal{P}(S)$ that maps an abstract value $\sigma \in \Sigma$ to the store set it denotes. In logic γ is called an *interpretation*, and Turchin uses the term *configuration* for such a store set description [33].

This idea is a cornerstone of abstract interpretation, where γ is called a *concretization function* [9,2,16]. Our approach can thus be described as *program specialization by abstract interpretation*. The abstract values are constructed 'on the fly' during program transformation to create new specialized program points. This is in contrast to most abstract interpretations, which iterate until the abstract values associated with the *original program*'s program points reach their collective least fixpoint.

Lemma 7. *If π_d is an $\overline{s}_0$-driven form of π, then for any $s_0 \in \overline{s}_0$ there is a computation*

$$(p_0, s_0) \rightarrow (p_1, s_1) \rightarrow (p_2, s_2) \rightarrow \ldots$$

if and only if there is a computation

$$((p_0, \overline{s}_0), s_0) \rightarrow ((p_1, \overline{s}_1), s_1) \rightarrow ((p_2, \overline{s}_2), s_2) \rightarrow \ldots$$

Proof. "If" follows from soundness, "only if" by completeness and invariance of $s \in \overline{s}$.

Corollary 8. $IO(\pi, \overline{s}_0) = IO(\pi_d, \overline{s}_0)$

Program specialization by driving. Informally, program π is transformed as follows:

1. Given π and an initial set of stores $\overline{s}_0$ to which π is to be specialized, construct a driven program π_d. In practice, π will be given in flow chart or other concrete syntactic form, and finite descriptions of store sets will be used.
2. Improve π_d by and removing unreachable branches, and by compressing sequences of one-way transitions

$$((p,\overline{s}),s) \to ((p',\overline{s'}),s') \to \ldots \to ((p'',\overline{s''}),s'')$$

into single-step transitions

$$((p,\overline{s}),s) \to ((p'',\overline{s''}),s'')$$

3. If $\pi = \pi^F$ where F is a given flow chart, then F_d is constructed and improved in the same way: by compressing transitions, and generating appropriately simplified commands as edge labels.

The idea is that knowing a store set $\overline{s}$ gives contextual information used to transform π_d to make it run faster. Conditions for correct code generation will be given after we discuss the choice of store sets and the use of alternative store representations in Section 3.

2.2 Extreme and intermediate cases

In spite of the close correspondence between the computations of π and π_d, there is a wide latitude in the choice of π_d. Different choices will lead to different degrees of optimization. For practical use we need intermediate cases for which π_d has finitely many program points, and its store sets $\overline{s}$ are small enough (i.e. precise enough) to allow significant code optimization.

We will see a pattern-matching example where a program with two inputs of size m, n that runs in time $a \cdot m \cdot n$ can, by specializing to a fixed first input, be transformed into one running in time $b \cdot n$ where b is independent of m.

One extreme case is to choose every $\overline{s}$ to be equal to S. In this case π_d is identical to π, so no speedup is gained. Another extreme is to define π_d to contain $((p,\overline{s}),s) \to_d ((p',\{s'\}),s')$ whenever $(p,s) \to (p',s')$, $s \in \overline{s}$, and $(p,\overline{s}) \in P_d$. In this case π_d amounts to a totally unfolded version containing all possible computations on inputs from $\overline{s}_0$.

State set choice and code generation. The extreme just described will nearly always give infinite programs. It is not at all natural for code generation, as it deals with states one at a time.

In flow chart form, a test amounts to two different transitions $p \overset{C1}{\Rightarrow} p'$ and $p \overset{C2}{\Rightarrow} p''$ from the same p. A more interesting extreme can be obtained from the following principle: *the driven program should contain no tests that are not present in the original program.* The essence of this can be described without flow charts as follows.

Definition 9. π_d *requires no new tests* if whenever π contains $(p,s) \to (p',s')$, $s \in \overline{s}$, and π_d contains $((p,\overline{s}),s) \to_d ((p',\overline{s}'),s')$, then

$$\overline{s}' \supseteq \{s_2 \mid \exists s_1 \in \overline{s}\,.\,(p,s_1) \to (p',s_2) \text{ is in } \pi\}$$

This defines the new store set $\overline{s}'$ to be *inclusive*, meaning that it contains every store reachable from any store in $\overline{s}$ by π transitions from p to p'. The target store set $\overline{s}'$ of a driven transition $((p,\overline{s}),s) \to_d ((p',\overline{s}'),s')$ includes not only the target s' of s, but also the targets of all its "siblings" $s_1 \in \overline{s}$ that go from p to p'.

For deterministic programs, this amounts to requiring that π_d can only perform tests that are also performed by π. This is a reasonable restriction for code generation purposes, but is by no means necessary: if one somehow knows that the value of a given variable x must lie in a finite set $X = \{a, b, \ldots, k\}$, new tests could be generated to select specialized commands for each case of $x \in X$. See the discussion on 'bounded static variation' in [19].

An $\overline{s}_0$-driven form of π can always be obtained by choosing equality rather than set containment for $\overline{s}'$, and choosing π_d to contain the smallest set of program points including $(p_0, \overline{s}_0)$ and closed under the definition above. This extreme preserves all possible information about the computation subject to the inclusiveness condition. It can be used in principle to produce a "most completely optimized" version of the given program, but suffers from two practical problems:

First, this $\overline{s}_0$-driven π_d will very often contain infinitely many specialized program points $(p, \overline{s})$. Second, its transition relation may not be computable.

Generalization. It is a subtle problem in practice to guarantee that the transformed program both is finite and is more efficient than the original program. A solution in practice is not to work with the mathematically defined and usually infinite store sets above, but rather to use finite descriptions of perhaps larger sets $\overline{s}'' \supseteq \overline{s}'$ that can be manipulated by computable operations.

Finiteness of the transformed program can be achieved by choosing describable store sets that are larger than $\overline{s}'$ but which are still small enough to allow significant optimizations.

Turchin uses the term *configuration* for such a store set description, and *generalization* for the problem of choosing configurations to yield both finiteness and efficiency [33,35].

2.3 Driven flow charts

We now reformulate the former abstract definition for flow charts. For now we leave commands unchanged, as Section 3 will discuss store modifications and code generation together.

Definition 10. Given flow chart $F = (P, E, p_0)$ and $\overline{s}_0 \subseteq S$, $F_d = (P_d, E_d, (p_0, \overline{s}_0))$ is an $\overline{s}_0$-*driven form* of F if $P_d \subseteq P \times \mathcal{P}(S)$ and F_d satisfies the following conditions.

1. $(p, \overline{s}) \overset{C}{\Rightarrow} (p', \overline{s}')$ in F_d implies $p \overset{C}{\Rightarrow} p'$ in F *soundness.*
2. $(p, \overline{s}) \in P_d$, $\overline{s} \neq \{\}$, and $p \overset{C}{\Rightarrow} p'$ in F imply that $(p, \overline{s}) \overset{C}{\Rightarrow} (p', \overline{s}')$ in F_d for some $\overline{s}'$ *completeness.*
3. $(p, \overline{s}) \overset{C}{\Rightarrow} (p', \overline{s}')$ in F_d and $s \in \overline{s}$ and $s' = \mathcal{C}[\![C]\!]s$ is defined imply $s' \in \overline{s}'$ *invariance* of $s \in \overline{s}$.

Theorem 11. *If F_d is an $\overline{s}_0$-driven form of F, then π^{F_d} is an $\overline{s}_0$-driven form of π.*

Proof. This is easily verified from Definitions 5 and 10, as the latter is entirely parallel to Definition 6.

2.4 An example

Collatz' problem in number theory amounts to determining whether the following program terminates for all positive n. To our knowledge it is still unsolved.

A: **while** $n \neq 1$ **do**
  B: **if** n even
    then (C: $n := n \div 2$;)
    else (D: $n := 3 * n + 1$;)
  fi
  od
G:

Its flow chart equivalent is $F = (P, E, 0)$ where $P = \{A, B, C, D, G\}$ and edge set E is given by the diagram in Figure 1. The program has only one variable n, so a store set is essentially a set of values.

We use just four store sets:

$$\begin{aligned} Even &= \{[n \mapsto x] \mid x \in \{0, 2, 4, \ldots\}\} \\ Odd &= \{[n \mapsto x] \mid x \in \{1, 3, 5, \ldots\}\} \\ \top &= \{[n \mapsto x] \mid x \in \mathcal{N}\} \\ \bot &= \{\} \end{aligned}$$

The flow chart F_d of Figure 2 is a driven version of F. Specialized program points $(D, \bot)$ and $(G, \bot)$ are unreachable since they have empty store sets. The driven version, though larger, contains two one-way transitions, from (A, Even) and (B, Even). (In the terminology of [32,15] these points are *imperfect.*) Transition compression redirects the branch from (D, Odd) to $(C, Even)$ to give a somewhat better program, faster in that two tests are avoided whenever n becomes odd.

3 Driven programs, with store transformations

According to Definition 6, a driven program π_d has exactly the same stores as π. As a consequence the only real optimizations that can occur are from

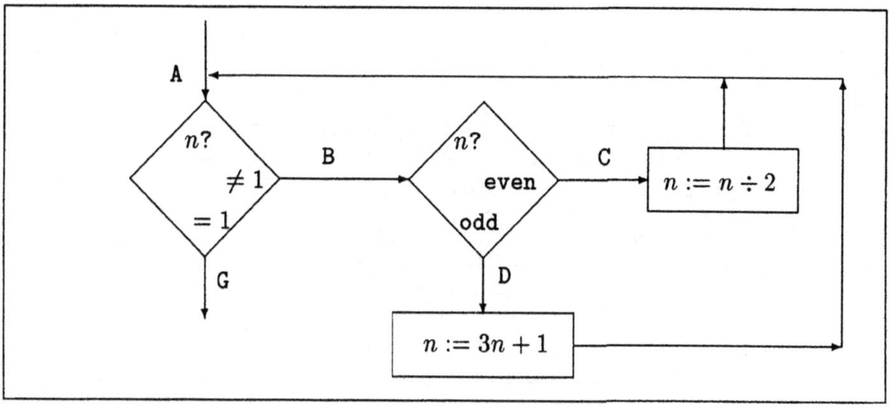

Figure 1: Diagram of a simple flow chart program

collapsing one-way transition chains, and no real computational saving happens. We now revise this definition, "retyping" the store to obtain more powerful transformations such as those of partial evaluation by projections [19,18,21] or arity raising [25].

3.1 Abstract formulation

From now on S_d will denote the set of possible stores in driven program π_d. Given the knowledge that $s \in \overline{s}$, a store s of π can often be represented in the driven program π_d by a simpler store $s_d \in S_d$. For example, if

$$\overline{s} = \{\ [\texttt{X} \mapsto 1,\ \texttt{Y} \mapsto y,\ \texttt{Z} \mapsto 3] \mid y \in \mathcal{N}\}$$

then $s \in \overline{s}$ at π_d program point $(p, \overline{s})$ can be represented by the value of Y alone since X, Z are known from context. In practice, $\overline{s}$ will be described finitely, e.g. by an abstract value σ in description set Σ:

$$\sigma = [\texttt{X} \mapsto 1,\ \texttt{Y} \mapsto \top,\ \texttt{Z} \mapsto 3].$$

together with concretization function (or interpretation) $\gamma : \Sigma \to \mathcal{P}(S)$. To formalize this abstractly, we assume given a function

$$\Delta : \mathcal{P}(S) \times S_d \stackrel{partial}{\longrightarrow} S$$

satisfying the following two properties (note that Δ is written in infix notation.):

1. $\overline{s}\Delta s_d \in \overline{s}$ whenever $\overline{s} \subseteq S$, $s_d \in S_d$, and $\overline{s}\Delta s_d$ is defined; and
2. $\overline{s}_0\Delta s_d = \overline{s}_1\Delta s'_d = s$ implies $s_d = s'_d$

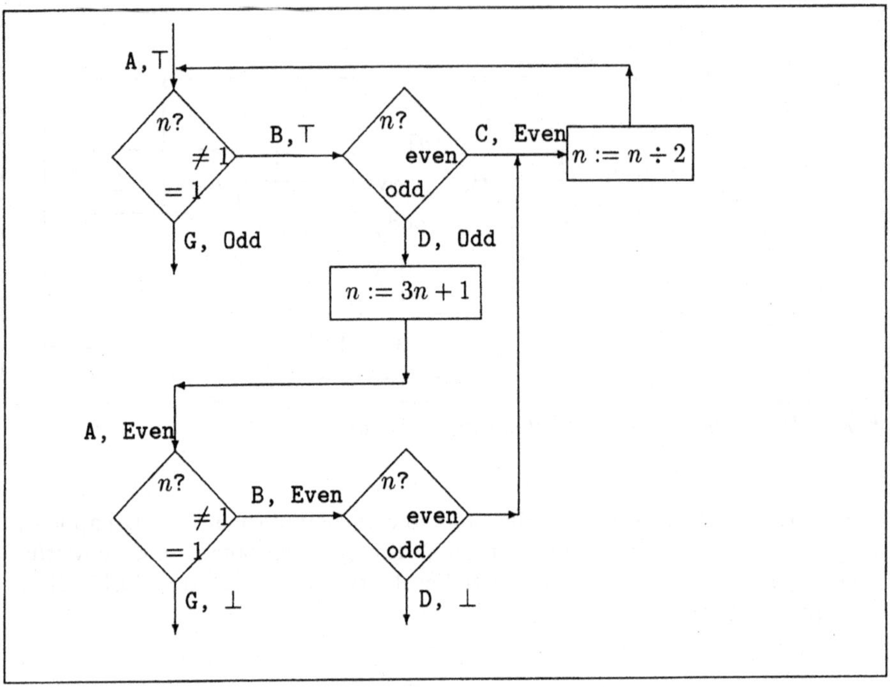

Figure 2: A driven version of the same program

One can think of Δ as a reconstruction function to build s from store set $\overline{s}$ and a driven store s_d. For example, if $\overline{s}$ is as above and if s_d is, say, $[Y \mapsto 5]$ then we would have $\overline{s}\Delta s_d = [X \mapsto 1, Y \mapsto 5, Z \mapsto 3]$.

The restriction $\overline{s}\Delta s_d \in \overline{s}$ says that s_d can only represent a store in the current $\overline{s}$. The second restriction says that Δ is injective in its second argument.

The previous formulation without store transformations is expressible by putting $S = S_d$, and letting $\overline{s}\Delta s_d = s_d$ when $s_d = s_d \in \overline{s}$, with $\overline{s}\Delta s_d$ undefined otherwise.

We will see that allowing alternative representations of the driven stores enables much stronger program optimizations. The new Definition 6 is as follows. The essential idea is that a transition

$$(p, s) \rightarrow (p', s') \quad = \quad (p, \overline{s}\Delta s_d) \rightarrow (p', \overline{s}'\Delta s'_d)$$

is transformed, by a kind of reassociation, into a specialized transition of form

$$((p, \overline{s}), s_d) \rightarrow_d ((p', \overline{s}'), s'_d)$$

Definition 12. Program $\pi_d = (P_d, S_d, \rightarrow_d, (p_0, \overline{s}_0))$ is an $\overline{s}_0$-*driven form* of $\pi = (P, S, \rightarrow, p_0)$ in case $P_d \subseteq P \times \mathcal{P}(S)$ and π_d satisfies the following conditions.

1. $((p,\overline{s}),s_d) \rightarrow_d ((p',\overline{s}'),s'_d)$ implies $s = \overline{s}\Delta s_d$ and $s' = \overline{s}'\Delta s'_d$ for some s, s', and $(p,s) \rightarrow (p',s')$. *soundness*

2. $(p,\overline{s}) \in P_d$, $s \in \overline{s}$, and $(p,s) \rightarrow (p',s')$ imply there are $s_d, s'_d, \overline{s}'$ such that $s = \overline{s}\Delta s_d$, $s' = \overline{s}'\Delta s'_d$, and $((p,\overline{s}),s_d) \rightarrow_d ((p',\overline{s}'),s'_d)$. *completeness*

3. $((p,\overline{s}),s_d) \rightarrow_d ((p',\overline{s}'),s'_d)$ imply $\overline{s}'\Delta s'_d \in \overline{s}'$

   invariance of $s \in \overline{s}$

Condition 3 is actually redundant, as it follows from 1 and the requirement on Δ.

Lemma 13. *If π_d is an $\overline{s}_0$-driven form of π, then for any computation*

$$(p_0, s_0) \rightarrow (p_1, s_1) \rightarrow (p_2, s_2) \rightarrow \ldots$$

with $s_0 = \overline{s}_0\Delta s_{0d}$ there is a computation

$$((p_0,\overline{s}_0),s_{d0}) \rightarrow_d ((p_1,\overline{s}_1),s_{d1}) \rightarrow_d ((p_2,\overline{s}_2),s_{d2}) \rightarrow_d \ldots$$

with $s_i = \overline{s}_i\Delta s_{di}$ for all i. Further, for any such π_d computation with $s_0 = \overline{s}_0\Delta s_{d0}$, there is a corresponding π computation with $s_i = \overline{s}_i\Delta s_{di}$ for all i.

The first part follows from initialization and completeness, and the second by soundness and invariance. The corollary on equivalent input/output behaviour requires a modification.

Corollary 14. *If every $s_0 \in \overline{s}_0$ equals $\overline{s}_0\Delta s_{0d}$ for some s_{0d}, then $IO(\pi,\overline{s}_0) =$*

$$\{(\overline{s}_0\Delta s_{0d}, \overline{s}\Delta s_d) \mid \overline{s}_0\Delta s_{0d} \in \overline{s}_0 \text{ and } (((p_0,\overline{s}_0),s_{0d}),((p,\overline{s}),s_d)) \in IO(\pi_d,\overline{s}_{0d})\}$$

3.2 Correctness of code in driven flow charts

We now redefine driven flow charts to allow different code in F_d than in F. Commands labeling edges of F_d will be given subscript d. Their semantic function is:

$$\mathcal{C}_d[\![\_]\!] : Command_d \rightarrow (S_d \stackrel{partial}{\longrightarrow} S_d)$$

The following rather technical definition can be intuitively understood as saying that for each paired $p \stackrel{C}{\Rightarrow} p'$ and $(p,\overline{s}) \stackrel{C_d}{\Rightarrow} (p',\overline{s}')$, the diagram corresponding to equation

$$\mathcal{C}[\![C]\!](\overline{s}\Delta s_d) = \overline{s}'\Delta(\mathcal{C}_d[\![C_d]\!]s_d)$$

commutes, provided that various of its subexpressions are defined.

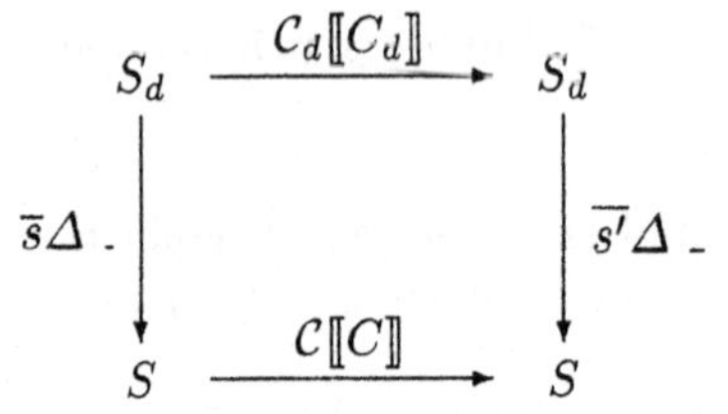

Definition 15. Given flow chart $F = (P, E, p_0)$ and $\overline{s}_0 \subseteq S$, $F_d = (P_d, E_d, (p_0, \overline{s}_0))$ is an $\overline{s}_0$-*driven form* of F if $P_d \subseteq P \times \mathcal{P}(S)$ and F_d satisfies the following conditions.

1. For each $(p, \overline{s}) \overset{C_d}{\Rightarrow} (p', \overline{s}') \in E_d$ there exists $p \overset{C}{\Rightarrow} p' \in E$ such that $s = \overline{s}\Delta s_d$ and $s' = C[\![C]\!]s$ are defined if and only if $s'_d = C_d[\![C_d]\!]s_d$ and $s' = \overline{s}'\Delta s'_d$ are defined *soundness*
2. If $p \overset{C}{\Rightarrow} p'$, $(p, \overline{s}) \in P_d$, and both $s = \overline{s}\Delta s_d$ and $s' = C[\![C]\!]s$ are defined, then F_d has an edge $(p, \overline{s}) \overset{C_d}{\Rightarrow} (p', \overline{s}')$ such that $s' = \overline{s}'\Delta(C_d[\![C_d]\!]s_d)$ *completeness*
3. $(p, \overline{s}) \overset{C_d}{\Rightarrow} (p', \overline{s}')$, $p \overset{C}{\Rightarrow} p'$, and both $s = \overline{s}\Delta s_d$ and $s' = C[\![C]\!]s$ are defined imply $C_d[\![C_d]\!]s_d \in \overline{s}'$ *invariance* of $s \in \overline{s}$.

Theorem 16. *If F_d is an $\overline{s}_0$-driven form of F, then π^{F_d} is an $\overline{s}_0$-driven form of π^F.*

Proof. This is easily verified from Definitions 5 and 15, as the latter is entirely parallel to Definition 12.

3.3 Partial evaluation by projections

Suppose there is a way to decompose or factor a store s into static and dynamic parts without loss of information (a basic idea in [18,19]). A *data division* is a triple of functions $(stat : S \to S_s, dyn : S \to S_d, pair : S_s \times S_d \to S)$. The ability to decompose and recompose without information loss can be expressed by three equations:

$$\begin{aligned} pair(stat(s), dyn(s)) &= s \\ stat(pair(v_s, v_d)) &= v_s \\ dyn(pair(v_s, v_d)) &= v_d \end{aligned}$$

An example. For example, a division could be given (as in [18,19]) by an $S-D$ vector, for instance SDD specifies the division of $S = \mathcal{N}^3$ into $\mathcal{N} \times \mathcal{N}^2$ where $pair(n, (x, a)) = (n, x, a)$, $stat(n, x, a) = n$, and $dyn(n, x, a) = (x, a)$. Using this, the program

$$\begin{aligned} f(n, x) &= g(n, x, 1) \\ g(n, x, a) &= \textbf{if } n = 0 \textbf{ then } 1 \textbf{ else } g(n-1, x, x * a) \end{aligned}$$

can be specialized with respect to known $n = 2$ to yield:

$$\begin{aligned} f_2(x) &= g_2(x,1) \\ g_2(x,a) &= g_1(x, x*a) \\ g_1(x,a) &= g_0(x, x*a) \\ g_0(x,a) &= 1 \end{aligned}$$

which by transition compression can be further reduced to

$$f_2(x) = x * x$$

Relationship between driving and projections. This method can be interpreted in current terms as specialization by using store sets that are equivalence classes with respect to static projections, i.e. every store set is of the following form for some $v_s \in S_s$:

$$\overline{s}_{v_s} = \{s \mid stat(s) = v_s\}$$

Store reconstruction can be expressed by defining: $\overline{s}_{v_s} \Delta v_d = pair(v_s, v_d)$. A specialized program π_d in [18,19] only contains transitions of form

$$((p, stat(s)), dyn(s)) \to ((p', stat(s')), dyn(s'))$$

where π contains $(p,s) \to (p',s')$. This corresponds to our soundness condition. The set "poly" in [18,19]) is constructed so if $(p_0, s_0) \to^* (p,s)$ by π for some $s_0 \in \overline{s}_0$, then poly and so π_d contains a specialized program point $(p, stat(s))$, ensuring completeness. Invariance of $s \in \overline{s}$ is immediate since every specialized state is of the form $((p, \overline{s}_{v_s}), v_d)$, and

$$\overline{s}_{v_s} \Delta v_d = pair(v_s, v_d) \in \{s \mid stat(s) = v_s\}$$

since $stat(pair(v_s, v_d)) = v_s$. The following definition is central in [18,19]:

Definition 17. Function $stat : S \to S_d$ is *congruent* if for any π transitions $(p,s) \to (p',s')$ and $(p,s_1) \to (p',s_1')$, if $stat(s) = stat(s_1)$, then $stat(s') = stat(s_1')$.

This is essentially the "no new tests" requirement of Definition 9.

4 An algorithm for driving

The driving algorithm of Figure 3 manipulates store descriptions $\sigma \in \Sigma$, rather than store sets. For the x^n example above, Σ is the set of all store descriptions σ of the form

$$\sigma = [n \mapsto u, x \mapsto \top, a \mapsto \top]$$

where $u \in \mathcal{N}$. We assume given a *concretization function* $\gamma : \Sigma \to \mathcal{P}(S)$ defining their meanings, and that the test "is $\gamma\sigma = \{\}$?" is computable, i.e. that we can recognize a description of the empty set of stores.

```
read F = (P, E, p₀);
read σ₀;
Pending := {(p₀, σ₀)};                           (* Unprocessed program points *)
SeenBefore := {};                                (* Already processed pgm. points *)
P_d := {(p₀, σ₀)};                               (* Initial program points *)
E_d := {};                                       (* Initial edge set *)
while ∃(p, σ) ∈ Pending do                       (* Choose an unprocessed point *)
  Pending := Pending \ {(p, σ)};
  SeenBefore := SeenBefore ∪ {(p, σ)};
  forall p =C=> p' ∈ E do                        (* Scan all transitions from p *)
    σ' := S(σ, C);                               (* Update store set description *)
    if γσ' ≠ {} then                             (* Generate code if nontrivial *)
      P_d := P_d ∪ {(p', σ')};
      if (p', σ') ∉ SeenBefore then add (p', σ') to Pending;
      C_d := G(σ, C);                            (* Generate code *)
      Add edge (p, σ) =C_d=> (p', σ') to E_d;    (* Extend flow chart by one edge *)
F_d := (P_d, E_d, (p₀, σ₀));
```

Figure 3: An algorithm for driving

In addition we assume given a *store set update* function

$$\mathcal{S} : \mathit{Command} \times \Sigma \rightarrow \Sigma$$

and a *code generation* function

$$\mathcal{G} : \mathit{Command} \times \Sigma \rightarrow \mathit{Command}_d$$

Correctness criterion. For any $C \in \mathit{Command}, \sigma \in \Sigma, s_d \in S_d$, let $\sigma' = \mathcal{S}(\sigma, C)$ and $C_d = \mathcal{G}(\sigma, C)$. Definition 15 requires $\mathcal{C}[\![C]\!](\gamma\sigma \Delta s_d) = (\gamma\sigma')\Delta(\mathcal{C}_d[\![C_d]\!]s_d)$ under certain conditions (where $t = t'$ means both are defined and the values are equal):

1. $s = (\gamma\sigma)\Delta s_d$ and $s'_d = \mathcal{C}_d[\![C_d]\!]s_d$ imply $\mathcal{C}[\![C]\!]s = (\gamma\sigma')\Delta s'_d$ — *soundness*
2. $s' = \mathcal{C}[\![C]\!]s$ and $s = (\gamma\sigma)\Delta s_d$ imply $s' = (\gamma\sigma')\Delta(\mathcal{C}_d[\![C_d]\!]s_d)$ — *completeness*
3. $s = (\gamma\sigma)\Delta s_d \in \gamma\sigma$ implies $\mathcal{C}_d[\![C_d]\!]s_d \in \gamma\sigma'$ — *invariance* of $s \in \overline{s}$.

4.1 Example: pattern matching in strings

A way to test a program transformation method's power is to see whether it can derive certain well-known efficient programs from equivalent naive and inefficient programs. One of the most popular of such tests is to generate, from a naive pattern matcher and a fixed pattern, an efficient pattern matcher as produced by the Knuth-Morris-Pratt algorithm. We shall call this *the KMP test* [27].

First we give a program for string pattern matching.

$$
\begin{aligned}
&match\ p\ s && = loop\ p\ s\ p\ s \\
\\
&loop\ []\ ss\ op\ os && = True \\
&loop\ (p:pp)\ []\ op\ os && = False \\
&loop\ (p:pp)\ (s:ss)\ op\ os && = \textbf{if}\ p = s\ \textbf{then}\ loop\ pp\ ss\ op\ os\ \textbf{else}\ next\ op\ os \\
\\
&next\ op\ [] && = False \\
&next\ op\ (s:ss) && = loop\ op\ ss\ op\ ss
\end{aligned}
$$

For conciseness in exposition, we specify the store sets that are encountered while driving *match AAB u* by means of terms containing free variables. These are assumed to range over all possible data values. Given this, the result of driving can be described by the configuration graph seen in the Figure ending this paper (where some intermediate configurations have been left out). More details can be seen in [27].

The program generated is:

$$
\begin{aligned}
&f\ u && = f_{AAB}\ u \\
\\
&f_{AAB}\ [] && = False \\
&f_{AAB}\ (s:ss) && = g\ s\ ss \\
\\
&g\ s\ ss && = \textbf{if}\ A = s\ \textbf{then}\ f_{AB}\ ss\ \textbf{else}\ f_{AAB}\ ss \\
\\
&f_{AB}\ [] && = False \\
&f_{AB}\ (s:ss) && = h\ s\ ss \\
\\
&h\ s\ ss && = \textbf{if}\ A = s\ \textbf{then}\ f_{B}\ ss\ \textbf{else}\ g\ ss \\
\\
&f_{B}\ [] && = False \\
&f_{B}\ (s:ss) && = \textbf{if}\ A = s\ \textbf{then}\ g\ s\ ss\ \textbf{else} \\
& && \quad \textbf{if}\ B = s\ \textbf{then}\ true\ \textbf{else}\ h\ s\ ss
\end{aligned}
$$

This is in essence a KMP pattern matcher, so driving passes the KMP test. It is interesting to note that driving has transformed a program running in time $O(m \cdot n)$ into one running in time $O(n)$, where m is the length of the pattern and n is the length of the subject string.

Using configurations as above can result in some redundant tests, because we only propagate positive information (what term describes the negative outcome of a test?). However this problem can easily be overcome by using both positive and negative environments, see [15].

Partial evaluators of which we know cannot achieve this effect without non-trivial human rewriting of the matching program.

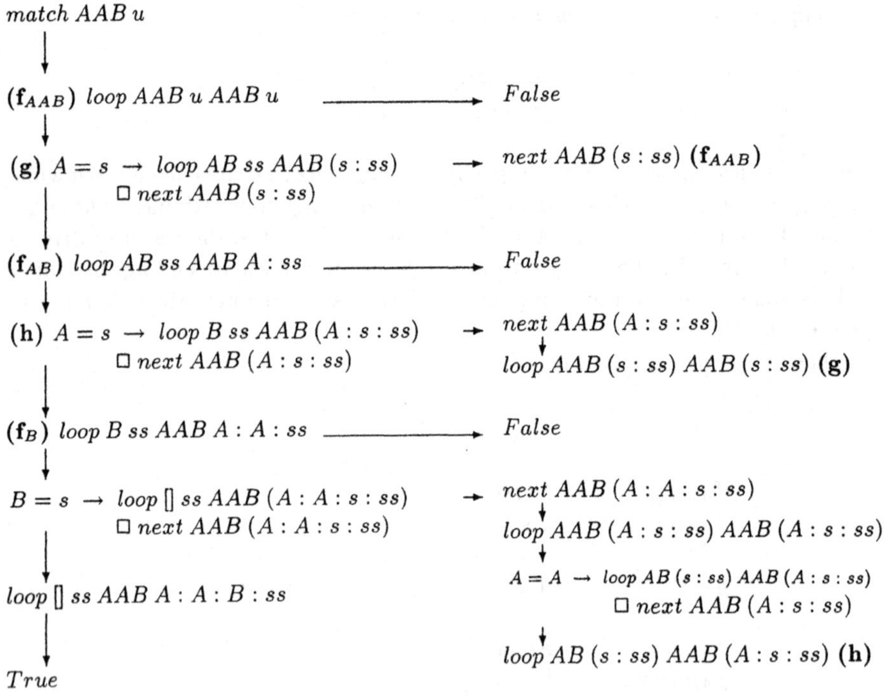
match AAB u
(f_AAB) loop AAB u AAB u
False
(g) A = s → loop AB ss AAB (s : ss)
□ next AAB (s : ss)
next AAB (s : ss) (f_AAB)
(f_AB) loop AB ss AAB A : ss
False
(h) A = s → loop B ss AAB (A : s : ss)
□ next AAB (A : s : ss)
next AAB (A : s : ss)
loop AAB (s : ss) AAB (s : ss) (g)
(f_B) loop B ss AAB A : A : ss
False
B = s → loop [] ss AAB (A : A : s : ss)
□ next AAB (A : A : s : ss)
next AAB (A : A : s : ss)
loop AAB (A : s : ss) AAB (A : s : ss)
A = A → loop AB (s : ss) AAB (A : s : ss)
□ next AAB (A : s : ss)
loop [] ss AAB A : A : B : ss
loop AB (s : ss) AAB (A : s : ss) (h)
True

4.2 Finiteness and generalization

Σ is usually an infinite set, causing the risk of generating infinitely many different configurations while driving. Turchin uses the term *generalization* for the problem of choosing configurations to yield both finiteness and efficiency [33,35].

The idea is to choose elements $\sigma' = \mathcal{S}(\sigma, C)$ which are "large enough" to ensure finiteness of the transformed program, but are still small enough to allow significant optimizations. This may require one to *ignore some information* that is available at transformation time, i.e. to choose descriptions of larger and so less precise store sets than would be possible on the basis of the current σ and C.

How to achieve termination without overgeneralization is not yet fully understood. Turchin advocates an online technique, using the computational history of the driving process to guide the choices of new σ' [35]. It is as yet unclear whether self-application for practical compiler generation can be achieved in this way, or whether some form of preprocessing will be needed. If offline preprocessing is needed, it will certainly be rather different from "binding-time analysis" as used in partial evaluation [19].

Acknowledgement

Many useful comments on this paper were made by Patrick Cusot, Robert Glück, Andrei Klimov, Sergei Romanenko, Morten Heine Sørensen, and Carolyn Talcott.

References

1. Sergei M. Abramov, Metacomputation and program testing. In: *1st International Workshop on Automated and Algorithmic Debugging.* (Linköping, Sweden). pp. 121-135, Linköping University 1993.
2. Samson Abramsky and Chris Hankin, editors. *Abstract Interpretation of Declarative Languages.* Ellis Horwood, 1987.
3. Alfred V. Aho, Ravi Sethi, and Jeffrey D. Ullman. *Compilers: Principles, Techniques, and Tools.* Addison-Wesley, 1986.
4. Lennart Augustsson, Compiling lazy pattern-matching. *Conference on Functional Programming and Computer Architecture,* ed. J.-P. Jouannoud. Lecture Notes in Computer Science 201, Springer-Verlag, 1985.
5. L. Beckman et al. A partial evaluator, and its use as a programming tool. *Artificial Intelligence,* 7(4), pp. 319–357, 1976.
6. D. Bjørner, A.P. Ershov, and N.D. Jones, editors. *Partial Evaluation and Mixed Computation. Proceedings of the IFIP TC2 Workshop.* North-Holland, 1988. 625 pages.
7. Wei-Ngan Chin, Safe fusion of functional expressions II: further improvements. *Journal of Functional Programming.* To appear in 1994.
8. Charles Consel and Olivier Danvy, Partial evaluation of pattern matching in strings. *Information Processing Letters,* 30, pp. 79–86, January 1989.
9. Patrick Cousot and Radhia Cousot, Abstract interpretation: a unified lattice model for static analysis of programs by construction or approximation of fixpoints. In *Fourth ACM Symposium on Principles on Programming Languages,* pp. 238–252, New York: ACM Press, 1977.
10. Edsger W. Dijkstra. *A Discipline of Programming.* Prentice-Hall, 1976.
11. Andrei P. Ershov. Mixed computation: Potential applications and problems for study. *Theoretical Computer Science,* 18, pp. 41–67, 1982.
12. Alex B. Ferguson and Philip Wadler, When will deforestation stop? *Glasgow Workshop on Functional Programming,* August 1988.
13. Yoshihiko Futamura and Kenroku Nogi, Generalized partial computation. In *Partial Evaluation and Mixed Computation,* Eds. A. P. Ershov, D. Bjørner and N. D. Jones, North-Holland, 1988.
14. Robert Glück and Valentin F. Turchin, Application of metasystem transition to function inversion and transformation. *Proceedings of the ISSAC '90,* pp. 286-287, ACM Press,1990.

15. Robert Glück and Andrei V. Klimov, Occam's razor in metacomputation: the notion of a perfect process tree. In *Static analysis Proceedings*, eds. P. Cousot, M. Falaschi, G. Filé, G. Rauzy. Lecture Notes in Computer Science 724, pp. 112-123, Springer-Verlag, 1993.
16. Neil D. Jones and Flemming Nielson, Abstract interpretation: a semantics-based tool for program analysis, 122 pages. In *Handbook of Logic in Computer Science*, Oxford University Press to appear in 1994.
17. Neil D. Jones, Flow analysis of lazy higher-order functional programs. In *Abstract Interpretation of Declarative Languages*, pp. 103-122. Ellis Horwood, 1987.
18. Neil D. Jones, Automatic program specialization: A re-examination from basic principles, in D. Bjørner, A.P. Ershov, and N.D. Jones (eds.), *Partial Evaluation and Mixed Computation*, pp. 225–282, Amsterdam: North-Holland, 1988.
19. Neil D. Jones, Carsten Gomard and Peter Sestoft. *Partial Evaluation and Automatic Program Generation.* Prentice Hall International, 425 pp., 1993.
20. Stephen S. Kleene, *Introduction to Metamathematics.* Van Nostrand, 1952, 550 pp.
21. John Launchbury, *Projection Factorisations in Partial Evaluation.* Cambridge: Cambridge University Press, 1991.
22. Andrei V. Klimov and Sergei Romanenko, A metaevaluator for the language Refal: basic concepts and examples. Keldysh Institute of Applied Mathematics, Academy of Sciences of the USSR, Moscow. Preprint No. 71, 1987 (in Russian).
23. Donald E. Knuth, James H. Morris, and Vaughan R. Pratt, Fast pattern matching in strings, *SIAM Journal of Computation*, 6(2), pp. 323–350, 1977.
24. Alexander Y. Romanenko, The generation of inverse functions in Refal, in D. Bjørner, A.P. Ershov, and N.D. Jones (eds.), *Partial Evaluation and Mixed Computation*, pp. 427-444, Amsterdam: North-Holland, 1988.
25. Sergei A. Romanenko, A compiler generator produced by a self-applicable specializer can have a surprisingly natural and understandable structure. In D. Bjørner, A.P. Ershov, and N.D. Jones (eds.), *Partial Evaluation and Mixed Computation*, pp. 445–463, Amsterdam: North-Holland, 1988.
26. Morten Heine Sørensen, *A grammar-based data flow analysis to stop deforestation.Colloquium on Trees and Algebra in Programming (CAAP)*, edinburgh, Scotland. Lecture Notes in Computer Science, Springer-Verlag, to appear in 1994.
27. Morten Heine Sørensen, Robert Glück and Neil D. Jones, Towards unifying partial evaluation, deforestation, supercompilation, and GPC. *European Symposium on Programming (ESOP).* Lecture Notes in Computer Science, Springer-Verlag, to appear in 1994.
28. Akihiko Takano, Generalized partial computation for a lazy functional language. *Symposium on Partial Evaluation and Semantics-Based Program Manipulation*, eds. Neil D. Jones and Paul Hudak, ACM Press, 1991.
29. Valentin F. Turchin, Equivalent transformations of recursive functions defined in Refal. In: *Teorija Jazykov i Metody Programmirovanija* (Proceedings of the Symposium on the Theory of Languages and Programming Methods). (Kiev-Alushta, USSR). pp. 31-42, 1972 (in Russian).
30. Valentin F. Turchin, Equivalent transformations of Refal programs. In: *Avtomatizirovannaja Sistema upravlenija stroitel'stvom.* Trudy CNIPIASS, 6, pp. 36-68, 1974 (in Russian).
31. Valentin F. Turchin, *The Language Refal, the Theory of Compilation and Metasystem Analysis.* Courant Computer Science Report 20, 245 pages, 1980.

32. Valentin F. Turchin, Semantic definitions in Refal and automatic production of compilers. *Semantics-Directed Compiler Generation*, Aarhus, Denmark. Lecture Notes in Computer Science, Springer-Verlag, pp. 441-474, vol. 94, 1980.
33. Valentin F. Turchin, The concept of a supercompiler. *ACM Transactions on Programming Languages and Systems*, 8(3), pp. 292–325, July 1986.
34. Turchin V. F., A constructive interpretation of the full set theory. In: *The Journal of Symbolic Logic*, 52(1): 172-201, 1987.
35. Valentin F. Turchin, The algorithm of generalization in the supercompiler. In D. Bjørner, A.P. Ershov, and N.D. Jones (eds.), *Partial Evaluation and Mixed Computation*, pp. 531-549, Amsterdam: North-Holland, 1988.
36. Philip L. Wadler, Deforestation: transforming programs to eliminate trees. European Symposium On Programming (ESOP). Lecture Notes in Computer Science 300, pp. 344-358, Nancy, France, Springer-Verlag, 1988.

Program Transformation via Contextual Assertions

Ian A. Mason and Carolyn Talcott

Stanford University, Stanford, California, 94305-2140, USA

Abstract. In this paper we describe progress towards a theory of tranformational program development. The transformation rules are based on a theory of contextual equivalence for functional languages with imperative features. Such notions of equivalence are fundamental for the process of program specification, derivation, transformation, refinement and other forms of code generation and optimization. This paper is dedicated to Professor Satoru Takasu.

1 Introduction

This paper describes progress towards a theory of program development by systematic refinement beginning with a clean simple program thought of as a specification. Transformations include reuse of storage, and re-representation of abstract data. The transformation rules are based on a theory of constrained equivalence for functional languages with imperative features (i.e. Lisp, Scheme or ML). Such notions of equivalence are fundamental for the process of program specification, derivation, transformation, refinement, and other forms of code generation and optimization. This paper is a continuation of our development of the Variable Typed Logic of Effects (VTLoE) introduced in [11,20,10]. VTLoE is inspired by the variable type systems of Feferman. These systems are two sorted theories of operations and classes initially developed for the formalization of constructive mathematics [2,3] and later applied to the study of purely functional languages [4,5]. VTLoE goes well beyond traditional programming logics, such as Hoare's [1] and Dynamic logic [9]. The programming language and logic are richer. It is close in spirit to Specification Logic [27], incorporating a full first order theory of data and the ability to express program equivalence, and to assert and nest Hoare-like triples (called *contextual assertions* in VTLoE). The underlying programming languages are quite different: Specification Logic concerns Algol-like programs that are strongly typed, can store only first-order data, and obey call-by-name semantics; while VTLoE concerns untyped ML- or Scheme-like languages that can store arbitrary values, and obey call-by-value semantics. The underlying programming language of VTLoE, $\lambda_{\mathtt{mk}}$, is based on the call-by-value lambda calculus extended by the reference primitives `mk`, `set`, `get`. The cornerstone of VTLoE is the notion of operational equivalence. Two expressions are operationally equivalent if they cannot be distinguished by any program context. Operational equivalence enjoys many nice properties such as being a congruence relation on expressions. It subsumes the lambda-v-calculus [26] and the lambda-c calculus [22]. The theory of operational equivalence for λ_{mk} is presented in [17,18].

In [10] we began the development of the full logic of VTLoE, including general properties of contextual assertions and valid forms of class comprehension. In this setting induction principles for reasoning about programs can derived using minimal and maximal fixed-points of class operators. Another important semantic technique for establishing properties of programs is induction on the length of computations. In this paper we focus on formalizing principles for program transformation based on computation induction. Rather than deal with the full λ_{mk} calculus, we restrict our attention to the first order fragment (where there are no higher-order procedures). This simplifies the presentation substantially. For this fragment we present four main tools: subgoal induction, recursion induction, peephole optimization, and a memory reuse principle. The subgoal and recursion induction principles generalize standard principles for purely functional languages. Subgoal induction reduces proving input-output assertions about recursively defined programs to finding suitable invariants and showing that they propagate across the functions defining bodies. Recursion induction reduces proving equivalence of two recursive programs to showing that each satisfies the others defining equation. The peephole rule answers affirmatively a conjecture in [13], p 178. This rule allows for the replacement of a program fragment with another fragment that is equivalent in the context of use. The memory-reuse principle captures many of the standard compiler optimizations concerning register and memory reuse. This principle strengthens recursion induction to account for local memory.

We give two examples of the use of these tools. The first is the transformation of a tail recursive program to a loop that utilizes a register. The second is the transformation of a simple, but non-trivial, rewriting program, known as the Boyer benchmark [8]. This example is part of a more extensive transformational development carried out in the process of developing parallel Lisp programs for symbolic manipulation [15].

The remainder of this paper is organized as follows. In section 2 we present the syntax and semantics of terms. In section 3 we describe the first-order fragment of VTLoE. In section 4 we present the main transformation tools. In section 5 these tools are used to transform the Boyer Benchmark. Section 6 contains concluding remarks and directions for future work.

We conclude this section with a summary of notational conventions. We use the usual notation for set membership and function application. Let X, Y, Y_0, Y_1 be sets. We specify meta-variable conventions in the form: let x range over X, which should be read as: the meta-variable x and decorated variants such as x', x_0, ..., range over the set X. Y^n is the set of sequences of elements of Y of length n. Y^* is the set of finite sequences of elements of Y. $[y_1, \ldots, y_n]$ is the sequence of length n with ith element y_i. $[Y_0 \to Y_1]$ is the set of functions f with domain Y_0 and range contained in Y_1. We write $\mathrm{Dom}(f)$ for the domain of a function and $\mathrm{Rng}(f)$ for its range. $\mathrm{Fmap}[Y_0, Y_1]$ is the set of functions whose domain is a *finite* subset of Y_0 and whose range is a subset of Y_1. For any function f, $f\{y := y'\}$ is the function f' such that $\mathrm{Dom}(f') = \mathrm{Dom}(f) \cup \{y\}$, $f'(y) = y'$, and $f'(z) = f(z)$ for $z \neq y, z \in \mathrm{Dom}(f)$. $\mathbb{N} = \{0, 1, 2, \ldots\}$ is the set of natural numbers and $i, j, n, n_0, \ldots$ range over $\mathbb{N}$.

2 The Syntax and Semantics of Terms

Our language can be thought of as a first-order untyped ML, or as a variant of Scheme in which naming of values and memory allocation have been separated. Thus there are explicit memory operations (`atom?`, `cell?`, `eq?`, `mk`, `get`, `set`) but no assignment to bound variables. The reason for the choice is that it simplifies the semantics and allows one to separate the functional aspects from the imperative ones in a clean way. We also include various forms of structured data such as numbers and immutable pairs. The presentation in this section is by necessity terse. A more detailed presentation can be found in [19].

2.1 The Syntax of Terms

We fix a countably infinite set of atoms, $\mathbb{A}$, with two distinct elements playing the role of booleans, `T` for *true* and `Nil` for *false*. We also fix a countable set $\mathbb{X}$ of variables and for each $n \in \mathbb{N}$ a countable set, $\mathbb{F}_n$, of n-ary function symbols. We assume the sets $\mathbb{A}$, $\mathbb{X}$, and $\mathbb{F}_n$ for $n \in \mathbb{N}$ are pairwise disjoint. We let $\mathbb{O}_n$ denote the set of n-ary operations, $\mathbf{F}_n$ denote $\mathbb{O}_n \cup \mathbb{F}_n$ and $\mathbf{F}$ denote $\bigcup_{n \in \mathbb{N}} \mathbf{F}_n$.

The operations, $\mathbb{O}$, are partitioned into memory operations and operations that are independent of memory. A memory operation may modify memory, and its result may depend on state of memory when it is executed. The memory operations are:

$$\{\mathtt{get}, \mathtt{mk}\} \subseteq \mathbb{O}_1 \quad \{\mathtt{set}\} \subseteq \mathbb{O}_2 .$$

The remaining operations neither affect the memory, nor are affected by the memory. In this paper we explicitly include operations for dealing with immutable pairs and assorted predicates.

$$\{\mathtt{cell?}, \mathtt{atom?}, \mathtt{nat?}, \mathtt{fst}, \mathtt{snd}, \mathtt{pr?}\} \subseteq \mathbb{O}_1 \qquad \{\mathtt{eq?}, \mathtt{pr}\} \subseteq \mathbb{O}_2$$

In addition there are operations on numbers which we shall not enumerate explicitly.

Definition ($\mathbb{V}$ $\mathbb{P}$ $\mathbb{S}$ $\mathbb{E}$): The set of value expressions, $\mathbb{V}$, the set of immutable pairs, $\mathbb{P}$, the set of value substitutions, $\mathbb{S}$, and the set of expressions, $\mathbb{E}$, are defined, mutually recursively, as the least sets satisfying the following equations:

$$\mathbb{V} = \mathbb{X} + \mathbb{A} + \mathbb{P}$$

$$\mathbb{P} = \mathtt{pr}(\mathbb{V}, \mathbb{V})$$

$$\mathbb{S} = \mathrm{Fmap}[\mathbb{X}, \mathbb{V}]$$

$$\mathbb{E} = \mathbb{V} \cup \mathtt{let}\{\mathbb{X} := \mathbb{E}\}\mathbb{E} \cup \mathtt{if}(\mathbb{E}, \mathbb{E}, \mathbb{E}) \cup \bigcup_{n \in \mathrm{N}} \mathbf{F}_n(\mathbb{E}^n)$$

We let a range over $\mathbb{A}$, x range over $\mathbb{X}$, v range over $\mathbb{V}$, f, g range over $\mathbb{F}$, σ range over $\mathbb{S}$, ϑ range over $\mathbb{O}$, and e range over $\mathbb{E}$. The variable of a `let` is bound in the second expression, and the usual conventions concerning alpha conversion apply. We write $\mathrm{FV}(e)$ for the set of free variables of e. $e^{\{x:=e'\}}$ is the result of substituting e' for x in e taking care not to trap free variables of e'. e^σ is the result of simultaneously substituting free occurrences of $x \in \mathrm{Dom}(\sigma)$ in e by $\sigma(x)$, again taking care not to trap free variables. For any syntactic domain Y and set of variables X we let Y_X be the elements of Y with free variables in X. A *closed expression* is an expression with no free variables. Thus $\mathbb{E}_\emptyset$ is the set of all closed expressions.

Definition ($\mathbb{C}$): Contexts are expressions with holes. We use $\bullet$ to denote a hole. The set of contexts, $\mathbb{C}$, is defined by

$$\mathbb{C} = \{\bullet\} + \mathbb{X} + \mathbb{A} + \mathtt{let}\{\mathbb{X} := \mathbb{C}\}\mathbb{C} + \mathtt{if}(\mathbb{C}, \mathbb{C}, \mathbb{C}) + \mathbf{F}_n(\mathbb{C}^n)$$

We let C range over $\mathbb{C}$. $C[e]$ denotes the result of replacing any hole in C by e. Free variables of e may become bound in this process.

Definition (Δ): The set of (recursive function-) definition systems is the collection of all finite sequences whose elements are of the form $f(x_1, \ldots, x_n) \leftarrow e$ where f is an n-ary function symbol. In symbols:

$$(\bigcup_{n \in \mathrm{N}} \mathbb{F}_n(\mathbb{X}^n) \leftarrow \mathbb{E})^*$$

Let Δ be a definition system. The defined functions of Δ are those $f \in \mathbb{F}$ for which there is a definition $f(x_1, \ldots, x_n) \leftarrow e$ occurring in Δ for some $x_1, \ldots, x_n$, and e. The variables $(x_1, \ldots, x_n)$ are called the formal parameters of the definition and e is the body. A definition system Δ is well-formed if no function symbol is defined more than once, and if for each $f(x_1, \ldots, x_n) \leftarrow e$ in Δ, the variables $x_1, \ldots, x_n$ are distinct, $\mathrm{FV}(e) \subseteq \{x_1, \ldots, x_n\}$, and the function symbols occurring in e are among the defined functions of Δ. We shall assume that definition systems are well-formed unless otherwise stated. Within a single definition the formal parameters are bound in the body and we may freely α-convert (subject to maintaining well-formedness).

In order to make programs easier to read, we introduce some abbreviations.

$\mathtt{seq}(e)$	abbreviates	e	
$\mathtt{seq}(e_0, \ldots, e_n)$	abbreviates	$\mathtt{let}\{d := e_0\}\mathtt{seq}(e_1, \ldots, e_n)$	d fresh
$\mathtt{cond}()$	abbreviates	`Nil`	
$\mathtt{cond}([e_0 \rhd e_0'], [e_1 \rhd e_1'], \ldots, [e_n \rhd e_n'])$	abbreviates	$\mathtt{if}(e_0, e_0', \mathtt{cond}([e_1 \rhd e_1'], \ldots, [e_n \rhd e_n']))$	

2.2 The Semantics of Terms

The operational semantics of expressions relative to a definition set Δ is given by a reduction relation $\overset{*}{\mapsto}$ on expressions. Computation is a process of stepwise reduction of an expression to a canonical form. In order to define the reduction rules we introduce the notions of *memory context*, *reduction context*, and *redex*. Redexes describe the primitive computation steps. A primitive step is either a `let`-reduction, branching according to whether a test value is `Nil` or not, unfolding an application of a recursively defined function symbol, or the application of a primitive operation.

Definition ($\mathbb{E}_{\mathrm{rdx}}$): The set of redexes, $\mathbb{E}_{\mathrm{rdx}}$, is defined as

$$\mathbb{E}_{\mathrm{rdx}} = \mathtt{if}(\mathbb{V},\mathbb{E},\mathbb{E}) \cup \mathtt{let}\{\mathbb{X} := \mathbb{V}\}\mathbb{E} \cup (\bigcup_{n\in\mathrm{N}} \mathbf{F}_n(\mathbb{V}^n) - \mathbb{P})$$

Note that the structured data, $\mathbb{P}$, are taken to be values (i.e are not redexes). Reduction contexts identify the subexpression of an expression that is to be evaluated next, they correspond to the standard reduction strategy (left-first, call-by-value) of [26] and were first introduced in [7].

Definition ($\mathbb{R}$): The set of reduction contexts, $\mathbb{R}$, is the subset of $\mathbb{C}$ defined by

$$\mathbb{R} = \{\bullet\} \cup \mathtt{let}\{\mathbb{X} := \mathbb{R}\}\mathbb{E} \cup \mathtt{if}(\mathbb{R},\mathbb{E},\mathbb{E}) \cup \bigcup_{n,m\in\mathrm{N}} \mathbf{F}_{n+m+1}(\mathbb{V}^n,\mathbb{R},\mathbb{E}^m)$$

We let R range over $\mathbb{R}$. An expression is either a value expression or decomposes uniquely into a primitive expression placed in a reduction context.

Definition ($\mathbb{M}$): The set of memory contexts, $\mathbb{M}$, is the set of contexts Γ of the form

$$\begin{array}{l}\mathtt{let}\{z_1 := \mathtt{mk}(\mathtt{Nil})\} \\ \quad \ddots \qquad\qquad \ddots \\ \qquad\qquad \mathtt{let}\{z_n := \mathtt{mk}(\mathtt{Nil})\}\mathtt{seq}(\mathtt{set}(z_1,v_1),\ldots,\mathtt{set}(z_n,v_n),\bullet)\end{array}$$

where $z_i \neq z_j$ when $i \neq j$. We include the possibility that $n = 0$, in which case $\Gamma = \bullet$. We let Γ range over $\mathbb{M}$.

We have divided the memory context into allocation, followed by assignment to allow for the construction of cycles. Thus, any state of memory is constructible by such an expression. We can view memory contexts as finite maps from variables to value expressions. Hence we define the domain of Γ (as above) to be $\mathrm{Dom}(\Gamma) = \{z_1,\ldots,z_n\}$, and $\Gamma(z_i) = v_i$ for $1 \le i \le n$. Two memory contexts are considered the same if they are the same when viewed as functions. Viewing memory contexts as finite maps, we define the modification of memory contexts, $\Gamma\{z := \mathtt{mk}(v)\}$, and the union of two memory contexts, $(\Gamma_0 \cup \Gamma_1)$, in the obvious way.

Definition ($\mathbb{D}$): The set of computation descriptions (briefly descriptions), $\mathbb{D}$, is defined to be the set $\mathbb{M} \times \mathbb{E}$. Thus a description is a pair with first component a memory context and second component an arbitrary expression. We let $\Gamma; e$ range over $\mathbb{D}$. A *closed* description is a description of the form $\Gamma; e$ where $\mathrm{Rng}(\Gamma) \cup \{e\} \subseteq \mathbb{E}_{\mathrm{Dom}(\Gamma)}$ (recall that $\mathbb{E}_{\mathrm{Dom}(\Gamma)}$ is the set of expressions whose free variables are among $\mathrm{Dom}(\Gamma)$). *Value descriptions* are descriptions whose expression component is a value expression, i.e. a description of the form $\Gamma; v$.

Single-step reduction ($\mapsto$) is a relation on *descriptions.* The reduction relation $\overset{*}{\mapsto}$ is the reflexive transitive closure of $\mapsto$. Officially, $\overset{*}{\mapsto}$ and $\mapsto$ should be parameterized by the definition system Δ, we will not make this parameter explicit here.

Definition ($\overset{*}{\mapsto}$): Single-step reduction is the least relation such that

(let) $\quad \Gamma; R[\mathtt{let}\{x := v\}e] \mapsto \Gamma; R[e^{\{x:=v\}}]$

(if) $\quad \Gamma; R[\mathtt{if}(v, e_1, e_2)] \mapsto \begin{cases} \Gamma; R[e_1] & \text{if } v \in (\mathbb{A} - \{\mathtt{Nil}\}) \cup \mathrm{Dom}(\Gamma) \\ \Gamma; R[e_2] & \text{if } v = \mathtt{Nil} \end{cases}$

(rec) $\quad \Gamma; R[f(v_1, \ldots, v_n)] \mapsto \Gamma; R[e^{\sigma}]$

$$\text{if } f(x_1, \ldots, x_n) \leftarrow e \text{ in } \Delta,\ \mathrm{Dom}(\sigma) = \{x_1, \ldots, x_n\} \text{ and } \sigma(x_i) = v_i$$

(atom) $\quad \Gamma; R[\mathtt{atom?}(v)] \mapsto \begin{cases} \Gamma; R[\mathtt{T}] & \text{if } v \in \mathbb{A} \\ \Gamma; R[\mathtt{Nil}] & \text{if } v \in \mathbb{P} \cup \mathrm{Dom}(\Gamma) \end{cases}$

(ispr) $\quad \Gamma; R[\mathtt{pr?}(v)] \mapsto \begin{cases} \Gamma; R[\mathtt{T}] & \text{if } v \in \mathbb{P} \\ \Gamma; R[\mathtt{Nil}] & \text{if } v \in \mathbb{A} \cup \mathrm{Dom}(\Gamma) \end{cases}$

(cell) $\quad \Gamma; R[\mathtt{cell?}(v)] \mapsto \begin{cases} \Gamma; R[\mathtt{T}] & \text{if } v \in \mathrm{Dom}(\Gamma) \\ \Gamma; R[\mathtt{Nil}] & \text{if } v \in \mathbb{P} \cup \mathbb{A} \end{cases}$

(eq) $\quad \Gamma; R[\mathtt{eq?}(v_0, v_1)] \mapsto \begin{cases} \Gamma; R[\mathtt{T}] & \text{if } v_0 = v_1,\ v_0, v_1 \in \mathrm{Dom}(\Gamma) \cup \mathbb{A}, \\ \Gamma; R[\mathtt{Nil}] & \text{otherwise and } \mathrm{FV}(v_0, v_1) \subseteq \mathrm{Dom}(\Gamma). \end{cases}$

(fst) $\quad \Gamma; R[\mathtt{fst}(\mathtt{pr}(v_1, v_2))] \mapsto \Gamma; R[v_1]$

(snd) $\quad \Gamma; R[\mathtt{snd}(\mathtt{pr}(v_1, v_2))] \mapsto \Gamma; R[v_2]$

(mk) $\quad \Gamma; R[\mathtt{mk}(v)] \mapsto \Gamma\{z := \mathtt{mk}(v)\}; R[z] \qquad \text{if } z \notin \mathrm{Dom}(\Gamma) \cup \mathrm{FV}(R[v])$

(get) $\quad \Gamma; R[\mathtt{get}(z)] \mapsto \Gamma; R[v] \qquad \text{if } z \in \mathrm{Dom}(\Gamma) \text{ and } \Gamma(z) = v$

(set) $\quad \Gamma; R[\mathtt{set}(z, v)] \mapsto \Gamma\{z := \mathtt{mk}(v)\}; R[\mathtt{Nil}] \qquad \text{if } z \in \mathrm{Dom}(\Gamma)$

In the definition of $\mapsto$ we have not restricted our attention to closed descriptions, thus allowing symbolic or parametric computation. Note however that in the `atom?` and `cell?` rules if one of the arguments is a variable not in the domain of the memory context then the primitive reduction step is not determined (i.e. it suspends due to a lack of information). This is also the case in the `eq?`, `get`, and `set` rules.

Definition ($\downarrow \uparrow \updownarrow$): A closed description, $\Gamma; e$ is *defined* (written $\downarrow \Gamma; e$) if it evaluates to a value description. A description is undefined (written $\uparrow \Gamma; e$) if it is not defined.

$$\downarrow(\Gamma;e) \Leftrightarrow (\exists\Gamma';v')(\Gamma;e \overset{*}{\mapsto} \Gamma';v')$$

$$\uparrow(\Gamma;e) \Leftrightarrow \neg\downarrow(\Gamma;e)$$

For closed expressions e, we write $\downarrow e$ to mean $\downarrow\emptyset;e$ and $e_0 \updownarrow e_1$ to mean that $\downarrow e_0$ iff $\downarrow e_1$.

2.3 Operational Equivalence of Terms

Operational equivalence formalizes the notion of equivalence as black-boxes. Treating programs as black boxes requires only observing what effects and values they produce, and not how they produce them. Our definition extends the extensional equivalence relations defined by [24] and [26] to computation over memory structures.

Definition ($\sqsubseteq$ $\cong$): Two expressions are operationally approximate, written $e_0 \sqsubseteq e_1$, if for any closing context C, if $C[e_0]$ is defined then $C[e_1]$ is defined. Two expressions are operationally equivalent, written $e_0 \cong e_1$, if they approximate one another.

$$e_0 \sqsubseteq e_1 \Leftrightarrow (\forall C \in \mathbb{C} \mid C[e_0], C[e_1] \in \mathbb{E}_\emptyset)(\downarrow C[e_0] \Rightarrow \downarrow C[e_1])$$

$$e_0 \cong e_1 \Leftrightarrow e_0 \sqsubseteq e_1 \wedge e_1 \sqsubseteq e_0$$

The operational equivalence is not trivial since the inclusion of branching implies that `T` and `Nil` are not equivalent. By definition operational equivalence is a congruence relation on expressions:

Lemma (Congruence):

$$e_0 \cong e_1 \Leftrightarrow (\forall C \in \mathbb{C})(C[e_0] \cong C[e_1])$$

In general it is very difficult to establish the operational equivalence of expressions. Thus it is desirable to have a simpler characterization of $\cong$. There are two simple characterizations of operational equivalence available in this setting. The first is called (**ciu**) equivalence and also holds for the full λ_{mk} calculus. The second is called strong isomorphism and holds only in the first order case.

The first result is that two expressions are operationally equivalent just if all closed instantiations of all uses are equidefined. This latter property is a weak form of extensionality.

Theorem (ciu [18,10]):

$$e_0 \cong e_1 \Leftrightarrow (\forall \Gamma, \sigma, R \mid \mathrm{FV}(\Gamma[R[e_i^\sigma]]) = \emptyset)(\Gamma[R[e_0^\sigma]] \updownarrow \Gamma[R[e_1^\sigma]]))$$

For the second we say two expressions e_0 and e_1 are strongly isomorphic if for every closed instantiation either both are undefined or both are defined and evaluate to objects that are equal modulo the production of garbage. By garbage we mean cells constructed in the process of evaluation that are not accessible from either the result or the domain of the initial memory. The result then is that operational equivalence and strong isomorphism coincide.

Theorem (striso [13,14]): $e_0 \cong e_1$ iff if for each Γ, σ such that $\Gamma[e_j^\sigma] \in \mathbb{E}_\emptyset$ for $j < 2$, one of the following holds:

(1) $\uparrow(\Gamma; e_0^\sigma)$ and $\uparrow(\Gamma; e_1^\sigma)$, or

(2) there exist v, Γ', Γ_0, Γ_1 such that $\mathrm{Dom}(\Gamma) \subseteq \mathrm{Dom}(\Gamma')$, $\Gamma'[v] \in \mathbb{E}_\emptyset$, $\mathrm{Dom}(\Gamma') \cap \mathrm{Dom}(\Gamma_j) = \emptyset$ and $\Gamma; e_j^\sigma \overset{*}{\mapsto} (\Gamma_j \cup \Gamma'); v$ for $j < 2$.

Using these theorems we can easily establish, for example, the validity of the let-rules of the lambda-c calculus [23]

Corollary ($\mathtt{let}_c$):

(i) $e^{\{x:=v\}} \cong \mathtt{let}\{x := v\}e$

(ii) $R[e] \cong \mathtt{let}\{x := e\}R[x]$

(iii) $R[\mathtt{let}\{x := e_0\}e_1] \cong \mathtt{let}\{x := e_0\}R[e_1]$

where in (ii) and (iii) we require x not free in R.

Another nice property that is easily established is that reduction preserves operational equivalence.

Lemma (eval): $\Gamma; e \mapsto \Gamma'; e' \Rightarrow \Gamma[e] \cong \Gamma'[e']$.

3 The Syntax and Semantics of the First-Order Theory

3.1 Syntax of Formulas

The atomic formulas of our language assert the operational equivalence of two expressions. In addition to the usual first-order formula constructions we add *contextual assertions:* if Φ is a formula and U is a certain type of context, then $U[\![\Phi]\!]$ is a formula. This form of formula expresses the fact that the assertion Φ holds at the point in the program text marked by the hole in U, if execution of the program reaches that point. The contexts allowed in contextual assertions are called *univalent contexts*, (U-contexts). The class of U-contexts, $\mathbb{U}$, is defined as follows.

Definition ($\mathbb{U}$):

$$\mathbb{U} = \{\bullet\} + \mathtt{let}\{\mathbb{X} := \mathbb{E}\}\mathbb{U}$$

The well-formed formulas, $\mathbb{W}$, of (the first order part of) our logic are defined as follows:

Definition ($\mathbb{W}$):

$$\mathbb{W} = (\mathbb{E} \cong \mathbb{E}) + (\mathbb{W} \Rightarrow \mathbb{W}) + (\mathbb{U}[\![\mathbb{W}]\!]) + (\forall\mathbb{X})(\mathbb{W})$$

We let Φ range over $\mathbb{W}$. Negation is definable, $\neg\Phi$ is just $\Phi \Rightarrow \mathtt{False}$, where $\mathtt{False}$ is any unsatisfiable assertion, such as $\mathtt{T} \cong \mathtt{Nil}$. Similarly conjunction, $\wedge$, and disjunction, $\vee$ and the biconditional, $\Leftrightarrow$, are all definable in the usual manner. We let $\Downarrow e$ abbreviate $\neg(\mathtt{seq}(e, \bullet)[\![\mathtt{False}]\!])$ and $\Uparrow e$ abbreviate its negation. Note that $\Downarrow e$ expresses the computational definedness of the expression e.

Given a particular U, for example $\mathtt{let}\{x := \mathtt{mk}(v)\}\bullet$, we will often abuse notation and write $\mathtt{let}\{x := \mathtt{mk}(v)\}[\![\Phi]\!]$ rather than $(\mathtt{let}\{x := \mathtt{mk}(v)\}\bullet)[\![\Phi]\!]$. Thus we write $\neg\mathtt{seq}(e, [\![\mathtt{False}]\!])$ rather than $\neg(\mathtt{seq}(e, \bullet)[\![\mathtt{False}]\!])$.

Note that the context U will in general bind free variables in Φ. A simple example is the law which expresses the effects of $\mathtt{mk}$:

$$(\forall y)(\mathtt{let}\{x := \mathtt{mk}(v)\}[\![\neg(x \cong y) \wedge \mathtt{cell?}(x) \cong \mathtt{T} \wedge \mathtt{get}(x) \cong v]\!])$$

For simplicity we have omitted certain possible contexts from the definition of $\mathbb{U}$. However those left out may be considered abbreviations. Two examples are:

(1) $\mathtt{if}(e_0, [\![\Phi_0]\!], [\![\Phi_1]\!])$ abbreviates

$$\mathtt{let}\{z := e_0\}[\![(z \cong \mathtt{Nil} \Rightarrow \Phi_1) \wedge (\neg(z \cong \mathtt{Nil}) \Rightarrow \Phi_0)]\!] \qquad z \text{ fresh.}$$

(2) $\vartheta(e_0, \ldots, e_n, U[\![\Phi]\!], e_{n+1}, \ldots)$ abbreviates $\mathtt{seq}(e_0, \ldots, e_n, U[\![\Phi]\!])$

In order to define the semantics of contextual assertions, we must extend computation to univalent contexts. The idea here is quite simple, to compute with contexts we need to keep track of the $\mathtt{let}$-conversions that have taken place with the hole in the scope of the $\mathtt{let}$. To indicate that the substitution σ is in force at the hole in U we write $U[\![\sigma]\!]$. Computation is then written as $\Gamma; U[\![\sigma]\!] \overset{*}{\mapsto} \Gamma'; U'[\![\sigma']\!]$ and is defined in full in [10]. For example if x is not in the domain of σ, then

$$\Gamma; \mathtt{let}\{x := v\}[\![\sigma]\!] \overset{*}{\mapsto} \Gamma; [\![\sigma\{x := v\}]\!].$$

3.2 Semantics of Formulas

In addition to being a useful tool for establishing laws of operational equivalence, (**ciu**) can be used to define a satisfaction relation between memory contexts and equivalence assertions. In an obvious analogy with the usual first-order Tarskian definition of satisfaction this can be extended to define a satisfaction relation $\Gamma \models \Phi[\sigma]$.

The definition of satisfaction $\Gamma \models \Phi[\sigma]$ is given by a simple induction on the structure of Φ.

Definition ($\Gamma \models \Phi[\sigma]$): $(\forall \Gamma, \sigma, \Phi, e_j)$ such that $\mathrm{FV}(\Phi^\sigma) \cup \mathrm{FV}(e_j^\sigma) \subseteq \mathrm{Dom}(\Gamma)$ for $j < 2$ we define satisfaction:

$$\Gamma \models (e_0 \cong e_1)[\sigma] \quad \text{iff} \quad (\forall R \in \mathbb{R}_{\mathrm{Dom}(\Gamma)})(\Gamma[R[e_0^\sigma]] \updownarrow \Gamma[R[e_1^\sigma]])$$

$$\Gamma \models (\Phi_0 \Rightarrow \Phi_1)[\sigma] \quad \text{iff} \quad (\Gamma \models \Phi_0[\sigma]) \text{ implies } (\Gamma \models \Phi_1[\sigma])$$

$$\Gamma \models U[\![\Phi]\!][\sigma] \quad \text{iff} \quad (\forall \Gamma', R, \sigma')((\Gamma; U[\![\sigma]\!] \overset{*}{\mapsto} \Gamma'; R[\![\sigma']\!]) \text{ implies } \Gamma' \models \Phi[\sigma'])$$

$$\Gamma \models (\forall x)\Phi[\sigma] \quad \text{iff} \quad (\forall v \in \mathbb{V}_{\mathrm{Dom}(\Gamma)})(\Gamma \models \Phi[\sigma\{x := v\}])$$

We say that a formula is *valid*, written $\models \Phi$, if $\Gamma \models \Phi[\sigma]$ for Γ, σ such that $\mathrm{FV}(\Phi^\sigma) \subseteq \mathrm{Dom}(\Gamma)$. Following the usual convention we will often write Φ as an assertion that Φ is valid, omitting the $\models$ sign. Note that the underlying logic is completely classical.

3.3 Contextual Assertion Principles

The theorem (**ca**) provides several principles for reasoning about contextual assertions: a simple principle concerning reduction contexts; a general principle for introducing contextual assertions (akin to the rule of necessitation in modal logic); a principle for propagating contextual assertions through equations; and a principle for composing contexts (or collapsing nested contextual assertions); a principle for manipulating contexts; three principles demonstrating that contextual assertions interact nicely with the propositional connectives, if we take proper account of assertions that are true for the trivial reason that during execution, the point in the program text marked by the context hole is never reached; and a principle (whose converse is false) concerning the quantifier. Finally a lemma demonstrating that contextual assertions interact nicely with evaluation. Proofs of the principles in this section can be found in [10].

Theorem (ca):

(i) $\Phi \Rightarrow R[\![\Phi]\!]$

(ii) $\models \Phi$ implies $\models U[\![\Phi]\!]$

(iii) $U[\![e_0 \cong e_1]\!] \Rightarrow U[e_0] \cong U[e_1]$

(iiii) $\models U_0[\![U_1[\![\Phi]\!]]\!] \Leftrightarrow (U_0[U_1])[\![\Phi]\!]$

(iv) $\mathtt{let}\{x := R[e]\}\, U[\![\Phi]\!] \Leftrightarrow \mathtt{let}\{y := e\}\mathtt{let}\{x := R[y]\}\, U[\![\Phi]\!]$ y fresh

(v) $U[\![\mathtt{False}]\!] \Rightarrow U[\![\Phi]\!]$

(vii) $U[\![\neg\Phi]\!] \Leftrightarrow (U[\![\mathtt{False}]\!] \vee \neg U[\![\Phi]\!])$

(viii) $U[\![\Phi_0 \Rightarrow \Phi_1]\!] \Leftrightarrow (U[\![\Phi_0]\!] \Rightarrow U[\![\Phi_1]\!])$

(viiii) $U[\![\forall x \Phi]\!] \Rightarrow \forall x\, U[\![\Phi]\!]$ where x not free in U

Lemma (eval):

$$\Gamma_0; U_0[\![\sigma_0]\!] \overset{*}{\mapsto} \Gamma_1; U_1[\![\sigma_1]\!] \text{ implies } (\Gamma_0 \models U_0[\![\Phi]\!][\sigma_0] \text{ iff } \Gamma_1 \models U_1[\![\Phi]\!][\sigma_1])$$

A simple use of (**ca**) is the following principle:

Lemma (cut):

$$\models \Phi \Rightarrow U[\![\Phi']\!] \text{ and } \models \Phi' \Rightarrow U'[\![\Phi'']\!] \text{ implies } \models \Phi \Rightarrow (U[U'])[\![\Phi'']\!]$$

Proof (cut): Assume $\models \Phi' \Rightarrow U'[\![\Phi'']\!]$. Thus

$\models U[\![\Phi' \Rightarrow U'[\![\Phi'']\!]]\!]$ by (**ca.ii**).

$\models U[\![\Phi']\!] \Rightarrow U[\![U'[\![\Phi'']\!]]\!]$ by (**ca.viii**).

$\models \Phi \Rightarrow (U[U'])[\![\Phi'']\!]$ by (**ca.iiii**) and classical logic.

3.4 Memory Operation Principles

This logic extends and improves the complete first order system presented in [16, 19]. There certain reasoning principles were established as basic, and from these all others, suitably restricted, could be derived using simple equational reasoning. The system presented there had several defects. In particular the rules concerning the effects of mk and set had complicated side-conditions. Using contextual assertions we can express them simply and elegantly. Their justification is also unproblematic.

The contextual assertions and laws involving mk, set and get are given below. The assertion, (**mk.i**), describes the allocation effect of a call to mk. While (**mk.ii**) expresses what is unaffected by a call to mk. The assertion, (**mk.iii**), expresses the totality of mk. The mk delay law, (**mk.iv**), asserts that the time of allocation has no discernable effect on the resulting cell. In a world with control effects evaluation of e_0 must be free of them for this principle to be valid [6]. The first three contextual assertions regarding set are analogous to those of mk. They describe what is returned and what is altered, what is not altered as well as when the operation is defined. The remaining three principles involve the commuting, cancellation, absorption of calls to set. For example the set absorption principle, (**set.vi**), expresses that under certain simple conditions allocation followed by assignment may be replaced by a suitably altered allocation. The contextual assertions regarding get follow the above pattern. They describe what is altered and returned, what is not altered as well as when the operation is defined.

Lemma (Memory Operation Laws):

(mk.i) $\mathtt{let}\{x := \mathtt{mk}(v)\}[\![\neg(x \cong y) \wedge \mathtt{cell?}(x) \cong \mathtt{T} \wedge \mathtt{get}(x) \cong v]\!]$

x fresh

(mk.ii) $y \cong \mathtt{get}(z) \Rightarrow \mathtt{let}\{x := \mathtt{mk}(v)\}[\![y \cong \mathtt{get}(z)]\!]$

(mk.iii) $\Downarrow \mathtt{mk}(z)$

(mk.iv) $\mathtt{let}\{y := e_0\}\mathtt{let}\{x := \mathtt{mk}(v)\}e_1 \cong \mathtt{let}\{x := \mathtt{mk}(v)\}\mathtt{let}\{y := e_0\}e_1$

$x \notin \mathrm{FV}(e_0),\ y \notin \mathrm{FV}(v)$

(set.i) $\mathtt{cell?}(z) \Rightarrow \mathtt{let}\{x := \mathtt{set}(z, y)\}[\![\mathtt{get}(z) \cong y \wedge x \cong \mathtt{Nil}]\!])$

(set.ii) $(y \cong \mathtt{get}(z) \wedge \neg(w \cong z)) \Rightarrow \mathtt{let}\{x := \mathtt{set}(w, v)\}[\![y \cong \mathtt{get}(z)]\!]$

(set.iii) $\mathtt{cell?}(z) \Rightarrow \Downarrow \mathtt{set}(z, x)$

(set.iv) $\neg(x_0 \cong x_2) \Rightarrow$

$$\mathtt{seq}(\mathtt{set}(x_0, x_1), \mathtt{set}(x_2, x_3)) \cong \mathtt{seq}(\mathtt{set}(x_2, x_3), \mathtt{set}(x_0, x_1))$$

(set.v) $\mathtt{seq}(\mathtt{set}(x, y_0), \mathtt{set}(x, y_1)) \cong \mathtt{set}(x, y_1)$

(set.vi) $\mathtt{let}\{z := \mathtt{mk}(x)\}\mathtt{seq}(\mathtt{set}(z, w), e) \cong \mathtt{let}\{z := \mathtt{mk}(w)\}e$

z not free in w

(get.i) $\mathtt{let}\{x := \mathtt{get}(y)\}[\![x \cong \mathtt{get}(y)]\!]$

(get.ii) $y \cong \mathtt{get}(z) \Rightarrow \mathtt{let}\{x := \mathtt{get}(w)\}[\![y \cong \mathtt{get}(z)]\!]$

(get.iii) $\mathtt{cell?}(x) \Leftrightarrow (\exists y)(\mathtt{get}(x) \cong y)$

We should also point out that officially we should make Δ a parameter of the satisfaction relation but, as in the presentation of the operational semantics, we will not usually make this parameter explicit. The only rule which depends on the definition system is the following unfolding rule, (**U**), it corresponds to the (**rec**) rule for single-step reduction.

Lemma (Unfolding law):

$$f(e_1, \ldots, e_n) \cong \mathtt{let}\{x_1 := e_1\} \ldots \mathtt{let}\{x_n := e_n\}e$$

where $f(x_1, \ldots x_n) \leftarrow e$ is in Δ and x_i are chosen fresh.

A simple example of a proof is the following lemma.

Lemma (if delay): If $z \notin \mathrm{FV}(e)$, then

$$\mathtt{let}\{z := \mathtt{mk}(x)\}\mathtt{if}(e, e_1, e_2) \cong \mathtt{if}(e, \mathtt{let}\{z := \mathtt{mk}(x)\}e_1, \mathtt{let}\{z := \mathtt{mk}(x)\}e_2)$$

Proof (if delay):

$$\mathtt{let}\{z := \mathtt{mk}(x)\}\mathtt{if}(e, e_1, e_2)$$

$$\cong \mathtt{let}\{z := \mathtt{mk}(x)\}\mathtt{let}\{y := e\}\mathtt{if}(y, e_1, e_2)$$

by (**congruence**) and ($\mathbf{let_c}$**.ii**)

$$\cong \mathtt{let}\{y := e\}\mathtt{let}\{z := \mathtt{mk}(x)\}\mathtt{if}(y, e_1, e_2) \qquad \text{by } (\mathtt{mk}\textbf{.iv})$$

So it suffices to show that if $z \notin \mathrm{FV}(e)$, then

$$\mathtt{let}\{z := \mathtt{mk}(x)\}\mathtt{if}(y, e_1, e_2) \cong \mathtt{if}(y, \mathtt{let}\{z := \mathtt{mk}(x)\}e_1, \mathtt{let}\{z := \mathtt{mk}(x)\}e_2)$$

First observe that static properties always propagate:

(i) $\neg(y \cong \mathtt{Nil}) \Rightarrow \mathtt{let}\{z := \mathtt{mk}(x)\}[\![\neg(y \cong \mathtt{Nil})]\!]$

(ii) $\neg(y \cong \mathtt{Nil}) \Rightarrow \mathtt{if}(y, e_1, e_2) \cong e_1$

Putting (**i**) and (**ii**) together via (**cut**) gives

$$\neg(y \cong \mathtt{Nil}) \Rightarrow \mathtt{let}\{z := \mathtt{mk}(x)\}\mathtt{if}(y, e_1, e_2) \cong \mathtt{let}\{z := \mathtt{mk}(x)\}e_1$$

A second application of (**ii**) gives

$$\neg(y \cong \texttt{Nil}) \Rightarrow$$
$$\texttt{let}\{z := \texttt{mk}(x)\}\texttt{if}(y, e_1, e_2)$$
$$\cong$$
$$\texttt{if}(y, \texttt{let}\{z := \texttt{mk}(x)\}e_1, \texttt{let}\{z := \texttt{mk}(x)\}e_2)$$

Similar reasoning under the hypothesis that $y \cong \texttt{Nil}$ provides

$$y \cong \texttt{Nil} \Rightarrow$$
$$\texttt{let}\{z := \texttt{mk}(x)\}\texttt{if}(y, e_1, e_2)$$
$$\cong$$
$$\texttt{if}(y, \texttt{let}\{z := \texttt{mk}(x)\}e_1, \texttt{let}\{z := \texttt{mk}(x)\}e_2)$$

Classical logic provides the rest. □

3.5 Reasoning about Newness

A very useful concept is that of a cell being new. A cell is considered *new* in a memory if it appears as if it was newly allocated, i.e. it is does not appear elsewhere in memory. We will use the newness assertions to recycle cells. Since a *new* cell is as good as a newly allocated cell. The definition of **new** requires an auxiliary program, *notin*, that checks whether z is not accessible from x via a chain of projections.

$$\begin{aligned} \mathit{notin}(z, x) \leftarrow \texttt{cond}([&\texttt{not}(\texttt{cell?}(z)), \texttt{T}] \\ [&\texttt{cell?}(x), \texttt{not}(\texttt{eq?}(x, z))] \\ [&\texttt{atom?}(x), \texttt{T}] \\ [&\texttt{pr?}(x), \texttt{and}(\mathit{notin}(z, \texttt{fst}(x)), \mathit{notin}(z, \texttt{snd}(x)))]) \end{aligned}$$

For convenience will will often write x *notin* y to abbreviate the assertion $\mathit{notin}(x, y) \cong \texttt{T}$.

Definition (**new**):

$$\texttt{new}(x) \quad \text{abbreviates} \quad \texttt{cell?}(x) \cong \texttt{T} \wedge (\forall y)(\texttt{cell?}(y) \Rightarrow x \;\mathit{notin}\; \texttt{get}(y))$$

A simple example of *newness* is given by the following lemma. It states that a cell is new immediately after it is created.

Lemma (new creation):

$$\texttt{let}\{x := \texttt{mk}(v)\}[\![\texttt{new}(x)]\!]$$

The next lemma provides some principles for propagating newness.

Lemma (new):

(i) $\mathtt{new}(x) \Rightarrow \mathtt{let}\{z := \vartheta(\bar{v})\}[\![\mathtt{new}(x)]\!] \qquad \vartheta \notin \{\mathtt{mk}, \mathtt{set}\}$

(ii) $\mathtt{new}(x) \wedge (x \mathit{\ notin\ } v) \Rightarrow \mathtt{let}\{z := \mathtt{mk}(v)\}[\![\mathtt{new}(x)]\!]$

(iii) $\mathtt{new}(x) \wedge (x \mathit{\ notin\ } v) \Rightarrow \mathtt{let}\{z := \mathtt{set}(y, v)\}[\![\mathtt{new}(x)]\!]$

(iiii) $U[\![\mathtt{new}(x)]\!] \Rightarrow (R[U])[\![\mathtt{new}(x)]\!]$

(iv) $\mathtt{seq}(e, [\![\mathtt{new}(x)]\!]) \Rightarrow \mathtt{if}(e, [\![\mathtt{new}(x)]\!], [\![\mathtt{new}(x)]\!])$

(v) $\mathtt{new}(x) \wedge \bigwedge_{w \in \mathrm{FV}(e)} x \mathit{\ notin\ } w \Rightarrow \mathtt{let}\{y := e\}[\![\mathtt{new}(x)]\!]$

Note that in (**new.iii**) the variables x and y could name the same cell. An important principle concerning newness is *reuse*:

Theorem (new reuse):

$$\mathtt{let}\{x := \mathtt{mk}(v)\}\mathtt{seq}(e_0, [\![\mathtt{new}(x)]\!]) \Rightarrow$$
$$(\mathtt{let}\{x := \mathtt{mk}(v)\}\mathtt{seq}(e_0, e_1)$$
$$\cong$$
$$\mathtt{seq}(\mathtt{let}\{x := \mathtt{mk}(v)\}e_0, \mathtt{let}\{x := \mathtt{mk}(\mathtt{get}(x))\}e_1))$$

4 Tools for Transformations

We now develop some tools for reasoning about recursively defined programs. These tools fall into three general classes: principles for proving input-output assertions, principles for proving program equivalence, and principles for manipulating memory. Contextual assertions play an important role here, especially in the formulation of rules for propagation of invariants.

We begin with some notation. In the following we let $\mathbf{x}$, $\mathbf{x}_i$, $\mathbf{y}$ be sequences of distinct variables, and let $\mathbf{v}$ be a sequence of value expressions. We let $\mathbf{f}$ be a sequence of function symbols and let f_i denote the i-th symbol of $\mathbf{f}$. We work in the context of an arbitrary but fixed system of definitions Δ. If the symbols of $\mathbf{f}$ are among those defined in Δ, we write $\Delta_{\mathbf{f}} \subseteq \Delta$ for the subsystem $[f_i(\mathbf{x}_i) \leftarrow F_i \mid i \leq n]$ where $n+1$ is the length of $\mathbf{f}$, and $f_i(\mathbf{x}_i) \leftarrow F_i$ is the definition of f_i in Δ for $i \leq n$.

We write $e\{f := \lambda\mathbf{x}.e'\}$ for the replacement of the function symbol f by the explicitly defined function $\lambda\mathbf{x}.e'$ in e. This is obtained by replacing each occurrence $f(e_1, \ldots, e_k)$ in e by

$$\mathtt{let}\{x_i := e_i \mid 1 \leq i \leq k\}e'.$$

Similarly, $e\{f_i := \lambda\mathbf{x}_i.e'_i\}$ denotes the simultaneous replacement of function symbols f_i by $\lambda\mathbf{x}_i.e'_i$ in e. We will use analogous conventions for sequences, $\mathbf{g}$ of function symbols.

4.1 Invariants

The central idea in this subsection is to formalize the notion of propagating an assertion to all important points in an expression, which in this case consists in all occurrences of recursive function calls. This is accomplished by defining the notion of a system of invariants, generalizing Floyd-style inductive assertions.

Definition (System of invariants): A system of invariants for $\mathbf{f}$ is a sequence of pairs of formulas (ϕ_i, ψ_i) for $i \leq n = |\mathbf{f}|$.

We let I range over systems of invariants. The ϕ_i are to be thought of as pre-conditions for f_i, while the ψ_i are post-conditions. We adopt the convention that the variable z will serve as the value of the output, and that $\mathbf{x}_i$ will serve as input variables for ϕ_i. Thus occurrences of these variables in the invariants will be used to name parameters in calls to the defined functions.

These invariants are used to propagate assertions across any calls to these functions. To make this precise we make the following definition.

Definition (I, f-propagation): Let I be a system of invariants for $\mathbf{f}$, and let θ, θ' be any invariants. We say that θ $(I, \mathbf{f})$-propagates across $\mathtt{let}\{z := e\}\bullet$ to θ' and denote this relation by

$$\models_{I,\mathbf{f}} \theta \Rightarrow \mathtt{let}\{z := e\}[\![\theta']\!]$$

just if one of the following holds:

(i) No element of $\mathbf{f}$ occurs in e and $\theta \Rightarrow \mathtt{let}\{z := e\}[\![\theta']\!]$.

(ii) $e = f_i(\mathbf{v})$, $\theta \Rightarrow (\phi_i)^\sigma$ and $(\psi_i)^\sigma \Rightarrow \theta'$, where $\sigma = \{\mathbf{x}_i := \mathbf{v}\}$;

(iii) $e = \mathtt{let}\{z_0 := e_0\}e_1$ and there is some θ_0 such that

$$\models_{I,\mathbf{f}} \theta \Rightarrow \mathtt{let}\{z := e_0\}[\![\theta_0^{\{z_0:=z\}}]\!]$$

$$\models_{I,\mathbf{f}} \theta_0 \Rightarrow \mathtt{let}\{z := e_1\}[\![\theta']\!]$$

(iv) $e = \mathtt{if}(e_0, e_1, e_2)$ and there is some θ_1, θ_2 such that

$$\theta \Rightarrow \mathtt{if}(e_0, [\![\theta_1]\!], [\![\theta_2]\!])$$

$$\models_{I,\mathbf{f}} \theta_1 \Rightarrow \mathtt{let}\{z := e_1\}[\![\theta']\!]$$

$$\models_{I,\mathbf{f}} \theta_2 \Rightarrow \mathtt{let}\{z := e_2\}[\![\theta']\!]$$

The key computational property of invariant propagation is expressed by the following lemma.

Lemma (I-prop): Let I be a system of invariants for $\mathbf{f}$, and let θ, θ' be invariants such that $\models_{I,\mathbf{f}} \theta \Rightarrow \mathtt{let}\{z := e\}[\![\theta']\!]$. If $\Gamma \models \theta[\sigma]$, and $\Gamma; e^\sigma \overset{*}{\mapsto} \Gamma'; v$ then

(a) $\Gamma; e^\sigma \overset{*}{\mapsto} \Gamma'; v$ without using $\Delta_{\mathbf{f}}$ and $\Gamma' \models \theta'[\sigma\{z := v\}]$; or

(b) $\Gamma; e^\sigma \overset{*}{\mapsto} \Gamma'; R[f_i(\mathbf{v})]$ (without using $\Delta_{\mathbf{f}}$) and (b.1) $\Gamma' \models \phi_i[\{\mathbf{x} := \mathbf{v}\}]$;

(b.2) $\models_{I,\mathbf{f}} \psi_i\{\mathbf{x} := \mathbf{v}\} \Rightarrow \mathtt{let}\{z := R[z]\}[\![\theta']\!]$

Definition (I-inductive): Let I be a system of invariants for $\mathbf{f}$. We say that $\Delta_\mathbf{f}$ is I-inductive if $\models_{I,\mathbf{f}} \phi_i \Rightarrow \mathtt{let}\{z := F_i\}[\![\psi_i]\!]$ for $i \le n$ (recall that $\Delta_\mathbf{f} = [f_i(\mathbf{x}_i) \leftarrow F_i \mid i \le n]$).

Theorem (Subgoal Induction): Let I be a system of invariants for $\mathbf{f}$. To prove

$$\phi_i \Rightarrow \mathtt{let}\{z := f_i(\mathbf{x}_i)\}[\![\psi_i]\!]$$

for $i \le n$, it suffices to prove that $\Delta_\mathbf{f}$ is I-inductive.

Proof : The validity of this principle is established by a simple computation induction, using (**I-prop**), showing the more general fact that if $\Delta_\mathbf{f}$ is I-inductive then $\models_{I,\mathbf{f}} \theta \Rightarrow \mathtt{let}\{z := e\}[\![\theta']\!]$ implies $\theta \Rightarrow \mathtt{let}\{z := e\}[\![\theta']\!]$. □

Corollary (Subgoal Induction): To prove $\theta \Rightarrow \mathtt{let}\{z := f_0(\mathbf{x}_0)\}[\![\theta']\!]$ it suffices to find a system of invariants I for $\mathbf{f}$, such that $\theta \Rightarrow \phi_0$, $\psi_0 \Rightarrow \theta'$, and $\Delta_\mathbf{f}$ is I-inductive.

As a simple example of the use of subgoal induction, we define $\mathtt{sum!}(n, c)$ that adds the numbers from 1 to n to the contents of c. We show that $\mathtt{sum!}$ returns c (call-by-reference), and preserves newness of c, and c always contains an number.

Definition (sum!):

$$\mathtt{sum!}(n, c) \leftarrow \mathtt{if}(\mathtt{eq?}(n, 0), c, \mathtt{seq}(\mathtt{set}(c, n + \mathtt{get}(c)), \mathtt{sum!}(n-1, c)))$$

Lemma (sum!):

$$(\mathtt{new}(c) \wedge \mathtt{nat?}(\mathtt{get}(c)) \cong \mathtt{T}) \Rightarrow$$
$$\mathtt{let}\{z := \mathtt{sum!}(n, c)\}[\![\mathtt{new}(c) \wedge \mathtt{nat?}(\mathtt{get}(c)) \cong \mathtt{T} \wedge c \cong z]\!]$$

Proof : This is proved by subgoal induction. Let

$$\theta = \phi_0 = \mathtt{new}(c) \wedge \mathtt{nat?}(\mathtt{get}(c)) \cong \mathtt{T},$$

$$\psi_0 = \theta' = \mathtt{new}(c) \wedge \mathtt{nat?}(\mathtt{get}(c)) \cong \mathtt{T} \wedge c \cong z,$$

be the system of invariants for $\mathtt{sum!}$. We must show that $\Delta_{\mathtt{sum!}}$ is I-inductive, i.e.

$$\models_{I,\mathtt{sum!}} \phi_0 \Rightarrow \mathtt{let}\{z := F_{\mathtt{sum!}}\}[\![\psi_0]\!]$$

where $F_{\mathtt{sum!}} = \mathtt{if}(\mathtt{eq?}(n, 0), c, \mathtt{seq}(\mathtt{set}(c, n + \mathtt{get}(c)), \mathtt{sum!}(n-1, c)))$.

By clause (iv) of the definition $\models_{I,\mathtt{sum!}}$ this reduces to showing

(0) $\models_{I,\mathtt{sum!}} \theta_0 \Rightarrow \mathtt{let}\{x := \mathtt{eq?}(n, 0)\}[\![\neg(x \cong \mathtt{Nil}) \Rightarrow \theta_1 \wedge x \cong \mathtt{Nil} \Rightarrow \theta_2]\!]$

(1) $\models_{I,\mathtt{sum!}} \theta_1 \Rightarrow \mathtt{let}\{z := c\}[\![\psi_0]\!]$

(2) $\models_{I,\mathtt{sum!}} \theta_2 \Rightarrow \mathtt{let}\{z := \mathtt{seq}(\mathtt{set}(c, n + \mathtt{get}(c)), \mathtt{sum!}(n-1, c))\}[\![\psi_0]\!]$

for some θ_1, θ_2. We take $\theta_1 = \theta_0 \wedge \mathbf{eq?}(n,0) \cong \mathtt{T}$ and $\theta_2 = \theta_0 \wedge \mathbf{eq?}(n,0) \cong \mathtt{Nil}$. Then (0) follows by clause (i), (**new.i**), (**ca**), and simple let laws. (1) follows by clause (i), (**new.i**), and simple let laws. For (2) we use clause (iii). Thus we must show

(3) $\models_{I,\mathbf{sum!}} \phi_0 \Rightarrow \mathtt{let}\{z' := \mathtt{set}(c, n + \mathtt{get}(c))\}[\![\theta_0]\!]$

(4) $\models_{I,\mathbf{sum!}} \theta_0 \Rightarrow \mathtt{let}\{z := \mathbf{sum!}(n-1, c))\}[\![\psi_0]\!]$

for some θ_0. Take $\theta_0 = \phi_0$, then (3) follows by clause (i), some simple properties of numbers and addition (c *notin* $n + \mathtt{get}(c)$) and (**new.iii**), and (4) follows by clause (ii).

□

4.2 General Principles for Establishing Equivalence

The recursion induction principle is based on the least-fixed-point semantics of recursive definition systems. Two systems can be shown to define equivalent programs by showing that each satisfies the others defining equations.

Theorem (Recursion Induction): To prove

$$\theta_i \Rightarrow f_i(\mathbf{x}_i) \cong g_i(\mathbf{x}_i)$$

for $i \leq n$, it suffices to find a system I of invariants for $\mathbf{f}$ (and $\mathbf{g}$), such that for $i \leq n$

(i) $\theta_i \Rightarrow \phi_i$;

(ii) $\Delta_{\mathbf{f}}$ and $\Delta_{\mathbf{g}}$ are I-inductive;

(iii) $\phi_i \Rightarrow g_i(\mathbf{x}_i) \cong F_i\{f_j := \lambda \mathbf{x}_j . g_j(\mathbf{x}_j) \mid j \leq n\}$, using $\Delta_{\mathbf{g}}$; and

(iv) $\phi_i \Rightarrow f_i(\mathbf{x}_i) \cong G_i\{g_j := \lambda \mathbf{x}_j . f_j(\mathbf{x}_j) \mid j \leq n\}$, using $\Delta_{\mathbf{f}}$.

Note that the condition (iii) says that $\mathbf{g}$ satisfies the defining equations for $\mathbf{f}$ and hence establishes that $f_i \sqsubseteq g_i$. Similarly (iv) establishes $g_i \sqsubseteq f_i$ (cf §2.3). As is the case of (**subgoal induction**) the validity of recursion induction is established by simple computation induction. This basic form of recursion induction can be generalized in many ways. The next theorem gives a generalization that allows for the functions being compared to have different argument lists.

Theorem (Recursion induction – elaborated): To prove

$$\theta_i \Rightarrow f_i(\mathbf{x}_i) \cong g_i(\mathbf{y}_i)$$

for $i \leq n$, (with the argument lists for for $\mathbf{g}$ possibly being different than those for $\mathbf{f}$) it suffices to find a system of invariants $I = [(\phi_i, \psi_i), i \leq n]$ and expressions $e_i^{\mathbf{f}}, e_i^{\mathbf{g}}$ such that for $i \leq n$

(i) $\theta_i \Rightarrow \phi_i$

(ii) $\Delta_{\mathbf{f}}$ and $\Delta_{\mathbf{g}}$ are I-inductive (taking the formal parameters to be $\mathbf{y}_i$ in the case of $\Delta_{\mathbf{g}}$).

(iii) $\phi_i \Rightarrow g_i(\mathbf{y}_i) \cong e_i^{\mathbf{g}} \cong F_i\{f_i := \lambda\mathbf{x}_i.e_i^{\mathbf{g}}, i \leq n\}$ using $\Delta_{\mathbf{g}}$,

(iv) $\phi_i \Rightarrow f_i(\mathbf{x}_i) \cong e_i^{\mathbf{f}} \cong G_i\{g_i := \lambda\mathbf{y}_i.e_i^{\mathbf{f}}, i \leq n\}$ using $\Delta_{\mathbf{f}}$.

The peephole hole rule relies on the fact that replacing a subexpression in the body of a definition by an expression that is equivalent independent of the interpretation of any function symbols that might appear.

Theorem (Peephole Rule): Let $\Delta_{\mathbf{g}}$ be obtained from $\Delta_{\mathbf{f}}$ by replacing some $F_i = C[e_0]$ by $G_i = C[e_1]\{\mathbf{f} := \lambda\mathbf{x}.\mathbf{g}(\mathbf{x})\}$. Suppose that $\theta \Rightarrow C[\![\theta_0]\!]$ and $\theta_0 \Rightarrow e_0 \cong e_1$ uniformly in $\mathbf{f}$, (i.e. established proof theoretically without using the unfolding rule for any f defined in $\Delta_{\mathbf{f}}$, or established semantically for arbitrary interpretations of the functions in $\mathbf{f}$). Then to prove

$$\theta \Rightarrow f_i(\mathbf{x}_i) \cong g_i(\mathbf{x}_i)$$

for $i \leq n$, it suffices to find a system of invariants $I = [(\phi_i, \psi_i), i \leq n]$ such that

- $\theta = \phi_i$, and
- $\Delta_{\mathbf{f}}$ is I-inductive.

We have chosen a simple instance of the peephole transformation so as not to get bogged down in notation. It is easy to generalize the peephole rule to allow for multiple replacements. Examples applications of the elaborated recursion induction principle and of the peephole rule can be found in the next section.

4.3 Principles for Introducing Memory Contexts

In this subsection we strengthen the recursion induction principle to allow for the introduction and manipulation of local memory context. For simplicity we focus on single cells contexts. We use c for the distinguished cell variable. Let L_v^c abbreviate $\mathtt{let}\{c := \mathtt{mk}(v)\}\bullet$. We narrow the scope of memory allocation via the memory allocation propagation relation, $L_v^c[e] \propto e'$. It is defined as follows.

(1) $L_v^c[e] \propto e$ if $c \notin \mathrm{FV}(e)$

(2) $L_v^c[\mathtt{get}(c)] \propto v$

(3) $L_v^c[\mathtt{seq}(\mathtt{set}(c, v'), c)] \propto \mathtt{mk}(v')$ if $c \notin \mathrm{FV}(v')$

(4) $L_v^c[\mathtt{if}(e_0, e_1, e_2)] \propto \mathtt{if}(e_0, e_1', e_2')$

if $c \notin \mathrm{FV}(e_0)$, and $L_v^c[e_j] \propto e_j'$ for $j \in \{1, 2\}$

(5) $L_v^c[\mathtt{let}\{x := e_0\}e_1] \propto \mathtt{let}\{c := e_0'\}\mathtt{let}\{y := \mathtt{get}(c)\}e_1'$

if $\mathtt{new}(c) \Rightarrow \mathtt{let}\{x := e_0\}[\![\mathtt{new}(c) \wedge c \cong x]\!]$, y is fresh,

$L_v^c[e_0] \propto e_0'$, and $L_y^c[e_1\{x := c\}] \propto e_1'$

(6) $L_v^c[\mathtt{let}\{x := e_0\}e_1] \propto \mathtt{let}\{x := e_0'\}e_1'$

if $\mathtt{new}(c) \wedge y \cong \mathtt{get}(c) \Rightarrow \mathtt{let}\{x := e_0\}[\![\mathtt{new}(c) \wedge c \mathrel{\mathit{notin}} x \wedge \mathtt{get}(c) \cong y]\!]$

(with y is fresh), $L_v^c[e_0] \propto e_0'$, and $L_v^c[e_1] \propto e_1'$

(7) $L_v^c[e] \propto L_v^c[e]$ otherwise

The following simple fact is established by simple structural induction.

Lemma (M-prop):

(1) If $L_v^c[e] \propto e'$ then $L_v^c[e] \cong e'$.

(2) If $e^* = e\{x := \mathtt{get}(c)\}$ and $c \notin \mathrm{FV}(e)$, then $L_x^c[e^*] \propto e$.

Definition (*New*): To usefully propagate cell allocation into an expression it is necessary for the expression to propagate newness. For this purpose we define the system of invariants $New^c = [(\phi_i, \psi_i), i \leq n]$ where $\phi_i = \psi_i = \mathtt{new}(c)$ for $i \leq n$.

The memory reuse theorem provides a principle for carrying out a transformation within the context of a newly allocated memory cell.

Theorem (M-reuse): To prove

$$\phi_i \Rightarrow L_x^c[g_i(\mathbf{y}_i, c)] \cong f_i(\mathbf{y}_i, x)$$

for $i \leq n$, it suffices to show that there are expressions H_i, over $\mathbf{f}, \mathbf{y}_i, x$ for $i \leq n$, and there are systems of invariants $I^l = [(\phi_i, \psi_i^l), i \leq n]$ for $l < 2$ such that

(1) $\Delta_{\mathbf{f}}$ is I^0-inductive

(2) $\phi_i \Rightarrow L_x^c[g_i(\mathbf{y}_i, c)] \cong F_i\{f_j := \lambda \mathbf{y}_j, x.L_x^c[g_j(\mathbf{y}_j, c)] \mid j \leq n\}$, for $i \leq n$

(3) $\Delta_{\mathbf{g}}$ is New^c-inductive and $\{f_i(\mathbf{y}_i, x) \leftarrow H_i \mid i \leq n\}$ is I^1-inductive

(4) $L_x^c[G_i] \propto H_i\{f_j := \lambda \mathbf{y}_j, x.L_x^c[g_j(\mathbf{y}_j, c)] \mid i \leq n\}$, for $i \leq n$ (using the invariants proved for $\Delta_{\mathbf{g}}$).

(5) $\phi_i \Rightarrow f_i(\mathbf{y}_i, x) \cong H_i$, for $i \leq n$

The memory reuse principle is similar in spirit to recursion induction. Conditions (1,2) show that

$f_i \sqsubseteq \lambda \mathbf{y}_i, x.L_x^c[g_i(\mathbf{y}_i, c)]$, while conditions (3,4,5) show that

$\lambda \mathbf{y}_i, x.L_x^c[g_i(\mathbf{y}_i, c)] \sqsubseteq f_i$.

4.4 Register Passing Style Transform

Many compiler optimizations for functional languages, object systems, and imperative functional languages such as ML, Scheme, and Lisp, can be considered as program transformations in $\lambda_{\mathbf{mk}}$. One objective of the VTLoE work is to be able to justify and provide soundness criteria for such optimizations. Consider the following Scheme example, suggested by Felleisen [6]. Assume that `C` is a context with holes only in tail position, and that `A`,`B` are expressions, such that `loop` is not free in `A`,`B`,`C`, and both expressions below are closed. Then

```
(letrec ([loop (lambda (x) C[(loop A)])]) (loop B))
```

maybe safely replaced by

```
(letrec ([loop (lambda () C[(begin (set! x A) (loop))])] [x B]) (loop))
```

As a first simple application of our reasoning tools, we formalize a variant of this transformation in the first-order VTLoE setting. First we elaborate the class $\mathbb{T}$ of contexts whose holes are all in *tail-recursive* position to allow indices on holes.

Definition ($\mathbb{T}$):

$$\mathbb{T} = \{\bullet_i\}_{i\in\mathbb{N}} + \mathbb{E} + \mathtt{let}\{\mathbb{X} := \mathbb{E}\}\mathbb{T} + \mathtt{if}(\mathbb{E}, \mathbb{T}, \mathbb{T})$$

We let T range over $\mathbb{T}$. We write $T[e_i]_i$ to mean that $\bullet_i$ is filled with e_i for i ranging over the indices of holes appearing in T. The general loop, `loop`, and its register passing variant, `rloop`, are defined by the following system.

$$\mathtt{loop}(x) \leftarrow T[\mathtt{loop}(e_i)]_i$$

$$\mathtt{rloop}(c) \leftarrow T^{\dagger}[\mathtt{seq}(\mathtt{set}(c, e_i^{\dagger}), \mathtt{rloop}(c))]_i$$

where $\mathtt{loop}, \mathtt{rloop}$ do not appear in $T[e_i]_i$, $T^{\dagger}$ abbreviates $T^{\{x:=\mathtt{get}(c)\}}$, and $e^{\dagger} = e^{\{x:=\mathtt{get}(c)\}}$. Note that the assumption of well-formedness of the definitions means that c is not free in T, or e_i.

Theorem (Reg-Passing): $\mathtt{loop}(x) \cong L_x^c[\mathtt{rloop}(c)]$

Proof : The proof is by (**m-reuse**) taking $n = 0$, $f_0 = \mathtt{loop}$, $g_0 = \mathtt{rloop}$, and ϕ_0 to be true. We take I^l to be the trivial invariant systems (all invariants true) for $l < 2$. To define H_0 we specialize the definition of $\propto$ to tail contexts with holes filled as in the definition of `rloop`. Thus we define

$$T^{\dagger}[\mathtt{let}\{y := e_i^{\dagger}\}\mathtt{seq}(\mathtt{set}(c, y), \mathtt{rloop}(c))]_i \propto H$$

by induction on the construction of T as follows. First note that

$$\mathtt{new}(c) \wedge x \cong \mathtt{get}(c) \Rightarrow \mathtt{let}\{w := e^{\dagger}\}[\![\mathtt{new}(c) \wedge c \mathit{\ notin\ } w \wedge x \cong \mathtt{get}(c)]\!]$$

for $e^{\dagger} = e\{x := \mathtt{get}(c)\}$ and $c \notin \mathrm{FV}(e)$. Thus (by (**mprop.2**)) $L_x^c[e^{\dagger}] \propto e$. The definition is according to the cases in the definition of T.

$T = \bullet_i$ $\quad H = \mathtt{let}\{y := e_i\}L_y^c[\mathtt{rloop}(c)]$

$T = e$ (with no holes), then $H = e$

$T = \mathtt{if}(e_0, T_1, T_2)$, then $H = \mathtt{if}(e_0, H_1, H_2)$ where

$$T_j^{\dagger}[\mathtt{let}\{y := e_i^{\dagger}\}\mathtt{seq}(\mathtt{set}(c, y), \mathtt{rloop}(c))]_i \propto H_j \text{ for } j \in \{1, 2\}$$

$T = \mathtt{let}\{x_0 := e_0\}T_1$, then $H = \mathtt{let}\{x_0 := e_0\}H_1$ where

$$T_1^{\dagger}[\mathtt{let}\{y := e_i^{\dagger}\}\mathtt{seq}(\mathtt{set}(c, y), \mathtt{rloop}(c))]_i \propto H_1.$$

We take H_0 to be H with $L_y^c[\mathtt{rloop}(c)]$ replaced by $\mathtt{loop}(y)$.

Now we only need to establish the conditions (1-5) of (**m-reuse**).

(1) $\Delta_{\{\mathtt{loop}\}}$ is trivially I^0-inductive

(2) $L_x^c[\mathtt{rloop}(c)] \cong F_0\{\mathtt{loop} := \lambda x.L_x^c[\mathtt{rloop}(c)]\}$ since $L_x^c[\mathtt{rloop}(c)] \cong H$ and $H_0 \cong F_0$ using no defining equations.

(3) $\{\mathtt{loop}(x) \leftarrow H_0\}$ is trivially I^1-inductive. $\Delta_{\{\mathtt{rloop}\}}$ is New^c-inductive by the propagation property of $e^{\dagger}$ noted above.

(4) $L_x^c[G_0] \propto H$ by construction

(5) $\mathtt{loop}(x) \cong H_0$ trivially ($H_0 \cong F_0$ using no defining equations)

□

5 Transforming the Boyer Benchmark

The source of this example is a Common Lisp version of the well known Boyer benchmark (cf. [8]) that was used as the starting point for developing a parallel version [15]. The heart of the Boyer benchmark program is a rewrite rule based simplifier that repeatedly tries to rewrite a term with a given list of rules. The original Boyer benchmark program used lists and list operations to represent composite terms and lemmas. Variables and operations were represented as Lisp symbols. We represented atomic terms, composite terms, operations and lemmas as abstract structures using the Common Lisp DEFSTRUCT facility. A simple matcher decides if a rule applies. The matcher returns two pieces of information: a flag to indicate success or failure, and a substitution in case of success. The original version returned `t` or `nil` depending on success, and if successful set the value of a global variable to be the resulting substitution. We used the Common Lisp multiple values feature to accomplish this. We also used higher-order mapping functions instead of mutually recursive definitions in several places.

Although use of structure definitions, multiple values, and other high-level constructs results in elegant and easy to understand code, these constructs are part of a rather complex machinery and may well not produce the most efficient implementation of the underlying algorithm. The original program can (essentially) be recovered by carrying out the simple set of transformations described below.

(1) Rerepresent composite structures as lists and omit structure definitions for variables and operations.

(2) Eliminate the use of multiple values in favor of simple conses.

(3) Eliminate the use of high-order mapping constructs

(4) Eliminate unnecessary storage allocation due to multiple values by cell reuse.

In fact, the original application of these transformation rules was in the converse direction. That is we started with the original Boyer benchmark program an equivalent program that did not rely on global variables and assignment. This was essential in order to parallelize the program. It is likely that similar transformations from programs optimized for sequential computation to more abstract version will play an important role in developing parallel versions of existing programs.

The first three transformations apply quite generally and can be carried out automatically. The final transformation requires more insight and care, and we focus on that transformation here. We first transform the matcher, and then transform the rewriter to use the transformed matcher efficiently.

We use the following abbreviations to write programs in the usual vanilla

Lisp style:

$\mathtt{not}(e)$	abbreviates	$\mathtt{if}(e, \mathtt{Nil}, \mathtt{T})$
$\mathtt{or}(e_0, e_1)$	abbreviates	$\mathtt{if}(e_0, \mathtt{T}, \mathtt{if}(e_1, \mathtt{T}, \mathtt{Nil}))$
$\mathtt{and}(e_0, e_1)$	abbreviates	$\mathtt{if}(e_0, \mathtt{if}(e_1, \mathtt{T}, \mathtt{Nil}), \mathtt{Nil})$
$\mathtt{null?}(x)$	abbreviates	$\mathtt{eq?}(x, \mathtt{Nil})$
$\mathtt{cons}(x, y)$	abbreviates	$\mathtt{pr}(\mathtt{mk}(x, y))$
$\mathtt{acons}(x, y, z)$	abbreviates	$\mathtt{pr}(\mathtt{pr}(x, y), z)$
$\mathtt{car}(x)$	abbreviates	$\mathtt{fst}(\mathtt{get}(x))$
$\mathtt{cdr}(x)$	abbreviates	$\mathtt{snd}(\mathtt{get}(x))$
$\mathtt{setcar!}(x, y)$	abbreviates	$\mathtt{seq}(\mathtt{set}(x, \mathtt{pr}(y, \mathtt{cdr}(x))), x)$
$\mathtt{setcdr!}(x, y)$	abbreviates	$\mathtt{seq}(\mathtt{set}(x, \mathtt{pr}(\mathtt{car}(x), y)), x)$
$\mathtt{setpair!}(x, y, z)$	abbreviates	$\mathtt{seq}(\mathtt{set}(x, \mathtt{pr}(y, z)), x)$

5.1 The matching transform

We begin by defining the basic data types to be used, as well as giving the definition of *match*, the abstract (specification) version of the matcher. Next we give an informal description of the transformation and the resulting final version of the program, and state the correctness of the transformation. Finally we outline the formal verification of the soundness of the transformation. This proves the correctness statement and provides additional information about the matcher.

A term is either an atomic term (variable) or a composite term obtained by application of an operation to a list of terms. Atomic terms and operations are just atoms, and application of an operation is represented by pairing it with the argument list. The abstract syntax of terms is thus represented as follows.

$$\mathit{term\text{-}mk}(o, a) \leftarrow \mathtt{pr}(o, a)$$
$$\mathit{term\text{-}op}(t) \leftarrow \mathtt{fst}(t)$$
$$\mathit{term\text{-}args}(t) \leftarrow \mathtt{snd}(t)$$

A substitution is a finite map from variables to terms. Maps are represented as lists whose entries are pairs consisting of an atom and a term, i.e. as Lisp-like alists (our alists are immutable in contrast to the usual Lisp alist). Maps are extended using $\mathtt{acons}(x, y, s)$ which abbreviates $\mathtt{pr}(\mathtt{pr}(x, y), s)$. A map is applied to an atom using *assoc* which returns the (first) pair whose `fst` is `eq?` to the atom, or `Nil` if no such pair exists. A substitution map is applied to a term using *app-sbst* which is defined as the obvious homomorphic extension of the substitution (mapping atoms not in the domain to themselves).

The specifying code for matching

The matcher *match* is given a pair of terms t_1, t_2 and a substitution s. The task of *match* is to determine whether or not t_1 is a substitution instance of t_2

via a substitution s' that extends s. *match* returns two pieces of information. Firstly, a boolean flag (T or Nil) indicating whether or not such a substitution exists, and secondly, when it exists, the substitution that achieves the match.

Definition (*match*):

```
match(t1, t2, s) ←
  cond([atom?(t2) ▷ let{b := assoc(t2, s)}
                      if(b,
                         if(term-eq(t1, snd(b)),
                            cons(T, s),
                            cons(Nil, Nil)),
                         cons(T, acons(t2, t1, s)))],
       [atom?(t1) ▷ cons(Nil, Nil)],
       [eq?(term-op(t1), term-op(t2))
             ▷match-args(term-args(t1), term-args(t2), s)],
       [T ▷ cons(Nil, Nil)])

match-args(a1, a2, s) ← if(and(null?(a1), null?(a2)),
                           cons(T, s),
                           if(or(null?(a1), null?(a2)),
                              cons(Nil, Nil),
                              let{w := match(car(a1), car(a2), s)}
                                if(car(w),
                                   match-args(cdr(a1), cdr(a2), cdr(w)),
                                   cons(Nil, Nil))))
```

Transforming match

We observe that the result produced by *match* is a new cell and in recursive calls the cell returned by subcomputations is discarded. We will transform the definition of *match* to a version *match!* that takes a new cell initialized so that the cdr is the input substitution. This cell is reused and eventually returned as the result (with contents suitably updated). Thus conses constructing the result are replaced by **setpair!**s on the reusable cell, and third argument to the call to *match!* from *match-args!* is now 'by reference'. The resulting definition of *match!* is the following.

Definition (*match!*):

```
match!(t1, t2, c) ←
```

$$\begin{aligned}
&\texttt{cond}([\texttt{atom?}(t_2) \rhd \texttt{let}\{b := \mathit{assoc}(t_2, \texttt{cdr}(c))\}\\
&\qquad\qquad \texttt{if}(b,\\
&\qquad\qquad\quad \texttt{if}(\mathit{term\text{-}eq}(t_1, \texttt{snd}(b)),\\
&\qquad\qquad\qquad \texttt{setcar!}(c, \texttt{T}),\\
&\qquad\qquad\qquad \texttt{setpair!}(c, \texttt{Nil}, \texttt{Nil})),\\
&\qquad\qquad\quad \texttt{setpair!}(c, \texttt{T}, \texttt{acons}(t_2, t_1, \texttt{cdr}(c))))],\\
&\quad [\texttt{atom?}(t_1) \rhd \texttt{setpair!}(c, \texttt{Nil}, \texttt{Nil})],\\
&\quad [\texttt{eq?}(\mathit{term\text{-}op}(t_1), \mathit{term\text{-}op}(t_2))\\
&\qquad \rhd \mathit{match\text{-}args!}(\mathit{term\text{-}args}(t_1), \mathit{term\text{-}args}(t_2), c)],\\
&\quad [\texttt{T} \rhd \texttt{setpair!}(c, \texttt{Nil}, \texttt{Nil})])
\end{aligned}$$

$$\begin{aligned}
\mathit{match\text{-}args!}(a_1, a_2, c) \leftarrow\ &\texttt{if}(\texttt{and}(\texttt{null?}(a_1), \texttt{null?}(a_2)),\\
&\quad \texttt{setcar!}(c, \texttt{T}),\\
&\quad \texttt{if}(\texttt{or}(\texttt{null?}(a_1), \texttt{null?}(a_2)),\\
&\qquad \texttt{setpair!}(c, \texttt{Nil}, \texttt{Nil}),\\
&\qquad \texttt{seq}(\mathit{match!}(\texttt{car}(a_1), \texttt{car}(a_2), c),\\
&\qquad\quad \texttt{if}(\texttt{car}(c),\\
&\qquad\qquad \mathit{match\text{-}args!}(\texttt{cdr}(a_1), \texttt{cdr}(a_2), c),\\
&\qquad\qquad \texttt{setpair!}(c, \texttt{Nil}, \texttt{Nil})))))
\end{aligned}$$

Although the intended domain of *match* constrains the first two arguments to be terms and the third argument to be a substitution, the transformation preserves equivalence under more general conditions.

Theorem (match):

$$\mathit{match}(t_1, t_2, s) \cong \texttt{let}\{c := \texttt{cons}(x, s)\}\mathit{match!}(t_1, t_2, c)$$

Proof (match): The proof of (**match**) uses (**m-reuse**). In order to use this principle as stated, we need to modify *match*, *match-args* to take a pair as their third argument, and ignore the first component. We show the modified form is equivalent to the original. We then establish the key invariants for *match!*, *match-args!*. Finally we use (**m-reuse**) to establish the equivalence of the modified matcher to the fully transformed matcher. Thus (**match**) follows directly from (**modified match**) and (**match'**) below. $\Box_{\mathbf{match}}$

We will use the following notation. *M*, *Ma* are the bodies of the defining equations for *match*, and *match-args* respectively. *M!*, *Ma!* are the bodies of the defining equations for *match!*, and *match-args!* respectively.

Definition (*match'*, *match-args'*): Let *match'*, *match-args'* be the modified matcher with defining equations

$$\mathit{match}'(t_1, t_2, y) \leftarrow M'$$

$$\mathit{match\text{-}args}'(a_1, a_2, y) \leftarrow Ma'$$

where M' is obtained from M by replacing: *match-args* by *match-args'*; the first three occurrences of s by $\mathtt{snd}(y)$; and the final occurrence (in the call to *match-args'*) by y. Ma' is obtained from Ma by replacing: *match* by *match'*; *match-args* by *match-args'*; the first occurrence of s by $\mathtt{snd}(y)$; and the second occurrence (in the call to *match'*) by y; and the occurrence of $\mathtt{cdr}(w)$ (in the call to *match-args'*) by $\mathtt{pr}(\mathtt{fst}(y), \mathtt{cdr}(w))$.

Lemma (modified match):

$$\mathtt{pr?}(y) \cong \mathtt{T} \wedge \mathtt{snd}(y) \cong s \Rightarrow$$

$$\mathit{match}(t_1, t_2, s) \cong \mathit{match}'(t_1, t_2, y) \wedge$$

$$\mathit{match\text{-}args}(a_1, a_2, s) \cong \mathit{match\text{-}args}'(a_1, a_2, y)$$

Proof : This is proved by (elaborated) recursion induction, taking

$$e_{\mathit{match}} = \mathit{match}(t_1, t_2, \mathtt{snd}(y))$$

$$e_{\mathit{match\text{-}args}} = \mathit{match\text{-}args}(a_1, a_2, \mathtt{snd}(y))$$

$$e_{\mathit{match}'} = \mathit{match}'(t_1, t_2, \mathtt{pr}(\mathtt{fst}(y), s))$$

$$e_{\mathit{match\text{-}args}'} = \mathit{match\text{-}args}'(a_1, a_2, \mathtt{pr}(\mathtt{fst}(y), s))$$

□

The key invariants for *match!* and *match-args!* are preservation of newness of the third argument, and the return of that argument. This is expressed in the following lemma.

Lemma (match-new): Let $\phi = \mathtt{new}(c) \wedge \mathtt{pr?}(\mathtt{get}(c)) \cong \mathtt{T}$, and let $\psi = \phi \wedge z \cong c$, then

$$\mathtt{new}(c) \Rightarrow \mathtt{seq}(\mathit{match!}(t_1, t_2, c), [\![\mathtt{new}(c)]\!])$$

$$\mathtt{new}(c) \Rightarrow \mathtt{seq}(\mathit{match\text{-}args!}(a_1, a_2, c), [\![\mathtt{new}(c)]\!])$$

$$\phi \Rightarrow \mathtt{let}\{z := \mathit{match!}(t_1, t_2, c)\}[\![\psi]\!]$$

$$\phi \Rightarrow \mathtt{let}\{z := \mathit{match\text{-}args!}(a_1, a_2, c)\}[\![\psi]\!]$$

Proof : By (**subgoal induction**) using an argument similar to that found in the proof of (**sum!**) in the previous section. □

Lemma (match$'$):

$$\mathit{match}'(t_1, t_2, y) \cong L^c_y[\mathit{match!}(t_1, t_2, c)]$$

$$\mathit{match\text{-}args}'(a_1, a_2, y) \cong L^c_y[\mathit{match\text{-}args!}(a_1, a_2, c)]$$

Proof : By (**m-reuse**). To see this, define H, Ha as follows: H is M'; and Ha is Ma' with the subexpression

$$\mathtt{let}\{w := \mathit{match}(\mathtt{car}(a_1), \mathtt{car}(a_2), s)\}\mathtt{if}(\mathtt{car}(w), \ldots, \ldots)$$

replaced by

$$\texttt{let}\{w := \mathit{match}(\texttt{car}(a_1), \texttt{car}(a_2), s)\}\texttt{let}\{p := \texttt{get}(w)\}\texttt{if}(\texttt{fst}(p), \ldots, \ldots).$$

Let Σ be the function substitution list

$$\mathit{match}' := \lambda t_1, t_2, y.L_y^c \mathit{match!}(t_1, t_2, c),$$

$$\mathit{match\text{-}args}' := \lambda a_1, a_2, y.L_y^c \mathit{match\text{-}args!}(a_1, a_2, c).$$

Then, by (**match-new**), the main work that remains is to show

(a) $L_y^c[M!] \propto H\{\Sigma\}$, and $L_y^c[Ma!] \propto Ha\{\Sigma\}$

(b) $L_y^c[\mathit{match!}(t_1, t_2, c)] \cong M'\{\Sigma\}$, and $L_y^c[\mathit{match\text{-}args!}(a_1, a_2, c)] \cong Ma'\{\Sigma\}$

(c) $\mathit{match}'(t_1, t_2, y) \cong H$, and $\mathit{match\text{-}args}'(a_1, a_2, y) \cong Ha$

(b) follows from (a) and (**m-prop**), (c) can easily be established using the Peephole rule. To establish (a) we use the definition of $\propto$. There are only three interesting points here. The first is the propagation of L_y^c across the subexpression $\texttt{let}\{b := \mathit{assoc}(t_2, \texttt{cdr}(c)\}\ldots$ in *match!*. Using (d) below we may apply clause (6) of the definition of $\propto$.

(d) $\texttt{new}(c) \wedge v \cong \texttt{get}(c) \Rightarrow$

$$\texttt{let}\{b := \mathit{assoc}(t_2, \texttt{cdr}(c))\}[\![\texttt{new}(c) \wedge v \cong \texttt{get}(c) \wedge c \mathrel{\mathit{notin}} b]\!]$$

(d) is easy to establish using the definition of new and the fact that *assoc* is purely functional.

The second point is the propagation of L_y^c across the subexpression

$$\texttt{seq}(\mathit{match!}(\texttt{car}(a_1), \texttt{car}(a_2), c), \ldots)$$

in *match-args!*. We expand the **seq**, replacing this subexpression by

$$\texttt{let}\{d := \mathit{match!}(\texttt{car}(a_1), \texttt{car}(a_2), c)\}\ldots).$$

Now, by (**match-new**) we may apply clause (5) of the definition of $\propto$.

The third point is the propagation of L_y^c across the subexpression

$$\texttt{if}(\texttt{car}(c), \ldots, \ldots).$$

We rewrite this (using the Peephole rule) to

$$\texttt{let}\{p := \texttt{get}(c)\}\texttt{if}(\texttt{fst}(p), \ldots, \ldots),$$

then using (e) below, we may again apply clause (6).

(e) $\texttt{new}(c) \wedge v \cong \texttt{get}(c) \Rightarrow$

$$\texttt{let}\{b := \texttt{get}(c)\}[\![\texttt{new}(c) \wedge v \cong \texttt{get}(c) \wedge c \mathrel{\mathit{notin}} b]\!]$$

□

5.2 Transforming the rewriter

We extend the abstract syntax for matching. A *lemma* has a left-hand side and a right-hand side, each of which is a term.

$$\textit{lemma-lhs}(x) \leftarrow \texttt{fst}(x)$$

$$\textit{lemma-rhs}(x) \leftarrow \texttt{snd}(x)$$

A lemma corresponds to an equation to be used as a rewrite rule in the left-to-right direction.

The specification code

The rewriter *rewrite* takes as input a term t and a list of lemmas l. If the term is atomic the program exits with that term as its value. Otherwise the term is a composite term consisting of an operation and an list of argument terms. The argument subterms are first rewritten and then the top-level rewriter *rewrite-top* is applied to the resulting whole term. The top-level rewriter applies the first lemma that matches (if any) and then restarts the rewriting process. This is repeated until no more rewriting can be done.

Definition (*rewrite*):

```
rewrite(t, l) ← if(atom?(t),
                   t,
                   let{t' := term-mk(term-op(t),
                                     rewrite-args(term-args(t), l))}
                     rewrite-top(t', l, l))
rewrite-args(a, l) ← if(null?(a),
                        Nil,
                        pr(rewrite(fst(a), l), rewrite-args(snd(a), l)))
rewrite-top(t, cl, l) ←
    if(null?(cl),
       t,
       let{w := match(t, lemma-lhs(car(cl)), Nil)}
         if(car(w),
            rewrite(app-sbst(cdr(w), lemma-rhs(car(cl))), l),
            rewrite-top(t, cdr(cl), l)))
```

Transformation steps

We transform *rewrite* into *rewrite!* just as we transformed *match* into *match!*.

Definition (*rewrite!*):

$$
\begin{array}{l}
\mathit{rewrite!}(t,l,c) \leftarrow \mathtt{if}(\mathtt{atom?}(t),\\
\qquad\qquad\qquad\qquad t,\\
\qquad\qquad\qquad\qquad \mathtt{let}\{t' := \mathit{term\text{-}mk}(\mathit{term\text{-}op}(t),\\
\qquad\qquad\qquad\qquad\qquad\qquad\qquad \mathit{rewrite\text{-}args!}(\mathit{term\text{-}args}(t),l,c))\}\\
\qquad\qquad\qquad\qquad\quad \mathit{rewrite\text{-}top!}(t',l,l,c))
\end{array}
$$

$$
\begin{array}{l}
\mathit{rewrite\text{-}args!}(a,l,c) \leftarrow \mathtt{if}(\mathtt{null?}(a),\\
\qquad\qquad\qquad\qquad\quad \mathtt{Nil},\\
\qquad\qquad\qquad\qquad\quad \mathtt{pr}(\mathit{rewrite!}(\mathtt{fst}(a),l,c),\\
\qquad\qquad\qquad\qquad\qquad \mathit{rewrite\text{-}args!}(\mathtt{snd}(a),l,c))
\end{array}
$$

$$
\begin{array}{l}
\mathit{rewrite\text{-}top}(t,cl,l,c) \leftarrow\\
\quad \mathtt{if}(\mathtt{null?}(cl),\\
\qquad t,\\
\qquad \mathtt{seq}(\mathtt{setpair!}(c,\mathtt{T},\mathtt{Nil}),\\
\qquad\quad \mathit{match!}(t,\mathit{lemma\text{-}lhs}(\mathtt{car}(cl)),c)\}\\
\qquad\quad \mathtt{if}(\mathtt{car}(c),\\
\qquad\qquad \mathit{rewrite!}(\mathit{app\text{-}sbst}(\mathtt{cdr}(c),\mathit{lemma\text{-}rhs}(\mathtt{car}(cl))),l,c),\\
\qquad\qquad \mathit{rewrite\text{-}top}(t,\mathtt{cdr}(cl),l,c)))
\end{array}
$$

The validity of the transformation is expressed by the following theorem.

Theorem (rewrite):

(rw) $\mathit{rewrite}(t,l) \cong \mathtt{let}\{c := \mathtt{cons}(\mathtt{T},\mathtt{Nil})\}\mathit{rewrite!}(t,l,c)$

(rwa) $\mathit{rewrite\text{-}args}(a,l) \cong \mathtt{let}\{c := \mathtt{cons}(\mathtt{T},\mathtt{Nil})\}\mathit{rewrite\text{-}args!}(a,l,c)$

(rwt) $\mathit{rewrite\text{-}top}(t,cl,l) \cong \mathtt{let}\{c := \mathtt{cons}(\mathtt{T},\mathtt{Nil})\}\mathit{rewrite\text{-}top!}(t,cl,l,c)$

6 Conclusion

In this paper we have presented rules for systematically transforming programs in the first-order fragment of a Lisp- (Scheme-, ML-) like language with first-order recursive function definitions and objects with memory. The validity of the transformations is based on a theory of constrained equivalence and contextual assertions. Subgoal and recursion induction are standard methods of proving properties of flow-chart and first-order programs acting on immutable data [21, 25]. We have generalized these methods to programs that act on mutable data structures. The contextual assertion notation allows one to express notions such as *exclusive use* which allow one to replace allocation by updating [12].

Even though the work presented here is at an early stage of development, we feel that much progress has been made towards practical application of formal methods to program development. Work is in progress to apply these methods to more substantial programming examples that arise in practice, and extend the methods to the full λ_{mk}-calculus.

For the transformational approach we have focused on methods for proving equivalence of definitions, as well as establishing invariants (partial correctness statements) needed to prove equivalence. For this purpose subgoal induction and recursion induction are appropriate. Treatment of total correctness requires the formulation of principles for induction on well-founded orderings. Examples of structural induction principles extended to the case of computations with effects are given in [19] and additional principles have been formulated to treat cases where the measure that is being decreased is not a simple structural property, but decreases due the effect that is produced by the computation. In [10] classes are used to express various forms of induction.

The atomic formula **new** treats the simplest case of a newly allocated structure. Another example to which we have applied our methods is the derivation of space efficient programs for manipulating polynomials. This requires formalizing the notion of newly allocated polynomial structures, either as a subtype of lists, or as a mutable abstract data type. Future work will extend the techniques presented in this paper to general mutable and immutable abstract data types.

Acknowledgements

We would like to thank Anna Patterson, Morten Heine Sørensen, and Scott Smith for helpful comments on an earlier draft. This research was partially supported by DARPA contract NAG2-703, NSF grants CCR-8917606, and CCR-8915663.

References

1. K.R. Apt. Ten years of Hoare's logic: A survey–part I. *ACM Transactions on Programming Languages and Systems*, 4:431–483, 1981.
2. S. Feferman. A language and axioms for explicit mathematics. In *Algebra and Logic*, volume 450 of *Springer Lecture Notes in Mathematics*, pages 87–139. Springer Verlag, 1975.
3. S. Feferman. Constructive theories of functions and classes. In *Logic Colloquium '78*, pages 159–224. North-Holland, 1979.
4. S. Feferman. A theory of variable types. *Revista Colombiana de Matématicas*, 19:95–105, 1985.
5. S. Feferman. Polymorphic typed lambda-calculi in a type-free axiomatic framework. In *Logic and Computation*, volume 106 of *Contemporary Mathematics*, pages 101–136. A.M.S., Providence R. I., 1990.
6. M. Felleisen, 1993. Personal communication.
7. M. Felleisen and D.P. Friedman. Control operators, the SECD-machine, and the λ-calculus. In M. Wirsing, editor, *Formal Description of Programming Concepts III*, pages 193–217. North-Holland, 1986.
8. Richard P. Gabriel. *Performance and Evaluation of Lisp Systems.* Computer Systems Series. MIT Press, Cambridge, Massachusetts, 1985.

9. D. Harel. Dynamic logic. In D. Gabbay and G. Guenthner, editors, *Handbook of Philosophical Logic, Vol. II*, pages 497–604. D. Reidel, 1984.
10. F. Honsell, I. A. Mason, S. F. Smith, and C. L. Talcott. A Variable Typed Logic of Effects. *Information and Computation*, ???(???):???–???, 199?
11. F. Honsell, I. A. Mason, S. F. Smith, and C. L. Talcott. A theory of classes for a functional language with effects. In *Proceedings of CSL92*, volume ??? of *Lecture Notes in Computer Science*, pages ???–??? Springer, Berlin, 1993.
12. U. Jø rring and W. L. Scherlis. Deriving and using destructive data types. In *IFIP TC2 Working Conference on Program Specification and Transformation*. North-Holland, 1986.
13. I. A. Mason. *The Semantics of Destructive Lisp*. PhD thesis, Stanford University, 1986. Also available as CSLI Lecture Notes No. 5, Center for the Study of Language and Information, Stanford University.
14. I. A. Mason. Verification of programs that destructively manipulate data. *Science of Computer Programming*, 10:177–210, 1988.
15. I. A. Mason, J. D. Pehoushek, C. L. Talcott, and J. S. Weening. A Qlisp Primer. Technical Report STAN-CS-90-1340, Department of Computer Science, Stanford University, 1990.
16. I. A. Mason and C. L. Talcott. Axiomatizing operational equivalence in the presence of side effects. In *Fourth Annual Symposium on Logic in Computer Science*. IEEE, 1989.
17. I. A. Mason and C. L. Talcott. Programming, transforming, and proving with function abstractions and memories. In *Proceedings of the 16th EATCS Colloquium on Automata, Languages, and Programming, Stresa*, volume 372 of *Lecture Notes in Computer Science*, pages 574–588. Springer-Verlag, 1989.
18. I. A. Mason and C. L. Talcott. Equivalence in functional languages with effects. *Journal of Functional Programming*, 1:287–327, 1991.
19. I. A. Mason and C. L. Talcott. Inferring the equivalence of functional programs that mutate data. *Theoretical Computer Science*, 105(2):167–215, 1992.
20. I. A. Mason and C. L. Talcott. References, local variables and operational reasoning. In *Seventh Annual Symposium on Logic in Computer Science*, pages 186–197. IEEE, 1992.
21. J. McCarthy. A basis for a mathematical theory of computation. In P. Braffort and D Herschberg, editors, *Computer programming and formal systems*, pages 33–70. North-Holland, 1963.
22. E. Moggi. Computational lambda-calculus and monads. Technical Report ECS-LFCS-88-86, University of Edinburgh, 1988.
23. E. Moggi. Computational lambda-calculus and monads. In *Fourth Annual Symposium on Logic in Computer Science*. IEEE, 1989.
24. J. H. Morris. *Lambda calculus models of programming languages*. PhD thesis, Massachusetts Institute of Technology, 1968.
25. J. H. Morris and B. Wegbreit. Subgoal induction. *Communications of the Association for Computing Machinery*, 20:209–222, 1976.
26. G. Plotkin. Call-by-name, call-by-value and the lambda calculus. *Theoretical Computer Science*, 1:125–159, 1975.
27. J.C. Reynolds. Idealized ALGOL and its specification logic. In D. Néel, editor, *Tools and Notions for Program Construction*, pages 121–161. Cambridge University Press, 1982.

On Coding Theorems with Modified Length Functions

Kojiro Kobayashi

Department of Information Science, Tokyo Institute of Technology,
Oh-Okayama, Meguro-ku, Tokyo 152, Japan

Abstract. Let $R = (r_1, r_2, \ldots)$ be an infinite sequence of real numbers ($0 < r_i < 1$). For a binary word (a bit sequence) w of length n, let $|w|_R$ denote the value "$-\log_2$(the probability that n coin-flippings of biased coins generate the sequence w, where the probability that the i-th coin-flipping generates 0 is r_i)". The usual length $|w|$ is the value $|w|_R$ for the special case $R = (1/2, 1/2, \ldots)$. Csiszar and Körner proved that, if there are $u > 0$, $v > 0$ such that $u \leq r_i \leq 1 - v$ for all i, then the coding theorem for memoryless sources holds even if $|w|_R$ is used as the length of a code word w instead of the usual length $|w|$. We prove that if $\lim_{i\to\infty} r_i/2^{-i} = 0$ then the coding thorem with this modified length $|w|_R$ does not hold true.

1 Introduction

The coding theorem for memoryless sources ([4]) concerns the following situation. Symbols $S_1, \ldots, S_m$ are generated independently with probabilities $p_1, \ldots, p_m$ respectively ($0 < p_i < 1$ for each i), and we are to encode these symbols with binary words (that is, sequences of bits 0, 1) $w_1, \ldots, w_m$ respectively. The code words $w_1, \ldots, w_m$ must constitute a prefix code. This means that $w_1, \ldots, w_m$ are different and that w_i is not a prefix of w_j for $i \neq j$. The problem is, for the given probabilities $p_1, \ldots, p_m$, to design code words $w_1, \ldots, w_m$ such that the average code length $\Sigma_{i=1}^m p_i|w_i|$ is as small as possible. Here, by $|w|$ we denote the length of a binary word w.

We denote the probability sequence $(p_1, \ldots, p_m)$ and the code word sequence $(w_1, \ldots, w_m)$ by D and C respectively (D for Distribution and C for Code). By H_D we denote the entropy $\Sigma_{i=1}^m - p_i \log p_i$ of a sequence D of probabilities. (Throughout in the present paper, the bases of all logarithms are 2.)

The coding theorem says that the following two statements are true:

CT(1) $\qquad \forall D\, \forall C\ H_D \leq \Sigma p_i|w_i|$

CT(2) $\qquad \exists c\, \forall D\, \exists C\ \Sigma p_i|w_i| < H_D + c.$

In the statement CT(2), we can select 1 as the constant c. By CT, we denote the conjunction of the two statements CT(1) and CT(2).

In the present paper, we modify the definition of the length $|w|$ of a binary word w, and see whether CT with the modified length is still true or not. Note that the length $|w|$ ($= n$) of a binary word w may be defined as follows:

$|w| =$
$-\log$ (the probability that n coin-flippings of a fair coin generate the sequence w).

Suppose that we have a sequence of infinite number of possibly biased coins and that, instead of using one fair coin repeatedly, we use these coins one after another. Let r_i be the probability that the i-th coin generates 0 ($0 < r_i < 1$), and let R denote the sequence $(r_1, r_2, \ldots)$ of the probabilities r_i. For each word w, let $|w|_R$ denote the corresponding value of the right hand side of the above equation. That is,

$|w|_R =$
$-\log$ (the probability that n coin-flippings generate the sequence w, where the probability that the i-th coin flipping generates 0 is r_i).

A more formal definition of $|w|_R$ is as follows. For each i and $a \in \{0,1\}$, let $|a|_{R,i}$ be defined by

$$|a|_{R,i} = \begin{cases} -\log r_i & \text{if } a = 0, \\ -\log(1 - r_i) & \text{if } a = 1, \end{cases}$$

and for each word $w = a_1 a_2 \ldots a_n$ ($a_i \in \{0,1\}$ for each i), let $|w|_R$ be defined by

$$|w|_R = |a_1|_{R,1} + \ldots + |a_n|_{R,n}.$$

The problem is to see whether CT with its length $|w_i|$ replaced by the modified length $|w_i|_R$ is still true or not. It is quite easy to see that CT(1) is true even if the modified length $|w_i|_R$ is used. Hence, the problem is whether CT(2) is true or not.

Concerning this problem, it is known that, if there exist $u > 0$, $v > 0$ such that $u \leq r_i \leq 1 - v$ for all i, then CT(2) with the modified length $|w_i|_R$ is true.

Theorem 1 (Csiszar & Körner ([2])). *If there exist constants $u > 0$, $v > 0$ such that $u \leq r_i \leq 1 - v$ for all i, then for any sequence of probabilities $D = (p_1, \ldots, p_m)$ there is a code $C = (w_1, \ldots, w_m)$ for D such that*

$$\Sigma p_i |w_i|_R \; < \; H_D + (-\log \min\{u, v\}).$$

In the present paper, we show that if $\lim_{i \to \infty} r_i / 2^{-i} = 0$ then CT(2) with the modified length $|w_i|_R$ does not hold true.

A comment on Theorem 1 is in order. Sciszar & Körner ([2]) obtained Theorem 1 from a more practical motivation than ours. They considered the situation where the cost $c(a)$ to send a symbol a depends on the symbol a to be sent, and the total cost $c(w)$ to send a binary word $w = a_1 a_2 \ldots a_n$ is the sum $c(a_1) + \ldots + c(a_n)$. They showed that CT is still true if we replace the length $|w_i|$ with the cost $c(w_i)$ and replace the value H_D with H_D / α_0, where $\alpha = \alpha_0$ is the root of the equation $2^{-\alpha c(0)} + 2^{-\alpha c(1)} = 1$.

Restricting to the case where the unit of cost is normalized so that $2^{-c(0)} + 2^{-c(1)} = 1$ and hence $\alpha_0 = 1$, the part CT(2) of their result corresponds to the statement of Theorem 1 for the special case $R = (r, r, \ldots)$, $r = 2^{-c(0)}$. However, their proof essentially proves the statement of Theorem 1.

The problem considered in the present paper is closely related to the problem of constructing Kolmogorov complexity and a priori (universal) distributions ([1], [3]).

2 The Main Result

Our main result says that, if $\lim_{i\to\infty} r_i/2^{-i} = 0$, then CT(2) with the modified length $|w_i|_R$ does not hold true.

Theorem 2. *If* $\lim_{i\to\infty} r_i/2^{-i} = 0$ *then for any* c *there is a sequence of probabilities* $D = (p_1, \ldots, p_m)$ *such that*

$$\Sigma p_i |w_i|_R \ - \ H_D \ \geq c$$

for any code $C = (w_1, \ldots, w_m)$ *for* D.

Proof. Let Δ be an arbitrary positive integer. Let I_Δ be an integer such that $r_i/2^{-i} \leq 1/\Delta$ for any $i \geq I_\Delta$.

Let r'_i be defined by

$$r'_i = \begin{cases} 1 & \text{if } 1 \leq i \leq I_\Delta - 1, \\ 2^{-i}/\Delta & \text{if } I_\Delta \leq i. \end{cases}$$

Then we have $r'_i \geq r_i$ for each i and $r'_1 \geq r'_2 \geq \ldots$. For a binary word $w = a_1 \ldots a_n$, let $|w|'$ be defined by

$$|w|' = \begin{cases} 0 & \text{if all of } a_1, \ldots, a_n \text{ are } 1, \\ -\log r'_i & \text{if } a_i = 0 \text{ and } a_{i+1} = \ldots = a_n = 1. \end{cases}$$

Then we have $|w|' \leq |w|_R$ for any $w = a_1 \ldots a_n$ because, if all of $a_1, \ldots, a_n$ are 1 then

$$|w|' = 0,$$
$$|w|_R = -\log(1 - r_1) - \ldots - \log(1 - r_n) \geq 0,$$

and if $a_i = 0$ and $a_{i+1} = \ldots = a_n = 1$ then

$$|w|' = -\log r'_i \leq -\log r_i,$$
$$|w|_R \geq -\log r_i - \log(1 - r_{i+1}) - \ldots - \log(1 - r_n)$$
$$\geq -\log r_i.$$

For each $t \geq 1$, let D_t be the sequence of probabilities $(1/2^t, \ldots, 1/2^t)$, and let $C = (w_1, \ldots, w_{2^t})$ be an arbitrary code for D_t. We prove that for all sufficiently large t, $\Sigma(1/2^t)|w_i|_R \ - \ H_{D_t} \geq \log \Delta - 2$. Since Δ may be arbitrarily large, this proves the theorem.

Let X_0 be the set of binary words

$$X_0 = \{1^i \mid i \geq 0\},$$

and for $j \geq 1$ let X_j be the set of binary words

$$X_j = \{a_1 \ldots a_{j-1}01^i \mid a_1, \ldots, a_{j-1} \in \{0,1\}, i \geq 0\}$$

(1^i denotes the binary word consisting of i 1's). Then $X_0, X_1, X_2, \ldots$ is a partition of the set of all binary words.

The following two properties are easy to see.

(1) The set X_0 contains at most one of $w_1, \ldots, w_{2^t}$, and, for $j \geq 1$, X_j contains at most 2^{j-1} of $w_1, \ldots, w_{2^t}$. The sum of these upper bounds for $X_0, \ldots, X_t$ is $1 + 1 + 2 + 2^2 + \ldots + 2^{t-1} = 2^t$, i.e., the number of symbols to be encoded.

(2) $|w|' = 0$ for any $w \in X_0$ and, for $j \geq 1$, $|w|' = -\log r'_j$ for any $w \in X_j$. Hence, if $j < k$ then $|u|' \leq |v|'$ for any $u \in X_j$, $v \in X_k$.

Hence, for any sufficiently large t, we have

$$\begin{aligned}
&\Sigma_{i=1}^{2^t}(1/2^t)|w_i|_R \;-\; H_{D_t} \\
&\geq \Sigma_{i=1}^{2^t}(1/2^t)|w_i|' \;-\; t \\
&\geq (1/2^t)(0 \cdot 1 + \Sigma_{j=1}^{t}(-\log r'_j)2^{j-1}) \;-\; t \\
&= (1/2^t)\Sigma_{j=I_\Delta}^{t}(j + \log \Delta)2^{j-1} \;-\; t \\
&\geq (1/2^t)(-c_\Delta + \Sigma_{j=1}^{t}(j + \log \Delta)2^{j-1}) \;-\; t \\
&\qquad (c_\Delta \text{ is a constant that depends only on } \Delta) \\
&= (1/2^t)(-c_\Delta + (\log \Delta)(2^t - 1) + t2^t - 2^t + 1) \;-\; t \\
&= \log \Delta - 1 + (-c_\Delta - \log \Delta + 1)/2^t \\
&\geq \log \Delta - 2.
\end{aligned}$$

□

The roles of two symbols 0, 1 are symmetrical. Hence, in Theorem 2 we can replace the assumption $\lim_{i \to \infty} r_i/2^{-i} = 0$ with $\lim_{i \to \infty}(1 - r_i)/2^{-i} = 0$. Although it is tempting to conjecture that the assumption $\liminf_{i \to \infty} r_i = 0$ is sufficient, at present it is unknown even whether the assumption $\lim_{i \to \infty} r_i/2^{-i} = 0$ can be replaced with a weaker one, for example, $\lim_{i \to \infty} r_i/2^{-i/2} = 0$.

Acknowledgments

The author thanks Dr. Tsutomu Kawabata who gave the author necessary technical information on coding theorems. The technical discussions with him were also quite helpful. The author also thanks Prof. Etsuya Tomita for much help concerning the present work.

References

1. Chaitin, G.: A theory of program size formally identical to information theory, *JACM* **22** (1975) 329 – 340
2. Csiszar, I., Körner, J.: *Information Theory: Coding Theorems for Discrete Memoryless Systems*, Academic Press (1981)
3. Kobayashi, K.: On malign input distributions for algorithms, *IEICE Trans. on Information and Systems* **E76-D** (June 1993) 634 – 640. (An extended abstract of this paper can be found in "Algorithms and Computation, Proc. of 3rd Int. Symp., ISAAC '92" (Ed. by T. Ibaraki et al.), Lecture Notes in Computer Science **650** (1992), 239 – 248.)
4. Shannon, C. E.: A mathematical theory of communication, *Bell System Tech. J.* **27** (1948) 379 – 423, 623 – 656

Thirty four Comparisons are Required to Sort 13 Items

Takumi Kasai, Shusaku Sawato, and Shigeki Iwata

Department of Computer Science, The University of Electro-Communications
1-5-1 Chofugaoka, Chofu-shi, Tokyo, 182 JAPAN

Abstract. The number of comparisons made in merge insertion sort [2] is known to be minimum to sort n items, $n \leq 12, n = 20, 21$. An exhaustive computation was carried out within 10 days by a workstation to show that the number is also minimum for $n = 13$. The problem has been open for nearly three decades since Mark Wells discovered the optimality of the sorting procedure for $n = 12$ in 1965.

1 Introduction

Merge insertion [2] is a sorting procedure using small number of comparisons. Manacher [4] has shown that the sorting procedure is not optimal. He gave a sorting algorithm using less comparisons than merge insertion for n items, $n \geq 189$. For $n < 189$ items, however, merge insertion uses the least comparisons ever known. The number of comparisons made in the merge insertion sort is $F(n) = \sum_{k=1}^{n} \lceil \log_2(\frac{3}{4}k) \rceil$, where the best lower bound of the number of comparisons to sort n items known to date is $L(n) = \lceil \log_2 n! \rceil$ (see [3, p.187].) The minimum number of comparisons $S(n)$ to sort n items satisfies in general

$$L(n) \leq S(n) \leq F(n),$$

and for $n \leq 11, n = 20, 21$, we obtain $L(n) = S(n) = F(n)$. Thus the number of comparisons of the sorting procedure is optimal for these n. By simple calculations, we obtain that $L(12) = 29$, $F(12) = 30$, $L(13) = 33$, and $F(13) = 34$.

In 1965 Mark Wells found that $S(12) = 30$ by an exhaustive search about 60 hours on a computer [1,3,5,6]. This implies that the merge insertion sort is optimal for $n = 12$ as far as the number of comparisons is considered.

We have made an exhaustive computation for $n = 13$ and discovered that $S(13) = 34$. The computer we used is NEC EWS4800/380 (98 mips) and the computation has taken about 230 hours. The amount of the main memory which we used during the computation was 100 mega bytes. The program is written in C language and consists of 8,800 lines. Compared with Mark Wells' computation, our program took 7 minutes to show that $S(12) = 30$.

2 The Exhaustive Computation

The purpose of our computation is to show the following:

Theorem 1. *There does not exist any sorting process with at most $L(13) = 33$ comparisons to sort 13 items.*

Assume that G be a directed acyclic graph (dag) with n nodes. If there is a path of length > 0 in G from node u to node v, then we write $u \prec v$, and if there is not any path then we write $u \not\prec v$. If $u \prec v$ and $v \prec w$, and if G contains the edge (u, w), then the edge is always eliminated from G, since we are concerned only with existence of a path among nodes in G. We call two dags $G_1 = (V_1, E_1)$ and $G_2 = (V_2, E_2)$ *isomorphic* if there exists a bijection $f : V_1 \rightarrow V_2$ such that $E_2 = \{(f(u), f(v)) \mid (u, v) \in E_1\}$. We call two dags $G_1 = (V_1, E_1)$ and $G_2 = (V_2, E_2)$ *quasi-isomorphic* either if they are isomorphic or if there exists a bijection $f : V_1 \rightarrow V_2$ such that $E_2 = \{(f(u), f(v)) \mid (v, u) \in E_1\}$. For a dag G, let $T(G)$ denote the number of possible permutations which assign integers $\{1, 2, \cdots, n\}$ to the nodes of G so that the number associated with u is less than the number associated with v whenever (u, v) is in G. If a graph G contains a cycle, then $T(G) = 0$. For two disjoint dags $G_1 = (V_1, E_1)$ and $G_2 = (V_2, E_2)$, let $G_1 \cup G_2$ denote the dag $(V_1 \cup V_2, E_1 \cup E_2)$. For a graph G and its node v, let $G - \{v\}$ denote the graph G after the deletion of both v and the edges adjacent to v. For a graph $G = (V, E)$ and a set of edges E' among nodes of V, let $G + E'$ denote the graph $(V, E \cup E')$.

Let us define the and-or labeled tree S_n. A label of each or-node of S_n is a dag with n nodes. A label of each and-node is the form $\langle G, (u, v)\rangle$ where G is a dag and u, v are nodes of G. We sometimes confuse a node of S_n with its label. The *root* of S_n is an or-node and is labeled with a graph of n isolated nodes. We say that an or-node of S_n is of *level* k if the length of the path from the root to the or-node is $2k$ ($k \geq 0$). An or-node of level k is a dag G with n nodes such that

$$E(G) = \frac{n!}{2^k T(G)} \geq \frac{n!}{2^{L(n)}}, \tag{2.1}$$

where $E(G)$ is the *efficiency* of G. (See [3, p.189].) A dag G is said to be *sorted* if for every pair u, v of nodes of G, either $u \prec v$ or $v \prec u$. Every son in S_n of an or-node G is an and-node, and is labeled with $\langle G, (u, v)\rangle$ for nodes u, v, such that $u \not\prec v$ and $v \not\prec u$ in G. The and-node $\langle G, (u, v)\rangle$ has exactly two sons G_1 and G_2 of or-nodes, $G_1 = G + \{(u, v)\}$, $G_2 = G + \{(v, u)\}$. If at least one of G_1 or G_2 does not satisfy equation (2.1), then $\langle G, (u, v)\rangle$ is eliminated from S_n. Thus an or-node of level k has an even number (possibly zero) of or-nodes of level $k + 1$ as its grandsons. The length of the path from the root to any node in S_n is restricted to at most $2L(n)$. Thus the level of each or-node in S_n is at most $L(n)$.

A leaf of S_n labeled with the sorted dag has the value *success*. The value of an and-node (or-node) is *success* if both values of its sons are (one of its sons is, respectively) success. The value of the node of S_n is *failure* if the value is not success. We note that if two dags labeled with or-nodes in S_n are quasi-isomorphic then they have the same values.

The proof of the theorem is to show that the value of the root of S_n is failure, if $n = 13$. Our objective is to make an exhaustive search on the and-or labeled tree S_{13}. In what follows, we focus our attention on the case $n = 13$.

The basic technique to cope with an exhaustive tree search is backtracking. Since the tree is huge, we need some unusual considerations.

To find or-nodes of S_{13} of the next level

For a matrix M, let $[M]_{ij}$ denote the ij-th element of M, and let M^T denote the transpose matrix of M. For a dag G consisting of nodes $x_1, x_2, \cdots, x_n$, let $C(G)$ be the $n \times n$ matrix, where

$$[C(G)]_{ij} = T(G + \{(x_i, x_j)\}).$$

(See [3, p.190].) If G is the label of an or-node in S_{13} of the level k ($0 \leq k < L(13)$), and if $1 \leq [C(G)]_{ij}, [C(G)]_{ji} \leq 2^{L(13)-(k+1)}$, then both dags $G + \{(x_i, x_j)\}$ and $G + \{(x_j, x_i)\}$ satisfy equation (2.1); thus G has a son (and-node) $\langle G, (x_i, x_j)\rangle$, and $\langle G, (x_i, x_j)\rangle$ has two sons (or-nodes) $G + \{(x_i, x_j)\}$ and $G + \{(x_j, x_i)\}$ of level $k + 1$ in S_{13}.

Proposition 2. *Let G be a dag with nodes $x_1, x_2, \cdots, x_n$, and let $\{x_1, x_2, \cdots, x_k\}$ be the set of all nodes such that $indeg(x_i) = 0$. For each ℓ ($1 \leq \ell \leq k$), let $G_\ell = G + \{(x_\ell, x_i) \mid 1 \leq i \leq k,\ i \neq \ell\}$. Then*

(1) $T(G) = \sum_{\ell=1}^{k} T(G_\ell)$,
(2) $T(G_\ell) = T(G - \{x_\ell\})$,
(3) $C(G) = \sum_{\ell=1}^{k} C(G_\ell)$,
(4) *the ℓ-th row vector of $C(G_\ell)$ is* $[\underbrace{T(G_\ell)\cdots T(G_\ell)}_{\ell-1}\ 0\ \underbrace{T(G_\ell)\cdots T(G_\ell)}_{n-\ell}]$
and the ℓ-th column vector is $[0\cdots 0]^T$; deletion of both the ℓ-th row and ℓ-th column from $C(G_\ell)$ results $C(G - \{x_\ell\})$.

Proof. (1) Since $indeg(x_\ell) = 0$ in G for all ℓ ($1 \leq \ell \leq k$), the number 1 will be assigned to one of the nodes x_ℓ. Then $T(G)$ is the summation over ℓ of the number of permutations where the number 1 is assigned to x_ℓ. In G_ℓ, the number 1 is always assigned to the node x_ℓ. Thus

$$\begin{aligned} T(G) &= \sum_{\ell=1}^{k} \{T(G), \text{ where } x_\ell \text{ is assigned to number } 1\} \\ &= \sum_{\ell=1}^{k} T(G_\ell). \end{aligned}$$

(2) Obvious.

(3) Assume that G is a graph with nodes $x_1, \cdots, x_n$, $indeg(x_i) = 0$ for all i, $1 \leq i \leq k \leq n$, and that $G_\ell = G + \{(x_\ell, x_i) \mid 1 \leq i \leq k,\ i \neq \ell\}$ for each ℓ $(1 \leq \ell \leq k)$. Note that G may contain a cycle. Then

$$T(G) = \sum_{\ell=1}^{k} T(G_\ell) \tag{2.2}$$

holds, since $T(G') = 0$ if G' contains a cycle. Thus

$$\begin{aligned} [C(G)]_{ij} &= T(G + \{(x_i, x_j)\}) \\ &= \sum_{\ell=1}^{k} T(G + \{(x_i, x_j)\} + \{(x_\ell, x_p) \mid 1 \leq p \leq k, p \neq \ell\}) \\ &\qquad\qquad\qquad\qquad\qquad\qquad \text{(by equation (2.2))} \\ &= \sum_{\ell=1}^{k} T(G_\ell + \{(x_i, x_j)\}) \\ &= \sum_{\ell=1}^{k} [C(G_\ell)]_{ij}. \end{aligned}$$

(4) Let $1 \leq i \leq n$. Then $G_\ell + \{(x_i, x_\ell)\}$ contains a cycle, and $T(G_\ell + \{(x_i, x_\ell)\}) = 0$. Thus

$$[C(G_\ell)]_{i\ell} = T(G_\ell + \{(x_i, x_\ell)\}) = 0.$$

Suppose that $1 \leq j \leq n$, $j \neq \ell$. Since G_ℓ contains the edge (x_ℓ, x_j),

$$[C(G_\ell)]_{\ell j} = T(G_\ell + \{(x_\ell, x_j)\}) = T(G_\ell).$$

Assume that $1 \leq i, j < \ell$. Then by (2)

$$\begin{aligned} [C(G_\ell)]_{ij} &= T(G_\ell + \{(x_i, x_j)\}) \\ &= T((G_\ell - \{x_\ell\}) + \{(x_i, x_j)\}) \\ &= [C(G_\ell - \{x_\ell\})]_{ij}. \end{aligned}$$

If $\ell < i \leq n$ or $\ell < j \leq n$, then we can similarly prove (4) as in the above case. □

Application of Proposition 2 to compute $C(G)$ and $T(G)$ causes recursion. If we apply Proposition 2 (1), (2) to compute $T(G)$, then many quasi-isomorphic dags appear during the computation. We use a hashing table with key G to hold the value $T(G)$. We compute $T(G)$ directly for $n \leq 8$, i.e., we generate the permutations of the integers $\{1, 2, \cdots, n\}$, and count the number of possible assignments of integers to the nodes of G such that (u, v) is an edge of G if and only if the number assigned to u is less than that to v.

Further if $G = G_1 \cup G_2$ is composed of two disjoint dags G_1 and G_2, then $T(G)$ and $C(G)$ can easily be computed. Let G_1 and G_2 consist of nodes $x_1, x_2, \cdots, x_n$ and $y_1, y_2, \cdots, y_m$, respectively. Then

$$T(G) = \binom{n+m}{n} T(G_1)T(G_2).$$

For i $(1 \leq i \leq n)$, j $(1 \leq j \leq m)$, let

$$\begin{pmatrix} i & < & j \\ n & & m \end{pmatrix} = \sum_{s=0}^{j-1} \binom{n-i+m-s}{n-i} \binom{i-1+s}{i-1},$$

and let $L(n,m)$ be the matrix where $[L(n,m)]_{ij} = \begin{pmatrix} i & < & j \\ n & & m \end{pmatrix}$. Assume that $A(G_1)$ is the $n \times n$ matrix, where $[A(G_1)]_{ij}$ is the number of consistent permutations of G_1 in which x_i is equal to j. The matrix product $A(G_1) \cdot L(n,m) \cdot A(G_2)^T$ is the $n \times m$ matrix, whose ij-th element would be the number of consistent permutations to assign integers $\{1, 2, \cdots, n+m\}$ to nodes of the dag $(G_1 \cup G_2) + \{(x_i, y_j)\}$. (For the matrices $L(n,m)$ and $A(G)$, see [3, pp.191–192].)

We have devised the way to compute $C(G)$ and $A(G)$ from $C(G_1)$, $C(G_2)$, $A(G_1)$, and $A(G_2)$. The equations to compute $C(G)$ and $A(G)$ are complicated but staightforward. So we omit the details.

Fig.1 shows the procedure *value*(G,k) to determine the value of G of the level k of S_{13}. The procedure requires values of dags of the level $k+1$, and it calls itself recursively to find these values of the level $k+1$. We explain local variables: integer ℓ is for a counter for sons (and-nodes) of G, integer m and boolean variable *undercomputing* are used for giving the value of G either success or failure. The pairs $(G_{\sigma(1)}, G_{\sigma(1)}'), (G_{\sigma(2)}, G_{\sigma(2)}'), \cdots, (G_{\sigma(\ell)}, G_{\sigma(\ell)}')$ of dags are of the level $k+1$, and the father of the pair $(G_{\sigma(i)}, G_{\sigma(i)}')$ is a son of G for $1 \leq i \leq \ell$. (See Fig. 2.) The conditions in line (1) are equivalent to $E(G \cup \{(x_i, x_j)\}) \geq \frac{13!}{2^{L(13)}}$ and $E(G \cup \{(x_j, x_i)\}) \geq \frac{13!}{2^{L(13)}}$, respectively. By the if statement in line (2), $T(G_i) \geq T(G_i')$ for $1 \leq i \leq \ell$. In line (4), we first examine *value*$(G_{\sigma(m)}, k+1)$ and if the value is failure then in line (5) we examine *value*$(G_{\sigma(m)}', k+1)$. *value*$(G_{\sigma(m)}, k+1)$ is first tested because the possibility that the value is failure is generally larger than the one that *value*$(G_{\sigma(m)}', k+1)$ is failure, since $T(G_{\sigma(m)}) \geq T(G_{\sigma(m)}')$. If it is failure then we can skip examining *value*$(G_{\sigma(m)}', k+1)$. Likewise, by (3), we obtain that $T(G_{\sigma(1)}) \leq T(G_{\sigma(2)}) \leq \cdots \leq T(G_{\sigma(m)})$. We examine in lines (4), (5) the values of $G_{\sigma(i)}$ and $G_{\sigma(i)}'$ before examining values of $G_{\sigma(j)}$ and $G_{\sigma(j)}'$ for $i < j$, because the possibility that both values of $G_{\sigma(i)}$ and $G_{\sigma(i)}'$ are success is generally larger than the one that both values of $G_{\sigma(j)}$ and $G_{\sigma(j)}'$ are success. If both values of $G_{\sigma(i)}$ and $G_{\sigma(i)}'$ are success, then the value of G is success and it is not necessary that we examine the values of $G_{\sigma(j)}$ and $G_{\sigma(j)}'$ for $j > i$.

Memory management

The number of the dags which appear in our exhaustive search of S_{13} is more than 10^6. (See Table 1.) We do not know the exact number. Our algorithm does not store all of the dags which appear in S_{13}. If our algorithm would try to hold all the dags in the computer memory, we might have not been able to complete the whole computation.

To make the exhaustive computation in a reasonable amount of time, it may generally be a good idea to store in the computer memory the information about dags which we have already computed, so that we retrieve the computed results if necessary, and will never make the same computation again. However S_{13} has an enormous number of dags (nodes), and we cannot hold all of the computed results. Here, each computed result of a dag G includes pointers to every connected component of G, the level of G, and a flag indicating whether we can reach the sorted dag or not from G in the and-or search tree. We therefore adopted the following criteria to store the information of the computed results: If there is a room for storing the computed result of a dag, then we store it. If the memory is full and is no more available to store information, then we delete the content of the memory, except (1) dags whose level is ≤ 12, (2) dags of the levels 13 and 15 whose exhaustive computations traverse edges of S_{13} more than 20 times; dags of the level 17 that traverse edges more than 15 times; and dags of the odd levels ≥ 23 that traverse more than 8 times. The dags of the kind (2) have already spent much "time" for its analysis, and are too valuable to throw away. We delete the computed information concerning dags of levels of an even number > 12, and of levels 19 and 21, to keep our total information small and to hold them in the computer memory. So many dags in S_{13} of levels 19 and 21 appear during our computation, and the number of the dags is too large for us to hold them all in the computer.

Table 1 shows the total numbers of dags in S_{13} of the levels $0, 1, \cdots, 33$, which are generated and are tested their values during the execution of our program. As described earlier, we throw some dags away when the memory is full, and may generate the same dag again which we have once deleted. Thus these values may count quasi-isomorphic dags more than twice, and the "real" number of the non-quasi-isomorphic dags in each level of S_{13} is smaller than the number in the table.

We prepared 50 mega bytes computer memory for storing the computed results of dags, 23 mega bytes for the work space of the computation of $T(G)$ and $C(G)$, 18 mega bytes for description of each connected component of graphs (nodes and edges), and 1.2 mega bytes for the stack of and-nodes and or-nodes of the search tree S_{13} to go back and forth on S_{13} which are necessary to maintain the backtracking.

Comments on the case $n = 12$

According to Knuth [3, pp.192–193], Wells' algorithm computes a set of dags such that if the computed set does not include the sorted dag, then we can conclude that $S(12) > L(12)$. The algorithm is shown in Fig. 3, where D_0 is the dag consisting of one node. Starting from the set $\{D_0\}$, the algorithm repeatedly tries to add an edge (u, v) to either one of the dags or to two dags in the set (the two dags may be the same) to form another dag G, and add (v, u) to form G'; and if $\frac{12!}{2^{L(12)}} \leq E(G) \leq E(G')$, then add G to the set *NewDagset*, unless G is quasi-isomorphic to a dag we already have obtained. Thus a dag in the set always consists of one connected component. [3] insists that the set obtained so far contains 1594 dags, and does not contain the sorted dag.

When adding a new dag to the set *NewDagset* of dags in lines (1),(2) of Fig. 3, a pair G and G' of dags appear such that $E(G) = E(G') \geq \frac{12!}{2^{L(12)}}$, that G and G' are not quasi-isomorphic, and that G and G' are not quasi-isomorphic to any dag in *NewDagset*. As a result it seems that we can show $S(12) > L(12)$ independent of whether we choose G or G' for the addition to the set. Several hundred pairs of dags G and G' appear during the whole computation where G and G' satisfy the above conditions. If we choose G for addition to the set, then the set may differ from the one if we choose G' for addition instead of G. Thus the set depends on the sequence of choices of these dags. We have tried to compute the set eight times by using a random number for choosing one of the two dags. The numbers of the computed sets were between 1492 and 1587. All dags we have searched among S_{12} had at most 24 comparisons. While in our search tree, the label of each node is a dag which may consist of some connected components. The numbers of the dags (consisting of some connected components) of the eight sets we have computed were between 1889 and 2055.

S_{13} has as a leaf a sorted dag after $L(13) = 33$ comparisons. If we compute the set of dags like Wells' algorithm does in Fig. 3, then the set will contain a sorted dag and we cannot prove that $S(13) > L(13)$ in that way. So we had to take care of the and-or search tree.

Acknowledgment

For our computation, we have used some work stations of the Computer Center of Tokai University by courtesy of the Center.

References

1. Aho, A.V., Hopcroft, J.E., Ullman, J.D.: *The Design and Analysis of Algorithms.* Addison-Wesley, (1974)
2. Ford, L.R., Johnson, S.M.: A tournament problem. Amer. Math. Monthly **66**, (1959) 387–389
3. Knuth, D.E.: *The Art of Computer Programming Vol.3: Sorting and Searching.* Addison-Wesley, (1973)
4. Manacher, G.K.: The Ford-Johnson sorting algorithm is not optimal. *Proc. of the 15th Allerton Conf. on Communication, Control, and Computing,* (1977) 390–397
5. Wells, M.B.: Applications of a language for computing in combinatorics. *Proc. IFIP Congress 65,* (1965) 497–498
6. Wells, M.B.: *Elements of Combinatorial Computing.* Pergamon Press, (1971)

```
     function value(G, k);
     begin
      comment determine the value of G of the level k in S13;
      if G is sorted then value := success
       else begin
        let x1, x2, ..., xn be the nodes of G;
        compute C(G);
        ℓ := 0;                  comment ℓ is a counter for sons of G;
        for i := 1 to n do     for j := 1 to n do
(1)      if 1 ≤ [C(G)]ij ≤ 2^(L(13)-k-1) and 1 ≤ [C(G)]ji ≤ 2^(L(13)-k-1)
         then begin
          comment both G ∪ {(xi, xj)} and G ∪ {(xj, xi)} are
           sons of ⟨G, (xi, xj)⟩, which is a son of G;
          ℓ := ℓ + 1;
(2)       if [C(G)]ij ≥ [C(G)]ji then
           begin Gℓ := G ∪ {(xi, xj)}; Gℓ' := G ∪ {(xj, xi)} end
          else
           begin Gℓ := G ∪ {(xj, xi)}; Gℓ' := G ∪ {(xi, xj)} end;
          comment T(Gℓ) ≥ T(Gℓ') holds
         end
         else;
        comment ℓ is the number of the sons (and-nodes) of G in S13;
(3)     let σ(1), σ(2), ..., σ(ℓ) be the permutation of 1, 2, ..., ℓ
         such that i < j implies T(Gσ(i)) ≤ T(Gσ(j));
        m:=1;
        undercomputing := true;
        while undercomputing and (m ≤ ℓ) do
         begin
(4)       if value(Gσ(m), k + 1) = success
(5)        then if value(Gσ(m)', k + 1) = success
            then begin
             undercomputing := false;
             value := success
            end
            else
           else;
          m := m + 1
         end;
        if undercomputing then value := failure else
       end
      end;
```

Figure 1 Procedure *value*(G, k).

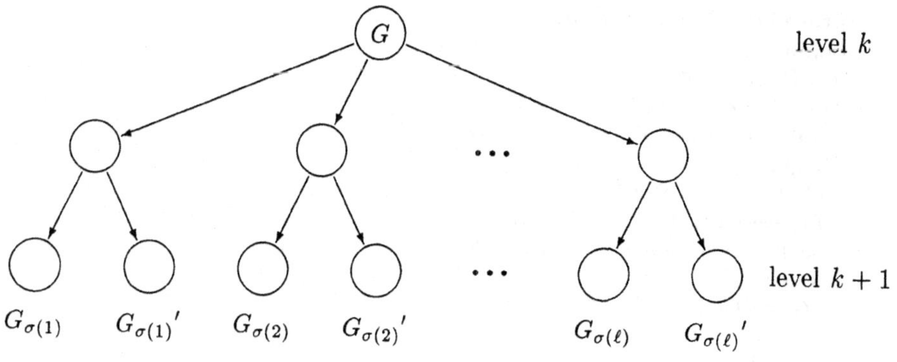

Figure 2 Or-node G in the level k and its 2ℓ grandsons in the level $k+1$.

level	number of dags	level	number of dags
0	1	17	351952
1	1	18	488678
2	2	19	542506
3	3	20	559716
4	7	21	448844
5	16	22	344103
6	27	23	184767
7	55	24	107683
8	155	25	46908
9	441	26	24877
10	1205	27	2734
11	3253	28	2415
12	8413	29	416
13	24441	30	355
14	66500	31	197
15	126530	32	114
16	241870	33	18

Table 1 Number of dags of S_{13} in our computation.

```
procedure Wells' Algorithm;
begin
 OldDagset := φ;
 NewDagset := {D0};
 while OldDagset ≠ NewDagset do
  begin
   OldDagset := NewDagset;
   for every dag D ∈ NewDagset
    and every node u, v of D, u ≠ v do
    begin
     G := D + {(u, v)};
     G' := D + {(v, u)};
     if 12!/2^L(12) ≤ E(G) ≤ E(G')
      and G is not quasi-isomorphic to any dag in NewDagset
(1)   then NewDagset := NewDagset ∪ {G} else
    end;
   for every dag D1, D2 ∈ NewDagset
    and every node u of D1 and v of D2, u ≠ v do
    begin
     comment D1 and D2 may be the same dag;
     G := (D1 ∪ D2) + {(u, v)};
     G' := (D1 ∪ D2) + {(v, u)};
     if 12!/2^L(12) ≤ E(G) ≤ E(G')
      and G is not quasi-isomorphic to any dag in NewDagset
(2)   then NewDagset := NewDagset ∪ {G} else
    end
  end;
 if a sorted dag is in NewDagset
  then
  else print "S(12) > L(12) is proved"
end;
```

Figure 3 Wells' algorithm.

Springer-Verlag and the Environment

Lecture Notes in Computer Science

For information about Vols. 1–714
please contact your bookseller or Springer-Verlag

Vol. 715: E. Best (Ed.), CONCUR'93. Proceedings, 1993. IX, 541 pages. 1993.

Vol. 716: A. U. Frank, I. Campari (Eds.), Spatial Information Theory. Proceedings, 1993. XI, 478 pages. 1993.

Vol. 717: I. Sommerville, M. Paul (Eds.), Software Engineering – ESEC '93. Proceedings, 1993. XII, 516 pages. 1993.

Vol. 718: J. Seberry, Y. Zheng (Eds.), Advances in Cryptology – AUSCRYPT '92. Proceedings, 1992. XIII, 543 pages. 1993.

Vol. 719: D. Chetverikov, W.G. Kropatsch (Eds.), Computer Analysis of Images and Patterns. Proceedings, 1993. XVI, 857 pages. 1993.

Vol. 720: V.Mařík, J. Lažanský, R.R. Wagner (Eds.), Database and Expert Systems Applications. Proceedings, 1993. XV, 768 pages. 1993.

Vol. 721: J. Fitch (Ed.), Design and Implementation of Symbolic Computation Systems. Proceedings, 1992. VIII, 215 pages. 1993.

Vol. 722: A. Miola (Ed.), Design and Implementation of Symbolic Computation Systems. Proceedings, 1993. XII, 384 pages. 1993.

Vol. 723: N. Aussenac, G. Boy, B. Gaines, M. Linster, J.-G. Ganascia, Y. Kodratoff (Eds.), Knowledge Acquisition for Knowledge-Based Systems. Proceedings, 1993. XIII, 446 pages. 1993. (Subseries LNAI).

Vol. 724: P. Cousot, M. Falaschi, G. Filè, A. Rauzy (Eds.), Static Analysis. Proceedings, 1993. IX, 283 pages. 1993.

Vol. 725: A. Schiper (Ed.), Distributed Algorithms. Proceedings, 1993. VIII, 325 pages. 1993.

Vol. 726: T. Lengauer (Ed.), Algorithms – ESA '93. Proceedings, 1993. IX, 419 pages. 1993

Vol. 727: M. Filgueiras, L. Damas (Eds.), Progress in Artificial Intelligence. Proceedings, 1993. X, 362 pages. 1993. (Subseries LNAI).

Vol. 728: P. Torasso (Ed.), Advances in Artificial Intelligence. Proceedings, 1993. XI, 336 pages. 1993. (Subseries LNAI).

Vol. 729: L. Donatiello, R. Nelson (Eds.), Performance Evaluation of Computer and Communication Systems. Proceedings, 1993. VIII, 675 pages. 1993.

Vol. 730: D. B. Lomet (Ed.), Foundations of Data Organization and Algorithms. Proceedings, 1993. XII, 412 pages. 1993.

Vol. 731: A. Schill (Ed.), DCE – The OSF Distributed Computing Environment. Proceedings, 1993. VIII, 285 pages. 1993.

Vol. 732: A. Bode, M. Dal Cin (Eds.), Parallel Computer Architectures. IX, 311 pages. 1993.

Vol. 733: Th. Grechenig, M. Tscheligi (Eds.), Human Computer Interaction. Proceedings, 1993. XIV, 450 pages. 1993.

Vol. 734: J. Volkert (Ed.), Parallel Computation. Proceedings, 1993. VIII, 248 pages. 1993.

Vol. 735: D. Bjørner, M. Broy, I. V. Pottosin (Eds.), Formal Methods in Programming and Their Applications. Proceedings, 1993. IX, 434 pages. 1993.

Vol. 736: R. L. Grossman, A. Nerode, A. P. Ravn, H. Rischel (Eds.), Hybrid Systems. VIII, 474 pages. 1993.

Vol. 737: J. Calmet, J. A. Campbell (Eds.), Artificial Intelligence and Symbolic Mathematical Computing. Proceedings, 1992. VIII, 305 pages. 1993.

Vol. 738: M. Weber, M. Simons, Ch. Lafontaine, The Generic Development Language Deva. XI, 246 pages. 1993.

Vol. 739: H. Imai, R. L. Rivest, T. Matsumoto (Eds.), Advances in Cryptology – ASIACRYPT '91. X, 499 pages. 1993.

Vol. 740: E. F. Brickell (Ed.), Advances in Cryptology – CRYPTO '92. Proceedings, 1992. X, 593 pages. 1993.

Vol. 741: B. Preneel, R. Govaerts, J. Vandewalle (Eds.), Computer Security and Industrial Cryptography. Proceedings, 1991. VIII, 275 pages. 1993.

Vol. 742: S. Nishio, A. Yonezawa (Eds.), Object Technologies for Advanced Software. Proceedings, 1993. X, 543 pages. 1993.

Vol. 743: S. Doshita, K. Furukawa, K. P. Jantke, T. Nishida (Eds.), Algorithmic Learning Theory. Proceedings, 1992. X, 260 pages. 1993. (Subseries LNAI)

Vol. 744: K. P. Jantke, T. Yokomori, S. Kobayashi, E. Tomita (Eds.), Algorithmic Learning Theory. Proceedings, 1993. XI, 423 pages. 1993. (Subseries LNAI)

Vol. 745: V. Roberto (Ed.), Intelligent Perceptual Systems. VIII, 378 pages. 1993. (Subseries LNAI)

Vol. 746: A. S. Tanguiane, Artificial Perception and Music Recognition. XV, 210 pages. 1993. (Subseries LNAI).

Vol. 747: M. Clarke, R. Kruse, S. Moral (Eds.), Symbolic and Quantitative Approaches to Reasoning and Uncertainty. Proceedings, 1993. X, 390 pages. 1993.

Vol. 748: R. H. Halstead Jr., T. Ito (Eds.), Parallel Symbolic Computing: Languages, Systems, and Applications. Proceedings, 1992. X, 419 pages. 1993.

Vol. 749: P. A. Fritzson (Ed.), Automated and Algorithmic Debugging. Proceedings, 1993. VIII, 369 pages. 1993.

Vol. 750: J. L. Díaz-Herrera (Ed.), Software Engineering Education. Proceedings, 1994. XII, 601 pages. 1994.

Vol. 751: B. Jähne, Spatio-Temporal Image Processing. XII, 208 pages. 1993.

Vol. 752: T. W. Finin, C. K. Nicholas, Y. Yesha (Eds.), Information and Knowledge Management. Proceedings, 1992. VII, 142 pages. 1993.

Vol. 753: L. J. Bass, J. Gornostaev, C. Unger (Eds.), Human-Computer Interaction. Proceedings, 1993. X, 388 pages. 1993.

Vol. 754: H. D. Pfeiffer, T. E. Nagle (Eds.), Conceptual Structures: Theory and Implementation. Proceedings, 1992. IX, 327 pages. 1993. (Subseries LNAI).

Vol. 755: B. Möller, H. Partsch, S. Schuman (Eds.), Formal Program Development. Proceedings. VII, 371 pages. 1993.

Vol. 756: J. Pieprzyk, B. Sadeghiyan, Design of Hashing Algorithms. XV, 194 pages. 1993.

Vol. 757: U. Banerjee, D. Gelernter, A. Nicolau, D. Padua (Eds.), Languages and Compilers for Parallel Computing. Proceedings, 1992. X, 576 pages. 1993.

Vol. 758: M. Teillaud, Towards Dynamic Randomized Algorithms in Computational Geometry. IX, 157 pages. 1993.

Vol. 759: N. R. Adam, B. K. Bhargava (Eds.), Advanced Database Systems. XV, 451 pages. 1993.

Vol. 760: S. Ceri, K. Tanaka, S. Tsur (Eds.), Deductive and Object-Oriented Databases. Proceedings, 1993. XII, 488 pages. 1993.

Vol. 761: R. K. Shyamasundar (Ed.), Foundations of Software Technology and Theoretical Computer Science. Proceedings, 1993. XIV, 456 pages. 1993.

Vol. 762: K. W. Ng, P. Raghavan, N. V. Balasubramanian, F. Y. L. Chin (Eds.), Algorithms and Computation. Proceedings, 1993. XIII, 542 pages. 1993.

Vol. 763: F. Pichler, R. Moreno Díaz (Eds.), Computer Aided Systems Theory - EUROCAST '93. Proceedings, 1993. IX, 451 pages. 1994.

Vol. 764: G. Wagner, Vivid Logic. XII, 148 pages. 1994. (Subseries LNAI).

Vol. 765: T. Helleseth (Ed.), Advances in Cryptology - EUROCRYPT '93. Proceedings, 1993. X, 467 pages. 1994.

Vol. 766: P. R. Van Loocke, The Dynamics of Concepts. XI, 340 pages. 1994. (Subseries LNAI).

Vol. 767: M. Gogolla, An Extended Entity-Relationship Model. X, 136 pages. 1994.

Vol. 768: U. Banerjee, D. Gelernter, A. Nicolau, D. Padua (Eds.), Languages and Compilers for Parallel Computing. Proceedings, 1993. XI, 655 pages. 1994.

Vol. 769: J. L. Nazareth, The Newton-Cauchy Framework. XII, 101 pages. 1994.

Vol. 770: P. Haddawy (Representing Plans Under Uncertainty. X, 129 pages. 1994. (Subseries LNAI).

Vol. 771: G. Tomas, C. W. Ueberhuber, Visualization of Scientific Parallel Programs. XI, 310 pages. 1994.

Vol. 772: B. C. Warboys (Ed.),Software Process Technology. Proceedings, 1994. IX, 275 pages. 1994.

Vol. 773: D. R. Stinson (Ed.), Advances in Cryptology - CRYPTO '93. Proceedings, 1993. X, 492 pages. 1994.

Vol. 774: M. Banâtre, P. A. Lee (Eds.), Hardware and Software Architectures for Fault Tolerance. XIII, 311 pages. 1994.

Vol. 775: P. Enjalbert, E. W. Mayr, K. W. Wagner (Eds.), STACS 94. Proceedings, 1994. XIV, 782 pages. 1994.

Vol. 776: H. J. Schneider, H. Ehrig (Eds.), Graph Transformations in Computer Science. Proceedings, 1993. VIII, 395 pages. 1994.

Vol. 777: K. von Luck, H. Marburger (Eds.), Management and Processing of Complex Data Structures. Proceedings, 1994. VII, 220 pages. 1994.

Vol. 778: M. Bonuccelli, P. Crescenzi, R. Petreschi (Eds.), Algorithms and Complexity. Proceedings, 1994. VIII, 222 pages. 1994.

Vol. 779: M. Jarke, J. Bubenko, K. Jeffery (Eds.), Advances in Database Technology — EDBT '94. Proceedings, 1994. XII, 406 pages. 1994.

Vol. 780: J. J. Joyce, C.-J. H. Seger (Eds.), Higher Order Logic Theorem Proving and Its Applications. Proceedings, 1993. X, 518 pages. 1994.

Vol. 781: G. Cohen, S. Litsyn, A. Lobstein, G. Zémor (Eds.), Algebraic Coding. Proceedings, 1993. XII, 326 pages. 1994.

Vol. 782: J. Gutknecht (Ed.), Programming Languages and System Architectures. Proceedings, 1994. X, 344 pages. 1994.

Vol. 783: C. G. Günther (Ed.), Mobile Communications. Proceedings, 1994. XVI, 564 pages. 1994.

Vol. 784: F. Bergadano, L. De Raedt (Eds.), Machine Learning: ECML-94. Proceedings, 1994. XI, 439 pages. 1994. (Subseries LNAI).

Vol. 785: H. Ehrig, F. Orejas (Eds.), Recent Trends in Data Type Specification. Proceedings, 1992. VIII, 350 pages. 1994.

Vol. 786: P. A. Fritzson (Ed.), Compiler Construction. Proceedings, 1994. XI, 451 pages. 1994.

Vol. 787: S. Tison (Ed.), Trees in Algebra and Programming - CAAP '94. Proceedings, 1994. X, 351 pages. 1994.

Vol. 788: D. Sannella (Ed.), Programming Languages and Systems - ESOP '94. Proceedings, 1994. VIII, 516 pages. 1994.

Vol. 789: M. Hagiya, J. C. Mitchell (Eds.), Theoretical Aspects of Computer Software. Proceedings, 1994. XI, 887 pages. 1994.

Vol. 790: J. van Leeuwen (Ed.), Graph-Theoretic Concepts in Computer Science. Proceedings, 1993. IX, 431 pages. 1994.

Vol. 791: R. Guerraoui, O. Nierstrasz, M. Riveill (Eds.), Object-Based Distributed Programming. Proceedings, 1993. VII, 262 pages. 1994.

Vol. 792: N. D. Jones, M. Hagiya, M. Sato (Eds.), Logic, Language and Computation. XII, 269 pages. 1994.